Creole Composition

LAUER SERIES IN RHETORIC AND COMPOSITION
Editors: Thomas Rickert and Jennifer Bay

The Lauer Series in Rhetoric and Composition honors the contributions Janice Lauer has made to the emergence of Rhetoric and Composition as a disciplinary study. It publishes scholarship that carries on Professor Lauer's varied work in the history of written rhetoric, disciplinarity in composition studies, contemporary pedagogical theory, and written literacy theory and research.

RECENT BOOKS IN THE SERIES

Creole Composition: Academic Writing and Rhetoric in the Anglophone Caribbean (Milson-Whyte, Oenbring, & Jaquette)
Retellings: Opportunities for Feminist Research in Rhetoric and Composition Studies (Enoch & Jack)
Facing the Sky: Composing through Trauma in Word and Image (Fox)
Expel the Pretender: Rhetoric Renounced and the Politics of Style (Wiederhold)
First-Year Composition: From Theory to Practice (Coxwell-Teague & Lunsford)
Contingency, Immanence, and the Subject of Rhetoric (Richardson)
Rewriting Success in Rhetoric & Composition Careers (Goodburn, LeCourt, Leverenz)
Writing a Progressive Past: Women Teaching and Writing in the Progressive Era (Mastrangelo)
Greek Rhetoric Before Aristotle, 2e, Rev. and Exp. Ed. (Enos)
Rhetoric's Earthly Realm: Heidegger, Sophistry, and the Gorgian Kairos (Miller)
   *Winner of the Olson Award for Best Book in Rhetorical Theory 2011
Techne, from Neoclassicism to Postmodernism: Understanding Writing as a Useful, Teachable Art (Pender)
Walking and Talking Feminist Rhetorics: Landmark Essays and Controversies (Buchanan & Ryan)

CREOLE COMPOSITION

Academic Writing and Rhetoric in the Anglophone Caribbean

Edited by Vivette Milson-Whyte,
Raymond Oenbring, and Brianne Jaquette

Parlor Press
Anderson, South Carolina
www.parlorpress.com

Parlor Press LLC, Anderson, South Carolina, USA

© 2021 by Parlor Press
All rights reserved.

Printed in the United States of America
S A N: 2 5 4 - 8 8 7 9

Library of Congress Cataloging-in-Publication Data on File

Names: Milson-Whyte, Vivette, editor. | Oenbring, Raymond, 1979- editor. | Jaquette, Brianne, editor.
Title: Creole composition : academic writing and rhetoric in the anglophone Caribbean / Edited by Vivette Milson-Whyte, Raymond Oenbring, and Brianne Jaquette.
Description: Anderson, South Carolina : Parlor Press, [2021] | Series: Lauer series in rhetoric and composition | Includes bibliographical references and index. | Summary: "Essays trace the history and current practices of, and ways forward for, teaching composition in the Anglophone Caribbean. They contextualize disciplinary developments related to rhetoric and composition and academic literacies in the Caribbean and explore how academic writing is viewed and taught in the region"-- Provided by publisher.
Identifiers: LCCN 2021029186 (print) | LCCN 2021029187 (ebook) | ISBN 9781643171111 (paperback ; acid-free paper) | ISBN 9781643171128 (hardcover ; acid-free paper) | ISBN 9781643171135 (pdf) | ISBN 9781643171142 (epub)
Subjects: LCSH: English language--Rhetoric--Study and teaching (Higher)--Caribbean, English-speaking. | Academic writing--Study and teaching (Higher)--Caribbean, English-speaking. | English language--Composition and exercises--Study and teaching (Higher)--Caribbean, English-speaking.
Classification: LCC PE1405.C27 C74 2021 (print) | LCC PE1405.C27 (ebook) | DDC 808/.0420711729--dc23
LC record available at https://lccn.loc.gov/2021029186
LC ebook record available at https://lccn.loc.gov/2021029187

2 3 4 5

Lauer Series in Rhetoric and Composition
Editors: Thomas Rickert and Jennifer Bay

Cover design by David Blakesley.
Front cover image: Photo by Jakob Owens on Unsplash.
Back cover image: "Caribbean Map," Uwe Dedering [CC BY-SA 3.0 (https://creativecommons.org/licenses/by-sa/3.0/)]

Printed on acid-free paper.

Parlor Press, LLC is an independent publisher of scholarly and trade titles in print and multimedia formats. This book is available in paper, cloth and eBook formats from Parlor Press on the World Wide Web at http://www.parlorpress.com or through online and brick-and-mortar bookstores. For submission information or to find out about Parlor Press publications, write to Parlor Press, 3015 Brackenberry Drive, Anderson, South Carolina, 29621, or email editor@parlorpress.com.

Contents

Preface: Hurricanes, Colonialism, and Language   *vii*
    Vivette Milson-Whyte, Raymond Oenbring,
    and Brianne Jaquette

Acknowledgments   *xiii*

Introduction: Expanding Linguistic Diversity   *3*
    Vivette Milson-Whyte, Raymond Oenbring,
    and Brianne Jaquette

Section One: Reflections on Linguistic Turmoil   *37*

1 Teaching Literacy Skills in the Jamaican Creole-Speaking Environment: A Reflection   *39*
    Carmeneta V. Jones

2 Building around Nation Language: A Critical Reflection on Teaching Composition at the University of The Bahamas   *76*
    Jacob Dyer Spiegel

Section Two: Empirical Studies of Attitudes and Time Management   *105*

3 Teaching on Island Time: Deadlines, Procrastination, and Composition at the University of The Bahamas   *107*
    Christine E. Kozikowski

4 Academic Writing in the Caribbean: Attitudes Matter   *125*
    Melissa L. Alleyne

Section Three: Perspectives on Language and Error   *155*

5 Understanding and Shifting a Marking Community's Response to Students' Writing: Lessons from Jamaican Instructors' "expression" Comments   *157*
    Annife Campbell

6 Balancing Composition and Grammar in the UTech, Jamaica Classroom   *178*
    Daidrah Smith and Michelle Stewart-McKoy

7 "African American" Anglophone Caribbean Writers in a
   Historically Black University Writing Center   *202*
      Kendra Mitchell

Section Four: Institutional Contexts   *221*

8 Administrators' and Lecturers' Perceptions of English
   Language-Mediated Academic Literacy Skills
   Development at a Jamaican University   *223*
      Clover Jones McKenzie and Beverley Josephs

9 Solving Problems and Signaling Potential in Writing
   Program Administration at The University of The West
   Indies, St. Augustine Campus (UWISTA)   *250*
      Tyrone Ali

Section Five: Regional Perspectives: Archipelagic Thinking   *269*

10 The Small Island *Polis*: Rhetorical Pedagogy
   in the Caribbean   *271*
      Raymond Oenbring

11 Transnational and Translingual Perspectives on Creoles in
   Education: Casting a Wider Net into the Caribbean Sea   *285*
      Valerie Combie

Section Six: A Way Forward   *301*

12 Academic Literacies: Literacy Facilitators'
   Framework for Self-Empowerment in the Anglophone
   Caribbean Postsecondary Context   *303*
      Clover Jones McKenzie and Tresecka Campbell-Dawes

13 Postcolonial Composition: Appropriation and
   Abrogation in the Composition Classroom   *320*
      Heather M. Robinson

Afterword: Creole Composition?   *343*

Contributors   *351*

Index   *355*

Preface: Hurricanes, Colonialism, and Language

Vivette Milson-Whyte, Raymond Oenbring, and Brianne Jaquette

On September 12, 2017, days after Hurricane Irma had devastated numerous Caribbean islands, the two major daily newspapers in the Bahamian capital, Nassau, went to press with the same above-the-fold headline (see Figure 1). Both papers were quoting Bahamian Prime Minister Dr. Hubert Minnis's assessment of the state of the tiny underdeveloped settlement of Ragged Island in the southern Bahamas; Ragged Island was "unlivable." Despite the seriousness of the plight of those affected by the storm, public and social media discourse in the Bahamas that day focused in significant part on a peculiar fact about the two competing headlines: the *Nassau Guardian* had spelled the word *unlivable* using the American spelling (Glinton, 2017), and the *Nassau Tribune* had spelled the same word using the distinctly British spelling *unliveable* (Russell, 2017). This peculiar incident placed in sharp relief the tension between British and American orthographies and educational cultures in the country, a tension that is no accident but stems from fact that the Bahamas is a former British colony heavily influenced by the language and culture of its geographically closer neighbor to the north, the United States—a situation that is mirrored in countries throughout the Caribbean region.

While popular and social media discourse in the Bahamas on September 12 started off as a discussion about the influence of American English and British English spellings, the conversation soon expanded to complex and broad issues regarding language, education, economics,

Figure 1.

and colonialism in the Bahamas and the broader Caribbean region. Bahamians chose to spend their time debating the correct spelling of the word *unliv(e)able* not just as a pedantic exercise, but also because the push and pull that such language choices have has a direct impact on their lived experiences. On a daily basis, Bahamians and other Caribbean people live with both the legacies of the British colonial system and encroaching American hegemony in language and education.

This instability of Caribbean linguistic identity is further complicated by the fact that in the region Standard Englishes exist side by side and are almost symbiotically linked with nonstandardized local Creole Englishes (that is, languages that developed in the colonial era from the contact of English with the numerous African languages spoken by black Caribbean people's slave ancestors).

No one in the Caribbean welcomed the twin hurricanes Irma and Maria in the fall of 2017, but they have caused scholars, activists, and columnists on both sides of the Atlantic and on both sides of the north/south divide to critically reassess the political, economic, and linguistic relationships between Western powers and their former and current colonies in the Caribbean basin. For example, UK barrister and former Attorney General of the British territory of Anguilla Rupert Jones argued in the UK's *Guardian* that when "the [British] foreign secretary arrives in the Caribbean, I hope he will maximise the UK's response to the devastation wreaked by Irma, as well as using it as an opportunity to discuss our relationship with the overseas territories. It's a conversation long overdue" (Jones, 2017). The government of the United States was also criticized for its slow response to Hurricane Maria in Puerto Rico and Hurricane Irma in the United States Virgin Islands. The power dynamics that result in these slow responses and lack of attention to former and current colonies are complicated and long-standing, but the focus on conversations that need to be had and what words, or spellings, should make up those conversations shows us how significant language and rhetorical ability will be to any change in the status quo of power relationships in the Caribbean. Furthermore, in an increasingly globalized world, the conversations about the Caribbean are of interest to people not only on the ground in the Caribbean but also elsewhere. Indeed, the participants of the discussion cross national boundaries, and the discussions themselves touch on issues of power and language in communities across the globe. Questions about how language is used, what kind of language has power, and who has the "right" to use that language are local, national, and global issues.

While words (and their spellings) are not financial resources or aid, both claiming and using language are important political and social tools. In the contemporary musical *Hamilton*, about the life of American statesman Alexander Hamilton told through hip-hop music, another hurricane marks a moment of pivot and opportunity—or to use rhetorical terminology, a point of *kairos*. In the play, the song "Hurricane" tells the story of how a hurricane was the impetus for Hamilton to move from St. Croix, presently in the United States Virgin Islands, to New York and, therefore, start his trajectory to becoming a founding father of the United States. The writer of *Hamilton*, Lin-Manuel Miranda, himself a descendant of Puerto Rican immigrants, makes the connection between the moment of the hurricane and Hamilton's leaving for a different life, but he does not attribute Hamilton's success to just his intelligence or his ambition. In Miranda's (2016) play, Hamilton's dexterous skill with the English language—especially his ability to write—leads him forward in life. The lyrics of "Hurricane" read: "I wrote my way out / Wrote everything down far as I could see / I wrote my way out." Indeed, in Miranda's account, it is Hamilton's ability with a pen that sends him forward in his life; language is not an isolated entity but a necessary part of Hamilton's success.

We agree with Miranda's sentiment about the power of language—in part. In this book, we argue that we need to recognize how the rhetorical power of language has shaped forces in the Caribbean. However, unlike Miranda's focus on Hamilton's movement out, we believe that there needs to be a reassessment of how best to give the tools of language to Caribbean citizens within the space of the Caribbean itself as well as in transnational spaces. We don't want to write our way out; we want to *write our way in*.

For centuries, debates about how to speak, how to write, and how to be in the Caribbean have been determined by colonial or imperial powers. What is standard or non-standard, allowed or stigmatized, affects the speech and writing choices that the people of the Caribbean make, and those choices influence their identity, as well as their educational, social, and economic experiences. Being told in school that you do not know how to write properly in standard English, or not getting a job working with tourists because of the way you sound, or hearing over and over again that your country is beautiful but backwards, or that your accent is "exotic" but hard to understand, can shape everything from how you feel about yourself to how much money you earn over your lifetime to how you participate in your world. The discussion around issues like *unliv(e)able*, then, is not just over-exacting but rather a debate about Caribbean identity and the (hopefully very *liv[e] able*) Caribbean future.

The essays in this collection, then, draw attention to how important ownership of language is in creating a sense of self, for both individuals and their islands. We recognize the fact that the issues of language play out in the writing of Caribbean students and how they are taught to write. Many individuals might view teaching students to write as merely an educational proposition, but it is in fact a political statement. How we teach students to view themselves as writers is inextricably linked to how we teach them to view themselves as people and as citizens of their countries and the world. This view of the writing classroom has not historically been a part of writing instruction in the Caribbean, but it is gaining prevalence as the pedagogy of composition is being more widely considered in the region.

Undoubtedly, one of the most fundamental political acts we can perform as teachers and scholars is to help students develop the tools to express their identities and their intellectual, economic, social, and cultural realities. One of the best ways to do this is to help them be better writers. For too long, students in the Caribbean—both at the K-12/13 level and at the postsecondary level—have been taught that their work is not good enough and that their writing is "atrocious." We need a new narrative to help students find power in their own voices. Much of the discussion around writing in the Caribbean has stemmed from outdated models of instruction that are a legacy of British colonialism or newer models imported from the United States. These mismatches have not been explored in enough detail; we need a conversation around what is being taught in the Caribbean, what is working and what is not, and how practitioners of writing can help students move forward with both self-confidence and skill. Complaints about how students are terrible writers do not move them forward. Throwing up our hands in frustration at their "errors" does not help them. What we need is real assessment of the situation of teaching writing in the Caribbean. We need to find out how we can create a praxis for teaching writing that is both uniquely Caribbean and also draws on previous international studies regarding best practices at the postsecondary level. We present this edited collection not as the answer to these issues but as part of the start of necessary discussions.

However, while this collection is rooted in the Caribbean and grows out of a need to define what writing instruction in the Caribbean means, it also speaks to a much wider audience, both colleagues who might have similar concerns regarding the power dynamics of their writing instruction and the growing body of scholars who are exploring how the discipline is crossing national boundaries as formalized academic writing becomes more common across the globe. Martins (2015) notes in his collection about transnational writing program administration that "transnational activities are thoroughly shifting the questions we ask about writing curricula, the space and the place in which writing happens, and the cultural and linguistic issues at the heart of the relationships forged in literacy work" (p. 1). This volume centers around similar questions of how to create writing pedagogy that does not replicate current power dynamics but acknowledges how teaching students to write can document and create shifts in networks of learning. Scholarship that focuses on international and transnational composition is still a developing field in the discipline of composition studies, and this collection is not only a part of the growing conversation generally but also an argument for the need to continually probe how, why, and where (academic) writing is taught.

References

Glinton, T. (2017, September 12). Unlivable. *The Nassau Guardian*. Retrieved from https://thenassauguardian.com/2017/09/12/unlivable-2/

Jones, R. (2017, September 12). Hurricane Irma has devastated British territories—so why such little aid? *The Guardian*. Retrieved from https://www.theguardian.com/commentisfree/2017/sep/12/hurricane-irma-british-territories-aid-anguilla

Martins, D. (2015). Transitional writing program administration: An introduction. In D. Martins (Ed.) *Transnational Writing Program Administration* (pp. 1–18). Boulder, CO: Utah State University Press.

Miranda, L. (2016). Hamilton: An American musical. In J. McCarter (Ed.), *Hamilton: The revolution* (pp. 23–26). New York: Grand Central Publishing.

Russell, K. (2017, September 12). Unliveable: PM urges remaining Ragged Island residents to evacuate. *The Tribune* (Nassau, Bahamas). Retrieved from http://www.tribune242.com/news/2017/sep/12/unliveable-pm-urges-remaining-ragged-island-reside/

Acknowledgments

Fitting for a study that crosses the waters of the Caribbean and beyond, this project has been worked on across islands, time zones, and continents. The collection was conceived of in The Bahamas, would not have taken off without input from Jamaica, and survived one of us moving to Norway. The ability to finish this book from three different locations was due not only to the blessings of technological advances but also to our own dedication to the project. Personal and professional circumstances pulled each of us away from the work at various times, but our collective belief in the need for an in-depth study of teaching academic writing in the Caribbean compelled us to the finish. As researchers, we have diverse backgrounds and different wells of knowledge. These were assets as we planned and executed the collection because we could offer our experiences and help one another consider ideas from new perspectives. While the book was often hard work, it was a joy to share the work with each other. Furthermore, it was a true pleasure to connect with all of the other players without whom this collection would not have succeeded. We thank them below.

First, we would like to thank David Blakesley at Parlor Press for his guidance through the process and his prompt and thorough work on the manuscript. At Parlor Press, we would also like to thank the Lauer Series in Rhetoric and Composition editors, Thomas Rickert and Jennifer Bay.

Second, the contributors included here created spaces to engage in reflection, research, writing, and yet more reflection. We thank them for their hard work, their specialized knowledge, and their thoughtful prose. Their contributions provided a vital expansion of scholarship about academic writing in the Caribbean. Other colleagues at The University of the West Indies, the University of The Bahamas, and Høgskulen på Vestlandet and in our larger academic circles listened to our project ideas and encouraged our work. To them, too, we are grateful.

Third, the various studies that inform the chapters would not have been possible without several cohorts of students and colleagues. We thank them for consenting to be included in investigations about academic writing education in the Caribbean and for Caribbean-origin students.

Fourth, we are thankful to Jared Jameson for his copyediting skills. Given the variety of terms, usages, and spellings present in the collection, his task was not a small one. We also owe a debt of gratitude to Høgskulen på Vestlandet for a grant that covered more than half of the indexing costs. We thank the anonymous indexer for creating an index that is of great value to this project and, we hope, to future studies of writing in the Caribbean.

Finally, we thank our families and friends for supporting us on this journey, especially in those periods that required almost total commitment to the work and for providing needed distraction at other times.

—*Vivette, Raymond, and Brianne*

Creole Composition

Introduction: Expanding Linguistic Diversity

Vivette Milson-Whyte, Raymond Oenbring, and Brianne Jaquette

A growing number of composition scholars acknowledge that the field of rhetoric and composition must move beyond its home base of universities in the United States if it is to overcome the solipsistic tendencies of an academic discipline based mostly in one country. Indeed, despite the fact that respect for cultural and linguistic diversity in all forms has long been a central tenet of the tradition of composition studies, an increasing number of North American compositionists recognize that the discipline continues to suffer from a lack of international involvement and international perspective. These concerns have provided impetus for important scholarship working to internationalize the discipline, including recent edited volumes by Bazerman et al. (2012), Horner and Kopelson (2014), Martins (2015), and Mueller et al. (2017), and have encouraged compositionists to look to and engage with contemporary scholarship produced by scholars in the UK and internationally under the banner of *academic literacies* (see, for example, Lillis, Harrington, Lea, & Mitchell, 2015).

Several of these scholars expressing concern regarding the seeming lack of international perspective in the field of composition studies have coalesced their interests under the banners of the terms *translingualism* and *translanguaging*, terms that do not explicitly imply international engagement. According to Canagarajah (2011), one of the scholars most closely associated with this movement, the term *translanguaging* involves the following assumptions:

> that, for multilinguals, languages are part of a repertoire that is accessed for their communicative purposes; languages are not discrete and separated, but form an integrated system for them; multilingual competence emerges out of local practices where multiple languages are negotiated for communication; competence doesn't consist of separate competencies for each language, but a multicompetence that functions symbiotically for the different languages in one's repertoire; and, for these reasons, proficiency for multilinguals is focused on repertoire building. (p. 1)

Within the tradition of composition studies, a number of recent studies have promoted the terms *translanguaging* and *translingualism* as organizing points of identity, including, Atkinson et al. (2006), Canagarajah (2013), Horner, NeCamp, and Donahue (2011), Lu and Horner (2013), Bawarshi (2016), and Williams and Condon (2016). We, the editors of this volume, contend, however, that international engagements and perspectives should be more central to attempts to internationalize and *translinguafy* the field. As an example, although notions of translanguaging may appear polemical in American academic contexts, translanguaging can appear to be a banal fact of everyday life in academic contexts outside North America. Accordingly, we believe that the tradition of rhetoric and composition has much to offer to—and, potentially, much to learn from—our particular sociolinguistically-fascinating translingual teaching and research site: the postcolonial Anglophone Caribbean.

Postsecondary Writing Pedagogy: Regional Divides

Although activists and educators in the postcolonial Caribbean have long desired to craft educational and linguistic identities for their nations distinct from those of their former (and in some cases current) colonial master Britain and the physically closer imperial power the United States, the project of decolonization of education in these small still materially developing states has been a slow-going process. While educational opportunities for the black majorities of the territories of the Anglophone Caribbean were severely limited under British colonial rule, the global wave of decolonization in the second half of the twentieth century corresponded with governments in the region seeking to dramatically increase educational opportunities for their citizens. However, in the years leading up to and following independence (1962 in Jamaica, 1962 in Trinidad & Tobago, 1966 in Barbados, 1973 in the Bahamas), postsecondary education in the Anglophone Caribbean, including English language instruction, largely followed British-inherited models (see Devonish, 1986). These colonial legacies in English-language teaching largely remain intact to this day, and include: English-as-mother-tongue traditions of instruction (despite the fact that the home languages of most individuals in the Anglophone Caribbean are English-based creoles rather than Standard English), and heavy reliance on timed and written examinations, tests that punitively assess "errors" stemming from students' nonstandard varieties of English—both of which have traditionally served to limit access to higher education in the region.

Due in part to British-inherited educational models and subsequent "colonial lag," pedagogical theories of postsecondary writing instruction advanced slowly in the postwar period in the Anglophone Caribbean. However, in the same time period in the United States, ever expanding postsecondary enrollment (driven in part by the G.I. bill), and the subsequent need for scholarship addressing the writing deficits of underprepared postsecondary learners, led to a dramatic increase in research in the teaching of writing at the postsecondary level (see, for example, Crowley, 1998). These innovations have led to the establishment of the theory base and professional institutions of a distinct academic discipline, rhetoric and composition. Because of this history, rhetoric and composition's intellectual home base in the past several decades has been institutions in the United States. Nonetheless, the discipline of rhetoric and composition has, somewhat unevenly, exported itself to other parts of the English-speaking world, including the Anglophone Caribbean, in the form of American-style first-year writing courses.

In the decades since achieving their independence from Britain, understandable concerns about the Americanization of their culture have made many Anglophone Caribbean nations prefer, at times, to look to the UK for guidance in terms of pedagogy. Nonetheless, the significant difficulties that Caribbean student writers face in composing in Standard English have led Caribbean postsecondary institutions to teach American-style college writing courses with the goal of improving the perceived deficits in their students' writing, often using textbooks written for the American college composition market. However, despite routinely looking to the American tradition of rhetoric and composition for guidance, many college composition programs in the Anglophone Caribbean have continued using traditional pedagogical models that have long since been replaced and/or challenged by the American rhetoric and composition tradition. That is to say, Caribbean postsecondary institutions have taught composition classes without an extensive rhetoric and composition knowledge base. For example, while compositionists in North America have largely discredited the modes of discourse taxonomy and pedagogies that emphasize formal and mechanical correctness over the communication of meaning and the student-writer's development, composition instructors in the English-speaking Caribbean maintain much of what is commonly derided by North American rhetoric and composition scholars as traditional (or current-traditional) pedagogy.

Consistent with an emphasis on *product* over *process*, many postsecondary institutions in the Anglophone Caribbean have traditionally placed greater institutional weight on the rhetoric of *excellence* rather than social *equity* and ease of *access* (see, for example, Milson-Whyte, 2015), a rhetoric which manifests itself as grading standards that can seem punitive to non-Caribbean faculty. In fact, the perceived greater rigor of their instruction, especially compared to that of American educational institutions, seems to be a primary point of professional identity for some Caribbean composition instructors (Oenbring, 2017). Hand in hand with the rhetoric of *excellence* rather than *equity* has been the maintenance of what may appear to outsiders as traditional attitudes to standard and nonstandard Englishes. These conservative linguistic attitudes are likely to strike outsiders as surprising, especially because the home languages of the majority of the population in most Anglophone Caribbean nations are English creoles. Indeed, from the colonial order—or perhaps more precisely from postcolonial Caribbeans' affectations of the trappings of colonial order—language education from K-12/13 and into the postsecondary level in the Caribbean has, for decades, maintained largely traditional attitudes to standard and nonstandard usage.

Additionally, despite the fact that first-year academic writing courses have been taught for decades in postsecondary institutions in the Caribbean, very little scholarship has been developed about the unique situation of teaching academic writing in the region. There have been few published academic studies from the perspective of composition theory or academic literacies analyzing the specific problems and potentials in teaching writing to Caribbean postsecondary students, with much of the existing scholarship on the teaching of writing in the Anglophone Caribbean coming from the tradition of applied linguistics. Moreover, the scholarship that does exist on teaching academic writing to students from Caribbean countries has come in significant part from American institutions (for example, Holm, 1986; Nero, 2001, 2005; Carney, 2009).

Working to expand the existing body of research literature about the teaching of writing at the postsecondary level in the Caribbean region, this collection consists primarily of essays written by teacher-researchers with experience teaching writing at postsecondary institutions in the Anglophone Caribbean. *Creole Composition* speaks to the disciplinary conversations of rhetoric and composition and academic literacies while addressing specific issues with teaching academic writing to Anglophone Caribbean students. The volume provides much-needed knowledge to the community of teacher-researchers in the Anglophone Caribbean and elsewhere in the fields of rhetoric and composition/writing studies/academic literacies. This collection builds off and adds to conversations in several different fields of composition and writing studies, including: strategies to accommodate speakers of nonstandard and stigmatized language varieties in the classroom (Perry & Delpit, 1998; Horner & Trimbur, 2002; Bell & Lardner, 2005; Canagarajah, 2006, 2013; Lockett & RudeWalker, 2016); scholarship working to internationalize the field of composition studies (Bazerman et al., 2012; Horner & Kopelson, 2014; Martins, 2015); and scholarship seeking to evaluate composition's international reach (Muchiri, Mulamba, Myers & Ndoloi, 1995; Donahue, 2009). This expansion of the knowledge base of rhetoric and composition outside its home in the United States will not only benefit scholars working internationally teaching composition but will also make the discipline more agile for meeting needs of diverse student populations in the United States. The editors and authors of this volume hope it will spark a broader discussion of best practices for developing students' academic writing skills in these diverse cultures.

THE CARIBBEAN ENGLISH CREOLES

While compositionists and linguists have long recognized the importance of respecting students' home languages in the classroom, many individuals (including educators) in the Anglophone Caribbean fail to recognize that the mother tongue of most people in the region is something other than international Standard English. Born of the contact of English varieties with the myriad African languages spoken by contemporary black Caribbean peoples' slave ancestors, the home languages of most individuals in the Anglophone Caribbean are what are referred to by linguists as *creole languages*: mixed languages of reduced morphology and syntax that are spoken as home or first languages (as opposed to *pidgin languages*, which develop at contact sites to facilitate communication and trade but are not spoken as first languages). English-based creoles are the mother tongues of the majority of the population in all of the following Caribbean territories: Jamaica (where the home language of most of the population is referred to by linguists as *Jamaican Creole* and the general population as *Patois/Patwa*); Trinidad & Tobago (*Trinidadian Creole*); Barbados (*Bajan Creole*); Grenada (*Grenadian Creole*); the Bahamas (*Bahamian Creole/Bahamian Dialect*); Belize (*Belizean Creole*); Guyana (*Guyanese Creole*); Antigua & Barbuda (*Antiguan Creole*); St. Kitts & Nevis (*St. Kitts Creole*); St. Vincent & the Grenadines (*Vincentian Creole*); and in the US and British Virgin Islands (*Virgin Islands Creole*). On the United States mainland, *Gullah* is an English-based creole language spoken by the Gullah/Geechee community in the coastal Carolinas and Georgia. Although African American Vernacular English (AAVE) shares a number of the linguistic features of creole languages, linguists generally classify contemporary AAVE to be a dialect of English rather than a creole (although it may have originated as a creole language [Rickford, 2015]).

Although the term *creole language* is presently accepted as a neutral technical term within the field of linguistics, the term *creole* itself undeniably has a sordid history. While the term *creole* is often used in the United States to refer to the culinary culture of Louisiana, the etymology of the term *creole* traces back (through a history as both a pejorative term and as a reappropriated point of identity) to the early colonial era in Latin America to a Portuguese term, *criollo*, used to describe non-indigenous persons born in the Americas (cf. Mufwene, 2015, p. 134). (In the colonial French West Indies, the term *créole* was used to describe Caribbean-born Europeans.) For centuries, both Europeans and Caribbean peoples believed creole languages to be "broken," "bastardized," or "bad" versions of European languages; however, linguists have long argued that the Caribbean creole languages are systematic, "proper" languages (see, for example, the classic textbook introductions to pidgin and creole languages developed by Holm [e.g., 2000].)

While traditional, negative attitudes to the local creole languages remain relatively common in the general populations of Anglophone Caribbean nations, progress has been made in recent decades in building the esteem of the general populations of Caribbean countries for their local creole languages (see, for example, Wassink, 1999; Mühleisen, 2001). In this regard, there are many parallels between sociolinguistic attitudes to local creoles in the Caribbean and attitudes in the African American community in the United States to AAVE. Also negatively affecting Caribbean people's attitudes to their local creoles is the fact that the languages are predominantly oral, rather than written—owing in large part to the lack of broadly-accepted government-sanctioned orthographies (that is codified sets of spelling) as have been developed for Haitian Creole French (see, for example, Milson-Whyte, 2018).

Whether based off English vocabulary or that of another European language such as French (from which Haitian, St. Lucian, and Dominican Creoles developed), the Caribbean creoles all followed broadly similar historical patterns of ontogeny: they all developed under the conditions of slavery, when enslaved Africans brought to the Americas to work in the plantation economies—intentionally separated from speakers of the same African languages to reduce the chances of revolt—developed simplified versions of European languages in order to communicate with one another and Europeans. However, like all adult learners of second languages, the first generations of slaves in the Americas developed language capacities demonstrating the phonological and syntactic influences of their first languages. When these languages were passed on to and expanded by subsequent generations, they became the Caribbean creoles. Common features of Caribbean English creoles include: the presence of loanwords derived from African languages; lack of inflection for past participles and past participles used as adjectives (e.g., *use car* [for *used car*]); consonant cluster simplification (e.g., *touris* and *respec* instead of *tourist[s]* and *respect*); distinct and nonstandard use of *to be*; nonstandard subject-verb agreement; and *palatalization* of consonants (so that *can't* becomes *kyan* and *gal* becomes *gyal*).

Admittedly, the imprint of African languages on contemporary Caribbean creoles can seem limited to the untrained eye because their lasting influence in present day creoles lies more in the areas of *phonology* (the sound patterns of language), *morphology* (word parts), and *syntax* (word order) rather than on the *lexicon* (vocabulary). Accordingly, linguists refer to the role of African languages in the formation of contemporary creoles as *substrate* languages. Conversely, those languages which provide the bulk of the vocabulary of creole languages are referred to by linguists as *superstrate* or *lexifier* languages, which in the case of Caribbean creoles are European languages. Accordingly, English creoles are sometimes referred to as *English-lexifier creoles*.

Nonetheless, in most Anglophone Caribbean nations there exists a broad range of sociolinguistic varieties, ranging from creole varieties to international Standard English (with the term *Standard English* being used in a broad range of educational and non-educational contexts and seemingly lacking much of the baggage that the term might carry in the United States). This range of varieties is referred to by linguists as a *(post-)creole continuum* (DeCamp, 1971; Rickford, 1987). Those speakers speaking varieties closest to international Standard Englishes are said by linguists to speak the *acrolect*. Those speaking the strongest variety of the creole, often older, and more rural, are said by linguists to speak the *basilect*. Those speaking a variety somewhere between the acrolect and the basilect are said to speak the *mesolect* (see, for example, Bickerton, 1975). Nevertheless, most Caribbean English creole speakers, including English composition students, have some ability, oftentimes quite significant, to code-mesh and code-switch between and within different language varieties, dialects and registers, both written and oral, when they choose to do so.

Apart from the creole languages used primarily in oral and informal communication, many Anglophone Caribbean nations have developed their own unique, though largely still unstandardized, varieties of Standard English used in formal and written contexts. Although not formalized through dictionaries and usage guides, these Caribbean Standard Englishes (e.g., Jamaican Standard English) are the varieties generally expected in formal situations, including: courts of law, parliament, national news programs, and classrooms. While British English spellings remain the official standard in many Caribbean territories, they are often (as explored in the preface) used interchangeably with American spellings. Perhaps the most distinctive feature of Caribbean Standard Englishes is their preference for markedly formal usage in contexts where British, American, and other international varieties might prefer more informal language (Sand, 1999; Christie, 2003; Deuber, 2010). For example, several Caribbean Standard Englishes demonstrate a preference for the legalistic term *persons* in many contexts when speakers of British and American English would use the term *people*.

While at least one study has found that several of these highly formal preferences for usage in Caribbean Standard Englishes appear to be largely carryover of patterns of usage from the colonial era while contemporary British (and American) Englishes have moved to a more informal style (Oenbring, 2015), it appears clear that a number of markedly formal patterns of English in Caribbean Standard Englishes are the result of *hypercorrection*: that is, attempts by speakers of a nonstandardized dialect to affect the linguistic patterns of what they believe to be "correct" language but in doing so creating something other than "correct" language. A common hypercorrection found among even acrolectal Caribbean speech is the addition of /r/ sounds after vowels and at the end of words, even in locations where no standard variety of English pronounces an /r/ (e.g., so that *Africa* becomes *Africar* and *Cuba* becomes *Cubar*)—a hypercorrection suggested by some scholars to be enacted by speakers who are overgeneralizing what they perceive to be "correct" American /r/ pronouncing speech (e.g., at the end of words such as *car*), despite the fact that many Caribbean varieties are /r/ dropping (e.g., pronouncing *car* as /ka/) (see, for example, Christie, 2003, p. 16). Similarly, although many Caribbean creoles pronounce the voiceless 'th' sound /θ/ (found in words such as Standard English *think*) as /t/ (so that *think* becomes *tink* in Caribbean creoles), some individuals, in their attempts to avoid creole structures, will pronounce /θ/ in locations where Standard English only has /t/, especially in words where the Standard English spelling has <th> but the word is pronounced in Standard English as /t/; that is, they will engage in hypercorrection and pronounce words such as *Thompson* as /θampsən/ rather than the Standard English /tampsən/.

THE ANGLOPHONE CARIBBEAN

Of course, to speak in broad strokes about the Anglophone Caribbean region is to gloss over the political, cultural, linguistic, and educational heterogeneity of the region. Indeed, to refer to an "English-speaking Caribbean" as such is, as creole linguist Carrington (1978) has argued, "a convenient inexactitude which excuses itself simply because English is the official language of the states" (p. 85). That is to say, the notion of an "Anglophone Caribbean" is, largely, a myth—and this is a book about it.

As previously suggested, most territories of the Anglophone Caribbean are former British colonies that achieved independence in the second half of the twentieth century, including: Jamaica (1962), Trinidad & Tobago (1962), Barbados (1966), the Bahamas (1973), Grenada (1974), Dominica (1978), St. Lucia (1979), St. Vincent & the Grenadines (1979), Antigua & Barbuda (1981), and St. Kitts & Nevis (1983). (St. Lucia and

Dominica are especially rich sociolinguistic environments, with their French-based creoles coexisting side-by-side with English and English creoles, a legacy of the battles for territory between European powers in the colonial era.) Although Guyana (1966) is in South America and Belize (1981) is in Central America, both are generally considered part of the Anglophone Caribbean due to their shared history of British colonial rule and their linguistic, cultural, and economic connections with the Anglophone Caribbean. Nonetheless, several Anglophone Caribbean territories remain UK colonies, each having some degree of internal self-government. These include: the Cayman Islands, Turks & Caicos, the British Virgin Islands, Anguilla, and Montserrat. Also, a current UK colony is Bermuda, an island well to the north of the Caribbean in the Atlantic, that for cultural and historical reasons is often considered part of the Caribbean.

But wait, there's more! The United States has two non-self-governing territories in the Caribbean basin: the United States Virgin Islands and Puerto Rico, the former being Anglophone and the latter being, of course, Hispanophone. Furthermore, Creole English is the primary language of daily communication in the Dutch Caribbean colonies of Sint Maarten, Sint Eustatius, and Saba, and is an important *lingua franca* in the former Dutch colony of Suriname. Finally, there are regions of Spanish-speaking Latin American countries where substantial portions of the population speak English-based creoles, including: Limonese Creole (derived from Jamaican Creole) in Costa Rica; Miskito Coast Creole (on the Caribbean coast of Nicaragua and Honduras); and San Andrés Creole (in the San Andrés and Providencia archipelago of Colombia).

Pre-Postsecondary English Instruction and Assessment in the Anglophone Caribbean

Stemming in large part from their British colonial heritage, Anglophone Caribbean nations maintain a tradition of assessing—and gatekeeping—students during their secondary education through a series of high-stakes tests that stem from the models of the British O-level, A-level, and General Certificate of Secondary Education (GCSE) examinations (that prevailed in the region until almost the end of the twentieth century). Generally, students who gain immediate entry into first-year writing courses in universities in the Anglophone Caribbean have attained the highest grades awarded in either of two current Caribbean regional examinations administered by the Caribbean Examinations Council (CXC). These are a Grade 1 in the Caribbean Secondary Education Certificate (CSEC) English Language examination or a Grade 1 or Grade 2 in Communication Studies in the Caribbean Advanced Proficiency Examination (CAPE). The CSEC English Language examination, usually done at the end of Grade 11, broadly tests language usage in narrative writing, descriptive writing, persuasive writing, summary writing, and grammar skills while the CAPE Communication Studies examination, done at the end of Grade 12 or 13, assumes additional language education regarding linguistic analysis in terms of appreciating creole languages. Students are also accepted into writing courses with equivalent qualifications from the previous examining body (Cambridge) in the region in the form of a Grade A in the General Certificate of Education (GCE) Ordinary (read: Secondary) Level English Language or a Grade A or B in the GCE General Paper. Students with equivalent passes from other recognized examining bodies in or outside of the region are usually allowed entry into the first-year academic writing courses following assessment of their qualifications.

Some postsecondary institutions administer an English Language Proficiency Test to students who do not have these qualifications (that is, at least a Grade 1 in CSEC English Language or its equivalent) while others routinely administer an English Language Proficiency Test to all incoming students to determine their placement in the general first-year writing course/s or in a developmental English Language course. The Language Proficiency Test, whether administered to some or to all new students in an institution, signals challenges regarding students' writing proficiency. These challenges are usually brought to the fore annually when regional English Language examination results are released or periodically when content area faculty complain about students' weak writing (see Milson-Whyte, 2015), but various studies have also confirmed difficulties experienced in writing in English by students who have gained entry into first-year academic writing courses (see, for example, McLaren & Webber, 2009; Rose, 2016).

For some faculty, these writing challenges are particularly troubling because students would have completed five to seven years of secondary education—beyond as many years at the kindergarten and primary levels—in which the medium of instruction was English. Educated in this system that involves much rote work, skills and drills, and high-stakes testing each year and at the end of select grades, students are expected to develop mastery of English, a critical marker of education in the Anglophone Caribbean. The reality, however, is that many students' limited mastery of English challenges assumptions about English as the medium of instruction. In other spaces, this medium would be considered the given; however, in the Anglophone Caribbean most students speak a creole language. Nevertheless, until very recently, the English Creoles were not accommodated in education in most countries in this region. Teaching was based on an English-as-mother-tongue tradition, the goal being to make children monolingual and mono-literate in English. Recent course syllabuses that include accommodation of children's home language in the early years of schooling suggest moving students to the target language (English) as quickly as possible, thereby still promoting a monolingual agenda. Additionally, arrangements are not in place for (consistently) teaching students via contrastive analysis so that they may perceive the differences in their language varieties (Craig, 2006; Milson-Whyte, 2018).

Given these arrangements, and because English is the lexifier for the English-based creoles, many predominantly creole-speaking children in the Anglophone Caribbean perform better in listening in English rather than in producing written English. Additionally, undergraduates frequently produce mixtures of English and creole—that they consider English—when they are required to write in English. Evidence of creole features in writing in English is often interpreted as undergraduates' difficulty in writing at length in English, leading to the not uncommon view that postsecondary writing instruction should continue the K-12/13 focus on proficiency/grammar concerns rather than address academic/university literacies.

POSTSECONDARY WRITING INSTRUCTION IN THE ANGLOPHONE CARIBBEAN

The previously discussed culture of secondary high-stakes testing extends in many Anglophone Caribbean nations to the postsecondary level, where at many institutions there remains a tradition of rigorously-graded course assignments, end-of-semester writing assignments, and timed essay final examinations. While some institutions have engaged in reforms, including ending end-of-semester timed essay exams and embracing the banner of *process writing*, these changes have often been surface level. As Milson-Whyte (2015) notes, sometimes these reforms equate to "superficial elements of process writing [being] grafted onto a product-driven system" (p. 152).

This superficial engagement with process-focused pedagogies often translates into a tendency for Caribbean composition instructors to focus on surface errors in students' writing and to expect or explain errors as being a result of the influence of creole use. The unique phonological and syntactic features of Caribbean creoles do, for certain, manifest themselves frequently in Caribbean postsecondary students' writing—as "errors" in Standard English expression (e.g., *several tourist* [from consonant cluster simplification] rather than *several tourists*). Nonetheless, most of the "errors" in Caribbean postsecondary students' writing cannot be directly attributed to the "interference" of their home languages; instead, many, if not most, of the errors in Caribbean first-year postsecondary students' writing are comparable to well-established patterns often found in basic writing (e.g., use of informal, personal language in formal writing [see Lunsford, 1980, p. 281]; and use of evidence and discourse conventions inappropriate for academic registers [see Miller, 1986, p. 295]). Perhaps more important in determining the formal written output of Anglophone Caribbean students than the direct influence of linguistic structures of their home languages are the orally-focused cultures of Anglophone Caribbean nations—cultures that often lead students to enter postsecondary learning environments with limited experience writing in formal Standard English and limited knowledge of the conventions of academic writing—despite the fact that Standard English is the *de jure* language of instruction from primary school on.

Also important to the stylistic proclivities of Anglophone Caribbean postsecondary student writers is the Caribbean esteem for highly formal language, what is referred to by one noted Caribbean linguist as *erudite English* (Roberts, 2007, p. 219). For example, Caribbean postsecondary students, mirroring Standard English writers throughout the region, tend to demonstrate a proclivity for frequent use of passive voice constructions, a well-known feature of legal and scientific writing (see, for example, Oenbring's [2010] study of Caribbean newspaper writing). Composition pedagogy has tended to treat passive voice constructions as stiltedly formal and undesirable in student writing. Thus, these distinct patterns of usage represent a conundrum for local and expatriate composition/writing instructors in the Caribbean: should these nonstandardized but, nonetheless, normalized national and regional proclivities in Caribbean Standard Englishes be treated as errors?

The Material Situation

Engagement with issues related to error or developments in writing studies scholarship in general is not something local Caribbean teacher-researchers readily do, in part, on account of material conditions. An outsider could easily conclude that there is, in the region, a lack of interest in professionalization. Apart from the apparent simple lack of desire by local scholars in institutionalizing the field of composition/writing studies in the region (which could be argued is a primary reason why rhetoric and composition/writing studies is significantly less developed as a field in Canada than it is in the United States) and the natural tendency toward institutional siloing that is exacerbated by the archipelagic nature of the Caribbean region (it's not our fault if our thinking is *insular*), a major hurdle in the advancement and professionalization of writing studies in the region is economic. As small still-developing states, Caribbean countries (and their public universities) are simply unable to provide students the same levels of service that western institutions provide. Bearing heavy teaching loads, Caribbean composition instructors have not traditionally been expected to engage with or in research. Moreover, significant issues remain for most Anglophone Caribbean universities in the areas of facilities, technology, and staffing. For example, many Caribbean universities lack resources for accommodating student disabilities, such as accessible classrooms and well-resourced disability support offices. Indeed, imagine a situation where ten or more full-time instructional staff—each teaching 140 or more writing students per semester—all attempt to support students through in-office consultations while sharing a single small office.

All this is to say, despite sun and sand vacation advertisements that paint the Caribbean as a paradise (see, for example, Strachan, 2003), teaching composition (and other courses) at Caribbean universities often means making the most of a decidedly unglamorous situation; our offices do not have ocean views (mostly). At many institutions this material/facilities situation fosters a teaching environment that rewards instructor resourcefulness. No computer-integrated classrooms with desktop computers available for instructional purposes to introduce students to library resources and research strategies? Ask students to bring in their laptops (or tablets [or smartphones]) and hope that the classroom's wi-fi signal is strong enough to support a virtual computer-integrated classroom. A/C in your classroom not working? You could send a report up the chain of command or submit a work order through the official channels and sweat the whole semester (the students will be used to it), or you could put your English PhD to use and try to hotwire the A/C unit outside (*editors' note: none of the editors or authors of this book have tried this *cough**).

While some institutions (such as The University of the West Indies [UWI] at Mona in Jamaica and the University of The Bahamas) have recently sought to increase the quality of their instruction by hiring more full-time academic writing faculty (often with PhDs), at other Caribbean postsecondary institutions writing courses are taught largely by cheaper part-time instructors, who are less likely to have training in composition/writing studies and unlikely to engage in research. (Advanced degrees with a focus on postsecondary writing instruction are only possible at one Anglophone Caribbean institution, UWI, Mona—and, even there, students can only approach the topic of writing instruction based out of other degree programs, such as education or linguistics, with co-supervision from one of those areas.) With the discourses of *writing program administration* being largely unknown in the Caribbean, the task of overseeing multi-sectional writing courses is often performed at Caribbean institutions by a *(section) coordinator* who is unlikely to have extensive course release to support their administrative work. Furthermore, the understandable desire of some Caribbean universities to employ their own nationals has discouraged cross-pollination of perspectives on writing instruction; many Caribbean institutions have a tendency to hire their own graduates as faculty.

CREOLE COMPOSITION

As the systematic study of strategies to develop postsecondary students' writing is still in its infancy in the Caribbean, we do not claim to present in this volume a unified approach to teaching college composition to Caribbean and Caribbean-origin students. Instead, we see this volume as both taking stock of the current state of postsecondary writing pedagogy in the Caribbean as well as driving the inchoate discipline forward. We have consciously chosen the title *Creole Composition* in part because it emphasizes the diversity of approaches and perspectives of Caribbean teacher-scholars to postsecondary writing instruction. In other words, *Creole Composition* refers both to the object of study of this collection and to the way it has been written—or composed: that is, including a *mixture* of perspectives on teaching writing at the postsecondary level in the Anglophone Caribbean and coming from teacher-scholars of varying personal and academic backgrounds. Accordingly, the volume includes work from both local Caribbean scholars and from non-Caribbean academics who either have experience teaching composition at postsecondary institutions in the Caribbean (i.e., expatriates) or from faculty working at institutions outside the Caribbean with a substantial number of Caribbean-origin students. Some chapters clearly reflect traditional Caribbean attitudes to postsecondary writing instruction; other chapters seek to reform these traditional practices. Some chapters' interventions come out of discussions in the field(s) of writing studies, while other chapters reflect their authors' primary training in other fields, such as applied linguistics, education, and literary studies. Moreover, the chapters use a variety of styles and methods, ranging from highly personal reflective essays to empirical studies following IMRaD format.

When choosing chapters for this collection, the editors consciously selected contributions from a broad geographic range in the region. This volume, therefore, brings together work from teacher-researchers from six different institutions in five different Caribbean territories: Jamaica, the Bahamas, Barbados, Trinidad and Tobago, and the United States Virgin Islands. Heavily represented among the contributors are faculty and graduates of the different campuses of The University of the West Indies, the premier regional research university. The collection also includes chapters from two scholars working at institutions in the United States, specifically in Florida and New York, who focus in their work on the writing development of Caribbean-origin students in postsecondary learning environments. Following are section overviews and introductions to individual chapters in the collection.

Section 1: Reflections on Linguistic Turmoil

Initiating a dialectic between endogenous and exogenous perspectives, the first section in the volume, entitled "Reflections on Linguistic Turmoil," contains two highly reflective essays by teacher-scholars working in the region. "Teaching Literacy Skills in the Jamaican Creole-Speaking Environment: A Reflection" by Carmeneta Jones and "Building around Nation Language: A Critical Reflection on Teaching Composition at the University of The Bahamas" by Jacob Dyer Spiegel are from a Caribbean-born scholar and a newly arrived expatriate, respectively. Both of these essays follow a long-established tradition in composition studies of personal and reflective scholarship. They highlight the importance of reflective practice in evaluating not only the teacher's place in the classroom but also how teachers relate to their students, design their courses, and encourage their students' own reflections. As Ryan (2013) argues, "treating 'self' as a subject of critical study" can create habits of learning that transcend far beyond the classroom (p. 145). These essays showcase the relevance of that idea both for the students and for the teacher as learner.

Furthermore, both essays in this section can also be read as a part of the tradition of personal narrative as academic work. Scholars have argued for the value of personal reflection not only in addition to scholarship but also *as* scholarship. This is a sentiment to which academic writing is often hostile. For example, Tompkins (1987) argues that there is a sense in academia that "you can't talk about your private life in the course of doing your professional work" (p. 169). While not only personal in nature, Jones and Dyer Spiegel's essays follow in the line of scholarship that acknowledges the role our personal lives play in our work, and, more than that, that personal experience and academic experience are not two separate strains of our existence. These essays could not have been written without the lived experience of the authors, and that is not something they shy away from but fully embrace.

Finally, the two chapters in this section also introduce a major thread that can be found in many chapters in the collection—the idea that the Caribbean writing classroom can and should be a place where students are allowed and encouraged to express themselves in their local creole language/s. While US-trained composition scholars will be familiar with analogous arguments in the American context—due to the 1974 CCCC "Students Rights to Their Own Language" resolution and more recent related work, such as Elbow (2002), Smitherman and Villaneuva (2003), Cobb Scott, Straker, and Katz (2008), and Gilyard (2011)—in the Caribbean, accommodating students' creole language/s in K-12/13 and postsecondary classrooms is a relatively new development. Indeed, in the first essay in the book, Carmeneta Jones traces her own growth as an educator starting when she was a young student facing stigmatization in the classroom due to her mother tongue's being Jamaican Creole. Instead of being turned away from learning by her negative experiences, she used them to develop her own teaching practice that pushed against the idea that there was no space in the classroom for the language that she spoke in other parts of her life. Jones outlines her time as a literacy and writing teacher at the primary, secondary, and postsecondary levels in Jamaica and argues that using texts, songs, and other media in local creole languages can increase student engagement in the learning of standard language forms and reduce student fear in the writing classroom. Jones's chapter also offers readers unfamiliar with the structures of Caribbean creole languages some inviting examples of eye dialect Jamaican Creole.

Keeping with the reflective style of the first chapter, Jacob Dyer Spiegel's chapter "Building around Nation Language: A Critical Reflection on Teaching Composition at the University of The Bahamas" discusses the author's experience using Caribbean philosopher and literary critic Kamau Brathwaite's notion of *nation language* as a theoretical frame to encourage composition students to engage with and write in their local creole tongue. Using examples of students' poetry and prose produced during the class, Dyer Spiegel notes that "composition teachers want students to be conscious of language, of the choices that we have as writers, and to produce content that is critical of our surroundings, influences, and the contexts that surround us. By using Brathwaite's *nation language*, by rooting language development in a historical trajectory, we anchor students' exploration of voice" (this volume). Like Jones, Dyer Spiegel offers insight into traditional Caribbean attitudes to Standard English (often referred to in the Bahamas with the deferential colonial epithet *the Queen's English*) and the *linguistic trauma* that many Caribbean students bring to the postsecondary composition classroom.

Section 2: Empirical Studies of Attitudes and Time Management

While many scholars in composition studies have argued for more personal and reflective student writing and composition scholarship, other compositionists have pushed in a very different direction—that is, encouraging the field to move more toward more empirical work traditionally characteristic of education and social science. Indeed, there has in recent years been in rhetoric and composition a broad move toward more empirical data-driven approaches to the assessment of writing programs and their outcomes. For example, survey and questionnaire-based research has become an established tradition in rhetoric and composition scholarship (e.g., Anderson et al. 2006; Edwards & Reyman, 2018; Wells & Söderlund, 2018). Arguing for data-intensive empirical studies of writing programs, Lang and Baehr (2012) contend that "writing program administrators, faced with increasing demands for accountability and assessment, as well as widely varying student populations, need to have ways of understanding the interactions of students, faculty, and administrators in their present program, both in the short term and longitudinally" (p. 173). This new direction toward more empirical work in composition studies dovetails nicely with previous studies of postsecondary student writing in the Caribbean—which have largely come from scholars working in the traditions of applied linguistics and education.

Accordingly, shifting modes from the highly personal and reflective essays of the first section—with the two sections placed side-by-side to put the different perspectives into relief—the second section, entitled "Empirical Studies of Attitudes and Time Management," consists of two chapters relying upon survey data that trenchantly analyze the effects of culture and psychology on student learning in the Caribbean context. Christine Kozikowski's "Teaching on Island Time: Deadlines, Procrastination, and Composition at the University of The Bahamas" analyzes the effects (and lack thereof) of the Caribbean phenomenon of *island time* (that is, events starting late for no apparent reason and taking much longer than they should) on student time management and learning. Using questionnaires, Kozikowski interrogates both how Bahamian students approach deadlines and how their instructors attempt to structure their classrooms in a teaching and learning environment where *island time* is pervasive. As Kozikowski notes, "with its high-output requirement, English composition provides a useful space to examine student and faculty perceptions of deadlines and time management" (this volume).

In the same way that culture influences students' learning and approaches to learning, students' previous traumatic experiences with writing (which, as previously noted, are very common in the Caribbean) also seem to influence their attitudes in academic writing classrooms. In this vein, Melissa Alleyne's "Academic Writing in The Caribbean: Attitudes Matter" is an incisive look at how Caribbean postsecondary students' feelings about and attitudes toward writing classes may influence their performance. Using surveys and interviews of students and faculty, Alleyne compares the attitudes toward writing of students in different areas of study. As she argues, "both attitudes and motivation can impact a learner's behavior, consciously or subconsciously, since even if attitudes and the reasons behind their motivation are subconscious, learners undoubtedly take conscious, active roles in many aspects of language learning" (this volume). In Alleyne's study, students expressed moderate self-confidence in their ability to write in academic English.

Section 3: Perspectives on Language and Error

The third section of the book, "Perspectives on Language and Error," highlights the range of theories of—and attitudes to—creole and standard varieties in the Caribbean and international academic environments, from highly theoretical to traditional to critical approaches. Adopting a critical perspective, Annife Campbell's "Understanding and Shifting a Marking Community's Response to Students' Writing: Lessons from Jamaican Instructors' 'Expression' Comments" analyzes problematic tendencies in the prevailing approaches used to teach and assess academic writing in the Caribbean, focusing on a particular idiosyncratic marginal comment made by Jamaican academic writing instructors: *expression*. As Campbell notes, in the Jamaican postsecondary environment the term *expression* has become a vague catchall comment for language-related issues in student papers (including grammar, mechanics, documentation, and unidiomatic language), which is thus not particularly helpful or insightful for guiding student revision, thereby exacerbating Caribbean writing instructors' tendencies to grade essays in a punitive, highly negative manner. Instead of merely punishing students for their linguistic transgressions, Campbell—mirroring calls made by Bartholomae (2001) among others—encourages Jamaican and Caribbean writing instructors to see/understand the "errors" that lead to the *expression* comment as evidence of the students' incomplete socialization into academic discourses. Campbell's chapter also overviews salient differences between grading practices in North America versus the Caribbean; while in North America commenting on student papers is largely a dialogue between individual instructors and their students, at many Caribbean institutions grading is a much more involved group activity, including multiple levels of grade norming and multiple readers/raters.

Campbell's essay is an important part of the collection's attempt to fill a gap, for whereas there is a significant sub-section of composition studies that addresses (teacher) response to student writing (see, Anson, 1989; Brannon & Knoblauch, 1982; Connors & Lunsford, 1993; Ferris, 2003, 2018; Sorcinelli & Elbow, 1997; Straub, 2000), the same interest is not evident in/from the Anglophone Caribbean. The essay is also likely to contribute to Caribbean scholar-teachers' engagement with proposals by advocates of academic literacies regarding differences in requirements in disciplines, differences that require students to wear multiple hats as they pursue studies in various academic disciplines.

Noteworthy in Campbell's essay and that following his by Smith and Stewart-McKoy is treatment (or omission) of recent proposals regarding accommodation of linguistic identity in composition. These proposals include code-meshing—blending of languages and styles in academic writing (Young, 2009; Canagarajah, 2006)—and translanguaging—working in and across multiple languages in one's repertoire (Canagarajah 2009) and requiring negotiation of meaning (Horner, Lu, Royster, & Trimbur, 2011). While it can be argued that code-meshing and translanguaging are commonplace language practices in the Caribbean—though not untouched by stigma attending use of some varieties, it would seem that such proposals could be particularly useful for Caribbean students' writing at the postsecondary level. Additionally, while Campbell's essay ultimately references some of the associated scholars, without explicitly naming their proposals, Smith and Stewart-McKoy's essay reflects the extent to which most of the little existing research on academic writing in the Caribbean occurs without reference to recent developments in writing studies (from the US).

Working, then, from the tradition of applied linguistics, the framework from which most previous research in the Caribbean on the teaching of writing at the postsecondary level has been conducted, Smith and Stewart-McKoy's chapter "Academic Writing in the Anglophone Caribbean Tertiary-Level Classroom: Balancing Composition and Grammar in the UTech, Jamaica classroom" is an empirical study of Standard English errors in university English proficiency entrance examinations. For the study, Smith and Stewart-McKoy categorized Standard English errors in a corpus of student entrance essays according to their type and number. Calling for more rhetorically-aware explicit grammar instruction in Caribbean postsecondary writing classrooms, Smith and Stewart-McKoy note:

> The traditional view of instructors at the tertiary level, including writing instructors, has been that grammar instruction should be given at the pre-tertiary level and has no place in the tertiary-level writing classroom. The writing that learners at this level produce, however, continues to dispel this myth. Consequently, the view about the teaching of grammar at the tertiary level has

been changing, with more and more persons admitting to the need to *meet the students where they are*. (this volume)

While some scholars may find Smith and Stewart-McKoy's understanding of grammar and pedagogical best practices problematic, their study does reflect commonly held traditional assumptions in Caribbean academic environments—assumptions that, perhaps, can shift with increased sharing of developments in and applications of writing studies scholarship.

Working from a poststructuralist and translingualist understanding of language, Kendra Mitchell's "'African American' Anglophone Caribbean Writers in a Historically Black University Writing Center" takes a richly theorized look at the boundaries of black language, focusing on interactions between Anglophone Caribbean students and an African American tutor at an American HBCU writing center. Mitchell reminds that black students from the Caribbean and around the world study at American HBCUs, often mixing their home languages with structures in African American Language (AAL), with many students coming to self-identify as African American. Accordingly, the boundaries of African American language and identity are fluid. As Mitchell argues "by including Anglophone Caribbean students who self-identified as African Americans in the writing studies and writing center scholarship, writing center practitioners and compositionists can nuance the fluid linguistic identity constructs of these students in historically Black universities where discrete language systems converge and diverge" (this volume). By implication, while such actions are justified, even discussions of language and identity in academic writing classrooms throughout the Anglophone Caribbean would be an important step toward making explicit for students (and instructors) the highly political nature of the act of (teaching academic) writing in English in an area that is heavily creole-speaking.

Section 4: Institutional Contexts

Moving from the discourses of the classroom, the writing center, and language/personal identity to institutional discourses, the fourth section in the volume, "Institutional Contexts," sheds light on the institutional factors that influence the teaching of writing and professionalization of writing instruction in the Anglophone Caribbean. Informing this section is awareness that composition studies is a field often considered by administrators, students, and even the instructors who teach the courses as not "true" academic work—as noted by Roemer, Shultz, and Durst (1999) based on the tendency for literature scholars to view the teaching of first-year writing courses as "scutwork" (p. 381). However, as a frequently marginalized academic field, composition studies has a long tradition of critically analyzing the work it does within broader societies and within postsecondary institutions; composition is a highly reflective discipline. Indeed, with its identity as a field perpetually in question, the place of the discipline's work within postsecondary institutions has been a major concern of compositionists, including noted scholars such as Crowley (1995; 1998); Berlin (1987); and Horner (2017). In the Caribbean, however, the professional identities of those teaching postsecondary writing courses are even more problematic than they are at American universities, as the discourses of composition studies are not well entrenched in the region. Perhaps not surprisingly, critical analysis of the place of writing instruction within Caribbean postsecondary institutions and the identity of the field have been major points of concern for the few extant studies operating within the traditions of composition studies in the region. For example, Milson-Whyte (2015) critically analyzes the historical development of writing pedagogies at The University of the West Indies, Mona in Jamaica, and Oenbring (2017) investigates the identity of postsecondary writing instruction in the region.

While many of the issues faced by Caribbean composition instructors will be familiar to American and international faculty (such as the persistent belief among content faculty that one or two English composition courses should be sufficient to "fix" all problems in student writing), the teaching of academic writing at Caribbean institutions has its own unique institutional and cultural peculiarities. In their chapter "Administrators' and Lecturers' Perceptions of English Language-Mediated Academic Literacy Skills Development at a Jamaican University," Clover Jones McKenzie and Beverley Josephs present a portion of a wider empirical study, focusing specifically on institutional stakeholders' perceptions of academic writing classes. Jones McKenzie and Josephs find that, while content faculty and administrators believe writing classes to be important, few expressed awareness of what goes on in writing classes and few focused directly on improving students' writing skills in their own content classes.

The next chapter, Tyrone Ali's "Solving Problems and Signaling Potential in Writing Program Administration (WPA) at The University of the West Indies, St. Augustine Campus (UWISTA)," traces the development of the writing program at UWI, St. Augustine, in Trinidad and Tobago, both before and during his tenure as writing program administrator. As Ali's account captures, writing program administration at Caribbean institutions is often focused on managing practical details under significant financial limitations (Ali notes, for example, the recent important development at UWISTA of all part-time writing instructors finally being issued genuine UWI email addresses). While some faculty members with experience teaching at Caribbean postsecondary institutions may potentially find Ali's representations of institutional functions at UWISTA overly rosy, Ali's account does reflect traditional Caribbean optimism that administrative/bureaucratic interventions have positive effects on institutional outcomes. Indeed, many Caribbean faculty members and administrators view administrative interventions such as standardization of multi-section courses and rigorous norming of essay final exams as important (particularly at multi-island institutions), especially because the part-time instructors who teach writing classes likely have fewer academic credentials and less specialization than most content faculty. In other words, Caribbean institutions have a long tradition of highly-restrictive (putatively) "teacher-proof" courses.

SECTION 5: REGIONAL PERSPECTIVES: ARCHIPELAGIC THINKING

In her famous account of life in her native Antigua, *A Small Place*, Caribbean-born author Jamaica Kincaid emphasizes both Caribbean peoples' seeming inability to resist the colonial legacies that keep them oppressed and their lack of perspective on their past, present, and future, suggesting that "the people in a small place cannot give an exact account, a complete account, of themselves" (Kincaid, 1988, p. 53). Expanding upon Kincaid's notion of *a small place*, Bahamian journalism scholar Storr (2016) notes in *Journalism in a Small Place* that the Caribbean is "a colonized society that cannot . . . escape its colonial history . . . and struggles with its ambivalent existence. For Kincaid, Antigua, like other Caribbean countries becomes the ultimate small place as it struggles to define itself against the larger places of the world" (p. 33). While the editors of this volume share Kincaid's unease over how material conditions, political structures, and colonial legacies of the small island states of the Caribbean negatively affect Caribbean people's abilities to express their identities both in writing and otherwise, we do not share Kincaid's famous pessimism. Instead, we believe that—although traditional "small" nationalistic thinking has failed the developing states of the postcolonial Caribbean—the socio-geographic constraints of small island states provide *potentials*, and not just *problems*, for building liv(e)able democratic societies.

Therefore, continuing to move outward from the discourses of the classroom and institutional discourses, the fifth section of the book, entitled "Regional Perspectives: Archipelagic Thinking," with the notion of *archipelagic thinking* being borrowed from the work of Glissant (1997), consists of two chapters that read the problems and potentials of writing instruction in the Caribbean through the geographic, linguistic, and political frames of the Caribbean region. Oenbring's chapter "The Small Island *Polis:* Rhetorical Pedagogy in the Caribbean" argues that the socio-geographic constraints of small islands, together with the Caribbean cultural proclivity to oratory and orality, makes the Caribbean postsecondary writing classroom a particularly productive location to recover the oratorical foundations of rhetorical pedagogy. Following other contemporary rhetoricians who have construed the *polis*/city state of classical antiquity as a potential (though admittedly romanticized) model for contemporary discourse communities, Oenbring claims that the *polis* can serve as an alluring ideal to describe the potentials of public discourse in small island Caribbean states such as the Bahamas. As a whole, Oenbring's chapter serves as a call to writing instructors working in the Caribbean region to utilize Caribbean students' cultural proclivities to orality and oratory to build their rhetorical skills and rhetorical awareness.

While Oenbring's chapter encourages rhetorical engagement within the confines of individual small island states, Valerie Combie argues in her chapter "Transnational and Translingual Perspectives on Creoles in Education: Casting a Wider Net into the Caribbean Sea" that what is limiting progress in institutionalizing awareness of and respect for local creole languages in the Caribbean is a lack of transnational and translingual perspectives in Caribbean pedagogical discourse. As Combie notes, to the extent that regional pedagogical discourses for accommodating creole languages in primary to postsecondary classrooms have developed, these discourses have largely been between and within the territories of the Commonwealth Caribbean (that is the former and current colonies of Britain [e.g., Jamaica, Trinidad and Tobago]). Working in the United States Virgin Islands (a current territory/colony of the United

States), Combie offers examples from her own institution, the University of the Virgin Islands, and outside the Anglophone Caribbean to expand scholars' perspectives on the problems and potentials of accommodating local creole languages in educational environments.

Section 6: A Way Forward

Ending where the first chapter began, the final section of the book, entitled "A Way Forward," consists of two chapters written by scholars working at postsecondary institutions in places called Jamaica—one on an island in the Caribbean, the other in a region of Queens in New York City. As the name of the section suggests, both chapters offer Caribbean writing instructors and writing program administrators (the latter often not called by that name in the Caribbean or afforded comparable benefits to WPAs at American institutions) potential organizing frameworks around which to build and further institutionalize writing studies in the region. Because writing studies is in some ways a nascent field in the Caribbean, there is the opportunity to build programs that take best practices from multiple writing traditions. It is in this vein that Clover Jones McKenzie and Tresecka Campbell-Dawes add another layer to the discussion by arguing for the inclusion of an academic literacies framework for postsecondary instruction. Academic literacies largely stems from educational discourses in the UK and, according to Jones McKenzie and Campbell-Dawes, can serve as a particularly beneficial schema for institutionalizing and deepening the discourses of postsecondary writing instruction in the Anglophone Caribbean. In their chapter "Academic Literacies: Literacy Facilitators' Framework for Self-Empowerment in the Anglophone Caribbean Postsecondary Context," the authors contend that academic literacies is useful for furthering the field of writing studies in the region due in part to the fact that, as a discourse, academic literacies encourages writing instructors and their students to critically interrogate their subject positions in the classroom and in postsecondary environments. This can be a crucial step to building a discipline that is not top-down but is an organic fit with the needs and aims of the writers, both student and teacher, in the Caribbean.

Building a framework where the needs of the actors in the Caribbean are centered is connected to the work of our final essay which comes from Heather M. Robinson. Robinson contends in "Postcolonial Composition: Appropriation and Abrogation in the Composition Classroom" that in order to avoid perpetuating monolingualist and white-supremacist ideologies, instructors of students in and from postcolonial nations need to teach writing through an explicitly postcolonial framework. Giving examples from a Jamaican-origin student writing at York College/CUNY, and expanding gender identity by using *they* instead of *he* or *she*, Robinson argues that postcolonial students should be taught to actively reject the language of empire through the self-conscious blending of their native tongues with international standard varieties. Robinson's emphasis on students as agents in their choice of language rather than merely as passive acceptors of imposed linguistic and cultural frames mirrors the emphasis on students' agency found in other chapters in the book (such as Oenbring's chapter).

Additionally, Robinson's chapter supports recent proposals in composition studies for radical multilingual perspectives on language (see, for example, Young [2009] and Canagarajah [2009, 2011]). Robinson acknowledges the efforts of noted compositionist Peter Elbow who argues for students doing early drafting in their home or native languages but editing out their non-standard language varieties from final drafts for grading. However, Robinson categorically rejects Elbow's (1999, 2012) proposal because for Robinson, as is it likely to be for other translingualists, editing out the language allowed in early drafts constitutes a form of prejudice against home or native languages. Robinson's work most clearly makes the argument undergirding many of the points of view in this collection—that writing and speaking in multiple languages or dialects is not a weakness but a strength that can be brought into and developed in the composition classroom.

Furthermore, Robinson's essay highlights the fact that while this collection is about teaching writing in the Caribbean, it is written during a moment when writing studies is globalizing—when "local" ideas can have much to say to diverse sites across the globe. Although based out of the metropole, Robinson's study is connected specifically to the conditions of the Caribbean and could be equally applicable in educational environments around the globe. Robinson notes that "a postcolonial approach to the teaching of writing is particularly appropriate in a Caribbean context, although the strategies that apply in the West Indies could be equally valuable in composition and academic English as taught in the 'metropolitan centres' of the United Kingdom and the United States" (this volume). Robinson's essay and the others in the collection speak specifically to Caribbean milieus including environments with

Caribbean-origin students; however, one of the major ways forward for composition/writing studies will involve inclusion of experiences from local spaces into global ones. Indeed, we expect that these chapters and ideas will provide fodder for making local-global connections in writing studies in the US, UK, Caribbean, and elsewhere.

GLOSSARY OF TERMS

Because this volume has a primary audience that crosses national and disciplinary boundaries, the following terms are defined in order to facilitate readers:

Commonwealth Caribbean	United States
Caribbean Advanced Proficiency Examination (CAPE)	a series of secondary school proficiency exit exams modeled on the British A-levels generally taken by Caribbean students at the end of grade 12 or 13
Caribbean Secondary Education Certificate (CSEC)	a series of secondary school proficiency exit exams modeled on the British General Certificate of Secondary Education (GCSE)/O-levels generally taken by Caribbean students at the end of grade 11
(cross-)moderation	grade norming
English language / language foundations / foundation course	first-year writing / composition
faculty (academic/s)	professor/s (general term)
faculty (sub-section of a University; e.g. Faculty of Law)	college (academic unit within a university)
instructor (with a teaching-intensive workload)	lecturer
lecturer (general term)	professor (general term)
lecturer (rank)	assistant professor
senior lecturer (rank)	associate professor
(section) coordinator	writing program administrator
script	exam paper or any assignment designed to be graded by team grading
tertiary	postsecondary

References

Anderson, D., Atkins, A., Ball, C., Millar, K. H, Selfe, C., & Self, R. (2006). Integrating multimodality into composition curricula: Survey methodology and results from a CCCC research grant. *Composition Studies, 34*, 52–84.

Anson, C. M. (Ed.) (1989). *Writing and response: Theory, practice and research.* Urbana, IL: NCTE.

Atkinson, D., Crusan, D., Matsuda, P., Ortmeier-Hooper, C., Ruecker, T., Simpson, S., & Tardy, C. (2015). Clarifying the relationship between L2 writing and translingual writing: An open letter to writing studies editors and organization leaders. *College English, 77*, 383–386.

Bartholomae, D. (2001). Inventing the university. In E. Cushman, E. Kingten, B. Kroll, & M. Rose (Eds.), *Literacy: A critical sourcebook* (pp. 511–524). Boston, MA: Bedford-St. Martin's.

Bawarshi, A. (2016). Beyond the genre fixation: A translingual perspective on genre. *College English, 78*, 243–249.

Bazerman, C., Dean, C., Early, J., Lunsford, K., Null, S., Rogers, P., & Stansell, A. (2012). *International advances in writing research: Cultures, places, measures.* Anderson, SC: Parlor Press.

Bell, A., & Lardner, T. (2005). *African American literacies unleashed: Vernacular English and the composition classroom.* Urbana and Carbondale, IL: NCTE and Southern Illinois University Press.

Berlin, J. (1987). *Rhetoric and reality: Writing instruction in American colleges, 1900–1985.* Urbana, IL: NCTE.

Bickerton, D. (1975). *Dynamics of a creole system.* Cambridge: Cambridge University Press.

Brannon, L., & Knoblauch, C. H. (1982). On students' rights to their own texts: A model of teacher response. *College Composition and Communication, 33*, 157–166.

Canagarajah, A. S. (2006). The place of world Englishes in composition: Pluralization continued. *College Composition and Communication, 57*, 586–619.

Canagarajah, A. S. (2009). Multilingual strategies of negotiating English: From conversation to writing. *JAC, 29*(1–2), 17–48.

Canagarajah, A. S. (2011). Translanguaging in the classroom: Emerging issues for research and pedagogy. *Applied Linguistics Review, 2*, 1–28.

Canagarajah, A. S. (Ed). (2013). *Literacy as translingual practice: Between communities and classrooms.* New York: Routledge.

Carney, W. (2009). Rhetorical preferences of Caribbean university students: An empirical study. *Intercultural Communication Studies, 2*, 249–257.

Carrington, L. (1978). *Education and development in the English-speaking Caribbean: A contemporary study.* Buenos Aires: UNESCO.

Christie, P. (2003). *Language in Jamaica.* Kingston, Jamaica: Arawak Publications.

Cobb Scott, J., Straker, D., & Katz, L. (Eds.). (2008). *Affirming students' right to their own language: Bridging language policies and pedagogical practices.* Urbana, IL: NCTE.

Connors, R. J., & Lunsford, A. A. (1993). Teachers' rhetorical comments on student papers. *College Composition and Communication, 44,* 200–223.

Craig, D. (2006). *Teaching language and literacy to Caribbean students: From vernacular to Standard English.* Kingston, Jamaica: Ian Randle Publishers.

Crowley, S. (1995). Composition's ethic of service, the universal requirement, and the discourse of student need. *JAC, 15,* 227–240.

Crowley, S. (1998). *Composition in the university: Historical and polemical essays.* Pittsburgh: University of Pittsburgh Press.

DeCamp, D. (1971). Towards a generative analysis of a post-creole speech continuum. In D. Hymes (Ed.), *Pidginisation and creolisation of languages* (pp. 349–370). Cambridge: Cambridge University Press.

Deuber, D. (2010). Modal verb usage at the interface of English and a related creole: A corpus-based study of can/could and will/would in Trinidadian English. *Journal of English Linguistics, 38*(2), 105–142.

Devonish, H. (1986). The decay of neo-colonial official language policies: The case of the English-lexicon Creoles of the Commonwealth Caribbean. In M. Görlach & J. Holm (Eds.), *Focus on the Caribbean* (pp. 23–52). Amsterdam: John Benjamins.

Donahue, C. (2009). "Internationalization" and composition studies: Reorienting the discourse. *College Composition and Communication, 61,* 212–243.

Edwards, M., & Reyman, J. (2018). Open access and the economics of scholarship in rhetoric and composition studies. *Rhetoric Review, 37*(2), 212–225.

Elbow, P. (1999). Inviting the mother tongue: Beyond "mistake," "bad English," and "wrong language." *JAC, 19*(3), 359–388.

Elbow, P. (2002). Writing, dialects, and the culture of literacy. In C. L. Schroeder, H. Fox, & P. Bizzell (Eds.), *ALT DIS: Alternative discourses and the academy* (pp. 126–138). Portsmouth, NH: Boynton/Cook-Heinemann.

Elbow, P. (2012). *Vernacular eloquence: What speech can bring to writing.* Oxford: Oxford University Press.

Ferris, D. (2003). *Response to student writing: Implications for second language students.* Mahwah, NJ: Lawrence Erlbaum.

Ferris, D. R. (2018). "They said I have a lot to learn": How teacher feedback influences advanced university students' views of writing. *Journal of Response to Writing, 4*(2), 4–33.

Gilyard, K. (2011). *True to the language game: African American discourse, cultural politics, and pedagogy.* New York: Routledge.

Glissant, É. (1997). *Traité du tout-monde.* Paris: Gallimard.

Holm, J. (1986). The creole core: Grammatical interference in college composition. *Standard English as a Second Dialect Newsletter, 5*(1), 1–7.

Holm, J. (2000). *An introduction to pidgins and creoles.* Cambridge: Cambridge University Press.

Horner, B. (2017). Writing language: Composition, the academy, and work. *Humanities, 6.* Retrieved from https://www.mdpi.com/2076–0787/6/2/11/htm

Horner, B., & Kopelson, K. (Eds.). (2014). *Reworking English in rhetoric and composition: Global interrogations, local interventions.* Carbondale, IL: Southern Illinois University Press.

Horner, B., Lu, M., Royster, J. J., & Trimbur, J. (2011). Opinion: Language difference in writing: Toward a translingual approach. *College English, 73,* 303–321.

Horner, B., NeCamp, S., & Donahue, C. (2011). Toward a multilingual composition scholarship: From English only to a translingual norm. *College Composition and Communication, 63,* 269–300.

Horner, B., & Trimbur, J. (2002). English only and U.S. college composition. *College Composition and Communication, 53,* 594–630.

Kincaid, J. (1988). *A small place.* New York: Farrar, Straus and Giroux.

Lang, S., & Baehr, C. (2012). Data mining: A hybrid methodology for complex and dynamic research. *College Composition and Communication, 64,* 172–194.

Lillis, T., Harrington, K., Lea, M., & Mitchel, S. (2015). *Working with academic literacies: Case studies towards transformative practice.* Anderson, SC: Parlor Press.

Lockett, A., & Rude Walker, S. (2016). Creative disruption and the potential of writing at HBCUs. *Composition Studies, 44,* 172–178.

Lu, M., & Horner, B. (2013). Translingual literacy, language difference, and matters of agency. *College English, 75,* 582–607.

Lunsford, A. (1980). The content of basic writers' essays. *College Composition and Communication, 31,* 278–290.

Martins, D. (2015). *Transnational writing program administration.* Boulder, CO: Utah State University Press.

McLaren, I., & Webber, D. (2009). Writing right: Enhancing student engagement and performance in an ecology course. *International Journal of Environmental & Science Education, 4*(4), 365–380.

Miller, S. (1986). What happens when basic writers come to college? *College Composition and Communication, 37,* 294–301.

Milson-Whyte, V. (2015). *Academic writing instruction for creole-influenced students.* Kingston, Jamaica: University of the West Indies Press.

Milson-Whyte, V. (2018). Caribbean creole-speaking cultures, language, and identity. In J. Liontas (Ed.) (Volume Editor: S. Nero). *The TESOL encyclopedia of English Language teaching, Vol. VI* (pp. 3483–3489). Oxford: John Wiley and Sons, Inc.

Muchiri, M., Mulamba, N., Myers, G., & Ndoloi, D. (1995). Importing composition: Teaching and researching academic writing beyond North America. *College Composition and Communication, 46*, 175–198.

Mueller, D., Williams, A., Wetherbee Phelps, L., Clary-Lemon, J. (Eds.). (2017). *Cross-border networks in writing studies.* Edmonton, AB & Anderson, SC: Inkshed and Parlor Press.

Mufwene, S. (2015). Pidgin and creole languages. In J. Wright (Ed.), *International encyclopedia of social and behavioral sciences* (pp. 133–145). Amsterdam: Elsevier.

Mühleisen, S. (2001). Is 'bad English' dying out? A diachronic comparative study of attitudes towards creole versus Standard English in Trinidad. *Philologie im Netz, 15*, 43–78.

Nero, S. (2001). *Englishes in contact: Anglophone Caribbean students in an urban college.* Cresskill, NJ: Hampton Press.

Nero, S. (2005). Language, identities, and ESL pedagogy. *Language and Education, 19*, 194–211.

Oenbring, R. (2010). Corpus linguistic studies of Standard Bahamian English: A comparative study of newspaper usage. *The International Journal of Bahamian Studies, 16*, 51–62.

Oenbring, R. (2015). Tracing the historical development of Standard Bahamian English: A first approach. *Journal of the Bahamas Historical Society, 37*, 18–27.

Oenbring, R. (2017). College composition in the Anglophone Caribbean: The search for a Caribbean identity. *Journal of Global Literacies, Technologies, and Emerging Pedagogies, 4*, 533–545.

Perry, T., & Delpit, L. (1998). *The real ebonics debate: Power, language, and the education of African-American children.* Boston: Beacon Press.

Rickford, J. (1987). *Dimensions of a creole continuum.* Stanford, CA: Stanford University Press.

Rickford, J. (2015). The creole origins hypothesis. In S. Lanehart (Ed.), *Oxford handbook of African American language* (pp. 35–56). Oxford: Oxford University Press.

Roberts, P. (2007). *West Indians and their language.* Cambridge: Cambridge University Press.

Roemer, M., Schultz, L., & Durst, R. (1999). Reframing the great debate on first-year writing. *College Composition and Communication, 50*, 377–392.

Rose, P. (2016). A case for academic literacies: Informed needs analysis. *UWI Quality Education Forum, 21*, 42–62.

Ryan, M. (2013). The pedagogical balancing act: Teaching reflection in higher education. *Teaching in Higher Education, 18*, 144–155. https://doi.org/10.1080/13562517.2012.694104

Sand, A. (1999). *Linguistic variation in Jamaica.* Tübingen: Gunter Narr Verlag.

Smitherman, G., & Villaneuva, V. (2003). *Language diversity in the classroom: From intention to practice*. Urbana and Carbondale, IL: NCTE and Southern Illinois University Press.

Sorcinelli, M. D., & Elbow, P. (Eds.). (1997). *Writing to learn: Strategies for assigning and responding to writing across the disciplines*. San Francisco, CA: Jossey-Bass Publishers.

Storr, J. (2016). *Journalism in a small place: Making Caribbean news relevant, comprehensive and independent*. Calgary, AB: University of Calgary Press.

Strachan, I. (2003). *Paradise and plantation*. Charlottesville, VA: University of Virginia Press.

Straub, R. (2000). *The practice of response: Strategies for commenting on student writing*. Cresskill, NJ: Hampton Press.

Tompkins, J. (1987). Me and my shadow. *New Literary History, 19*, 169–178.

Wassink, A. B. (1999). Historic low prestige and seeds of change: Attitudes toward Jamaican Creole. *Language in Society, 28*, 57–92.

Wells, J., & Söderlund, L. (2018). Preparing graduate students for academic publishing: Results from a study of published rhetoric and composition scholars. *Pedagogy, 18*, 131–156.

Williams, J., & Condon, F. (2016). Translingualism in composition studies and second language writing: An uneasy alliance. *TESL Canada Journal, 33*, 1–18.

Young, V. (2009). "Nah, we straight": An argument against code switching. *JAC, 29*(1–2), 49–76.

Section One: Reflections on Linguistic Turmoil

Me tink me did done wid English at high school, Miss.

1 Teaching Literacy Skills in the Jamaican Creole-Speaking Environment: A Reflection

Carmeneta V. Jones

Prologue

Reflective practice is an invaluable means by which educators critically view different aspects of their profession, including pedagogical methods, language issues, teaching materials, students' attainment, and other concerns that are related to their field. Making reference to experiences I have had teaching students at the primary, secondary, and tertiary levels of the Jamaican education system for almost three decades, this chapter focuses on literacy instruction in the Jamaican Creole-speaking environment. There exist multiple literacy realities in Jamaica, including layers of complexities that affect students' acquisition of literacy skills. In this instance, these skills are interpretive reading, critical thinking, good writing, analytical viewing, active listening, and informed speaking. These skills are fundamental to life-long learning (Hanemann, 2015), and the ways in which Jamaicans function in their private and public domains. The teaching and learning of these critical literacy skills in the Jamaican classroom, like educational settings in the Caribbean and beyond, are complex processes that require careful thought and innovation.

Growing up in their Creole-speaking environment, most Jamaican students hear and use their Creole as an effective transactional means. This is the language they know; it is the mode of communication that works well for them as they interact with others. However, when they start formal schooling, there is the need for them to become proficient users of the target language, Jamaican Standard English. This can be demanding and challenging for teachers as well as students. The reality is that these students learn English as a second language. Playing on an idea by one Jamaican educator of English, researcher, and author, I propose that the last thing that Jamaican stakeholders of literacy education should do is to turn a blind eye to students who are stuck "Between two Grammars" (Bryan, 2010). Ultimately, Jamaican students have to develop the art of code switching from their Creole to the Jamaican Standard English and vice versa, because this will help them to be able to adapt their use of language as appropriate for different contexts and purposes. I believe that this is one area in which Jamaican educators can make a big difference in their students' literacy development. Bryan's (2004) advice is that Jamaican educators should use instructional methodologies that focus on immersion, practice, scaffolding, and contrast, and I have been guided by this invaluable insight since I discovered its significance in the teaching of literacy skills in the Jamaican Creole-speaking environment. In this chapter, I present retrospective accounts of my learning experiences and my attempts at using a bilingual/bi-literacy approach in which I employed Jamaican Creole and Jamaican Standard English in literacy instruction. Samples of students' writing, for which permission was obtained for inclusion in the chapter, are strategically integrated in the work.

Jamaican Creole-Speaking Learners' Multiple Realities

Jamaican Creole-speaking students, like their counterparts in other regions, are complex beings who engage in complex processes in order to develop their literacy skills. Having worked with Jamaican students from three levels of the education system for three decades, I discovered their multiple realities (Breen, 2011; Nath, 2014). Born and reared in their Jamaican Creole-speaking homes and communities, these students use their home language to satisfy the functions of language, as postulated by Halliday (1973): instrumental, regulatory, interactional, personal, imaginative, heuristic, and informative. Naturally, the knowledge that these students acquire outside of the formal school setting during their emergent literacy years is generated in Jamaican Creole. It is less structured and is used in informal conversations with peers, parents, siblings, and other significant people with whom they come into contact.

A dramatic change occurs when proficient Jamaican Creole-speaking students start formal education because the official language of instruction, the acrolect, is Jamaican Standard English (Kennedy, 2018). However, there is a lack of cohesion between the language culture of the home and that of the school (Bryan, 2004 & 2010; Craig, 1999; Honeyghan, 2000; Pollard, 1998; Shields, 1989; Taylor, 2002). In fact, some Jamaican Creole-speaking students become "victims" because of their home language, for, as observed by Taylor (2011), the formal school environments in Jamaica do not always accept and affirm these students' native tongue. These students are rendered wordless, voiceless, and powerless at the start of their formal education.

Without their words, voices, and power, Jamaican Creole-speaking students are likely to become passive receptacles who depend on their teachers' language for their literacy learning to take place. It is impossible for these students to depend solely on their teachers' language to generate new knowledge. Without healthy social and affective relations and meaningful interaction, the classroom becomes a dull and drab place where silence abounds (Delpit, 1988; Waddell, 1998–1999). This kind of silence can be damaging because it can leave some students with permanent psychological scars; it can be a lethal classroom weapon that can be fatal to students' communicative competence and social responsiveness. Referring to this as the *silenced dialogue*, Delpit explained that when students are not afforded opportunities to use their home language, they feel repressed. This is a recipe for affective learning issues including incidences of *wounded silence* (Waddell). Since teaching and learning should be a reciprocal, interactional arrangement, Creole-speaking students' words, voices, and power should also be as equally important as their teachers' in their lifelong literacy learning (Hanemann, 2015).

Waddell's (1998–1999) assertion invites me to do a quick flashback to an experience I had on my first day of primary school. When I arrived, I saw many unfamiliar faces in the frightful classroom; but the one that intimidated me was that of my teacher. She totally ignored every attempt that I made at communicating with her because I did not *speak properly*. I was so petrified that I refused to even ask my teacher to use the bathroom—and the *inevitable* happened. Because of that *losing of my face* experience, I pledged that I would never be a part of any exercise or movement that intentionally or unintentionally renders my students silent. Although that incident occurred more than fifty years ago, it is still etched in my memory; however, I have not allowed it to deter me.

It is a constant reminder for me that in assuming my roles in the capacity of literacy/writing educator I should be careful and sensitive enough to not use a problematic phrase such as *speaking properly* when I engage my students in conversations. Rather, I use a more empowering term—*appropriate*. The horrible incident I experienced has caused me to be alert about matters that concern my Jamaican Creole-speaking students. I have been committed to discovering and understanding their concerns and realities.

LITERACY LEARNING CONCERNS OF JAMAICAN CREOLE-SPEAKING LEARNERS

Working at different levels in education over the last thirty years has made it possible for me to accumulate a significant repertoire of knowledge about the multiple realities of Jamaican Creole-speaking students. I observed that at the primary level, some students were apprehensive about making the transition from home to school. The students experienced the trepidation of venturing into the unknown, which for them is to use Jamaican Standard English. I made similar observations about some secondary and tertiary students. For example, like the primary school students, some of them were fearful about making the transition to a high school setting. Some recurring sentiments that my secondary students expressed, especially at the start of the term or school year, were *Me caan do English, Miss* (I am not good at English, Miss.) or *Me hate reading, Miss* (I hate reading, Miss) or *Miss, me not a good writer* (Miss, I am not a good writer) or *Me not a critical thinker, Miss* (I am not a critical thinker, Miss) or *Me is not a language person, Miss* (I am not a language person, Miss). Though expressed in different ways, the sentiments of my secondary school students are similar to those of some of my university students who take mandatory foundation writing courses: *Me tink me did done wid English at high school, Miss* (I thought I had finished with English at high school, Miss) and *English again*!. Clearly, my university students had a misconception; they thought that in the context of their writing courses, English and writing were used synonymously. I have found it difficult to demystify this notion.

JAMAICAN CREOLE-SPEAKING LEARNERS' PROFILES

It behooves me at this point to focus on the *profiles* of my Jamaican Creole-speaking learners. Being a sensitive educator and a staunch apologist of the tacit dimension conceptualized by Hungarian philosopher-chemist Michael Polanyi (as cited in Gill, 2000), I have come to appreciate the importance of tacit knowledge in my pedagogy. Summarized, tacit knowledge is untapped, unspoken, and concealed insight that is generated and stored in the internal repositories of human-beings. These insights evolve based on individuals' lived experiences, socio-cultural and linguistic backgrounds, and psychological make-up. Tacit knowledge may be retrieved by associates who closely observe, thoughtfully get to know, and tactfully forge and maintain meaningful connections with others through collaborative effort (Polanyi, as cited in Gill). It was with such an understanding, lessons learned from my first day of primary school experience, and the conviction that I got when I read a soul-stirring story about a teacher who did an altruistic act by reaching out to and saving a sixth grade seemingly hopeless child from a worst case scenario (Wubbles, 1995), that I thought it was incumbent on me to gradually develop a learner profile of each Jamaican Creole-speaking student I nurtured, so I could get a deeper understanding of his or her "otherness which means that I put myself in the place of [each] conceptually" (Baer, 2017, para. 8).

MULTIPLE SELVES AND THE JAMAICAN CREOLE-SPEAKING LEARNER

Habitually drawing upon my lived experiences as a Jamaican Creole-speaking student, I train my eyes to detect different behavior patterns to ensure that I compile comprehensive accounts of students' lived realities as literacy learners. In the classroom, I read my students' eyes, and they tell me many untold stories. My inward search for a deeper understanding of the nature and quality of the experiences of my Jamaican Creole-speaking students has helped me to discover that each student has multiple identities (selves): seeking selves, enduring selves, and endangered selves (Spindler & Spindler, 2000). The composite selves portrayed by any one student or group of students represent variety and complexity. To contextualize it, in the Jamaican Creole-speaking classroom environment, seeking selves were all of the students in the quest of literacy education. The enduring selves searched for acceptance for their home language and hoped for opportunities to use their organic knowledge as they connect their past experiences to unknown ones (Moll, Amanti, Neff, & González, 2005). The endangered selves were the *at risk* students. They were *fearful, anxious,* and *uncertain* about how their literacy-learning events would unfold. Together, they represented situated selves who have the need for favorable literacy learning outcomes. These outcomes were fundamental to not only their cognition but also other aspects of their development, including their affective, aesthetic, and creative dimensions, among others. Carlo and Bengochea (2011) suggested that best practices in literacy education use holistic approaches. These methodologies focus on multiple ways of knowing (Gardner, 1983; Gurm, 2013) and the simultaneous building of these dimensions in all students despite their socio-cultural and linguistic backgrounds, their psychological make-up, and their developmental stages. The essence of these approaches is that all teachers should pay keen attention to the building of the whole person.

Retrospectively, given the profiles that I developed of Jamaican Creole-speaking primary, secondary, and tertiary level students over the years, the essence of my philosophy of teaching in this context is that most Jamaicans, despite their distinctive life circumstances and linguistic backgrounds, have the potential of both becoming functionally literate and making invaluable contributions to personal, community, and national development. Therefore, I have made an unwavering commitment to draw upon a variety of strategies, such as Bryan's (2004) immersion, practice, scaffolding, and contrast, in a *balanced, innovative, interactive,* and *eclectic* approach in literacy teaching and learning in Jamaica. The definition of this approach that best aligns with my philosophy of teaching follows:

> one of the premises of eclecticism is that teaching should serve learners not methods. Thus, teachers should feel free in choosing techniques and procedures inside the classroom. There is no ideal approach in language learning. Each one has its merits and demerits. There is no royalty to certain methods. Teachers should know that they have the right to choose the best methods and techniques in any method according to learners' needs and learning situation[s]. Teachers can adopt a flexible method and technique so as to achieve their goals. They may choose

whatever works best at a particular time in a particular situation. (Wali, as cited in Mwanza, 2017, p. 56).

Obviously, teachers need appropriate training to be efficient at this and every instructional methodology.

A Newly Trained Teacher's Dilemma: Issues and Resolutions

I started teaching literacy skills at an all-girls, privately-run primary school in Jamaica in 1988. The students came from different backgrounds and, even those who were from more affluent homes, used or were exposed to Jamaican Creole. Fresh out of college, I felt confident that I was ready to assume my teaching responsibilities because, as I perceived it, my training had prepared me to do careful planning, effective delivery, and daily evaluation of the lessons I would teach in literacy across the curriculum. My teachers' college program had emphasized theories of teaching and learning in the language arts: reading, thinking, speaking, listening, and writing. As part of the program, I was required to apply the theories while I did sixteen weeks of teaching practice, two in the second year of my teacher training and twelve in the final year.

Evaluating my first week's lessons at the affluent primary school, I noted that some students spoke Jamaican Creole fluently and others mixed it with Jamaican Standard English in their oral and written tasks. I was not fully equipped for my teaching journey. Although I had acquired appreciable theoretical knowledge about teaching the language arts, I was not adequately prepared to interface the theoretical and practical components of language usage in literacy instruction for Jamaican Creole-speaking students. Therefore, I realized there was much for me to learn.

To resolve the issue concerning inadequate training to facilitate the learning of Jamaican Creole-speaking students, in 1994, I enrolled to read for my undergraduate degree in Literatures in English with a minor in Education. During that program, I registered to do *Language Teaching and Learning in a Creole-Speaking Environment*, a course that focused on preparing teachers to examine the demands of teaching English in the Anglophone Caribbean and similar environments. While doing this useful course, I read works by researchers who had studied the language situation in Jamaica, including Craig (1999), Devonish (1986), and Bryan (1997), and started getting a deeper understanding of the art of teaching literacy in the Jamaican Creole-speaking environment. I discovered from the course and these experts that in the Jamaican context, English should be taught as a second language and that there was the need for all stakeholders of literacy education to not only value Jamaican Creole as a powerful means of communication but also to establish practical ways of using it as an instructional tool. After I completed my undergraduate degree in 1997, my thirst for knowledge on issues relating to teaching in the Jamaican Creole-speaking environment grew exponentially when an angry primary school boy told me that he hated comprehension because his teacher did not teach him; rather, she only tested those skills, and because of that, he requested my help.

Teaching Primary School Learners Comprehension and Writing the Bilingual/Bi-literacy Literature-Based Way

Passionate about helping the angry boy and other Jamaican Creole-speaking students with similar problems, I applied to read for a master's degree in literacy education in 1998. I designed a bilingual/bi-literacy literature-based instructional model for improving comprehension and writing in the Jamaican Creole-speaking environment for my master's project (Jones, 2000). I incorporated immersion, practice, scaffolding and contrast in this intervention (Bryan, 2004). While I was gathering information for the thesis, I found a profound assertion articulated by one of my literature professors:

> The English language is struggling for survival in this country, and unless Jamaicans develop 'the spirit of literacy,' it will not survive here. . . . We should see ourselves as a bilingual people and should be proud of the English language and our Creole (patois) . . . But it is the English that is under threat. (Baugh, as cited in Shields, 1989, p. 43)

This statement made an indelible mark on my mind as I tried to diversify the literature-based approach by integrating Jamaican Creole resources. The students were more fluent in Jamaican Creole than in Jamaican Standard English as manifested in their oral and written assignments. In my experience as student, researcher, and educator, I discovered that Baugh was partially correct: Jamaican Creole was also under threat for different reasons.

When I conducted literacy workshops for teachers at several schools across the island, I recognized that the use of Jamaican Creole for instructional purposes was not welcomed by many stakeholders in the education system. I observed that some administrators and teachers did not accept the notion that students' mother tongues, like the official languages of their countries, are vital to literacy development (Bühmann & Trudell, 2007; Rollnick & Rutherford, 1996). Baugh's idea caused me to start reflecting more deeply on my future practice and the charges given to me by other professors: to use the best of what my students know and that which is readily available to them to teach them what they do not know and to equally nurture the cognitive, affective, and aesthetic aspects of their literacy learning. Provoked by Baugh's assertion, inspired by these charges, and driven by the work I was doing for my master's project, I was motivated to kindle my students' enthusiasm and to lift their spirit of literacy above and beyond survival levels.

I was further enlightened and encouraged on my master's degree journey when I read an interesting account of the early experiences of a Jamaican literacy educator (Honeyghan, 2000). The experience that resonated with me was that at the age of six and a half years, when she started her formal education, she described her learning environment as a "schoolhouse full of horror" (p. 410). She remembered the "[British] Standard English demanded by the teacher" (p. 410). This demand required Jamaican Creole-speaking students to instantaneously understand how the English language worked. I wondered whether Honeyghan's perception of her Jamaican primary school being a setting "full of horror," might have been partly triggered by her teacher's unrealistic demands. In many ways, her experience reminded me of the horrible one I had on my first day of primary school when I was reduced to an object of ridicule—my tongue and bladder were simultaneously rendered powerless—I could not *speak properly*—I was afraid to communicate my urgent physiological need to my teacher. The psychological baggage was heavy for a child aged six years.

From an enlightened perspective, I can deduce that when my teacher expected me to *speak properly*, it was an implied demand for me to speak Jamaican Standard English, a tongue that was unknown to me. However, looking back, I am convinced that my teacher had to conform and make that demand because it was a requirement of the island's education policymakers, curriculum developers, and other relevant authorities who unquestioningly followed the tenets of the British system, which embraced an *English-only* ideology because of the perception that *anything black nuh good* (anything that is black is not good). Aptly put by Bennett-Coverley (ShakaRaSpeaks, 2011), there was the perception in some quarters that English is *derived* (from other European languages such as German and French), but Jamaican Creole is *corrupt.*

This perception is still lingering in erudite quarters today because although the highest office of education in Jamaica drafted a language policy seventeen years ago, in which it is stated, "Teacher training programmes should adequately prepare teachers for delivering language and literacy instruction to varying ability levels in primary and secondary schools" (Ministry of Education, Youth, and Culture [MOEYC], 2001, p. 4), it has not been formalized. According to Nero (2014), this document "was not formally ratified owing to a refusal by the Jamaican Parliament to accept its central premise that Jamaica is a bilingual country" (p. 227). This means that it is mere *paper talk*, and now, more than ever, such talk is destructively cheap.

The resistance against officially declaring Jamaica a bilingual country has been a time-ridden issue. However, negative attitudes toward Jamaican Creole have never affected my belief that it is a useful teaching tool. The strong resistance that I got from administrators and some colleagues at the school for girls when I was persistent in experimenting with innovative ways of integrating Jamaican Creole and Jamaican Standard English in my literacy teaching did not affect my tenacity. Citing factors that contribute to such perceptions and resistance, Nero (2010) explained:

> the reality of evolving language and discourses defy our perceptions of, and desire for, fixed linguistic codes and discourses; and . . . the assumption that acquisition or affirmation of one discourse comes at the expense of another which is related to the differential power attached to particular discourses. (pp. 142–143)

Like Devonish (2012), Nero (2010), and Warner-Lewis (2015), I believe that the acquisition of the Standard Jamaican English should not cause the death of the Jamaican Creole. Such a death has the potential of rendering young Jamaican Creole-speaking learners incapable of making appreciable progress in their literacy education. Cummins (2001) emphasizes that "when the message, implicit or explicit, communicated to children in the school is, 'Leave your language and culture at the schoolhouse door,' children also leave a central part of who they are—their identities—at the schoolhouse door" (para. 19). In reality, they leave themselves; their lived experiences; and, most importantly, their language behind. This has the potential of making them feel like the classroom is a place of horror (Honeyghan, 2000). The lack of the home and school connection makes it impossible for some students to become functionally literate.

In contrast to many of her early experiences in the classroom, Honeyghan (2000) describes memories of her early language experiences: "I remember the interaction of the Creole spoken by my villagers" (p. 410). She also reminisced about her primary school teachers' use of Jamaican art forms including poems, proverbs, songs, and stories in her literacy education. Inspired by Honeyghan's revelation, I was determined to do likewise. While teaching a group of grade four students at the all-girls school where I started teaching when I graduated from teachers' college, for the first term of the year 1998 to 1999, I experimented with an idea introduced by American author Beverly Cleary (Harper Collins, 2013): Drop Everything And Read (DEAR). After lunch break each day, the girls did fifteen to twenty minutes of uninterrupted silent sustained reading (McCracken, 1971) from a variety of literature, and the girls fell in love with books and reading.

The girls' love of reading and books motivated me to introduce a new dimension in the second term. Drawing on the DEAR idea (Harper Collins, 2013), as well as reading aloud, I came up with *drop everything and listen* (DEAL). The *deal* was that after lunch, I read aloud to the class, starting with a chapter-a-day reading of a big book version of *Charlotte's Web* (White, 1980). Each day, the girls used a variety of local discarded and natural materials to create a large mock-up of the chapter that was read. By the time I finished reading the book, the classroom walls teemed with life and color, and the girls were mentally and aesthetically pleased as they did analytical viewings of their self-instructed panoramic design of the story. At the core of their hearts and the middle of the pictorial display, was the sign Charlotte had wondrously woven, "*SOME PIG,*" to save Wilbur's life.

I capitalized on these treasures by continuing the momentum. I started reading to students Anansi stories authored by the mother of Jamaican folklore, the Right Honorable Louise Bennett-Coverley. Cherry (2010) notes that "Anansi stories were introduced to Jamaica in the 1600s by the Akan people of the Gold Coast, who were brought to the

New World as slaves" (p. 71). Bennett-Coverley (ShakaRaSpeaks, 2011) and Cherry further stated that the stories were told in Ashanti, Fanti, and Akwapim, Twi dialects that were among the languages from which Jamaican Creole was derived. Discovering that the Anansi stories were aesthetically appealing to the students, I decided to teach them how to write contemporary Anansi stories. The students put a creative twist and personal touch to their stories based on their preferences for, and interest in, different subject areas. They used ideas that they had learned in subjects across the Jamaican primary school curriculum to compose their narratives. Using the web idea presented in *Charlotte's Web* and Brer Anansi's schemes as motifs, the writer of the following story drew on ideas from literature, computer studies, and mathematics.

Anansi and the Abacus (Original Student Work)

Once upon a time, about five thousand years ago in Egypt, there lived a tricky spider man called Anansi. One day, Anansi went for a walk and heard an outstanding announcement that would change history forever.

It was, "Attention! Attention please!" It was the voice of a scribe who worked for a merchant. He continued, "I have a speech to make today. The great, wise and rich merchant Pepyankhe Abu has created a marvellous counting machine. He calls it the abacus."

Anansi was furious when he heard the bad bad news. Just then, he had an idea. He would change his work attitude. He would no longer play tricks but work his brain to build something much better than the abacus, something high tech.

Anansi did not waste time. He started working right away. He worked and worked both day and night. He was designing and building and thinking and thinking. "Gosh! It's too much work doing this over and over again," said Anansi. "But I am not giving up." After five days of hard work, Anansi was thirsty and hungry. So he made a plan. He rushed to Sister Camel's house. When he got there, he said "Sister Camel, if you get food and water fi mii every day, I will give you the product I am inventing for free. Then you won't have to spend time counting on the abacus."

Sister Camel thought about what Anansi had said for a minute. Then she said, "Ok, but you must let me try to work on the machine also. I have to help and I have to work." "Then let us work together!" said Anansi.

Soon they were working together. Anansi felt satisfied with his food and water every day, but he did not want Sister Camel to do more work than him. He wanted to get all of the glory. So he worked much more.

Some years later, Anansi invented the calculator. He was still not satisfied. So he worked and worked hard again, until a few years later he invented a computer. He was still not satisfied. So he worked and worked again. Finally, he was satisfied when he created the internet. He was very glad. That is why when we turn our computers on to the internet, we see Anansi on the web.

Story done!

It was fun! (Jones, 1999, pp. 54–55)

The students' confidence soared to new heights when their collection of Anansi stories was launched and celebrated at a special all-school assembly. I also used the bilingual approach to teach the grade four girls literacy skills in science. This provided an opportunity for my students to use their Creole and target language simultaneously (Bryan, 2004; Cummins, 2001; Devonish, 2011; Devonish & Carpenter, 2007, 2010; Pollard, 2003, Siegel, 2005, 2010).

Open Mic/Dancehall and Poetry Creation

Contemporary societies have seen the birth and diffusion of new literacies (NCTE, 2013). Among these are "new skills, strategies, dispositions, and social practices that are required by new technologies for information and communication" (Leu, O'Byrne, Zawilinski, McVerry, & Everett-Cacopardo, 2009, p. 266). Users of new literacies need to be proficient in interpretive reading, critical thinking, good writing, analytical viewing, active listening, and informed speaking to function in a virtually digital world where they are required to use applications and resources including chats, YouTube videos, and instant text messages. If teachers intend to remain current and relevant in the classroom, the onus is on them to strategize as the changes take place.

In the school year 2003–2004, I implemented a yearlong literacy intervention program, Jamaican Art-based Multi-method Instructional Network (JAMIN), for a group of inner-city grade four boys for my doctoral study (Jones, 2009). I used the "open mic" strategy noted by Fisher (2003, 2005). First, I did a picture walk, a strategic preview (Milne, 2014) of the colorful illustrations of a Jamaican story, *The Tangerine Tree* (Hanson, 1995). Secondly, I did another picture walk, but this time I asked the boys to make predictions. I, then, read the entire story after which I invited the boys to respond to parts of the narrative they liked best using a medium/form of their choice. Eagerly holding up his hand, one boy said, "Me miss! Me miss!" When he was given the opportunity to respond, he grabbed his pencil as if he were holding a microphone and imitating the structure and rhythm of a song entitled *Pon de river, pon de bank* (On the river, on the bank), by a popular dancehall artist Elephant Man (Bryan, 2007), he created the following:

Jamaican Creole Verse	***Standard English Translation***
I've seen nuff trees before	*I have seen many trees before*
But a never see no tree like dis.	*But I have never seen a tree like this.*
I've seen nuff trees before,	*I have seen many trees before*
But a never see no tree like dis.	*But I have never seen a tree like this.*
Refrain	
Tangerine! Tangerine!	*Tangerine! Tangerine!*
Tangerine! Tangerine!	*Tangerine! Tangerine!*
Mek a tell you likl bout tangerine. (x 2)	*Let me tell you a little about tangerine.* *(x 2)*

(Jones, 2009, p. 158)

This student performed the dancehall song once, and thereafter, responding to the music mnemonics (Kelly, 2017; Ong, 1982), the other boys joined in the refrain. The spontaneous creation and performance of the dancehall song reminded me of the talking music approach that is used to enhance language learning (Harrison & Pond, 1996) and the *new Jamaican orature*, the terminology that Devonish (1998) used to refer to Jamaican dancehall music. It was clear that the natural synergy exuded from this performance was second nature for the boys. Their engagement in the activity marked a turning point in their literacy learning because they were motivated to learn. Their confidence and word power increased exponentially. Gradually, the synergistic interaction that initiated their creation of the dancehall single, *Tangerine Tree*, became a transformative force that caused them to establish a strong bond that lasted for the duration of their year-long literacy intervention. It is noteworthy that at the end of the intervention, these Jamaican Creole-speaking boys (including the one described as being *not responsive* by his class teacher at the beginning of their literacy intervention), had preserved their vernacular (Craig, 2006; Devonish, 2012; Elbow, 2012) and were more proficient in Jamaican Standard English (Jones, 2009). Their writing also showed appreciable improvement.

It is important to emphasize that the performance aspect of the open mic strategy was aesthetically and intellectually rewarding for the boys. Given the opportunity to use a self-selected medium, the boys chose their home language and the dancehall genre, expressions that abound in their inner-city communities—expressions that they knew best. Bailey (2014) attests to the fact that "historically, Caribbean peoples have used a variety of performance styles as vehicles for self-expression" (p. 6). From an intellectual stance, the strategy invited the students' active participation in multiple literacies (Fisher, 2003; 2005). The boys did not only *raid di ridim* ("ride the rhythm") (Devonish, 1998, p. 44), but also engaged in active listening, quick thinking, and creative use of language when they deconstructed parts of the story and used them to *construct* their dancehall ensemble. Looking back, I feel that by getting the opportunity to engage in the open mic activity, the boys were aware that their language, style, and identity were affirmed.

Proverbs and Dancehall Lyrics as Prompts for Teaching Inferential Comprehension at the Secondary Level

I also used the eclectic bi-lingual/bi-literacy to address problems that my secondary school students had with comprehension. Some students were able to read and recall information that was explicitly stated, but they had difficulties making inferences and generating new ideas. I designed a strategy called the Jamaican Proverbs Connection (JPC). I also asked second formers to listen, think, and write about and to read aloud the ideas they generated about the proverbs like "Lawn fe danse a yaad befoe yu go abraad/Learn to dance at home before you go abroad" (Morris-Brown, 1988, p. 71). Find a Proverb Project was another strategy that I used. Each student was required to select an unfamiliar Jamaican proverb and use their own words to explain the meaning of the chosen proverb in no more than three sentences. The proverb chosen by one student was, *One han caan clap*. The student's translation and explanation are presented in Table 1.

Table 1
Jamaican Creole proverbs, students' original English translations and explanations

Jamaican proverb	English translation	Student's explanation
One han caan clap.	One hand cannot clap.	People have to depend on the help and support of others to complete some tasks. It is impossible for one person to successfully do some things.

This activity facilitated the students' literacy learning in many ways. It appeased their aesthetic and affective domains. They engaged in purposeful, concise writing when they translated the proverbs from Jamaican Creole to Jamaican Standard English and explained their meanings. This activity facilitated the students' engagement in different stages of the writing process. *A proverb a day* was another concept that I introduced. The students selected a Jamaican proverb. Then working individually or collaboratively they extrapolated meaning from it and did a *quick interpretive write* (QIW) in which they linked the proverb to the theme and their lives.

The students' attempt at doing collaborative writing was very useful in that they shared the responsibilities, and as a result, the task was more manageable and attainable. Though used in different contexts, Elola and Oskoz (2010), Hirvela (1999), and Storch (2005) observed similar benefits in collaborative writing for students who were learning second languages. However, this activity posed challenges and some conflicts emerged, but the students learned to compromise and this facilitated affective learning.

Controversial Reggae Lyrics/Texts as Stimuli for Critical Thinking

I used various genres of popular Jamaican music for teaching literacy skills at the secondary level. Danley (2007) provided a useful definition of popular culture: "the vernacular *or* people's culture that predominates in a society at a point in time" (para. 1). With an understanding that what they know best can be used in transformative pedagogy for young people (Barrett, 2013; Christenson & Roberts, 1998; Weinstein, 2006), I asked second formers to listen to and do oral and written responses to lyrics, stories, and topical issues presented in selected Jamaican Creole dancehall and reggae lyrics/texts (Lloyd, 2003). They engaged in heated conversations on *bleaching*. *Bleaching* is the use of a variety of creams and other substances to lighten dark skin tone—a practice that is predominant in Jamaican dancehall culture and has sparked national debates (Hope, 2011). Lyrics from *Dem a bleach* (Henderson, Willis, & Dunbar, 1992) and *Odd Ras* (McNaughton, 2013) were selected for this activity (see Table 2).

Table 2
Lyrics of Jamaican Creole songs and Jamaican Standard English translations

Dancehall lyrics (Jamaican Creole)	Jamaican Standard English Translation
Dem a bleach (Nardo Ranks, stage name) And dem a bleach Dem a bleach out dem skin Dem a bleach Fi look like a browning Dem a bleach Dem a bleach out dem skin Dem a bleach Fi look like a browning	**They are bleaching (Nardo Ranks, stage name)** And they are bleaching They are bleaching their skin They are bleaching To lighten the hue of their skin And they are bleaching They are bleaching their skin They are bleaching To lighten the hue of their skin
Odd Ras (Chronixx, stage name) Mi nah falla nobody And when the whole Jamaica a bleach dem face Mi nah falla nobody . . . All when a mi alone a sing rightous song Mi nah falla nobody	**Odd Rastafarian (Chronixx, stage name)** I will not be influenced by anybody Even if all Jamaicans are bleaching their faces I will not be influenced by anybody . . . Even if I am alone when singing this righteous song I will not be influenced by anybody

In their discussion, the students did comparative analysis, which constitutes a high order literacy skill as exemplified in one student's writing:

A Student's Comparison of Controversial Dancehall Lyrics (Original Student Work)

> In comparing *Dem a bleach* recorded by Nardo Ranks and *Odd Ras* by (Chronnix) it is seen that the issue of skin bleaching is

raised in both songs. Ranks portrays bleaching, an issue which is prevalent in the Jamaican dancehall culture. In this song, he speaks of "bleaching" as an activity which is accepted and practised by Jamaica's dancehall culture fans. He presents his lyrics in a matter of fact way. On the other hand, in presenting his stance on the issue in Odd Ras, Chronixx speaks of himself as an *odd* one who does not indulge in this glorified practice in the dancehall culture. He states that he will not be influenced by those individuals who alter their skin complexion and participate in other unacceptable activities. Chronnixx also implies that despite the fact that some dancehall artistes portray bleaching as an acceptable practice, even if he is the only one to sing a song of this "righteous" nature, he will not be influenced by others who embrace it.

This student's response, as well as those presented by others that were submitted, illustrates that there is a place for popular culture in the teaching of literacy skills to Jamaican Creole-speaking students. Morrell (2004) attested to the fact that young people are constantly in touch with popular culture, so they have appreciable knowledge that teachers can strategically tap to foster their literacy learning. Based on the students' oral and written responses to reggae and dancehall genres, I agree with Alverman, Moon, and Hagwood (1999) and Weinstein (2006) who suggest that popular culture, and in this case popular music, can make literacy instruction intellectually stimulating and pleasurable. However, successful use of Jamaican popular culture requires careful selection of resources that are appropriate for the classroom and effective planning and implementation by teachers. First, I create learner profiles to learn about learners' interests, preferences, and developmental stages. Second, I select appropriate Jamaican Creole teaching resources and strategically integrate them with appropriate Jamaican Creole and Jamaican Standard English materials in lessons so that they are juxtaposed. I also monitor my students' use of language and celebrate them when they respond in both languages. Furthermore, I capitalize on teachable moments and model the target language when necessary. With these considerations, cultural relevance (Wurdeman-Thurston & Kaomea, 2015), purposefulness, and appropriateness are guaranteed.

VIDEOS AND POEMS FOR AFFECTIVE AND AESTHETICALLY APPEALING TERTIARY WRITING PEDAGOGY

When I started teaching writing to university students in Jamaica in 2000, I was of the view that university-level students would not experience such challenges as "poor" grammar, lack of comprehension, inability to write coherent compositions, and weak listening and speaking skills. I assumed that since these tertiary-level students had completed their primary and secondary education, they would have mastered those fundamental skills. This assumption was unfounded and caused me to have unrealistic expectations of my students regarding their learning outcomes. However, by understanding the fact that although they were postsecondary students, they had not obtained mastery in literacy skills, I was in a better position to assume my teaching roles, which included identifying and addressing their concerns. They were afraid of doing oral presentations and writing of compositions.

Use of Videos to Allay Students' Fear of Oral Presentations

A part of the students' fear for oral presentations was that some were not fully aware when they mixed Jamaican Creole and Jamaican Standard English in their formal oral communication (Kennedy, 2018). Since 2010, I have been addressing this issue by engaging the students in the analytical viewing of videos including the following: *Miss Lou: Fi wi language: (Jamaican patwah)* (ShakaRaSpeaks, 2011), *Writing Jamaican the Jamaican Way (Raitin Jamiekan di Jamiekan wie)* (thejamaicanlangco, 2009), *Nobody Canna cross it* (kevy2c, 2011), Everything flood out CVM funny video (Jamaican Truckers, 2013), *Aubrey Stewart's introduction to President Obama* (Stewart, 2015), and Barack Obama in Jamaica (Patois) *"Greetings massive! Wha gwaan Jamaica?"* ([S]itgan 2015). It was deliberate on my part to ask the students to do analytical viewing of these videos.

By asking the students to view and listen to excerpts from the recordings, I intended to show them Jamaican Creole and Jamaican Standard English in action. I wanted to make the point that the two languages are equally capable of transmitting messages as exemplified in the video by the Jamaican Language Unit (thejamaicanlangco, 2009) and Stewart (2015). I also wanted the students to view different presenters using formal and informal language for different purposes and to get them to observe how they adapted their tone, register, and diction and engaged in code switching, as was the case in the excerpt with President Obama's opening remark when he addressed young people at a town hall meeting at The University of the West Indies, Mona, when he visited Jamaica in 2015. President Obama's first utterances to the audience were informal, *"Greetings massive! Wha gwaan Jamaica?"* (Good afternoon, Jamaicans! How are you?). His use of the Jamaican Creole was an effective strategy employed to establish common ground with his young audience, and, given the applause that it aroused, it worked well. Thereafter, President Obama switched to American Standard English and maintained its formal tone for the rest of his presentation. Like the president, Aubrey Stewart used a formal tone in his articulate Jamaican Standard English introduction of the president.

Although the viewing of the videos helped the students to get a better understanding of the need to use appropriate diction and register in their formal presentations, it was apparent that even at the university level, they had not mastered the art of completely switching from Creole to Jamaican Standard English in the formal oral presentation of their documented (research) essays in progress. Explaining Jamaica's language situation, Kennedy (2018) asserted that "generally, in even the most formal setting Creole rules have infiltrated and affected the supposed acrolect without speakers being aware of it" (p. 41). This is also the case with academic writing.

Use of Poetry to Allay Students' Fear of Academic Writing

Some of my Jamaican Creole-speaking university students are fearful of academic writing. Academic writing is "written scholarly discourses that academics produce in conformity with the conventions and expectations of their disciplines" (Milson-Whyte, 2015, p. 7). While teaching academic writing courses to students from different disciplines, such as the social sciences, science and technology, medicine, and the humanities at two Jamaican universities, I observed that students' fear of writing was linked to the difficulties they experienced when they made attempts at conforming to the conventions of this genre of writing. The students found it difficult to switch from Jamaican Creole to idiomatic Jamaican Standard English in their formal writing. I also found that when the students did their first writing assignments, the ones who confidently declared that they did not speak Jamaican Creole, combined the two languages. Lack of preparedness to make the transition from secondary to tertiary level academic writing was a glaring issue. Milson-Whyte

(2015) suggests writing is needed at the tertiary level for knowledge making. She explained, "students in—their quest to increase their learning in new subjects—are expected to comprehend, evaluate, challenge and eventually produce such discourses in order to communicate effectively in writing in the university and beyond" (p. 7). However, some students' fear of academic writing was so crippling that even when they were aware of the stages of the writing process they had difficulties with starting their expository essays. I used what I like best to address that concern.

Bilingual Poetry and Reader's Theatre for Introduction to the Writing of Exposition

Drawing upon principles postulated in the transactional theory, which suggest that reading and writing are events that require engagement with texts (Rosenblatt, 1994, 2013), in the 2017 to 2018 academic year, I used bilingual poetry and reader's theatre to introduce the writing of exposition to my students who were pursuing a writing course designed for majors in Science and Technology and Medical Sciences. Reader's theatre involves "readers reading a script adapted from literature, and the audience picturing the action from hearing the script being read aloud . . . Performers bring the text alive by using voice, facial expressions, and some gestures" (Cornwell, 2018, para. 1). Rather than telling the students what the writing of exposition entailed, I invited them to do an interpretative reading (Olson, Land, Anselmi, & AuBuchon, 2010) of a bilingual adaptation of John Godfrey Saxe's (1872) *The blind men and the elephant* (Philosophy, 2002), a poem in which I integrated Jamaican Creole:

The Blind Men of Jamaica

Six men of Jamaica
To learning inclined
Went to circus to see a circus elephant
Though all of them were blind
Each based on his lived experience
Tried to *'sel aff'* his perspective.
The first approached to the elephant
And happening to fall
Against his broad and sturdy side
At once began to bawl
"Good to go! Dis ya elephant

Is nothing but a wall."
The second feeling round the tusk
Approached with a lot of haste
Said he, *"Yu sii mii! Dis is mighty sharp*
Dis long and pointed instrument
Feel exactly like a machete."
The third man approached the Circus King
And happening to shake
The squirming trunk in his hand,
In his own language spake,
"Tek way yu self! Dis massive creature,
Can only be a snake!"
The fourth reached out his eager hand
And fell on bended knees
"Irie! Jah bless I and I eyesight
Dis wicked beast
Is mighty clear I see
Has got to be and nothing else,
Except a whole a cotton tree."
The fifth by chance
Quickly touched the elephant's ear.
Quote he, *"Cool! Cool!*
On this I have to swear
This strange and rounded creature
Has the resemblance of a fan."
The sixth who had heard each foregoing detail
Help up the elephant's tail
And gave a haughty Jamaican shout,
"Dis ya rhum rham! Who can beat this?
Dis marvelous, wonder elephant
Is a piece a rope fii real"
And so these blind Jamaican men
Argued loud and very long
Each defending his opinion
In his voice so clear and strong
And though each convinced
That he was absolutely right
Was proven very wrong.

Although all except two of the students in one class were Trinidadians, I still took the risk to experiment. I distributed copies of the poem and asked the students to read it silently. I, then, negotiated with the Trinidadian male students regarding who would volunteer to play the roles of the blind men. A Jamaican female student did the narration. The volunteers read their parts and the other members of the class read silently to follow the proceedings in a practice session. The narrator read the first verse and then did shared reading with the readers of the second to seventh verse respectively.

Each male reader's part (written in Jamaican Creole) presented each blind man's perspective of the elephant based on the part of its body that he touched. The narrator then read the concluding verse. Thereafter, the actual transactional reading (Rosenblatt, 1994, 2013) took place. All of the students participated in extrapolating meaning from the poem. The benefits derived from the reading of the poem were manifold as suggested in four students' reflections, two Jamaicans who provided insiders' views and two Trinidadians who zoomed in on the exercise through external lenses:

Jamaican Female Student's Comments (Original Student Work)

> The poem "The Blind Men of Jamaica" was ingeniously used by my partner in learning to illustrate to students the working parts of an expository piece. The perspectives of the blind men were in Jamaican Creole and students were asked to embody and voice each perspective aloud. This tactic gave the poem an authentic feel and it is this authenticity I believe my tutor wanted to see embodied in the individual expositions. It also established that structure and the importance of critically analyzing information prior to writing an exposition to ensure its validity are fundamental to a quality expository essay. I believe it's a strategy that should be adopted by other writing tutors as it is an exciting way of getting students to conceptualize the various aspects of exceptional expository essay writing.

Trinidadian Female Student's Comments (Original Student Work)

> 'The Blind Men of Jamaica,' a poem which I had no prior knowledge of has now become solidified in my memory after

one faithful day at my weekly Critical Reading and Writing class. My lecturer presented this piece to us requesting a dramatic reading of it by the members of the class. The memory is a particularly fond one of mine as the sound of many foreigners attempting to replicate the Jamaican Creole accent was humorous to say the least. Amidst all the laughter, I wondered what this piece could have to teach us in terms of our critical reading and writing skills, but soon I began to see the method to my lecturer's 'madness.'

The poem was used as a means of preparing us to write exposition, one of our many writing assignments. In the poem, even though the blind men were all touching the same elephant, based on what portion of the elephant they chose to focus on, their perspective or impression of the animal varied. I found this concept to be applicable to our exposition since in the poem, the blind men operated on opinion versus actual facts in terms of their interpretation of the elephant. This thus caused each of them to miss the mark and misidentify the creature altogether, something which we were all warned to avoid doing in analysing articles for our expositions.

Thus, I viewed that the exercise was extremely beneficial as it helped the class to grasp various teaching points in a very enjoyable and practical way. Furthermore, the writing of the piece in Jamaican Creole created an air of cultural inclusivity within the class which, being an English writing course, could sometimes be clouded with Western influence.

Jamaican Male Student's Comments (Original Student Work)

"The blind men of Jamaica," a poem used to establish and demonstrate exactly what expository writing is that was made vivid in the reading of my verse from the poem, further augmented by each reader creating the setting in their voice, embodying the characters due to the use of code switching for personification and differentiation. As I read, I tried to embody my character in an eloquent exposition suited for the performance of the poem. The author's intent became evident, illustrating that the truth has several angles dependent on the perspective of the analyzers, therefore distinguishing facts versus opinions. This I believe is key to precise and interpretive expository writing, as I first needed to understand to reproduce information to assess its credibility because this is a vital component in expository writing.

Trinidadian Male Student's Comments (Original Student Work)

> It is in my opinion that 'The Blind men of Jamaica' effectively depicted a solid and vivid representation of 'perspectives.' Being given the opportunity to read the lyrics aloud in class amongst my peers, simultaneously generated a sense of excitement and appreciation for the Jamaican culture, as I attempted to verbalise the Jamaican Creole in the poem. After the analytical class discussion about the lessons to be extrapolated from this poem, I obtained a more profound understanding of the interpretive skills necessary to write a 'damn good' expository piece. I learned that I had to carefully analyse potential sources, and effectively utilise the information available to appropriately develop a claim or idea with clarity. Furthermore, I greatly appreciated the aesthetic value of the reading since it elicited a sense of enjoyment in this learning experience, which allowed me to better understand and remember the lessons provided.

The local and regional perspectives presented by the Jamaican and Trinidadian university students, respectively, indicate that a bilingual approach is a plausible way of integrating the efferent and aesthetic stances (Rosenblatt, 1988) in the teaching of writing to not only Jamaican Creole-speaking university students but also learners from other countries in the Anglophone Caribbean. It represents one way in which university writing educators can heed Devonish's (2011) call to "value the bilingual or two language nature of Jamaica, with the slogan, 'Tuu langwij beta dan wan/Two languages are better than one' or 2>1" (para. 9), as demonstrated in the reading of the bilingual poem. In fact, the Jamaican female student suggested that all tutors should adopt the exciting strategy.

First, the reading of the bilingual poem engaged the students mentally because it created an opportunity for interconnected literacy learning: reading, speaking, listening, thinking, and writing (Hagwood, 2009; Roberts & Billings, 2008). Second, its performance provided entertainment as was evident in the Trinidadian male students' use of theatrical techniques to articulate the blind men's perspectives of the elephant.

The reading of the bilingual poem may be best situated at the middle of Rosenblatt's (1988) efferent/aesthetic continuum. Rosenblatt asserted that "the kind of reading in which attention is centered predominantly on what is to be carried away or retained after the reading event [is called] 'efferent' (after the Latin *efferre*, to carry away" (p. 5). Rosenblatt also stated that "the predominantly aesthetic stance covers the other half of the continuum. In this kind of reading, the reader adopts an attitude of readiness to focus attention on what is being lived through during the reading event" (p. 5). Since the reading of the bilingual poem was equally efferent and aesthetic, it added a novel and interesting dimension to the student-driven learning about the writing of exposition. The poem represented effective global organization: the introduction of an idea, the development of the idea, and the concluding statement. As suggested by the Jamaican and Trinidadian male students, students need interpretative skills to present multiple perspectives, including their voices in their expositions. Also, as demonstrated in the poem, they can use Jamaican Creole perspectives at strategic points to retain authenticity of voice in their expositions if it is relevant to the focus of their essays, but like President Obama did in his speech ([S]itgan, 2015), they must consider appropriateness and adaptability and, in the next breath, switch to Standard English to maintain a formal tone in their academic writing.

Initially some of the students resisted the idea of reading aloud in class. It could be that they, like the Trinidadian female students, thought that the bilingual activity was *madness*. Some thought that it was inappropriate for the university level, while others felt uncomfortable about doing it. Some even declared that they hated reading aloud in the classroom setting. Despite the students' initial responses, the active participation and excitement made the learning experience a valuable and memorable one, for, as Center for Teaching (n. d.) and Gibson (2008) suggest, there are numerous benefits that university students can derive by reading aloud with a purpose, including celebration of their home language. An important benefit here was that they felt free to be themselves (Lopez, 2011); this was demonstrated in the Trinidadian male student's unrestricted use of *damned good* in his description of exemplary exposition. This augured well for the use of local culture for positive effects in writing pedagogy (Nurlia & Arini, 2017). Sometimes the negative past experiences that students had with writing affect their learning. This is an important aspect of writing education that is oftentimes ignored or not adequately addressed at the university level since the focus is mostly on writing cognition. Larson observed over three decades ago that writing instructors had the tendency to separate cognition from emotions (as cited in Lee, 2003). Like Larson, I believe that the nurturing of students' affective domain can make a big difference in how they view, engage, and perform in writing activities.

POETRY, AFFECTIVE LEARNING, AND ACADEMIC WRITING

I also used my own poetry as a means of allaying the anxiety that some of my humanities students had about the writing of exposition. The following poem, which was written for that purpose, was presented to them during the week when they wrote the first drafts of their research (documented) essays:

Nothing Came to Mind

I put my pen to paper, and my mind went blank.
No thought, no theme, no focus . . .
No idea flowed on my narrowed topic.
My mind went blind.
Nothing came to mind.
I sat there . . . I wondered what to write
Started to write . . . it turned out not right
Even though I'd created a blueprint,
consulted current and reputable sources . . .
and over time.
refined my essay outline
'til the claims were all mine . . .
Nothing came to mind . . .
I could not move beyond the physical.
My mind had turned grey . . .
Though I thought I had so much to say
I could not write . . . or said another way . . .
My fingers turned numb . . . as stiff as spike
My brain cells walked out on a strike . . .
Nothing came to mind . . .
Being a Creole-influenced student
Struggling for survival in the academy
I got stuck Between two grammars . . .
Despite numerous attempts,

> I could not connect the dots . . .
> The habit of the mind thing eluded me . . .
> *Nothing came to mind . . .*
> As far as I can remember,
> When I put my pen to paper
> *Nothing came to mind . . .*
> *Nothing came to mind . . .*
> N-O-T-H-I-N-G!
> *Do you understand this Creole-influenced writer's plight?*

Before I displayed the poem electronically, I shared an experience I had with the writing of the third chapter of my Caribbean Study, a significant assignment I had to do for the completion of my undergraduate degree. Although I had worked assiduously at preparing for the writing of this chapter, I could not write it. I started writing it on several occasions but got diminishing returns. However, I kept writing for several weeks until I got it done. After sharing that experience, I displayed the poem on the multi-media screen and read it for the students. I, then, asked them: "Why do you believe I shared this poem with you?" I did not invite responses. This was deliberate. My intention was to let the poetry do the teaching—and it did. The reflections of a younger and more mature student (respectively) on the activity are powerful testimonies:

Younger Student's Reflection (Original Student Work)

> As my tutor read the poem "Nothing Came to Mind" I could relate to the creole-influenced student who experienced a writer's block when he/she was trying to produce an academic paper. The writer could not focus and was unable to think critically. Being a Jamaican native, this poem resonated with me as sometimes I find it very difficult to follow the structure of the Standard English in my academic writing or to think logically about the ideas I wish to communicate to the reader. Furthermore, this poem also reflects the situation that many students who do essay writing courses face. For this reason, I believe that my lecturer read it to us the week when I was writing what I considered the most important component of my course, the documented essay. I believe that since she was such a caring teacher, she was aware that this has happened to many students she taught before and that it would have most likely happened to those in my year

group. As a fellow writer, I believe that my lecturer empathized with us as she had experienced writer's block many times before. The poem's repetition of "Nothing came to mind" caused me to think that it could have been a reoccurring event for her. This poem is an accurate representation of what I experienced when I was getting ready to write my documented essay. I had difficulty in communicating my ideas on paper for academic purposes. The "stuck between two grammars" reminded me of the struggle I faced formulating the correct grammar, syntax and diction and making my ideas coherent. I felt that it would be a very tedious task, but in understanding that writer's block was so common, it also prepared me to overcome this obstacle.

Mature Student's Reflection (Original Student Work)

Emptiness of mind was what came to my mind as the poem was being read by my sensitive partner in learning. As usual her intention was to motivate me to do some soul searching because I had discussed the fear I was experiencing when I consulted with her as I prepared to face the mammoth task of writing the dreaded documented essay and I was also having a writer's block experience. The student, a Creole speaker was having a more difficult job writing English than the average student as she was accustomed to a different language. The writer described in the poem had a variety of discouraging distractions which affected critical thinking. The writer's experience was a stormy one. The poem's display of empathy forced me to think positively. Therefore, I was not concerned about the completion of my documented essay because the poem made me feel that there is always calm after a storm. I knew that once I started writing the essay it would finally sort the ideas in my brain and my thoughts would work out themselves, they would begin to flow in sequence and become a beautiful masterpiece.

The students' reflections on my purpose for using the poem mirrored my thoughts. Based on my experiences taking and teaching writing courses at the university level, I was aware of my students' concerns and decided to be tactfully proactive rather than insensitively reactive. I empathized with them and intended to use my experiences as well as those of the persona in the poem to establish common ground with them for, as McLeod (1997) and Richmond (1999–2000) note, the practice of an ethics of empathy in the writing classroom provides manifold opportunities for mutual understanding and the forging of healthy teacher-student connections. McLeod (1997) reiterated, "empathetic understanding is usually seen not only as an ability to understand the other person's affective world but also to communicate this understanding to the other in a sensitive, caring way" (p. 114). Indeed, my Jamaican Creole-speaking university students figured that I understood their plight and that I embraced an *I care* philosophy in my writing pedagogy.

Epilogue

Jamaican Creole-speaking students, like their counterparts who are schooled in the Anglophone Caribbean, learn English as a second language. The experiences I have gained from being a student and teacher at the different levels of the education system have taught me how to approach teaching Jamaican students and also have shown me that many teachers are not trained to teach English as a second language. The consequences are inevitable. When Jamaican Creole-speaking students enter the formal education system, some teachers do not have the expertise to help these children make the transition in terms of their use of language. This is where the issues begin. If the language-related literacy learning concerns that emerge at the primary level are not adequately addressed, they reside with these learners as they pass through the system, and only the strong ones survive. It is highly probable that even the strong ones will grow weak if timely, appropriate interventions are not implemented.

With language issues unresolved, teachers, like students, get frustrated and the blame game begins. Having experimented with the use of Jamaican Creole alongside Jamaican Standard English in literacy instruction over the years, I can attest to the fact that it holds great promise for the intellectual, affective, and aesthetic dimensions of learning that are equally important for primary, secondary, and tertiary students. Jamaica is abundantly blessed with natural talents and other resources, the Jamaican Creole being the lifeblood of its culture. It cannot be easily discarded; therefore, as aptly articulated by Pollard (1998), "what we need to do is to fit everyone to switch codes as the situation arises" (p. 3).

Many things have changed in the field of education and other related disciplines. In fact, the realities have become even more complex with the introduction of new literacies. However, the language situation that exists in Jamaica remains the same. All stakeholders of the Jamaican education system should take the initiative to use the best of what students know, and in this case, I refer to using the rich, colorful, rhythmic, versatile Jamaican Creole, to move them beyond their first world. I, therefore, charge:

- government officials to put a sense of urgency in their undertakings to move the language policy beyond the paper talk stage.
- administrators at teacher-training institutions to design and offer a mandatory course for all students with a title such as *Teaching literacy skills across the curriculum in the Jamaican Creole-speaking environment*; in-service teachers should be offered the option of pursuing this course as a part of their ongoing professional development.
- teachers at all levels of the Jamaican education system to accept and celebrate Jamaican Creole as most of their students' known tongue and make a concerted effort to use it alongside Jamaican Standard English for intellectual affective, aesthetic culturally responsive lifelong literacy learning across the curriculum.
- university writing facilitators to handle the fears that students associate with writing with great care because in many instances these students are fragile and would benefit greatly from an ethics of empathy.

References

Alverman, D. E., Moon, J. S., & Hagwood, M. C. (1999). *Popular culture in the classroom: Teaching and researching critical media literacy*. Newark: International Reading Association.

Baer, M. B. (2017). The connection between empathy toward others and ethics. *Psychology Today*. Retrieved from https://www.psychologytoday.com/us/blog/empathy-and-relationships/201701/the-connection-between-empathy-toward-others-and-ethics

Bailey, C. (2014). *A poetics of performance: The oral-scribal aesthetics in Anglophone Caribbean fiction*. Kingston, Jamaica: University of the West Indies Press.

Barrett, C. (2013). (Re)imagining TESOL through critical hip hop literacy. *International Journal of Critical Pedagogy, 4*(3), 100–115.

Breen, M. P. (2011). Teaching language in the postmodern classroom. Retrieved from http://www.raco.cat/index.php./bells/article/viewFile/102825/149230

Bryan, B. (1997). Investigating language in a Jamaican primary school: Perceptions and findings of a group of primary school teachers. *Changing English, 4*(2), 251–258. Retrieved from http://www.mona.uwi.edu/des/pages/bBryan.htm

Bryan, B. (2004). Language and literacy in a Creole-speaking environment: A study of primary schools in Jamaica. *Language, Culture and Curriculum, 17*(2) 87–96. doi.org/10.1080/07908310408666685

Bryan, B. (2010). *Between two grammars: Research and practice for language learning and teaching in a Creole-speaking environment.* Jamaica: Ian Randle Publishers.

Bryan, O. (2007). Pon de river [Recorded by Elephant Man]. On *Good 2 go* [CD]. Kingston, Jamaica: VP Records.

Bühmann, D., & Trudell, B. (2007). *Mother tongue matters: Local language as a key to effective learning.* Paris: UNESCO.

Carlo, M. S., & Bengochea, A. (2011). Best practices in literacy instruction for English language learners. In L. M. Morrow & L. B. Gambrell (Eds.), *Best practices in literacy Instructions* (4th ed., pp. 117–138). New York: The Guildford Press.

Center for Teaching (n. d.). What are the benefits of reading aloud?: An instructional format for college-age learners. Retrieved from https://teach.its.uiowa.edu/sites/teach.its.uiowa.edu/files/docs/docs/What_are_the_Benefits_of_Reading_Aloud_ed.pdf

Cherry, R. (2010). From Africa to reggae: The Anansi connection. *American Entomologist,* 70–72.

Christenson, P. G., & Roberts, D. F. (1998). *It's not only rock and roll: Popular music in the lives of adolescents.* New York: Hampton Press.

Cornwell, L. (2018). What is readers theater? Retrieved from http://www.scholastic.com/librarians/programs/whatisrt.htm

Craig, D. (1999). *Teaching language and literacy: Policies and procedures for vernacular situations.* Georgetown, Guyana: Education and Development Services.

Craig, D. (2006). *Teaching language and literacy to Caribbean students: From vernacular to Standard English.* Kingston, Jamaica: Ian Randle Publishers.

Cummins, J. (2001). Bilingual children's mother tongue: Why is it important for education? *Sprogforum, 7*(19), 15–20. Retrieved from http://www.iteachilearn.com/cummins/mother.htm

Danley, T. (2007). Pop culture: An overview. Retrieved from https://philosophynow.org/issues/64/Pop_Culture_An_Overview

Delpit, L. (1988). The silenced dialogue: Power and pedagogy in educating other people's children. *Harvard Educational Review, 58*(3), 280–299.

Devonish, H. (1986). *Language and liberation: Creole language politics in the Caribbean.* London: Karia Press.

Devonish, H. (1998). Electronic orature: The deejay's discovery. *Social and Economic Studies, 47*(1), 33–53.

Devonish, H. (2011). A horse of a different colour: A language with a different name. Retrieved from https://icclr.wordpress.com/2013/06/26/a-horse-of-a-different-colour-a-language-with-a-different-name/

Devonish, H. (2012, August 26). Stop demonising Patois: From a semi-lingual to a bilingual Jamaica. *The Gleaner.* Retrieved from http://jamaicagleaner.com/gleaner/20120826/cleisure/cleisure2.html

Devonish, H., & Carpenter, K. (2007). Towards full bilingualism in education: The Jamaican Bilingual Primary Education Project. *Social and Economic Studies, 56*(1&2), 277–303.

Devonish, H., & Carpenter, K. (2010). Swimming against the tide: Jamaican Creole in education. In B. Migge, I. Leglise, & A. Bartens (Eds.), *Creoles in education: An appraisal of current programs and projects* (pp. 167–182). Amsterdam: John Benjamins.

Elbow, P. (2012). *Vernacular eloquence: What speech can bring to writing.* Oxford: Oxford University Press.

Elola, I., & Oskoz, A. (2010). Collaborative writing: Fostering foreign language and writing conventions development. *Language Learning & Technology, 14*(3), 1–71. Retrieved from http://llt.msu.edu/issues/october2010/elolaoskoz.pdf

Fisher, M. T. (2003). Open mics and open minds: Spoken word poetry in African diaspora participatory literacy communities. *Harvard Educational Review, 73*(3), 362–389.

Fisher, M. T. (2005). From the coffee house to the schoolhouse: The promise and potential of spoken word poetry in school contexts. *English Education, 37*(2), 115–131.

Gardner, H. (1983). *Frames of mind: Multiple intelligences.* New York: Basic Books.

Gibson, S. (2008). Reading aloud: A useful learning tool. *English Language Teachers Journal, 62*(1) 29–36.

Gill, J. H. (2000). *The tacit mode: Michael Polanyi's postmodern philosophy.* New York: SUNY Press.

Gurm, B. (2013). Multiple ways of knowing in teaching and learning. *International Journal for the Scholarship of Teaching and Learning, 7*(1), 1–7. doi.org/10.20429/ijsotl.2013.070104

Hagwood, M. (2009). Designing learning with new literacies. In M. Hagwood (Ed.), *New literacy practices: Designing literacy learning* (pp. 1–6). New York: Peter Lang.

Halliday, M. (1973). *Explorations in the functions of language.* London: Edward Arnold.

Hanemann, U. (2015). Lifelong literacy: Some trends and issues in conceptualising and operationalising literacy from a lifelong learning perspective. *International Review of Education, 61*(3), 295–326.
Hanson, R. (1995). *The tangerine tree*. New York: Clarion Books.
Harper Collins. (2013). Drop Everything And Read. Retrieved from http://www.dropeverythingandread.com/
Harrison, C., & Pond, L. (1996). Talking music: Empowering children in as musical communicators. *British Journal of Music Education, 13*(3), 233–42.
Henderson, G., Willis, L., & Dunbar. S. (1992). Dem a bleach. [Recorded by Nardo Ranks]. On *Bam Bam Riddim* [CD]. Kingston, Jamaica: VP Records.
Hirvela, A. (1999). Collaborative writing instruction and communities of readers and writers. *TESOL Journal, 8*(2), 7–12.
Honeyghan, G. (2000). Rhythm of the Caribbean: Connecting oral history and literacy. *Language Arts, 77*(5), 406–413.
Hope, D. (2011). From browning to cake soap: Popular debates on skin bleaching in the Jamaican dancehall, *The Journal of Pan African Studies, 4*(4), 165–194.
Jamaican Truckers. (2013, July 11). *Everything flood out CVM funny video* [Video File]. Retrieved from http://lgcatv.com/watch/Mviu3RUtEnU
Jones, C. (Ed.). (1999). *Contemporary Jamaican Anansi stories* (Unpublished manuscript). Kingston, Jamaica.
Jones, C. (2000). *Literature-based instruction: A model for improving comprehension and writing in the Jamaican Creole-speaking environment* (Unpublished master's thesis). Oakland University, Rochester, Michigan.
Jones, C. (2009). *The unfolding: Phenomenological perspectives of a group of grade four inner-city primary school boys engaged in a Jamaican Arts-based Multi-method Instructional Network [JAMIN]* (Unpublished doctoral dissertation). The University of the West Indies, Kingston, Jamaica.
Kelly, M. (2017). Mnemonic devices for students. Retrieved from https://www.thoughtco.com/mnemonic-devices-tools-7755
Kennedy, M. M. (2018). *What do Jamaican children speak?: A language resource*. Kingston, Jamaica: University of the West Indies Press.
kevy2c. (2011, June 15). *Nobody Canna Cross It Twanging (Refix Video) - DJ Powa* [Video File]. Retrieved from https://www.youtube.com/watch?v=hknVoAoyy-k
Lee, S. (2003). Teaching EFL writing in the university: Related issues, insights, and implications. *Journal of National Taipei Teachers College, 16*(1), 111–36. Retrieved from http://www-o.ntust.edu.tw/~syying.lee/publications/Lee_JNTTC2003.pdf
Leu, D. J., O'Byrne, W. I., Zawilinski, J., McVerry, G., & Everett-Cacopardo, H. (2009). Expanding the new literacies conversation. *Educational Researcher, 38*(4), 364–369.

Lloyd, C. V. (2003, June). Song lyrics as texts to develop critical literacy. *Reading Online, 6*(10). Retrieved from http://www.readingonline.org/articles/art_index.asp?HREF=lloyd/index.htm

Lopez, A. (2011). Culturally relevant pedagogy and critical literacy in diverse English classrooms: A case study of a secondary English teacher's activism and agency. *English Teaching: Practice and Critique, 10*(4), 75–93

McCracken, R. K. (1971). Initiating silent sustained reading. *Journal of Reading, 14*(8), 582–583.

McLeod, S. H. (1997). *Notes on the heart: Affective issues in the writing classroom.* Carbondale, IL: Southern Illinois University Press.

McNaughton, J. (2013). Odd Ras [Recorded by Chronnix] on *The music for grand theft auto v* [CD]. Kingston, Jamaica: Digital Vibez Entertainment.

Milne, E. (2014). Taking a picture walk. *Hands & Voices.* Retrieved from http://www.handsandvoices.org/articles/education/ed/V11-2_picturewalk.htm

Milson-Whyte, V. (2015). *Academic writing instruction for creole-influenced students.* Kingston, Jamaica: University of the West Indies Press.

Ministry of Education, Youth, and Culture (MOEYC) [Jamaica]. (2001). Language education policy. Retrieved from http://dlpalmer.weebly.com/uploads/3/5/8/7/3587856/language_education_policy.pdf

Moll, L., Amanti, C., Neff, D., & González, N. (2005). Funds of knowledge for teaching: Using a qualitative approach to connect homes and classrooms. In N. González, L. Moll, & C. Amanti (Eds.), *Funds of knowledge: Theorizing practices in households, communities, and classrooms* (pp. 71–88). New York: Routledge.

Morrell, E. (2004). *Linking literacy and popular culture: Finding connections for lifelong learning.* Norwood, MA: Christopher-Gordon Publishers, Inc.

Morris-Brown, V. (1988). *The Jamaica handbook of proverbs.* Mandeville, Jamaica: Island Heart Publishers.

Mwanza, M. D. (2017). The eclectic approach to language teaching: Its conceptualisation and misconceptions. *International Journal of Humanities Social Sciences and Education, 4*(2), 73–67. doi.org/10.20431/2349 - 0381.0 402 0 06

Nath, S. (2014). The concept of reality from postmodern perspectives. *Journal of Business Management & Social Sciences Research, 5*(3) 26–30.

NCTE. (2013). The NCTE definition of 21st century literacies. Retrieved from http://www2.ncte.org/statement/21stcentdefinition/

Nero, S. (2010). Discourse tensions, Englishes, and the composition classroom. In B. Horner, M. Lu, & P. K. Matsuda (Eds.), *Cross-language relations in composition* (pp. 142–157). Carbondale, IL: Southern Illinois University Press.

Nero, S. (2014). De facto language education policy through teachers' attitudes and practices: A critical ethnographic study in three Jamaican schools. *Language Policy, 13,* 221–242.

Nurlia, R., & Arini, F. (2017). Effect of bringing local culture in English language teaching on students' writing achievement. *KnE Social Sciences, 1*(3), 187–194.

Olson, C. B., Land, R., Anselmi, T., & AuBuchon, C. (2010). Teaching secondary English learners to understand, analyze, and write interpretive essays about theme. *Journal of Adolescent and Adult Literacy, 54,* 245–256.

Ong, W. (1982). *Orality and literacy: The technologizing of the world.* London: Routledge.

Philosophy. (2002). Blind men and the elephant. Retrieved from https://www.allaboutphilosophy.org/blind-men-and-the-elephant.htm

Pollard, V. (1998). Code switching and code mixing: Language in the Jamaican classroom. *Caribbean Journal of Education, 20,* 21–29.

Pollard, V. (2003). *From Creole to Standard English: A handbook for teachers.* Kingston, Jamaica: University of the West Indies Press.

Richmond, K. J. (1999–2000). The ethics of empathy: Making connections in the writing classroom. *Journal of the Assembly for Expanded Perspectives on Learning, 5,* 37–46.

Roberts, T., & Billings, L. (2008). Thinking is literacy, literacy thinking. *Educational Leadership, 65*(5), 32–36.

Rollnick, M., & Rutherford, M. (1996). The use of mother tongue and English in the learning and expression of science concepts: A classroom-based study. *International Journal of Science Education, 18,* 91–103. doi:10.1080/0950069960180108

Rosenblatt, L. M. (1988). Writing and reading: The transactional theory. Retrieved from https://www.ideals.illinois.edu/bitstream/handle/2142/18044/ctrstreadtechrepv01988i00416_opt.pdf

Rosenblatt, L. M. (1994). *The reader, the text, the poem: The transactional theory of literary work.* Carbondale, IL: Southern Illinois University Press.

Rosenblatt, L. M. (2013). The transactional theory of reading and writing. In N. Unrau, N. J. Unrau, & R. B. Ruddell (Eds.), *Theoretical models and processes of reading* (6th ed., pp. 923–956). Newark, DE: International Reading Association.

ShakaRaSpeaks. (2011, January 25). Miss Lou: Fi wi language: (Jamaican patwah). [Video File]. Retrieved from https://www.youtube.com/watch?v=W58MtDzanqA

Shields, K. (1989). Standard English in Jamaica: A case of competing models. *English World-Wide, 10*(1), 41–53.

Siegel, J. (2005). Literacy in Pidgin and Creole languages. *Current Issues in Language Planning, 6*(2), 143–163.

Siegel, J. (2010). Bilingual literacy in Creole contexts. *Journal of Multilingual and Multicultural Development, 31*(4), 383–402. doi: 10.1080/01434632.2010.497217

[S]itgan. (2015, April 9). *Barack Obama in Jamaica (Patois) Greetings massive! Wha gwaann Jamaica?* [Video File]. Retrieved from https://www.youtube.com/watch?v=vucnSelKio

Spindler, G., & Spindler, L. (2000). *Fifty years of anthropology and education.* Mahwah, NJ: Lawrence Erlbaum Associates.

Stewart, A. (2015 April 30). *Aubrey Stewart introduction of President Obama: Youth town hall meeting* [Video File]. Retrieved from https://www.youtube.com/watch?v=dCYbhjtHwD4

Taylor, M. (2002). Walking a cultural tightrope in the classroom: Does affirming the home language imply 'ghettoizing' the bilingual learner? Paper presented at the Second Conference on Caribbean Culture, University of the West Indies, Mona, January 9–12.

Taylor, M. (2011). *Connecting the dots: Anatomy of verbal interaction in Jamaican English language classrooms.* Kingston, Jamaica: Arawak Publications.

thejamaicanlangco. (2009, June 1). *Writing Jamaican the Jamaican way (Raitin Jamiekan di Jamiekan wie)* [Video File]. Retrieved from https://www.youtube.com/watch?v=2rx4FAIxaTEthe

Waddell, D. (1998–1999). When a student ends a wounded silence. *The Journal of the Assembly for Expanded Perspectives on Learning, 4,* 61–70.

Warner-Lewis, M. (2015, October 5). Patois not enemy of English. *The Gleaner.* Retrieved from http://jamaica-gleaner.com/article/commentary/20151005/patois-not-enemy-english

Weinstein, S. (2006). A love for the thing: The pleasures of rap as a literate practice. *Journal of Adolescent & Adult Literacy, 50*(4), 270–81.

White, E. B. (1980). *Charlotte's web.* New York: HarperCollins Publishers.

Wubbles, L. (1995). *One small miracle.* Bloomington, MN: Bethany House.

Wurdeman-Thurston, K., & Kaomea, J. (2015). Fostering culturally relevant literacy instruction: Lessons from a Native Hawaiian classroom. *Language Arts, 92*(6), 424–434.

2 Building around Nation Language: A Critical Reflection on Teaching Composition at the University of The Bahamas

Jacob Dyer Spiegel

This critical reflection explores the use of *Bahamian Creole English* (broadly referred to in the Bahamas as *Bahamian Dialect*, *Bahamianese*, or, more simply, *Dialect*) in first-year composition courses at the University of The Bahamas. My courses were designed to celebrate language diversity, and they began by redefining *dialect* as a word-site attached to ongoing colonial constructs. The use of *dialect* in the classroom and in assignments, re-approached from a Caribbean and postcolonial perspective, encouraged students to claim and exalt their multiple languages and allowed students to look at course material through at least two cultural lenses. Despite initial resistance to writing in dialect, the use of multiple language varieties in the classroom created a safe space for expression that empowered students, allowed them to look at cultural patterns through language paradigms, enhanced their critical ability to move between audiences across power structures, and, for many students, sparked a joy for words and expression that had not been felt in previous writing courses. Indeed, students became the teachers of their languages, actively created course content by sharing lived-experience, and by working so closely with the medium of the course—language and expression—their awareness of how audience, context, and purpose shape language use was sharpened significantly. Students thrived when their mother tongues were supported, and they took new risks with language and writing. These experiments with orality, liberties taken that might have been punished in secondary schooling, transformed the classroom experience and by the end of the course, students eagerly sent me their course writing and final reflections knowing that they might be included in the present volume. (All students cited throughout requested that their names be published and gave full consent.) This chapter looks closely at the student experience so that teachers of composition can be open to perspectives—regardless of their fluency in multiple languages and registers—that enliven and inspire a class, particularly in places where colonialism and ongoing colonial legacies marginalize certain language varieties.

As a newly hired, foreign professor trained in Caribbean literatures and African diaspora studies, I found the possibility of having students interrogate colonial definitions of dialect and standard English, and elevating dialect to the status of language, of great personal interest. Even more incredible was the opportunity to introduce the great poet, historian, linguist, and philosopher, Kamau Brathwaite to the class, particularly his concept of *nation language*. Describing this concept, Brathwaite (1984) stated:

> What I am going to talk about . . . is language from the Caribbean, the process of using English in a different way from the 'norm.' English in a new sense as I prefer to call it. English in an ancient sense. English in a very traditional sense. And sometimes not English at all, but *language*. (p. 5)

He explained further that nation language is

> the submerged area of dialect which is much more closely allied to the African aspect of experience in the Caribbean. It may be in English: but often it is in an English which is like a howl, or a shout or a machine-gun or the wind or a wave. It is also like the blues. And sometimes it is English and African at the same time. (p.13)

It was here, in the wind and water that moves between West Africa and the Caribbean, that students in my writing classes experimented with multiple ways of defining their first languages—Bahamian nation language for most of the students, the nation language of Haiti and of Jamaica for other students. In Brathwaite's poetically historicized version of "English in an ancient sense" that cuts across colonial legacies, nation language became an avenue much more allied with the students' own sense of history and self for writing about language and culture.

Importantly, the collective act of defining (and using) languages so close to the students' lived-experience was, at least by the end of the course, empowering and revelatory of the complex series of relationships that students could "read" through language. For example, in a first draft, a student wrote towards the middle of her essay: "Language tells the story of who we are and where we came from . . . Each language is important . . . To erase languages would mean to erase history" (Sashae Duncan). In the final draft, after discussions on Brathwaite, that same student reworked her essay and issued the following decree:

> *I born, bred an ga ded Bahamian*, and nobody can stop that, just like nobody can stop our language from being a language. My language is beautiful, unique and filled with striking content that leaves the ears it falls upon captivated by its indifference. As we Bahamians call it, "Bahamianese" is our language; it is our form of expression, communication and culture. Our dialect is our story, it defines us, it shows us where we've been and what we've accomplished. (Sashae Duncan)

What happened between these drafts charts the story of a classroom opening to the poetics and possibilities of nation language.

As a concept, nation language, what Brathwaite (1984) describes as "the kind of English spoken by the people who were brought to the Caribbean, not the official English . . . but the language of slaves and labourers, the servants who were brought in by the conquistadors" (pp. 5–6), embodies a radical shift of consciousness in which, he claims, Caribbean language highlights a history of imposed metropolitan languages and decolonizes language use. Brathwaite's nation language subverts colonial power structures by elevating dialect to the status of a language that is capable of expressing Caribbean realities, poetics, cultural patterns, memories, and geographies. The pejorative associations that are invoked through the word *dialect*, then, are reversed as nation language—and perhaps nation language alone—is posited as the communicative medium that can allow the Caribbean, its writers, its artists, and its speakers to express realities particular to the region and its history. For Brathwaite, nation language may be, on one level, partially shaped by English, but *nation language* reaches far beyond the British metropole to include African, Asian, and Amerindian languages and worldviews. Further, nation language is part of Brathwaite's refashioning of imported forms in a Caribbean region that has often, through ongoing colonial practices, privileged European modes of expression—even if they are inadequate in terms of expressing from the perspective of the Caribbean. The hurricane, as Brathwaite asserts, "does not roar in pentameters," (p. 10) and since the hurricane is at the core of wind patterns linking Africa and the Caribbean—much like the languages and religions that Brathwaite invokes in his poetry and philosophy—nation language makes possible methods of description and captures the poetics of the (is)lands.

I began the writing classes at the University of The Bahamas (UB) with students discussing ideas surrounding language. After several class meetings focused on language, we moved to learning about dialect, nation language, and notions of standard English. Though several students fully embraced—and, at least in retrospect, found great comfort in—a classroom experience that could include multiple forms of language, it became clear that many students resisted writing in nation language until the very end of the course. Nation language may have been inspiring as a model and as a form of *speech* that opened up doors into themes previously unexplored in a classroom, it seemed, but the initial resistance to writing was apparent. The exception to this resistance came in the form of improvised sharing of writing far outside of the formal structure of the course—in the form of spontaneous emails, unsolicited printouts left on my desk, and direct messages through the online course management platform. As part of this study, I share some reasons why this resistance may have happened, highlighting the tension between colonial patterns of language policing and the empowerment that Brathwaite's (1984) definition of nation language can bring to a classroom in the Anglophone Caribbean and certainly beyond, wherever languages meet across power constructs. Indeed, while this teaching praxis and approach to celebrating language diversity was built into the teaching in the Bahamas, the incorporation of nation language and the elevation of dialect can hopefully inform approaches where the languages imposed by colonialism and colonial legacies are interwoven with "local" languages.

By fully exploring and engaging nation language in the classroom and by applying Brathwaite's (1984) method of equating standard English and dialect, the course affirmed students' unique written voices and respected student orality. It is what Heather M. Robinson, in this volume, might define as teaching composition by using a postcolonial definition of language itself. I argue that when nation language is brought into a classroom as even a possible vehicle for expression and reflection, the result can be inspiring, invigorating, and re-centering. One student reflected on the impact of nation language in the classroom as a kind of linguistic awakening:

> I was able to find myself in my writing. I was able to express myself in ways that I could never even fathom doing in high school. I opened my heart and my mind, and I let all of my pent-up anger and insecurities bleed into my writing. I said what I wanted to say and my dialect was heard and understood and accepted for once. One thing you will learn is that dialect isn't "wrong" or "forbidden" or "improper." In this class, it wasn't any of those things. It was an art. It was a masterpiece. It was a language. It brought colour and cultural flair to the classroom and that flair set the tone for rest of the course. (Curstin Mazuir)

Brathwaite's nation language set a tone of acceptance, reinforced writing as an outlet, and, despite initial resistance, allowed students to navigate expression from a space of empowerment.

Walking with Linguistic Purpose

There is a backstory to the inclusion of dialect and nation language in the course. Even weeks before the semester began, now onsite in New Providence, I was not sure if I would include a language-centric component in my courses, much less begin with it. I had no idea what to expect from the students: Would they find the concept of *dialect as language* obvious and cliché, would they reject being asked direct questions on spoken language in a writing classroom, would the education system have taught such rigid definitions of language that there would be no room for debate, would there simply be silence? As hopeful as I was that students would actively construct the definitions of our course's medium (language, words, written expression) by including their linguistic heritage, I could not produce a single word of Bahamian Creole English without the community's constant phonetic guidance, and I had never set foot in the *Anglophone* Caribbean before a few days prior. I had worked with university students in Brazil and Cuba on similar themes (and *in* dialects), often interrogating European cultural imposition through the very definition of standard Portuguese, Spanish, and regional language varieties. I had also worked with students from across Latin America, the Anglophone Caribbean, and Caribbean diasporas in the US at the University of Massachusetts-Amherst and the New York City public school system, and the writing and literature courses that I led usually began with the idea that colonial legacies continue to shape the way that societies define and approach dialects, sociolects, pidgins, and creoles. Yet, this was a different context. The Bahamas is a much younger independent nation than most Latin American countries, having gained independence from the UK in 1973, and the discourse surrounding language and empire—even hearing Bahamians affectionately refer to *Queen's English* as the esteemed language variety—made me wonder how new (and perhaps how uncomfortable) it would be for students to question values associated with the language of the British metropole. So, in the weeks preceding the course, I did what Cadogan (2016) outlines in his Benjaminian ruminations through the streets of New York City and Kingston: I walked.

I walked with linguistic purpose throughout downtown Nassau and the neighborhoods of New Providence, the island that is the major population center of the Bahamas, striking up conversations on language and dialect with jitney bus drivers and passengers, store owners, university professors, local bankers, potential landlords, political speech writers, cultural affairs attachés, families hanging out at the beach, maintenance staff on campus, and people at food stands (among others). I was trying to understand how students might respond to questions on language, how people valued Bahamian Creole/Bahamian Dialect, and what they thought about dialect coming into the university classroom. I wanted to know the culture-scape of linguistic identity. If the inclusion of dialect would be a contentious topic—some were perplexed, even amidst the booming bass of Soca on the jitneys, about why *anyone* would ask students about dialect at a university—I wondered how a teaching style built around empowering dialect and privileging lived-experience would work.

Initially it seemed a relatively large section of the community in New Providence considered the inclusion of themes relating to dialect to be inappropriate, and so new questions emerged: What would the community think about teaching methods that tap into students' lived-experience and allow that wisdom to shape the course content? Would the students actively participate, sharing lived-experience, especially through the prism of language? If I could not draw from student diglossia or bilingualism—highlighting the way in which dialect carries a rich worldview—how would students respond to an interactive approach based on discussion? At UB, professors are, as a British colonial legacy, generally called *lecturers* by students and faculty alike: how would I break the norms surrounding the *lecturer* title, especially considering that I deliver my writing courses as workshops that involve very little lecturing at all? The answers, I decided, depended on the delivery of the themes and the relationship built in the classroom, yet my informal interviews continued.

While discussing language throughout the capital city in the three weeks before the semester began, I was struck by a few patterns in the responses. Some of the people that I spoke to believed that dialect should simply be prohibited from the classroom, removed altogether, banished the moment one stepped foot on the university campus. "Haven't you seen the 'No Profanity' signs all around campus," a group at a conch stand in the neighborhood of Gambier asked me, "that's the way it should be, because they need to be speaking *Queen's English*." Others on a crowded jitney explained (in Bahamian Creole English/Bahamian Dialect I should note) that bringing dialect into the classroom was risky because the students would not take me seriously—a course in English composition should prevent the informalities afforded by dialect and, in order to manage the classroom experience successfully, students had to respect the lecturer by speaking "properly." Dialect, in this view, was improper and relegated to specific situations and spaces. Similarly, standard English was equated with the bestowing of respect and true leaders had to be addressed in the language of monarchy. I was learning.

Another group of younger, recent college graduates from universities in Nova Scotia and Ontario who had returned to work in The Bahamas a year earlier saw a possibility for engagement. "If you want to reach the students," they explained, "showing them that dialect is just as rich a form of expression could be a powerful lesson." I had imagined that most students already viewed dialect as a rich expressive language and was hesitant to make assumptions. I wanted students to show me where they stood in terms of language appreciation. Several community members that I met at a local conch stand, even though they supported my linguistic stance, declared that I would most definitely land myself in trouble with university administration should I incorporate dialect into my lesson plans (they were incorrect, I would later learn). "And never," they said between lessons on ways of serving conch, "let them call you anything other than *Dr. Dyer Spiegel*, as this is the only way they will respect your status as lecturer."

Finally, and especially among groups that lived for longer periods abroad, some community members were hesitant: "Dialect is what we use when we don't want foreigners to understand us—it's secret, it's our way of undermining power, it's ours—it's not appropriate to force them to divulge the secrets, especially as a foreigner." This was, without a doubt, the response that I found most revealing: dialect is a sacred code and a tool for resistance. Questions emerged: Would students feel, upon asserting dialect as a language, that they would be forced to reveal aspects of the culture to an outsider? Teachers from outside of the cultural system who bring dialect into a classroom, must recognize that they are entering a position of power in a classroom, and the idea that students could feel forced to divulge secrets was an alert that I carried with me throughout the language-focused course. Instead of requiring use of dialect, I would always give students space to choose their language of narration, oral and written production, and analysis.

The warning that students might feel forced to divulge secrets posited Bahamian Dialect as a kind of mask: the outsider may think he or she is "understanding" the culture, yet the moment a conclusion is drawn the meaning system could shift. Later in the course, several students would explore dialect as a secret code used when foreigners are close, so that they cannot penetrate the culture. As one student would write: "We are taught to speak properly when communicating with tourists and to not let our other side show. It's as almost if there is a mask we put on to entertain them, while only showing a fraction of our identity" (Raymond Ward). The ability to articulate this inside/outside relationship, I would discover, came through the students' attention to language. Writing about language, once given the tools, allowed students to explore and analyze language and power relationships across language varieties. Writing about language also allowed students to be more self-reflective about language itself and how to adapt written text for specific audiences.

BUILDING TOWARDS NATION LANGUAGE

Despite some of the warnings as to the appropriateness of "elevating" dialect and encouraging the use of multiple language varieties in a classroom, I went forward with my plan to build the initial course unit around nation language. Discussion and readings, however, started with themes on language and culture (I would have to scaffold towards nation language) and students shared some of the most probing, thoughtful responses and definitions of language that I had ever witnessed in a university classroom. Some students were only sixteen years old, others had several children themselves, but across the range of experiences and ages, we heard that language is a living, communicative code that can connect (or tear apart) communities, families, or even the individual to (or from) the core self. Students probed language as a vessel that carries culture, memory, emotion, and hope—a vehicle for expression that allows us to unite and achieve the greatest feats. One student wrote, "language frames and grounds our realities. Cultures are built on language and the memories that it carries. It is the collective sounds, symbols, patterns, and behaviours that give meaning to our existence, through which we express our existence. Language transcends time. . . . Language is the rhythm of the people" (Xan-Xi Bethel).

Reflection on language proved to be stimulating, and as the semester progressed, I brought in more prompts and questions that students responded to in oral and written form, in small groups and individually. We all have access to this mysterious force of communication, one prompt began, let us use our own experience with this *being* to define it. Once I saw how lively the discussion could be, I let the language-centric theme spread out across several weeks as students considered the following: "What is language? What can words do? What are these mysterious things that can connect people or lead to all out war? What is dialect? What are the powers of those words? And what is the difference between language and dialect?" We read fragments of Anzaldúa's (1999) *Borderlands/La Frontera*, and students wrote accounts of their own multilingualism and brief odes to the power of words. Though it was not my intention to "legitimize" dialect by including statements on language from outside of the Caribbean, students recognized and found inspiration in patterns in language philosophy shared across cultural geographies and contexts. Several students discussed the capacity of words to carry prayer and as emanations of God's grace.

And then several class meetings later we considered the question, "What is dialect?" Response: a long, heavy silence. I tried to read the tension without interrupting the silence. It was the best attempt at an intuitive probing I could manage given the short amount of time I had lived in New Providence: Does he want to hear what we were taught, what we actually think, what we should think, do we have to think the same way now that we are at a university, will he grade us, and what will our classmates think? Perhaps, I mused in the silence, teachers had never asked this question before.

In sharp juxtaposition to the incredible statements on language and the power of words earlier in the week, my question on dialect—like many on the jitneys shared with blaring Rake n' Scrape classics in the background—seemed to require a series of translations. Discussion of dialect in a classroom was not the same as my walks through the city, and this defining of expression and worldview took on new meaning inside the space of the nation's only public university. "But," a student began, breaking the silence, "dialect is just poor English; it is slang, just broken English." The group of students all nodded in agreement. "Dialect is badly spoken English, it's meant to get an idea across as fast as possible—you don't write in it or use it for anything other than *communicating*." Students across the two courses continued: "dialect is low class, uneducated, nobody will hire you if you speak improperly." Was this the spoon-fed response that students were taught? Was this the response meant to protect the sacred language from outsider appropriation? Or was this part of the colonial legacy passed on through numerous structures of power?

As I tried to advance the discussion, students continued to reiterate and support the colonial attitudes on dialect. "But, last class," I reminded the students, "didn't we say that language, like dialect, was meant to *communicate* an idea of some kind?" Silence. It was almost as if students wanted or expected me to affirm the views on dialect that had been taught in the past, though—especially when reinforcing what we had defined as language during previous class periods—there was an undercurrent of suspicion that I may not exactly be buying the whole prepackaged concept of linguistic inferiority. Students seemed enthused to find out why I was visibly connecting certain statements that they made about *language proper* and the more positive utterances on dialect. They sensed that I was not opening the course with such a direct inclusion of dialect as a way to bash it.

When I asked the class if there were things that could be said in dialect that could not be said in so-called standard English, the students' suspicions were confirmed: the new guy was up to something. "Yes," many replied emphatically, and the journey into the expressive capacity of dialect began. And then I asked about proverbs, words their grandparents used, stories passed down through generations in dialect. Students ransacked my marker supply and went to the white boards, eager to share and discuss sayings and words specific to their island, to their parents' islands. I had never seen a board fill up so quickly. Impromptu impersonations, skits, students acting out the meaning of certain words, and, of course, the phonetics lessons began: they were teaching the teacher and teaching each other. The teaching mode continued into the written assignments and moved from lexicon to syntax, and from Bahamian nation language to that of Jamaica:

> Two of the most iconic words in the language are 'nuh' and 'náh' (pronounced with a long 'aah' sound as in the word last). These two words are misused by most, if not all non-Jamaicans . . . The word 'nàh' is used with the verb 'to be,' while the word 'nuh' is used with the verb 'to do.' For example, if one wants to say "I **am not** moving," ('am' is a form of the verb 'to be') one is supposed to say "Mi náh move." If one says "Mi nuh move," he or she is saying "I **did not** move" ('did' is past tense of the verb 'to do'). (Todd Denton)

These lessons allowed students to teach the professor and claim their languages. Importantly, though standard English drives the description, all of the students writing about nation language adopted a unique perspective *inside* of the nation language-culture, *inside* of the standard English audience, and *between* these groups. This ability to be inside and between multiple language varieties strengthened the students' skills at adapting their writing for specific audiences and for different purposes. The student-driven grammar lessons continued for several class meetings and the classroom volume prompted neighboring teachers to inquire as to the lesson plan. While some passersby looked concerned, one colleague from the English Studies program waited for the class to end, smiled, and gave me Glinton-Meicholas's (1995) *More Talkin' Bahamian*. "I heard you have the students considering dialect," she said enthusiastically; "you might find this book useful." That was, to me, the symbolic passing of the key and indirect invitation to continue.

For homework, I asked the students to try to define dialect and to refer to the classroom discussions, especially considering what Standard English might not be able to transmit. In written form, I found that many of the more vocal advocates for the far-reaching poetic capacity of dialect took a turn into the engrained, accepted position (that of dialect as substandard, uneducated English). Others expanded upon the conclusions that we reached in the oral, performative classroom context and wrote such things as, "dialect is home, it is our way, we know instantly where people are from based on the sound of it, it is what we miss most when we are away from home, it is our history" (Sashae Duncan). That same student exclaimed, "dialect is our identity, it is *ours*, nobody can take it from us."

At this point, I assigned Brathwaite's (1984) *A History of the Voice* and, in class, we looked closely at several key statements, including the ones I used to open the chapter; we explored how nation language is, "allied to the African aspect of experience in the Caribbean. It may be in English: but often it is in an English which is like a howl, or a shout or a machine-gun or the wind or a wave" (p. 13). The idea of language and wind resonated. Hurricane season was beginning, and news of the "classic Cape Verdean storm," Hurricane Irma, had been announced the day before. Students naturally built from previous class discussion on the transmission of story and proverb. They began to look at dialect, now framed by Brathwaite as language, as a vehicle to carry thought, instinct, memory, and culture between generations. Students interviewed family members and neighbors about their language, all the while reflecting how nation language can carry an African experience and sensibility.

Writing in Nation Language

Building from this momentum, and using the students' in-class responses as a model, I asked that students try something new: adapt the previous assignment in which dialect was defined and discuss nation language: "How are these two language varieties different? What does Brathwaite mean when he writes, "language like a machine-gun . . . language that is African and English at the same time"? And the crucial piece of the assignment: "Try to do this defining of nation language *in* nation language—give examples, and feel free to write in nation language." Everyone came to class the next day, eager to share the adaptation. To my surprise, however, only a few students of approximately ninety-five, across two courses and four sections, actually wrote more than a few words *in* Bahamian Creole English/nation language. The students were far more comfortable writing in standard English about their own language. It was a fascinating decision that they made, one that highlighted their masterful code-sliding capacities, a double-lens announced through the translative movement inside and outside of dialect.

In an oral context, students were willing to describe nation language and even teach variants of nation language as spoken across the Bahamian archipelago and, to a lesser extent given our student body demographics, in Haiti and Jamaica. Though I was surprised that this enthusiasm did not transfer into the written assignment, it was evident the writing *about* dialect exercised the students' ability to engage critically with cultural legacies, interrogate social norms, and articulate colonial power dynamics — core goals of many college composition courses.

The poetic, critical reach of the small group of students who chose to write in dialect (or partially in dialect) about dialect was transcendental, and peer celebration of their work, much more than my praise, let students know that expressive exploration would be rewarded. After riveting written definitions of nation language in which some students even offered brief grammar lessons and "translations" of key terminologies, one student whose work throughout the semester consistently built from the lessons on nation language, Xan-Xi Bethel, raised her hand and recited a poem:

>Sisters to the sea
>Stones in the ocean
>We are-
>Hispaniola
>half-side
>of a pot pourri
>sweet, spicy flavor
>mix-up
>fixup
>boil together for
>hot pepper-pot
>Beautiful flower
>Haiti
>[. . .]
>We are-
>Rocks on the
>same water
>We are
>from the same Africa
>Man!
>the same Africa land
>Shared the same womb

> sucked the same
> tits-
> Tell Me
> Why you want to
> fight your brother-Man
> Deny your mother
> Come on Man
> Sisters to the sea
> Stones in the ocean
> We are-
> Skin pressed
> glistening
> black
> Our pasts move together
> close

As if synchronized, the final syllable of the poem led to the eruption of applause and shouting: the poem, which was about nation language (written between nation language and standard English), was fully celebrated by the class. For the lyrical subject in this poem, nation language is a possible mirror in which Bahamians can see themselves in "other" Caribbean immigrant communities in the Bahamas, where Haitian immigrant communities remain stigmatized. (In fact, one major reason why Bahamians prefer the label *Bahamian Dialect* over *Bahamian Creole* to describe their language is that they associate the term *creole* with the stigmatized Haitian minority [see, for example, Hackert, 2004].) To deny nation language, for the speaker, means to deny a possibility for cross-cultural understanding and to deny the historical ties that link the Bahamas and Haiti.

Moving into the second draft, Bethel alters form (the poem begins its transition into an essay) and situates the narration in what is sometimes called "the Haitian Village," a community in New Providence, providing an interesting example of how building from nation language allowed for a unique voice in essay form:

> Take a walk with me, through the brush, along a narrow, rocky path. Prickles will cling to your pant legs, pay them no mind. They are a minor inconvenience. What you are about to see will baffle you, blow your mind, yet, bring you to a greater awareness of your own self... Deep, in the village, beyond the prickly

bush, the rugged thatch, the love vine, and just past the poinciana trees—live a people, of us, with us, from us, but apart. Here we are. The acrid smell of burning castor greets us. It snakes into our nostrils, clings to the sinuses. The women are burning bush for oil. A sacred secret . . . Suddenly your gaze is broken by the squeal of a small child as he rushes past. He chases a little dog with a stick. Then a throng, all small, all brown, all gleeful, follow; leaving billowing clouds of dust in their wake. They shout and laugh in a strange language. It does not roll like Spanish, or sing like French—but still, you feel you know it. It sounds like Gambier and Obeah and Sisi and Kanep. And like juju and gimme and yinna, and so much like ya'sef! Odd, this feeling, this knowing, but unknowing.

The exploration of the Haitian Village, and by extension Haiti itself, in which the author moves between nation language and standard Englishes, develops into a moment of possibility—unity across Caribbean cultures that is a reconciliation of historical ties between the Bahamas and Haiti, or a failed connection in the form of ongoing assumptions regarding the Haitian *other*. The "you" could be a Bahamian national seeing the self in what they have *othered*, the Haitian-Bahamian of "The Village": "He says, me and you, me and you are the same. See? Bantu, Yoruba, Congoland, Ifa, Africa. You are Duvalier? He asks. You say yes, From Cat Island. He says, yes, From Ayiti." Bethel—through her detailed account of language and sound, by tracing the commonalities of nation language across nations—has crafted a language-centric refutation of xenophobia. To push against the linguistic norms that I had been warned of during the initial days of arrival in New Providence, to elevate nation language *with* students (not as a lecture, but as a collaborative act), and to allow students to define language on their own terms was what prompted many students to take control of their incredibly potent critical voices. Yet, not all of the students chose to write in nation language.

When I asked the class, the next day, why most had chosen to write about nation language in standard English, many explained that they did not think about it—*Queen's English* just came naturally. Others avoided my question with nervous laughter or silence, as if they had done something wrong. "Was he expecting us to do that," they were probably thinking, "will there be a punishment through the grading, a kind of reverse from the K-12 years of language enforcement?" That void space was layered and could only be described fully at the end of the course, once students were more comfortable. At the time, it became clear that for most of the students—despite what was shared in class discussion—dialect could be used in an oral context but was not a language to dwell in for long, at least in written form (see, for example, Milson-Whyte, 2013). As a *formal* element of the course, with the exception of the hybrid poem-essay that was read *aloud*, students were willing to consider the expressive capacity of nation language as long as that reflecting was done in standard English. At that time, however, I was not aware that almost all written assignments were perceived by the first-year students as equally "formal": drafting was a new process to many and even in-class brainstorming in written form felt more like an exam room than the writing workshops I had been accustomed to. Even though framed as a generative writing assignment, the fact that it was *assigned* signified norms, conformity to past teaching requirements, and insecurity with regards to what I was really looking for.

After the assignment, many students seemed to return to their original conclusions, refuting claims that dialect is also a language—just as rich, just as expressive—and even questioned their own bilingualism that we had celebrated in class only days before. It seemed that the brief encounter with writing in nation language (or even the request to write in nation language) triggered a return to the earlier definitions from class: "Maybe it is like the wind, but dialect is not written," a student exclaimed, "it is substandard, there's no central, standard for grammar and spelling—we just invent it daily." Students proceeded to give examples: "The word *bey* is spelled *bae* and *beuy*; *whatchu sayin* becomes *chu sayin*—we can't even agree on how to spell that!" Even though we had defined language as an expressive world in constant flux, many of the students now refuted this alleged bilingualism that I was celebrating. (Nonetheless, Oenbring [2013] demonstrates that Bahamians have normalized, though not officially codified, eye dialect spellings for many Bahamian Creole words.) I had touched upon something uncomfortable, but the time was not yet right to explore exactly why.

New Communicative Channels

However, to my surprise, in these changing climes of language attitudes, several students took to sending unsolicited and unassigned poems and stories through email, our online course platform, and sometimes on paper printouts left on my desk. It was a student-generated break from the perceived formality of an assignment—a genuine opening of a new space to match the level of informality that students felt was necessary in order to write in nation language. Through this student-initiated space outside of the framework of the course, a new communicative channel naturally emerged, and students took to the sending and sometimes printing of poems, notes, essay fragments, and stories in nation language.

There, outside of the boundaries of the course, beyond the margins of all graded materials, the use of dialect was thriving and its interaction with standard English seemed most natural. One student—in this student-driven, unsolicited, completely organic channel—even started sending her grandfather's poetry. Generations of poetic voice were piping in through this tributary that students, finally, controlled. As long as the writing was far beyond the perceived confines of the syllabus, course progression, and the power structure of grades, sharing was safe. Outside of grammatical scrutiny and comfortable in the mode of code-sliding, students seemed to develop an inside/outside perspective and a voice that could move seamlessly between the analytical and critical thinking goals of the college composition courses while developing a genuine interest in the stylistic aspects of expression. One afternoon, the following poem appeared in my inbox: "Who you is? / . . . You live down South Beach aye? / Or you live where gates grow? Is it da constituency of Carmichael? / . . . You ean know where or how we live / You ean know about our struggles / You ean know what we had to give" (Keneisha Johnson). The initial "you" is the upper-class Bahamian disconnected from Carmichael, Bain Town, Fox Hill, and the working-class communities of New Providence, and then—perhaps *because* she is writing in nation language—that "you" figure changes and addresses the foreigner: "How can you tell bout my country? Is it all graphs and signs?" The student's critique, based on language and articulated through movement between languages, is that the displacement of the upper classes mirrors the foreign tourist. The critique is accentuated *through* language, specifically Bahamians that speak in standard English, abandoning the culture. Language (and conscious exploration of language varieties) allows the students to interrogate norms and expose issues: "Are you ashamed of our Bahamianese? Seems like ya tryin to hide, / the people we really are. / Sure, show dem the beaches out west, / or the best restaurants by far. / Looka pigs in Exuma / . . . Hide behind dem hotel smiles, Where our Bahamian pride?" (Keneisha Johnson).

In a few instances, I would reply to the senders of these informal emails—often without any subject or title, sometimes without a name on the top of the page—hoping that they might try to include more nation language and to take the poem deeper into Brathwaite's (1984) *howl*. They always resisted. Later, often weeks later, a new series of notes, poems, or essay pieces would emerge. It was almost as if *any* trace of formalization or directive could hinder the creative act, leaving that same initial empty space and silence from the class meeting when I asked students to define dialect. One thing was certain: some of the greatest student writing I have ever seen came in those emails and informal moments of sharing. How, then, could I bring the openness that students felt outside of the boundaries of the formal course—a space of critical engagement—into the structure of the course? And should I?

My role, if I wanted students to develop their expressive capacity about language (sometimes in nation language, and sometimes across language varieties), was to encourage these creative acts by allowing students to use nation language in the spaces they saw most fit. And, likewise, some of the most dynamic, creative, probing arguments emerged in oral contexts, in the one-on-one meetings when I would ask students to *tell* me their position or argument on a given topic, a teaching strategy that mirrors approaches suggested by Elbow (2012), among others. As I worked as their transcriber, students produced riveting arguments and sometimes entire outlines to complex themes. There was a clear parallel to this oral performance and the *translation* of oral to written that I was encouraging—the elevating of dialect and orality that nation language demands gave students a base from which to articulate. It was an oral base, a voice rooted in oral experience, that could easily turn into powerful, student-generated thesis statements. Once oral production was supported and revered, students felt comfortable developing intricate positions on a range of topics (on language and far beyond) with creative supporting arguments. At the end of our one-on-one meetings, I, the transcriber, would simply tear out the notebook pages I had used and hand to them the work that they had created. Sometimes students were amazed at how articulate and thorough their statements had been. By bringing nation language into the very beginning of the course—at that critical point at which relationships with each other, with language, and with the teacher form—students learned that their voice could emerge from *any* context (oral, written, image-based, sound-based, hybrid). Further, students no longer had to separate oral production from the written.

Linguistic Traumas

At the end of the course, now in reflective mode, I returned to those first few weeks of linguistic exploration and asked students to think back to the decision to write in standard English despite the encouragement to experiment with writing in nation language. This time they laughed: "Mr. Jacob, we didn't think you would understand if we wrote in Bahamianese." They did not want me to feel insulted, monolingual, and left out of the communicative act, and so their decision was to translate *for* me—the students were doing me a favor (or at least that was how they were spinning it). Yet, there was more to it. "Mr. Jacob," they continued, "writing in dialect was strange. It felt awkward. We never did that before. Actually, we would be fined for writing in *Bahamianese* in school." One student, confirming the fines mentioned in Milson-Whyte (2015) regarding Jamaica and other Caribbean territories (pp. 71–72), explained that the fine for speaking in dialect was twenty-five cents per word. "We knew we'd be fined because we liked to use our language, so one day we decided to bring in a sack of funds to pay the fine ahead of time." In the elementary and public schools, the students explained, some teachers took a piece of chalk to the floor, marking the doorway, the threshold where dialect ended and where *Queen's English* began. That symbolic point of entry was where Bahamianese was to be abandoned and—from primary school through university—the remnants of that chalk could be traced.

Stories of corporal punishment, meted out by Bahamian-Creole-speaking teachers, the consequence of using dialect in the classroom (and sometimes in written form), also came to the surface. Most students who spoke of corporal punishment came from the rural, underpopulated "family islands" and always from the public schools across the Bahamian archipelago. Several students shared more elaborate stories of punishments for using dialect: once "caught" using dialect, they were to fetch the stick, wrap it in tape, and hand it to the teacher so that he or she could strike them in front of the class. While some students joked about the beatings they received for having spoken in dialect, others only discussed the punishments in private during office hours. There had been, in a way, a kind of *linguistic trauma* in some of those classrooms. One student, reflecting on primary schooling, described how hard it was to be told that the language she used at home, with family and friends, was always "wrong." Another student, on the topic of punishments, travelled instantly back to first grade and to one word in particular: *Saturday*, which he made the mistake of referring to as *Satday*. Though nearly two decades later, the student remembered each moment vividly: "The teacher picked me up by my shirt collar in front of the whole class, pushed me against the wall, my feet dangling in the air, and demanded that I say *Saturday* properly. I always remember that moment each time I hear the days of the week, even today."

By the end of the semester, after units on protest and writing for social change, students opened up about that first experience with nation language in the course, especially in the final reflective activities and writing pieces. "I felt cheated in school," one student shared, "like the language we used at home and with the people closest to us was a disgrace, there was constant attacking and correcting, it hurt to be told that the language I always used was incorrect." Another student described feelings of sadness, as early as primary school, when the language used with family and friends was removed. She recalled numerous types of punishments, especially when she would try to be creative with language, and then stated with pride, "but they could never take it away from me." She had a copy of her latest nation language poem in hand.

For her, and many others, nation language continued to thrive elsewhere, though always outside of the classroom. "We're trained as children to demonize this language that we were born with," a student confided, "it was taboo to speak the Bahamian dialect, and that causes you to be afraid of using the language you use at home in the classroom or any formal setting. On the playground, as long as there were no adults around, we could use dialect." This was only a decade ago. Students were coming into these college writing classrooms with what seemed like multiple layers of recent linguistic trauma (a phenomenon that I had seen in the US public education system in which students were forced to abandon their first languages as if their multilingualism were an obstacle). The standard English language learning process, then, was sometimes marked by a violent—even on a physical level—stamping out of dialect, something that must have made writing *in* nation language quite difficult during their first weeks of class. Yet, this demonizing of dialect must have also made writing in standard English, about any topic, an experience that involved overcoming a history of language enforcement in the school setting. What does it mean, I thought, that many students are using the English variety required at the university with this type of emotive experience attached to it? How might linguistic trauma impact their reading and writing across the disciplines? And what is the role of the composition course in the context of this experience, a course built around the experience of fines, punishment, and policing? If the act of writing, and perhaps reading, conjures forms of trauma for many students, then alleged "poor results" on the country's standardized exams—especially in writing—take on another sphere of meaning. To build a course around respect for all language, to bring in Brathwaite's nation language, may be the first step in accessing, identifying, and reversing some of that history with language. It is certainly a step in the direction of making composition courses more engaging and carries the possibility of reversing some of the negative experiences students attribute to college writing courses.

There is no immediate response to these questions, but it would appear to anyone sensitive to language, trauma, and language development that a reidentification with language itself may be in order. In that vein, Brathwaite's (1984) nation language becomes even a therapeutic intervention. Our teaching methods, then, can allow for movement between languages, between "Englishes," between dialects. During a presentation in New Providence, Dr. Chanti Seymour, a linguist who teaches composition courses at the University of The Bahamas (UB), described her employment of the practices that bilingual education specialists have adopted. Her call for the composition courses at UB—drawing from conclusions that bilingual students perform best when their "mother tongue" and the "second" language are supported concomitantly—was for teachers to "use" dialect as a teaching aid. Some of her tools involved repeating key composition phrases and lessons in Bahamian Creole and Standard English, moving between the two language varieties. Dr. Seymour's praxis, then, places the teacher into a bilingual speech performance model that Tymoczko (2002) delineates for translators.

The translator, according to Tymoczko (2002), is in Language 1 (L1, or the Source Text Language), Language 2 (L2, or the Target Text Language), and the space between languages and cultures—what is termed Language X (or Lx). Lx, located at a boundary between languages, is one way of describing the space that translators occupy or dwell in as they transfer meaning between systems. It is also the inside/outside space that students worked from when writing about nation language, even if in standard English. Lx is a crossroads space, marked by an "x," and—for Brathwaite and those who pursue Yoruba and Kongo religious philosophies as the core of their aesthetic engagement with Caribbean writing and arts—it is the space of the great deity of language and communication itself, *Eshu-Eleggua*. It is also where Brathwaite locates the rise of nation language: in the watery crossroads of the "Black Atlantic" (see Gilroy, 1993) and in the wind that carries thought across the Atlantic between continents. The method of supporting L1 with the objective of full L2 development positions the teacher in Lx, in the space of translation and transfer, and therefore deep into the religious cosmos that nourishes much of the impetus behind Brathwaite's (1984) nation language. This teaching praxis may hold the restorative capacity to allow students to work beyond whatever colonial and neocolonial language-based trauma has been imposed: it is a decolonizing act even though situated in a postcolonial moment.

Questions are bound to emerge regarding the linguistic training and background of composition instructors who teach language-centric writing courses, especially given the possibilities for the potentially radical shift in students' development in the context of linguistic trauma. While it certainly aids the classroom experience to have fluency in (or access to) nation language(s), what is more essential is a *sensibility* to language itself and a working—even if unarticulated by the instructor—definition and recognition of language as a conduit of ancestral memory, a tool that grants access to the wisdom of lived-experience. In terms of training, a composition instructor need not be fluent in all language varieties present in a classroom. Especially in a Caribbean context or wherever power dynamics emerge through languages in contact, the instructor should, however, have an appreciation and respect for nation language and a built-in sensitivity that dialect is also a language in its own right. In the end, standard languages emerge through dialects and languages in contact. What if the interview process for composition instructors were to include Brathwaite's brief yet transcendent statement on language that opened the present chapter? An ideology emerges through such a response and one can gauge an instructor's willingness to create a safe, secure space of written expression. One student put it best: "For the first time in my life, and in my relationship with language, I was able to explore my *mother tongue* without shame and fear of reproach. A dignity was attached to something that had previously been associated with poverty and a lack of education" (Xan-Xi Bethel). Bethel's comments are important to consider for the cultural linguist or education theorist who holds close to heart the understanding that we must fully support students' mother tongues to enhance all forms of language development.

Student Reflections

For many of the students, the decision early on in the semester not to write about nation language *in* nation language was at least partially rooted in the history of punitive, linguistic patrolling with the intention of stamping out Bahamian Creole from the education experience. There was a long, often painful history to the awkwardness that many students may have felt in relation to the assignment. For the final project, I led several in-class generative writing exercises so as to give raw material for the final course reflection in which the students explore: their development throughout the course, the choices they made as writers throughout the semester, the ways in which audience, context, and purpose changed their writing across drafts or units, or changes relating to the relationship with language and expression, even the definitions of language and dialect.

One of these generative exercises took the form of a response to those who view dialect as inferior, incapable of expression, illegitimate, and substandard. Speaking back to racism, exposing oppression, and writing for change was always a source of inspiration in the composition courses, and, now at the end of the course, I wanted to have students return to the theme of language. In that way, they could look side-by-side at writing from the first weeks of the course and the very end of the semester to measure the ways in which their writing may have changed. I told the students not to worry about form and translating for me, and certainly not to worry about a grade—this was extra credit and could be written in *any* language. I explained that "no self-censoring" was the goal and that the response could take the form of an audio recording, a performed skit, a video recording of a skit, a written rebuttal, or some hybrid merging of all of the aforementioned forms. Students could work alone or in groups. No rules.

This time, many students wrote prose and poetry and most, in the space of the classroom, shared the writing:

> My Language een' standard Mr. Lexicographer, please spare me! My blood is a unique concoction of Turks and Caicos sass, afro-Trinidadian spunk and Bahamian creativity—and so is my tongue. Is it you who aids in the creation of dictionaries? Those modern day conquistadors imprisoning my Caribbean people all over again, raping our freedom of culture and imposing this "imperial English" upon our homes and schools. How dare you?

> Well, I tink ya standard language is beautiful . . . but dialect is beautiful too. . . . Language is expression, it is art, it is identity and so is dialect. (Shavante Simms)

The pride in nation language was on full display and students appeared more comfortable writing *in* nation language (especially at the height of critique and where emphasis was needed), yet the predominant language of narration was still standard English. The standard English, however, was informed by dialect—orality was the core of the written account.

The success of bringing Brathwaite's nation language into the composition course was felt in the atmosphere of support for all language and expression, something that students detected early on and that motivated them to push their writing to the limits without fear: "You ain kno the stress I been thru just tuh speak, propa English. I had tuh pretend tuh be propa knowing propa wasn in my blood. I get cuthip almost every day fuh speaking in my dialect jus cause we have to live up to yinna expectations of speaking propa English" (Aaliyah Charlton). The "you," being addressed here, is the standard English language: Charlton writes *to* this history of valuing the colonial norms, *to* language, and, in that way, reflects upon a history of imposition through language. Our goals as teachers include enhancing students' awareness regarding audience, purpose, and context; sharpening self-reflexive capacities during the writing act so that the different rhetorical strategies become clear and accessible; and, through practice and a process writing approach, opening a safe space for the development of a written voice that is critical and personalized. I see these goals crystallizing through the incorporation of nation language in the composition courses at UB.

Conclusion

It is important to note that while Brathwaite's definition of nation language is rooted in the Anglophone Caribbean and applicable to communities across the African diaspora, the concept of nation language can be extended to many languages, cultures, and geographies. Therefore, the teaching approach outlined here can apply to the Cape Verdean communities of New Bedford and Fall River, Massachusetts, where code-sliding between standard US English, Crioulo Kabuverdiano/Cabo-Verdiano, standard continental Portuguese, and the Brazilian-Portuguese absorbed through novelas, popular music, and the large Brazilian community of New England is a norm; to Indian communities of Jackson Heights,

Queens, where Hindi and standard Englishes of multiple nations cross; and to Salvador da Bahia, Brazil, where speakers move fluidly between Baianês—a Portuguese-based nation language infused with Yoruba and Kongo languages—and standard Brazilian-Portuguese. Brathwaite's nation language grants a historicity to the development and use of language in the Caribbean and, because the definition is as rooted as it is open to interpretation, it opens a path for students to critically engage colonial legacies through their own experiences with language.

In the end, composition teachers want students to be conscious of language, of the choices that we have as writers, and to produce content that is critical of our surroundings, influences, and the contexts around us. By using Brathwaite's nation language, by rooting language development in a historical trajectory, we anchor students' exploration of voice. Further, an approach to teaching that reveres and elevates dialect echoes an urgent call from our field: "rhetoric and composition is increasingly recognizing that the demarcation of a single, stable, monolithic internally uniform set of forms known as 'English' is inadequate to practices of English locally and globally . . . 'English' is seen as in need of pluralization—to 'Englishes'" (Horner, 2014, p. 1). Teaching around a pluralized notion of English, especially through Brathwaite and a postcolonial perspective rooted in the Caribbean, can yield transformative results. Indeed, the contents of this chapter suggest that one can radically change the classroom experience by including units on standard language and (local) dialect and by celebrating nation language.

Despite moments of resistance and discomfort in the beginning of the course—to be expected given the linguistic policing and possible trauma associated with the use of dialect in the classroom, a history I only learned of at the end of the course—many final student reflections focused on the feeling of acceptance that came through our direct work around dialect. Most students had not worked from a perspective that empowered the mother tongue and, therefore, reinforced the tenacity and brilliance of nation language cultures. One student wrote:

> 'Bahamianese' is an original work of art in which we create with our tongues each time we converse with our own. Our words are fluid and they roll off our tongues familiarly without the need to stress about pronunciation or context or even panic about who is around to hear us. . . . The most rewarding and thrilling part of this course was being able to create without being confined to rules or regulations as we were previously accustomed to in sec-

ondary school and, most importantly, to express our originality without the fear of being inadequate. (Shavante Simms)

Read outside of the Bahamas/the Caribbean, Simms's statement may appear obvious. Yet here, there is something revolutionary in what she is saying and claiming. In fact, through Brathwaite and the lively discussions on language, Simms and many of her classmates took control of a worldview when they declared and employed nation language as an "original work of art."

As Harris (2007) notes, "the concept of language is one which continuously transforms inner and outer formal categories of experience" (p. 142). The act of defining one's language in the space of a composition course—especially language(s) that have historically been defined and controlled by the world's colonial superpowers—can be re-constitutive. For Harris, like Brathwaite, language opens a "vision of consciousness [.] . . . [T]he peculiar reality of language provides a medium to *see* in consciousness . . . and to *hear* with consciousness the 'silent' flood of sound by a continuous inward revisionary and momentous logic of potent explosive images evoked in the mind" (p. 142). In a Bahamian context, students seeking to explore, define, or write in nation language are engaging a potentially transformative, redefining of self and community, one that holds the possibility of accessing and tapping into the wisdom of multiple voices—what we have come to call critical and analytical frameworks, the development of which is the very goal of composition courses. In the embrace of Bahamian Dialect/Bahamian Creole English/nation language, and through Brathwaite's (1984) poetic refashioning of dialect into a language of far-reaching capacity, also lays a reassessment of the students' self-perceived multilingualism, capacity to translate, and fluid movement across cultures.

We are challenging students to find and develop a written voice in these composition courses—if Brathwaite's (1984) nation language allows students to feel rooted, supported, and empowered as they navigate the terrain of putting words to thought and reflecting on the choices they face as writers, all the more reason to invoke this foundational text. *A History of the Voice* allowed students to find safety in developing their own voices—a trajectory and map was etched onto the pages for them:

> To be able to delve into the nuances of language as it comes, devoid of pretense and affect, was quite wonderful. I also enjoyed Brathwaite's work on Nation language, working in class to find

> our voice, and describing our own Nation language with the same kind of flair and class that Brathwaite does. Language to me now, is movement, motion, fury, and sweet melody. Language is that magical medium that comes forth from the ether, creating bridges between us; tethering us in an infinite number of ways. Language is a code that carries memories, pains, joys. Language is a time machine. (Xan-Xi Bethel)

Brathwaite's nation language awoke a sense of pride in language itself, inspired critical thought into lived-experience, and sparked a passion for creativity inside what had often been a linguistically exclusive classroom space.

Students flourished when Bahamian Creole English was brought into the classroom as a mode of expression and as a bridge into their unique range of experiences. At the very least, my hope in sharing this reflection is that teachers of students of all ages—especially in The Bahamas but also wherever languages come into contact—can embrace dialect as *nation language*. Students' written development can be strengthened by "elevating" dialect and building around nation language, and since student learning is our goal, what better way to end than with the student perspective on a semester that deeply engaged language itself:

> 'Dialect' . . . is normally used in a pejorative manner, invoking the history of assigned inferiority and suffering. On the other hand, Nation Language, as Brathwaite calls it, exalts these languages, dignifies them, makes them human. Nation languages . . . defy the rules and fight for their right to be. Just like the people who speak them. The African languages' cadence and rhythm march through the imperial tongues, cutting. Slicing, and fighting the imperious master. The term 'nation language' makes our backs straighten and our lips curl in defiance. No longer does the 'dialect' bear us down and crush us under the boot of stupidity. We are able to say yes! Yinna, wunna, unnah, not gine keep we downpress na more! (Xan-Xi Bethel)

References

Anzaldúa, G. (1999). *Borderlands/la frontera*. San Francisco: Aunt Lute Books.
Brathwaite, E. K. (1984). *History of the voice: The development of nation language in Anglophone Caribbean poetry*. London: New Beacon Books.

Cadogan, G. (2016). Walking while black. Retrieved from http://www.lithub.com/walking-while-black/.
Elbow, P. (2012). *Vernacular eloquence: What speech can bring to writing.* Oxford: Oxford University Press.
Gilroy, P. (1993). *The black Atlantic: Modernity and double consciousness.* Cambridge, MA: Harvard University Press.
Glinton-Meicholas, P. (1995). *More talkin' Bahamian.* Nassau, Bahamas: Guanamina Press.
Hackert, S. (2004). *Urban Bahamian Creole: System and variation.* Amsterdam: John Benjamins.
Harris, W. (2007). *Selected essays of Wilson Harris* (A. Bundy, Ed.). London: Routledge.
Horner, B. (2014). Introduction. In B. Horner & K. Kopelson (Eds.), *Reworking English in rhetoric and composition: Global interrogations, local interventions* (pp. 1–12). Carbondale, IL: Southern Illinois University Press.
Milson-Whyte, V. (2013). Pedagogical and sociopolitical implications of code-meshing in classrooms: Some considerations for a translingual orientation to writing. In S. Canagarajah (Ed.), *Literacy as translingual practice: Between communities and classrooms* (pp. 115–127). New York: Routledge.
Milson-Whyte, V. (2015). *Academic writing instruction for creole-influenced students.* Kingston, Jamaica: University of the West Indies Press.
Oenbring. R. (2013). Bey or buoy: Orthographic patterns in Bahamian Creole English on the web. *English World-wide, 34*(3), 341–364.
Tymoczko, M. (2002). Translation in oral tradition as a touchstone for translation theory and practice. In S. Bassnett & A. Lefevere (Eds.), *Translation, history and culture* (pp. 46–55). London: Pinter.

Section Two: Empirical Studies of Attitudes and Time Management

The window box air conditioner had a hard time combating the tropical heat, and I was feeling drenched with sweat in no time. . . . As the clock ticked toward 6 P.M., my room remained empty. Typical first day, I thought. I figured the students were finding their way, and we'd start a bit late. By 6:10 P.M., only one student had taken her seat, so I stepped outside to see if others were on their way. Indeed, cars were still arriving. A few of the students gathered in small groups, and a couple of professors were outside having casual conversations. To me, the atmosphere felt unusually calm for a first day.

—Bruce, 2015, p. 123

3 Teaching on Island Time: Deadlines, Procrastination, and Composition at the University of The Bahamas

Christine E. Kozikowski

Like many postsecondary students throughout the Anglophone Caribbean, students at the University of The Bahamas (UB) are often unsuccessful in English composition classes for a variety of reasons: poor preparedness, lack of effort, multiple conflicting responsibilities, and problems with time management. Of these reasons, time management is one of the most critical and pervasive problems that undermine student success. In his reflective essay for English 300, an advanced composition course, one of my students described his greatest challenge as time management and the consequences of his struggle; he wrote, "at times, I felt I was bombarded with a proliferation of assignments, tests, projects, and research papers not only from English 300 but from other classes. Lack of time management led me to be late for all of my assignments during the course of this semester." This student's commentary is not unique in that students in large numbers at UB either fail or barely pass composition due to late work or missed work; furthermore, this student's commentary is not unique to UB since university students globally struggle with time management, procrastination, and deadlines (Ackerman & Goss, 2005; Akpur, 2017; Balkis & Duru, 2017; Onwuegbuzie & Jiao, 2000; Prohaska, Morrill, Atiles, & Perez, 2000; Saleem & Rafique, 2012). As a part of the process of educating students, university faculty are tasked to continue the training students began in primary and secondary school on the importance of deadlines and demonstrating consequences of failing to meet them; however, countering these behaviors in university students is challenging, and even more so in the Caribbean, where time and deadlines are often fluid. Therefore, to examine students' time management and work production, this study sought both student and faculty perspectives about deadlines, procrastination, and late penalties in the composition classroom.

With its high output requirement, English composition provides a useful space to examine student and faculty perceptions of deadlines and time management. Unlike other academic disciplines that may have only two or three assignments per semester, current pedagogical trends in composition studies emphasize that to improve their writing, students must write continuously, which often leads to multiple close deadlines and requires students to manage their time effectively. Although students may procrastinate for a variety of reasons, including but not limited to anxiety, boredom, a lack of overall caring, low self-esteem, or the prioritization of other activities, procrastination, for whatever reason, nearly always adversely affects student performance (Ackerman & Goss, 2005; Balkis & Duru, 2017; Humphrey & Harbin, 2010; Patrzek, Sattler, van Veen, Grunschel, & Fries, 2015). Reducing these behaviors in college writing courses is challenging, and understanding student attitudes towards deadlines may help professors more effectively respond to students or develop policies that provide positive redirection.

At UB, all students enrolled in bachelor's programs must take a series of three English writing classes as part of the general education core: English Writing 119 and 120 are the first-year writing sequence, and English 300 is an advanced composition course for junior- and senior-level students. As one may expect, at the first-year level, students write fewer pages in total and focus on basic academic writing skills: thesis generation, citation styles, paragraph construction, and following essay prompt instructions. In years previous, these courses followed the modes of discourse taxonomy, focusing separately on expository writing and argumentative writing; however, their current pedagogical track concentrates more on writing in different genres. Students in advanced composition, English 300, write longer papers, which are often more discipline specific and require a higher level of sophistication, and include genres such as literature reviews, discourse analyses, and empirical research studies. All three composition classes are portfolio courses that have as many as three to four high-stakes essays, three or more low-stakes assignments, and a revision/portfolio requirement. In a given semester, English Studies runs approximately fifty sections of composition, which are each capped at twenty students.

As in the rest of the Caribbean, research on composition pedagogy and practice at the tertiary level in the Bahamas is limited. Most recently, Oenbring, Jaquette, Kozikowski, and Higgins (2016) assessed student perceptions of their composition experience at UB via an exit survey given to first-year composition students. Overall, the students responded that English 119, the first course in the first-year writing sequence, helped them think and write critically about sources; however, they felt neither prepared by their high school training to write nor empowered to write when the semester ended. While Oenbring et al.'s study did not examine time or deadlines, one of the statements that students responded to has some relevance for the current study. In Oenbring et al., students were asked to respond to the statement *I completed all the work according to the assignment requirements*; of the ninety-nine students who responded, thirty-eight students selected *highly agree*, forty-four selected *agree*, fifteen responded *neutral*, and one selected *disagree* (with none selecting *highly disagree*). While there was no qualification about how students interpreted this statement, whether their responses focused on the word *completed* or the words *assignment requirements* (and whether students considered assignment deadlines), 82% of the students responded positively, which stands, as Oenbring et al., note, in contrast to actual student performance. Students in the study, on average, presented a more positive picture of their engagement in class than the reality demonstrates.

Also relevant to the current study are Bruce's (2015) reflections on her experience teaching business writing and world literature at Nova Southeastern University's Bahamas Student Educational Center. Five times over a ten-week period, Bruce flew from Florida to the Bahamas to teach a combined six hours over two days, and in her essay, she described one of her greatest challenges as accepting "a new expression of time" (p. 128). She noted that her initial expectations of time stem from an assumption that "US academic culture would have been transplanted along with the campus and the professors" (p. 126). Although Bruce's conclusions were directed towards transnational writing program administration as opposed to assessing assignment deadlines, her descriptions of *island time* where her students arrive late and leave early reflect behavior and attitudes similar to UB students.

Beyond the Bahamas and Caribbean, significant research has been done on procrastination and time management. Studies have been conducted on the procrastination habits of students across the disciplines, their reasons for procrastination, and the relationship between academic work and emotional factors. For example, Ackerman and Goss (2005) focused on students in marketing and found that when they perceive the assignment to be more interesting, students are less likely to procrastinate. Further, the more skills the project or task requires, the earlier students will start working on it. On the other hand, Akpur (2017) examined the relationship between anxiety and motivation in foreign language classes and found that motivation based on joy or contentment is a positive factor in academic achievement as opposed to motivation based upon stress. Surveying students who use the writing center, Fritzsche, Young, and Hickson (2003) found that students indicate that they procrastinate on writing more than any other assigned academic task; however, students who receive feedback on their writing tend to perform better and procrastinate less. Other research has considered the role that gender plays; Balkis and Duru's (2017) survey compared general life satisfaction and academic procrastination of females and males, finding that females in the study procrastinated less and had greater life satisfaction overall. Perhaps the most research has been conducted on the relationship between anxiety and time management; nearly all research on academic procrastination references anxiety or stress. Onwuegbuzie & Jiao (2000), for example, claimed that the main reason for procrastination—for up to 95% of undergraduates and 60% of graduate students—is due to anxiety, which may develop from issues associated with performance, comfort with the material, or understanding the assignment requirements.

In this chapter, I examine the connections between student time management and procrastination in the Anglophone Caribbean, analyzing the relationship between attitudes towards time and place in Caribbean academic contexts. For the study, I address time through two different lenses: the practice of time in the university and the practice of time in the Caribbean region. To begin, the university system in the way that it is structured and practiced reflects Western attitudes toward time. At its core, the university system is a product of the medieval European West with its focus on a liberal arts education and further reinforced through the humanistic philosophies that began with Plato and incorporated various rebirths throughout centuries (Peters, 2015). Two factors further shaped time in both the university and the west as a linear construction: first, Christianity's emphasis on starting "in the beginning" (Gen. 1:1 King James Version) and tracing a timeline of events forward, and second, the capitalistic concept of time as money (e.g., *I don't have time to spend on this*).

In addition to its historical underpinnings, the modern Western university separates its units into time: a four-year degree; separate fall, spring, and summer semesters; full- and half-semester classes; units of learning measured within classes; and finally, assignments with strategic due dates. Achievement of any academic degree equates with the successful management of each of these elements of time. Deadlines form the backbone of the university system, not just for students' classwork but also for administrative progress. Dozens of book titles promise students handy tips to succeed academically: *Skillful Time Management!*; *How to Be A Student: 100 Great Ideas and Practical Habits for Students Everywhere*; and *Last Minute Term Papers*. At the university level and most places in the professional world, deadlines function in a way that supports a linear timeline, where certain tasks must be completed before others. When students learn to meet deadlines, they are also learning linear time. For faculty, particularly composition teachers, it can be essential that students meet assignment deadlines so that faculty have time to devote to commenting on and grading essays thoroughly and fairly. Furthermore, and most importantly, when deadlines are built into a class schedule, they provide ways to assess student learning. Students who wish to turn their work in all at once risk missing steps essential to the learning and writing process; indeed, current pedagogical trends treat writing as a process as more sophisticated and advanced skills are layered on top of the basics. Additionally, students who miss deadlines do not give themselves sufficient time for the next assignment.

In contrast, time in the Caribbean is neither perceived nor practiced in a linear form. In many ways, time is a suggestion; events, appointments, or other functions not only do not begin on time but are also not expected to begin on time. Theoretically, through displacement and colonization, the disruption of time has influenced the way that people perceive time; this cultural trauma disrupted ancestral histories and reconditioned social perceptions (Edwin & Bonnelame, 2012; Glissant, 1989; Thomas, 2016). According to philosopher and critic Glissant (1989), Caribbean people do not perceive time as something with a clearly designated starting point or end but as a continuum or a contradiction, an "instinctive response against the ambition of imposing a 'single' historical time, that of the west" (p. 92). Although Glissant is talking about writing and creative agency, his description of time is still applicable outside of the intended focus: "Because the Caribbean notion of time was fixed in the void of an imposed nonhistory, the writer must contribute to reconstituting its tormented chronology; that is, to reveal the creative energy of a dialectic reestablished between nature and culture in the Caribbean" (p. 65). Likewise, Thomas (2016) describes an example of a Jamaican woman who was asked to talk about the Tivoli Incursion that occurred in 2010. In her story, the woman began with a description of her son's death in 2008; by using the events from 2008 to discuss 2010, she folds time "in a way that suggests a simultaneity of time" (p. 185) instead of providing a progression. This confusion or contradiction of time is the cultural perception that students experience prior to coming to the university and that lays at odds with the time management required to successfully complete classes and a degree.

Methods

For the current study, both UB students and teachers were surveyed about assignment deadlines using specially designed questionnaires that contained ten questions each. Students' surveys asked about student feelings about writing, reasons for missing deadlines, and general feelings about deadlines while teachers' surveys focused on their policies and penalties for late work. The responses gathered from these surveys indicate the general approach of both students and English faculty toward the making and the keeping of deadlines.

The student survey, created with the web-based questionnaire software SurveyMonkey, was posted on the student-run Facebook page (*UB Survival Guide*) and was available to students over a four-month period; reminders for students were periodically posted to the group. Students who had completed any UB composition class, regardless of level, were encouraged to complete the survey; only students who were over the age of eighteen, or legally adults in The Bahamas, were allowed to complete the survey. The objective was to discover what affects students' abilities to complete work on time or complete activities fully.

The faculty survey was also created with SurveyMonkey and disseminated through the English Studies department email list. Faculty questions focused mainly on policy but also addressed typical interactions with students about deadlines and late work. The questions were designed to discover if faculty members' policies on deadlines are similar and to compare their assumptions about students' attitudes toward deadlines. (Per UB policy, faculty are granted significant intellectual freedom to establish policies regarding late work and to penalize late work.) Responses were then examined in relation to current research on deadlines and academic procrastination as well as cultural perceptions of deadlines.

Results

Student Survey Results

The UB student population is approximately 5,000 full and part-time students, and, of those, 127 students who completed varying levels of composition responded to the survey. Although this number is small, representing approximately only 2% of the student population, it provides a place to start assessing student perception versus their actual practice during writing courses. While respondents reported having taken their most recent English composition course as far back as six years before the date of the study, the majority of student responses came from individuals who had completed writing courses within the previous two years. Respondents who were no longer students, either because they had graduated or dropped out, could have completed the survey. Students answered ten questions about deadlines, essay writing, penalties for missed deadlines, and procrastination; the first and last questions allowed respondents to write in responses.

Q1.

	119	120	300	No course indicated
What was your most recent English writing class? Please indicate semester and year.	15	41	52	19

Although students were asked to write which semester and year their most recent composition class took place, only ninety-five students answered this question completely. The remaining thirty-two respondents answered with either the year only, the course only, or in one case, an English class that was not a composition class. Because of the inaccurate reporting, I chose to list only the course numbers provided.

Q2.

In general, which best describes how you feel about deadlines?	Response	Percent of total
They motivate me to get my work done.	57	45.2%
They make me anxious.	52	41.3%
They don't bother me.	12	9.5%
They don't matter.	5	4.0%
Skipped	1	

Almost equally, respondents found deadlines to be motivating and anxiety inducing. This response is unsurprising in that it reinforces the research on deadlines and procrastination, particularly Akpur (2017) and Fritzsche, Young, and Hickson (2003).

Q3.

Now thinking about the deadlines associated with your major writing assignments in your English classes, how did an approaching deadline make you feel? (Choose all that apply)	Response	Percent of total
Anxious	60	47.6%
Overwhelmed	75	59.5%
Stressed	78	61.9%
Prepared	18	14.3%
Skipped	1	

From Q2 to Q3, students' predominant responses turned equally negative when writing was added to the question. Students at UB, in general, displayed high levels of anxiety about academic writing, citing general dislike or dismissing their abilities.

Q4.

Did your English instructors impose strict due dates on your assignments?	Response	Percent of total
Yes	69	54.8%
No	7	5.6%
Sometimes	50	39.7%
Skipped	1	

Although over half of the respondents indicated that their instructors imposed strict deadlines, the response *sometimes* could indicate how policies lead to student confusion; if professors do not always require students to adhere to deadlines, then students may not understand their importance.

Q5.

How often did your writing instructors penalize you for missed deadlines?	Response	Percent of total
Always	33	26.4%
Most of the time	23	18.4%
Occasionally	30	24.0%
Never	39	31.2%
Skipped	2	

Based on Q4, which asked about students' awareness of instructors' policy, the results in Q5 are surprising and seemingly contradictory. If instructors consistently imposed strict deadlines, students' perceptions of applied penalties would be higher; *never* was the most frequent response, suggesting a disconnect between the written or stated deadline and the penalties applied.

Q6.

When thinking about the essays you had to write for English, how often did you procrastinate?	Response	Percent of total
Always	42	33.6%
Most of the time	34	27.2%
Sometimes	42	33.6%
Never	7	5.6%
Skipped	2	

The top two responses here together, *always* and *most of the time*, equal 60%, which means that students reported procrastinating on over half of their writing assignments. However, as students' comments indicated, procrastination does not always lead to missed deadlines.

Q7.

In your English writing classes, do you think the grade deductions associated with turning in your essays late	Response	Percent of total
Helped you turn your work in on time	74	60.7%
Had no effect on your timing	32	26.2%
Paralyzed you to inactivity	16	13.1%
Skipped	5	

This question was useful to assess students' motivations for meeting deadlines and their reactions to the consequences for missing them.

Q8.

Thinking about the essays you had to write, what were some of the reasons you procrastinated? (Choose all that apply)	Response	Percent of total
Bored or uninterested in the topic	82	65.6%
Assignments for other classes were more important	66	52.8%
Fear that you would do poorly on the assignment	32	25.6%
Underestimated the time it would take to write the essay	76	60.8%
Other non-school related activities were more important	14	11.2%
Didn't procrastinate	9	7.2%
Skipped	2	

The results of this question are unsurprising; the most chosen response could illustrate a gulf between what faculty think is interesting and what students are interested in. Students in 119 and 120 are provided a booklet with readings that faculty can choose from; English 300 focuses on an instructor-designated theme. It is common for students to perceive academic work as boring or difficult or less fun than other activities; this perception can lead to academic procrastination and inattention to deadlines. The second highest number in Q8, *Underestimated the time it would take to write the essay*, reinforces students' lack of awareness of time management or their overestimation of their own skills.

Q9.

How often were your major essay assignments late?	Response	Percent of total
Always	1	0.8%
Most of the time	4	3.2%
Occasionally	28	22.2%
Never	93	73.8%
Skipped	1	

Students' responses here are extremely surprising. If these patterns were imposed on a standard composition section that has twenty people, then there would only be five or six students who occasionally submit assignments late. In my composition classes, I rarely see only five or six students who submit their major assignments late. As a comparison, I informally surveyed the number of late research essays submitted by my composition classes since the fall of 2015, when I began using Turnitin to receive and grade student work. Since then, I have taught 280 students to completion in seventeen classes, and 122 of them have either submitted their final research paper late or not at all. In my seventeen classes, only seven of them had numbers that correlate to the percentages in the student responses.

Q10 offered students the opportunity to write in any comments they had about deadlines, procrastination, and grade deductions. Twenty-one students out of 127 wrote in comments, but only three commented specifically that procrastination resulted in poorer grades; for example, one student said, "procrastination never helps it reduces the chances of getting good grades" [*sic*]. Ten of the comments, on the other hand, describe academic procrastination as a positive motivator and stated that deadlines with associated penalties are effective ways to ensure assignment submission. Two students remarked that unforeseen circumstances or family responsibilities affected their ability to achieve deadlines; three students commented that boredom or "cliché" topics contributed to their procrastination habits. One of these respondents wrote: "as a student that does not favor English as a subject, the irrelevant topics and unreasonable due dates especially those associated with assignments carrying the most weight, added to the anticipated stress of college. Personally, this stress led to anxiety attacks, chest pains and even occasional depression." Notably, two students described that unclear instructions or assignment guidelines caused them to procrastinate, with one writing: "often time, there are no clear instructions regarding what should be done when writing an essay which almost always leads to low grades. Other times, you're told by your lecturer that your essay is good after following their instructions and then they still give you a low grade."

Faculty Survey Results

In a department of sixteen fulltime English faculty, twelve faculty members responded to ten questions, three of which were open-ended. These questions examined how composition faculty treat deadlines and perceive student attitudes toward deadlines. At UB, all faculty teach between one and four composition classes per semester and choose which level of composition they prefer to teach.

Q2.

	Yes	No	Sometimes
Do you have a written late work policy on your syllabus or on the assignment prompt?	9	1	2

Clear written policies help students to follow guidelines; a late work policy is particularly important for providing structure and mitigating confusion.

Q3.

	Yes	No	Sometimes
When thinking about essay assignments only, do you accept submissions after the set deadline?	4	1	7

Without clarification, it is not possible to know in what circumstances assignments were accepted late, so further research could provide better direction for this response. This question correlates to Q4 in the student survey, which asks *Did your English instructors impose strict due dates on your assignments?* Positive faculty responses (33%) were lower than student responses (69%), which suggests that most faculty place a high level of importance on this policy; however, the percentage of *sometimes* for both groups was selected approximately half the time. The high number of respondents choosing *sometimes* suggests that deadlines are not strict or that strict deadlines and policies are less strict in practice.

Q4.

	Yes	No	Sometimes	I don't accept essays after the deadline
If you do accept essays after the deadlines, do you impose late penalties on your students' paper grade?	6	0	5	1

This number contrasts to Q5 in the student survey, *How often did your writing instructors penalize you for missed deadlines?*, where *never* received the highest percentage of responses at 31.2%. Zero faculty respondents selected *no* while thirty-nine students indicated that they were never penalized for late work. Q5 allowed faculty to write in their average deduction for late work. Ten supplied faculty responses ranged from 10% per day to 1 point per day to being dependent on the circumstances.

Q6.

	As soon as the deadline passes	One week or less	Two weeks	Three weeks	I accept work at any time.
Thinking about essay assignments only, how late is too late to turn in work?	1	6	2	0	2

Q7 (which expanded on Q6 above) asked respondents to write in the most common reasons why they believe that students do not turn in essays on time or at all. Out of the eleven responses, poor time management and procrastination were featured in eight of the comments. Other common responses include problems with technology and family responsibilities.

Q8.

	Yes	No	Sometimes
Do you think that penalizing students for not turning in work on time or not at all is useful for student education?	4	0	8

This question provides a useful line of inquiry; if penalizing students for late work is only sometimes useful for student education, then what strategies could be more effective? Research shows that conferencing with students and providing more detailed feedback helps them with time management (Fritzsche, Young, and Hickson, 2003), while rewarding students for early submission has mixed results (Humphrey & Harbin, 2010).

Q9.

	Yes	No	Sometimes
Do you think that students' attitudes towards deadlines reflects cultural attitudes towards deadlines and timeliness?	6	2	4

The results of this question are interesting because of the background of the faculty in English Studies at UB. Of the sixteen fulltime faculty in the 2016–2017 academic year, eleven are from the Caribbean, while the other five are from the US, Great Britain, and India. As indicated in the beginning of the essay, culture affects individuals' concepts of time; however, regardless of ethnic background or nationality, most of the faculty have been educated in the US school systems.

Finally, Q10 allowed faculty to write in any further comments they have about deadlines, late work deductions, and procrastination. Perhaps the most meaningful comment suggested that research on student attitudes toward deadlines should be conducted on secondary school students since student practices are solidified before they reach the university. On the other hand, another instructor acknowledged the punitive functions of their late work penalties, stating, "however, with around 80 students a semester, it is hard to keep up with my grading, let alone trying to go back and follow up with late work. Maybe my policy has taught a few students lessons, but even if not, I find it necessary to manage my own workload." It is necessary for faculty to have enough time to grade and respond to student writing; furthermore, spacing out the workload allows them to assess student writing and address or readdress problem areas.

Overall, the faculty survey indicates a wide variety of policies toward late work, from no penalty given to no late work accepted. While no penalty and no late work accepted are the outliers on either end of the spectrum, most UB English faculty assess some measure of penalty on a per-day scale, as seen in Q5, *Thinking about the essay assignments only, what is your average deduction or penalty for late student work?* In addition, most faculty, nine out of twelve, provide a late policy either on the syllabus or the assignment, which helps students to be mindful of their deadlines. However, the overwhelming response reflects that UB professors believe that students have issues with time management, regardless of reason.

Discussion

The student and faculty survey results are mostly consistent with recent research on procrastination and deadlines in that students struggle with time management for similar reasons and that it nearly always affects them negatively (Ackerman & Goss, 2005; Akpur, 2017; Rabin, Fogel, & Nutter-Upham, 2011). When students were asked in Q6, *When thinking about the essays you had to write for English, how often did you procrastinate?*, 42 students, or 33%, answered *Always* while 34 students, or 27%, responded *Most of the time*, which taken together is consistent with the research about procrastination. Procrastination, however, does not always lead to missed deadlines as a few of the students noted in the write-in response (Q10): "I'm just a procrastinator. I normally got good results when I took longer to write my paper, however, my assignments were never late. I ultimately got an A- [in] my engw300 class." Rather, it is indicative of a lack of time-management strategies.

Differences lie, however, with students' perceptions of their own levels of procrastination. As indicated in Q9 of the student survey, *How often were your major essay assignments late?*, 93 students, or almost 74%, indicated that their work was never late, a statement that is comparative to their response that deadlines and penalties helped them to get their work in on time. This number stands in contrast to their responses about procrastination and grade penalties. Several reasons are possible for these results. On the one hand, although the survey was anonymous, it is possible that some students may have believed that there was a way to track their results, and therefore, they misrepresented their submission practices. On the other hand, and more likely, students may be unaware or inattentive to their own work production, which was a conclusion also reached by Ackerman and Goss (2005) and Oenbring et al. (2016). Based on the informal survey of my own seventeen composition classes, most classes had a missed deadline percentage of their final research essay that ranged from 45% to 55% of students, or 8 to 11 students in a class of 20. While this is by no means conclusive, it demonstrates a clear disconnect between student practice and perception. Further research on late or missing assignments at UB could be useful for course and degree completion statistics.

As a cultural practice, student perception, and even faculty to an extent, aligns with the less strict Caribbean attitude towards time and timeliness. Time and attention to time is a learned behavior that is reflected in students' attitudes toward deadlines; because of their cultural consciousness, students may feel less pressure to meet academic deadlines. Students, therefore, are caught between cultural practice and learned practice. Spears and Amos (2012) argue:

> individuals construct an orientation toward time that has its roots not only in the society in which they are immersed but in sociodemographic factors such as social class, age, gender, and education. Sociodemographic factors and cultural context work in concert to influence time orientation. In essence, individuals develop a temporal structure that is composed of both their personal perception of time and their perception of society's view of time. (p. 190)

In their nonacademic lives, students live time that is fluid; however, when they come to the university, that fluidity is rejected. This further explains the disconnect between the perception and practice.

However, this rationale of cultural consciousness stands in contrast to the research that demonstrates that academic procrastination and associated issues with time management are global problems, occurring both in countries that were colonized and in the countries that colonized them, as well as in countries that perceive linear temporalities and those that perceive nonlinear temporalities, at rates that range from 40% to 95% of surveyed students (Akpur, 2017; Fritzsche, Young, & Hickson, 2003; Onwuegbuzie, & Jiao, 2000).

This study provides a useful framework for faculty to compare their policies and practices and student practices versus their perceptions. In the tradition of rhetoric and composition, writing is commonly taught as a *process,* so potentially rethinking deadlines and the way that assignments are built could lessen the frequency that students miss them. Furthermore, as one English faculty member suggested, research on primary and secondary schools could demonstrate more clearly where students learn academic time management skills, leading to more outreach or communication between primary, secondary, and tertiary institutions. And although it can be difficult for students to break learned habits, it is not impossible, as demonstrated by my English 300 student who concluded in his reflection:

> It was after receiving so many reductions in my scores for my English assignments that I began to stick to a strict schedule and forced myself to complete tasks when I scheduled myself to complete them. I began to see some progress towards the ending of the semester when I was able to effectively carry out the research aspect of my research essay while juggling the preparations for my presentation and effectively completing other tasks like studying for an exam and completing math labs in a timely manner.

While this student missed every deadline, this comment demonstrates the learned value of time management for students. For faculty, on the other hand, activities such as calendar building, bulleting, and task management could be built into the semester's schedule to help students manage their time and work as a reward system to reinforce the importance of meeting deadlines and managing one's time well.

References

Ackerman, D. S., & Goss, B. L. (2005). My instructor made me do it: Task characteristics of procrastination. *Journal of Marketing Education, 27*(1), 5–13.

Akpur, U. (2017). Predictive and explanatory relationship model between procrastination, motivation, anxiety and academic achievement. *Eurasian Journal of Educational Research, 69*, 221–240.

Balkis, M., & Duru, E. (2017). Gender differences in the relationship between academic procrastination, satisfaction with academic life and academic performance. *Electronic Journal of Research in Educational Psychology, 15*(1), 105–125.

Bruce, S. (2015). So close, yet so far: Administering a writing program with a Bahamian campus. In D. Martins (Ed.), *Transnational writing program administration* (pp. 117–137). Boulder, CO: Utah State University Press.

Edwin, M., & Bonnelame, N. (2012). Fragmented temp(oralities): A Caribbean perspective of time in literature and art. *Journal of Writing in Creative Practice, 5*(2), 189–203.

Fritzsche, B. A., Young, B. R., & Hickson, K. C. (2003). Individual differences in academic procrastination tendency and writing success. *Personality and Individual Differences, 35*, 1549–1557.

Glissant, É. (1989). *Caribbean discourse: Selected essays.* Charlottesville, VA: University of Virginia Press.

Humphrey, P., & Harbin, J. (2010). An exploratory study of the effect of rewards and deadlines on academic procrastination in web-based classes. *Academy of Educational Leadership Journal, 14*(4), 91–98.

Oenbring, R., Jaquette, B., Kozikowski, C., & Higgins, I. (2016). First-year English at the College of The Bahamas: Student perceptions. *International Journal of Bahamian Studies, 22,* 43–53.

Onwuegbuzie, J. A., & Jiao, Q. G. (2000). I'll go to the library later: The relationship between academic procrastination and library anxiety. *College and Research Libraries, 61,* 45–54.

Patrzek, J., Sattler, S., van Veen, F., Grunschel, C., & Fries, S. (2015). Investigating the effect of academic procrastination on the frequency and variety of academic misconduct: A panel study. *Studies in Higher Education, 40*(6), 1014–1029.

Peters, M. A. (2015). The humanist bias in western philosophy and education. *Educational Philosophy & Theory, 47*(11), 1128–1135.

Prohaska, V., Morrill, P., Atiles, I., & Perez, A. (2000). Academic procrastination by nontraditional students. *Journal of Social Behavior & Personality, 15,* 125–34.

Rabin, L. A., Fogel, J., & Nutter-Upham, K. E. (2011). Academic procrastination in college students: The role of self-reported executive function. *Journal of Clinical and Experimental Neuropsychology, 33*(3), 344–357.

Saleem, M., & Rafique, R. (2012). Procrastination and self-esteem among university students. *Pakistan Journal of Social and Clinical Psychology, 9*(3), 50–53.

Spears, N., & Amos, C. (2012). Revisiting Western time orientations. *Journal of Consumer Behavior, 11,* 189–197.

Thomas, D. A. (2016). Time and the otherwise: Plantations, garrisons and being human in the Caribbean. *Anthropological Theory, 16*(2–3), 177–200.

4 Academic Writing in the Caribbean: Attitudes Matter

Melissa L. Alleyne

Introduction

The difficulty encountered in Standard English language use by Caribbean students at almost all educational levels is often lamented by educators, linguists, politicians, and private/public sector employers in the Caribbean (Warrican, 2005). Visible at all levels, the challenges Caribbean students face with Standard English use are compounded when they enter university by the fact that an even higher level of English usage is expected of them for both speaking and writing purposes. This higher level, referred to generally as *academic English*, is crucial to the students' academic success. Yet, success in the speaking and writing of academic English is predicated on a mastery, or at least proficiency, in Standard English, something that many students struggle with even after completing twelve years of primary and secondary school education. Caribbean linguists have long noted that Standard English (even Caribbean Standard English) is not the first language of the majority of Caribbean children (Craig, 2006; Roberts, 2007). Despite this, in school, students are taught using English as Mother Tongue traditions (Craig, 2006), which do not appear to be able to effectively provide for the acquisition of the Standard English variety in light of all of the complicating factors of the Caribbean linguistic context.

The University of the West Indies (UWI), therefore, admits undergraduate students who may not all be as proficient in standard or academic English as they should be. To these students, UWI offers, at all four of its campuses, a number of courses intended to provide instruction and practice in academic writing. However, the effectiveness of these courses continues to be discussed both within the institution and in the wider society, where after graduates enter the world of work their writing skills are often called into question. Reasons linked to factors such as instructional approach, intelligence, language aptitude of students, and the language background of the students are often cited for this perceived ineffectiveness of the academic writing courses. One element that is at times overlooked in these discussions is that of affective factors. These affective factors may influence learning just as much or sometimes more than the cognitive and sociolinguistic factors that are traditionally associated with learning the conventions of academic writing. These affective factors, which include attitudes, motivation, and anxiety, can play a critical role in the success of any learning endeavor (Brown, 2014). Attitude is a key consideration because of the well-established link that it has to student achievement, seemingly inextricably linked to motivation (Brown, 2014; Gardner, 1985; McIntyre, 2002; Petric, 2002; Popham, 2016; Warrican, Leacock, Thompson, & Alleyne, 2014). In fact, study habits, skill, and attitude have been found to be effective predictors of academic performance, rivalling standardized tests and previous grades (Credé & Kuncel, 2008).

The current study sought to investigate the attitudes that undergraduate university students in the Caribbean have toward academic English and academic writing courses. Focus was placed on the affective factors of attitudes, motivation, and self-confidence and the circular nature of how they impact student performance in all areas, but specifically in writing tasks. Findings of previous studies on the relationship between various affective factors and student performance are explored, and the specific factors of interest in this study are outlined. Finally, the usefulness of this study to anyone who is interested in teaching or developing a program or course in academic writing is discussed.

An important starting point in any discussion on the importance of attitudes and motivation on language learning is Robert Gardner, one of the pioneers of research in this area. Gardner (1985) viewed the construct of attitude as a mental state involving belief structures, feelings, values, and dispositions to act in certain ways. He stated that the attitudes that students possess are most likely developed in their home environment, affected by their community, and reinforced by their peers, but he noted that attitudes to language often become salient for the first time in language class (Gardner). Not only do learner attitudes have an impact on the level of proficiency achieved in a second language by a learner, but the attitudes may themselves be influenced by the proficiency or success achieved (Ellis, 2008). The importance of attitudes to achievement appears to lie in their connection to motivation, which refers to the combination of effort and desire on the part of the student to achieve the goal of learning (Gardner, 1985). A distinction made in studies on motivation is that of intrinsic and extrinsic motivation: intrinsic motivation is when people engage in activities for their own pleasure or interest and not because of a perceived reward, and extrinsic motivation is when activities are engaged in because of an expected reward, such as high grades, positive feedback, or prizes, or even to avoid punishment or ill opinion (Ryan & Deci, 2017). Both attitudes and motivation can impact a learner's behavior, consciously or subconsciously, since even if attitudes and the reasons behind their motivation are subconscious, learners undoubtedly take conscious, active roles in many aspects of language learning.

The relationship between attitudes and motivation, however, is not always present, and if it is, it may not be a strong, direct relationship. Attitudes are complex for a number of reasons, especially since positive attitudes do not necessarily guarantee or predict behavior needed for success (Petric, 2002; Popham, 2016). Indeed, researchers have noted that it is not unusual for there to be an inconsistency between student attitudes and their writing behavior (Petric, 2002). However, it has been suggested that it is possible that student attitudes play a larger role in achievement in language learning than in other subjects (Gardner, 1985, 2001). Throughout his work, Gardner posits that language, as the root of human communication, is strongly impacted by social power dynamics, prejudices, and other value judgements that may unconsciously affect attitudes.

As mentioned earlier, a critical link between attitudes and student achievement is motivation. Even important factors of learning, such as aptitude or intelligence, cannot overrule the importance of motivation, since once a learner is not motivated to take the necessary steps towards mastery of a subject, there is a general acceptance that their achievement is likely to suffer. Speaking of the Caribbean situation, but with universal implications, Roberts (2014) noted that "imposing a purely formal standard and requiring the individual to conform to it would not achieve much, unless there is a sound political and ideological basis and unless the power possibilities of the language are apparent or are revealed to the learner" (p. 82). The power possibilities Roberts speaks of would contribute greatly to the attitudes and motivation of Caribbean people to learning Standard English. Research has shown that when students are able to perceive the value of a learning task the result is better learning outcomes (Pintrich, 1999; Pintrich & Schunk, 2002), since they are more likely to employ strategies of self-regulated learners (Denzine & Brown, 2015) and transfer skills they have learned, for example in writing, to other courses (James, 2012).

Another key consideration in this discussion on factors important to language learning is that of self-confidence. Brown (2014) stated that "no successful cognitive or affective activity can be carried out without some degree of self-esteem, self-confidence, knowledge of yourself, and belief in your own capabilities for that activity" (p. 145). It is possible that students may have positive attitudes towards learning a subject and a strong motivation for learning it, but without confidence in their ability to succeed in that subject it is highly improbable that they will do so. If students believe that they are capable of reaching their goal, they may devote more effort and persistence towards reaching it (Rushidi, 2012; Tavani & Losh, 2003; Tremblay & Gardner, 1995). However, if students experience repeated failures or have been in a learning situation where their behavior or effort did little to improve their situation, they may believe that their actions will not bring about success and reduce what effort they put forth in both that course and future endeavors (Crookes & Schmidt, 1991; Uckun, Tohumoglu, & Utar, 2011).

One pair of researchers who examined the relationship among students' academic performance, expectation, motivation, and self-confidence among 4,012 high school students at a southeastern university in the United States discovered significant positive correlations among these variables and noted they were also significant predictors of the participants' academic performances (Tavani & Losh, 2003). These researchers noted that when the motivation levels of the students increased, there was an accompanying increase in their expectations of academic success (Tavani & Losh). Relatedly, a study which investigated the relationship between attitudes and motivation in learning English for academic purposes (EAP) at a European university found that earlier experiences in learning English affected students' attitudes and motivation in this regard (Uckun, Tohumoglu, & Utar, 2011). The researchers determined that participants with positive attitudes towards English-medium education were more desirous to learn English, possessed stronger motivational intensity, and achieved higher scores on instrumental and integrative motivation measures. Those with positive previous language-learning experiences tended to have less anxiety about learning English, prompting the researchers to conclude that a history of success in learning English at high school had the strongest relationship with achievement in English-medium tertiary education, linked to the importance of self-confidence in academic achievement (Uckun, Tohumoglu, & Utar).

Another factor that can affect attitudes and motivation to writing is the complexity, real and perceived, of the task. It is often not easy to determine whether it is the complexity of writing that affects overall attitudes and motivation or whether it is that poor attitudes and weak motivation affect students' perceptions of the complexity of the writing tasks. This is then compounded in second or foreign language learning situations, as noted in many of the studies reviewed in this chapter. In the context of the current study, the language-learning environment is not a full-fledged second or foreign language-learning situation. As mentioned earlier, however, it is also not a first or native language-learning situation. Rather, the majority of the students already speak a variety of English and may feel that they can not only participate fully in society with their current variety but also successfully complete university education with it. Their attitudes and motivation towards academic writing courses may, therefore, depend on what practical use such courses have from their perspective. The perceived practical use of the courses could ultimately have an impact on the degree of success that students achieve.

Although there is an acceptance of the interconnectivity of attitudes and motivation, the principal focus of this chapter is student attitudes. While it does not ignore motivation, it seeks primarily to answer the question: *What are the attitudes of students to academic English and academic writing courses?* In the exploration of this question, consideration was given to the pertinent factors of sex, age, and faculty of the student, even as it delved into the interconnectivity with related factors of self-confidence and the practical value of academic writing courses. The expectation is that the answers received will be helpful for university administrators and faculty to understand what may be contributing to the perception that student writing is not at the required level either upon entry or at the time of exit and to understand why the courses designed to assist students in developing their skill in academic writing are perhaps not as successful in this regard as intended. They will also allow the instructors of the academic writing courses to plan how to address issues surrounding student attitudes as well as plan instruction with knowledge of student attitudes to academic English, academic writing, and the academic writing courses, recognizing the impact that student attitudes can have on their performance.

THE CONTEXT

This study was conducted at one campus of The University of the West Indies. UWI has three physical campuses, in Barbados, Jamaica, and Trinidad and Tobago, as well as one that is virtual. It admits students with varying entry-level qualifications: some have only the current official Caribbean Secondary Education Certificates (CSEC) or an equivalent such as the British General Certificate of Examination (GCE) secondary level (the previous official certification in the region). In other cases, some have CSEC and Caribbean Advanced Proficiency Examination (CAPE) certificates or the British advanced level equivalent or CSEC and an Associate Degree or other postsecondary qualification.

One of the requirements for entry to UWI is that an English Language Proficiency Test (ELPT) be taken by all students who did not receive a Grade 1 in CSEC English Language, a Grade A in GCE Secondary Level English Language, a Grade 1 or 2 in CAPE Communication Studies, or a Grade A or B in the GCE General Paper. Although the exemptions do not explicitly mention examining bodies from outside of the region, as indicated in the introduction to this volume, an assessment is usually done on a case-by-case basis for students entering the university with such qualifications. Students who fail the ELPT must complete a basic course in fundamentals of written English, which aims to increase students' competence in Standard English and key essay-writing skills. After students have successfully completed this course, they can then go on to register for the required number of other compulsory writing courses, referred to here as the academic writing courses. Students who pass the ELPT skip straight to the compulsory courses and are required to take either one or two of them depending on the faculty in which they are registered. While these courses are compulsory for the majority of students (the exception being students in the Faculty of Law with a Grade 1 in CAPE Communication Studies), they can be taken at any time during their program and did not, at the time of data collection (before 2014), count towards students' Grade Point Average (GPA).

METHODS

The study was conducted primarily using a survey and supplemented by interviews. The survey was conducted to, among other reasons, obtain a sense of the attitudes of undergraduate students toward the concept of *academic English* and the courses designed to improve students' academic writing. For the survey, a questionnaire was developed by modifying the well-known and widely used Attitudes/Motivation Test Battery (AMTB) first developed by Gardner and later extended by Gardner and Smythe in 1975 (Gardner, 2001) to make it more relevant to the Caribbean linguistic context. The original version of the AMTB was created to assess motivation to learn a second language, specifically English-speaking students learning French. Some of the areas that the AMTB sought to explore were attitudes towards French Canadians, interest in foreign languages, attitudes towards French speakers from Europe, attitudes towards learning French, French class anxiety, parental encouragement, and integrative and instrumental orientation. Due to its length, with over one hundred questions and taking approximately thirty minutes to complete, the AMTB has been adapted to suit different cultural and linguistic situations across the world but remains the foundation for any research into the affective factors involved in second language learning. With the special language context of the Caribbean in mind, only those items that were applicable were retained (such as attitudes to the language/register being investigated, desire to learn the language/register, instrumental orientation, and motivational intensity), and others more specific to the current context were added (items particular to academic English, self-confidence, attendance, and participation).

After expert review and piloting, forty-three items were settled on: forty-two questions on a five-point Likert scale and one open-ended question. The forty-two Likert scale questions were divided into seven subscales, measuring students' attitude to course(s), attitude to course instructor, attitude to lecturer (where applicable, since for one writing course at the time of the research there was one person conducting lectures and several conducting tutorials where students had the opportunity to practice in small groups), motivational direction, motivational intensity, self-confidence, and practical use of the course(s). For the purposes of this chapter, twenty-eight of the original forty-two closed-ended items were used to create four subscales, divided as follows: four items measuring students' self-confidence in academic writing (Cronbach's alpha = 0.70); nine measuring their attitude to academic English and academic writing (Cronbach's alpha = 0.80); twelve measuring their attitude to the academic writing courses (Cronbach's alpha = 0.87); and three measuring their perceptions of the practical use of the courses (Cronbach's alpha = 0.67). The Cronbach's alpha coefficient for the overall scale was 0.91, indicating good internal consistency. The questionnaire was administered among 2,679 undergraduate students via email. Of these, 667 students completed the questionnaire, representing a 25% response rate. The demographic data of the questionnaire respondents are provided in Table 1.

Table 1
Demographic Data of Respondents

Variable	Category	Number	Percentage
Sex	Male	181	27%
	Female	486	73%
	Total	667	100%
Age	Under 30	527	80%
	Over 30	140	20%
		667	100%
Faculty	Clinical Medicine and Research	8	1%
	Humanities and Education	152	23%
	Law	23	3%
	Pure and Applied Sciences	120	18%
	Social Sciences	364	55%
	Total	667	100%

In addition to the questionnaires, interviews were conducted with students, instructors of the academic writing courses (that is, those who only teach academic writing courses to students from all faculties), and content-area lecturers from four of the five faculties on the campus. Fifty (50) students were interviewed utilizing convenience sampling methods. The interviews with the instructors of the first-year writing courses and the lecturers from the different faculties were arranged by means of contacting each individually and requesting an interview. Eight of the twelve academic writing course instructors and twelve lecturers from various disciplines were interviewed. Overall, the purpose of the interviews was to gather more detailed information on the topic of academic English and the academic writing courses from the students than could be obtained from the questionnaire and also to obtain the perspective of the academic writing course instructors and the content area lecturers from the various Faculties. All interview participants were assigned pseudonyms for the purpose of anonymity.

The survey data were analyzed using SPSS. Descriptive statistics were run, taking into consideration the key factors of the study (age, sex, and Faculty of student). Means were calculated for each respondent for each of the subscales to facilitate investigation of the results obtained from the questionnaire. The mean scores were then divided into three groups: means of less than 2.9 were taken to signify negative attitudes, 3.0–3.9 a moderate attitude and over 4.0 a positive attitude. One-way analysis of variance (ANOVA) and two-way between groups ANOVA tests, respectively, were employed to enable comparisons and measure interaction effects between the independent variables as measured on the questionnaire. The interview data were analyzed for common themes, patterns and contradictions. Excerpts from the interviews are used jointly with the questionnaire data either to support or refute a finding.

RESULTS

Students have severe difficulty with writing—structure, spelling, having a beginning, a middle and an end to an essay. English really seems to be a foreign language for many students. Punctuation is a thing of the past. I am surprised they got past CSEC English sometimes! But these problems are mainstream now and it's getting worse. When I get a paper now without a lot of problems I notice it, rather than it being the other way around.

—Dr Clarke, lecturer in Psychology, Faculty of Social Sciences

The sentiments expressed by this lecturer were broadly shared by the twelve lecturers interviewed for this study. Comments such as the one above served as the initial inspiration for this research into possible reasons for the perceived poor writing standard of university students in the Caribbean. While several factors may be involved in this issue, the focus of this study is primarily the attitudes of university students to academic English and academic writing. Attention was paid to subfactors, such as students' self-confidence in academic writing, their attitudes to academic English and to the academic writing courses offered by UWI, as well as perceptions of the practical use of these courses. Results for each of these subfactors will be examined overall and then by the sex, age, and faculty of student.

As established earlier, a student's attitude and motivation to a subject can have a significant impact on their success in learning that subject. The primary research question guiding this study was, therefore, *What are the attitudes of students to academic English and academic writing courses?* The answers to this research question were gathered from an exploration of the data from the questionnaires and interviews. However, the self-confidence of students regarding academic writing courses was explored before the examination of students' attitudes to academic English. The literature shows that there is a link between self-confidence and attitudes (Brown, 2014; Rushidi, 2012). Four items were, therefore, included on the questionnaire to determine students' self-confidence in academic writing.

The data suggest (see Table 2) that overall the students possessed moderate self-confidence in their academic writing. A two-way between groups ANOVA was run to determine the impact of sex and age on the student's self-confidence in academic English and academic writing. The six original age group categories were recoded into two categories: thirty and under and over thirty. The interaction effect between sex and age was not significant [$F(1, 663) = 0.332; p = 0.565$]. Sex also had no significant main effect [$F(1, 663) = 0.665; p = 0.415$]. A significant main effect was found for age [$F(1, 663) = 8.988; p = 0.003$], suggesting that students under thirty ($M = 3.63$, $SD = 0.75$) were more likely to have higher self-confidence than students over thirty ($M = 3.40$, $SD = 0.73$).

Table 2
Means and Standard Deviations of Four Questionnaire Subscales

Subcategories	N	Mean	SD
Self-confidence	667	3.58[2]	0.75
Attitude to Academic English	667	3.92[2]	0.66
Attitude to Course	667	3.35[2]	0.72
Practical Use of Course	667	3.27[2]	0.91

[1] < 2.9 = low attitude
[2] 3.0–3.9 = moderate attitude
[3] > 4.0 = high attitude

A one-way ANOVA was run to investigate whether any differences existed in the self-confidence means according to the faculty of the students. The test revealed a significant difference among the means ($F[4, 662] = 3.26$; $p = 0.012$). Further exploration was done using the least significant difference (LSD) post-hoc test to ascertain exactly where differences existed among each faculty. The results of the LSD revealed the following:

- The Faculty of Medical Sciences ($M = 4.03$, $SD = 0.80$) had significantly higher means than the Faculty of Pure and Applied Sciences ($M = 3.48$, $SD = 0.75$)
- The Faculty of Humanities and Education ($M = 3.68$, $SD = 0.73$) had significantly higher means than the Faculty of Pure and Applied Sciences ($M = 3.48$, $SD = 0.75$)
- The Faculty of Law ($M = 3.91$, $SD = 0.73$) had significantly higher means than the Faculty of Pure and Applied Sciences ($M = 3.48$, $SD = 0.75$)
- The Faculty of Law ($M = 3.91$, $SD = 0.73$) had significantly higher means than the Faculty of Social Sciences ($M = 3.54$, $SD = 0.75$).

The results, therefore, suggested that students possessed moderate self-confidence in their ability to write using academic English, and both age and faculty appeared to have an impact on the level of self-confidence possessed. With the overall finding that the students have only moderate self-confidence in writing using academic English, it seems reasonable to investigate whether their moderate self-confidence translates into similarly moderate attitudes to academic English and academic writing courses, taking into consideration the same factors of sex, age, and faculty, especially in light of the fact that some significant differences were found among students within the subgroups of age and faculty.

A two-way between groups ANOVA was run to determine the impact of sex and age on the students' attitudes to academic English. With the recoded age group categories, thirty and under and over thirty, the ANOVA results showed that the interaction effect between sex and age was not significant [$F (1, 663) = 2.208$; $p = 0.138$]. Age also had no significant main effect [$F (1, 663) = 1.731$; $p = 0.189$]. Sex of student showed a significant main effect [$F (1, 663) = 10.305$; $p = 0.001$], suggesting that female students ($M = 3.97$, $SD = 0.64$) were more likely to have more positive attitudes towards academic English than male students ($M = 3.78$, $SD = 0.69$).

A one-way ANOVA was run to investigate whether any differences existed in the means in attitude to academic English according to the faculty of the students. The test revealed a significant difference among the means ($F [4, 662] = 3.83$; $p = < 0.0005$). Further exploration was conducted using the LSD post-hoc test to determine where differences existed between each Faculty. The results of the LSD revealed:

- The Faculties of Humanities and Education ($M = 4.05$, $SD = 0.67$), Law ($M = 3.96$, $SD = 0.63$), and Social Sciences ($M = 3.95$, $SD = 0.63$) had significantly higher means than the Faculty of Pure and Applied Sciences ($M = 3.66$, $SD = 0.66$).

The results of the questionnaire on students' attitudes to academic English were borne out in the interviews of both students and the academic writing course instructors. Maria, an under thirty Faculty of Humanities and Education student, clearly expressed both an understanding of academic English and an appreciation for courses being provided in the university setting to assist students in improving their academic writing. She stated:

> I think academic English is absolutely vital and that all university students should have an appreciation for the skill of writing academically. There is no disadvantage to using the language correctly and effectively, and recognizing its place in the world of academia.

However, a frequently observed sentiment of students was that while they understood the concept and appreciated the potential benefit the courses offer students, they did not believe that the academic writing courses should be compulsory for all students. In response to the one open-ended item on the questionnaire, Patrick, an under thirty student from the Faculty of Humanities and Education, stated:

> My honest opinion of the importance of learning English suited to academic work is that while it may prove extremely useful, with regard to preparation for future job interviews and such, it does not necessarily do much to expand the knowledge of some students who are already proficient, not only in the use of English on a whole but specifically in the use of English suited to academic work.

Some students, however, stated that they failed to see the importance of either the concept of academic English or the courses. Kimberley, an under thirty student from the Faculty of Social Sciences, remarked, "I never really understood the term 'academic English.' I don't think everyone should have to take the courses. I don't see the relevance of it for me, in accounting, or for science students." Comments such as these suggest that the students viewed both academic writing and the academic writing courses as a necessary evil: something that is necessary for them to graduate but not something they look forward to. While many students appeared to see the value in such courses, they felt little enthusiasm to take them. Rather, students appeared to feel ambivalent about their individual need for the courses and about their experiences in taking them.

Some students stated that one of their problems with the academic writing courses was that they do not count towards their GPAs, even though students were awarded credit for passing the courses. This suggests that for some students, the usefulness of a course that may benefit them personally and professionally is limited unless it counts towards their GPA. One under thirty female questionnaire respondent from the Faculty of Social Sciences, in response to the open-ended item on the questionnaire, said that:

> Learning language suited to academic purposes is a good idea but seeing that after working to pass the course and it does not count to your GPA, it's a waste of time. Some people may not be able to adequately present information in written form but are very capable of using an oral method to present information. Heavy reliance on the written word is very unfortunate for those

> persons who know the work but are penalised for not being able to write it in proper or academic English.

The notion of a course offered to help with students' academic writing but that is graded on a pass/fail basis, therefore, seems to be considered unnecessary by many students. Also of concern to this student was that knowing the subject matter should be of more importance than expressing it in a more formal register than that used in everyday speech. While some scholars do advocate for alternative means of assessment (Popham, 2013), assessment at the university level will always contain a dimension of writing, and exposure to academic writing instruction will remain important for students. It would be counterintuitive to assess a *writing* course through any means other than writing, so this student's preference for extensive nonwritten assessment does not seem feasible.

Many students were steadfast in their opinion that the courses should not be compulsory for all students but rather only for those who fail to meet certain criteria. One under thirty male questionnaire respondent from the Faculty of Pure and Applied Sciences stated the following:

> In my opinion, English for academic purposes is indeed an important course, as are the other academic writing courses. I do, however, believe that they are more important to some persons, i.e., those persons who left school without being adequately qualified. It is the responsibility of the university to find out which persons are in need of the English courses as opposed to forcing everyone to do them.

Investigation into the attitudes of students to the academic writing courses was conducted after their attitudes to academic English as a concept were established. The questionnaire contained a number of items designed to explore students' attitudes to the academic writing courses. As with self-confidence and attitude to academic English, the data suggest that students possessed a moderate attitude to the academic writing courses, but on the lower end of the moderate band (see Table 2).

A two-way between groups ANOVA was run to determine the impact of sex and age on the students' overall attitude to the academic writing courses. When the two recoded age-group categories were used, the ANOVA results showed that the interaction effect between sex and age was not significant [$F (1, 663) = 0.042; p = 0.837$]. Sex also had no significant main effect [$F (1, 663) = 0.812; p = 0.368$]. A significant main effect was found for age [$F (1, 663) = 20.132; p = < 0.0005$], suggesting that students over thirty (M = 3.66, SD = 0.66) were more likely to have a more positive attitude to the academic writing courses than students under thirty (M = 3.27, SD = 0.72).

Age was indeed identified as a factor by the instructors of the academic writing courses. The instructors who noted age as a factor said that in their experience the more mature students, especially those in the workforce, were able to appreciate the practical application of the skills they were learning since they could benefit from them in the workplace. The younger students took longer to appreciate the potential benefits of the courses. This is what two of the instructors had to say:

> At the beginning of semester students will sometimes come in and ask why they have to do the course; they say they are not English students, why should they have to do English? They say they don't need it. What I find is that age makes a difference in this: the day groups have younger students who say they don't think they need to do it and the night groups tend to have more mature students who are working and who recognize the need for the course.—Sharon Springer, academic writing course instructor

> With younger students, I would say indifference is the biggest cause of failure. They don't come to the classes, don't submit the assignments, and show up at the end of semester trying to make up for it with three essays to hand in at the same time.—Mary Joseph, academic writing course instructor

It is also possible that since the younger students possessed higher self-confidence in academic writing, they may feel even less need to take the academic writing courses.

Not only were differences found according to the age of the student but also according to the faculty to which the student belonged. A one-way ANOVA was run to investigate whether any differences existed in the means in overall attitude to course according to the faculty of the students. The test revealed a significant difference among the means (F [4, 662] = 3.032; p = 0.017). Further exploration was done using the LSD post-hoc test to determine where differences existed between each Faculty. The results of the LSD revealed that:

- The Faculty of Humanities and Education (M = 3.48, SD = 0.74) had significantly higher means than the Faculty of Pure and Applied Sciences (M = 3.17, SD = 0.69)
- The Faculty of Social Sciences (M = 3.36, SD = 0.72) had significantly higher means than the Faculty of Pure and Applied Sciences (M = 3.17, SD = 0.69).

These results were also observed in the interviews with the academic writing course instructors. Five of the eight instructors interviewed stated that in their observation not only does the faculty of the student make a difference to approach to the academic writing courses but also students from the Faculties of Pure and Applied Sciences and Social Sciences show the most resistance. Ms Springer, one of the instructors, explained, "I find in my experience that Pure and Applied students show the most resistance. They say they don't do any writing, that it's all numbers or short sentences and that their lecturers only want the points from them and essays are not necessary." However, one of the lecturers from the Faculty of Pure and Applied Sciences interviewed for this study spoke directly to this belief, stating that her course (in microbiology) required an extensive amount of writing in the form of laboratory reports, literature reviews, test responses, and essays. This suggests that some of the interviewees from the Faculty of Pure and Applied Sciences possessed misconceptions concerning the amount of writing required of students in their faculty.

Two of the eight instructors interviewed of their own volition contrasted students from the Faculty of Humanities and Education with students from the Faculties of Pure and Applied Sciences and Social Sciences. These instructors stated that humanities and education students tend to be more receptive to writing and the writing process in general and are less negative about the number of writing assignments because they expect to have numerous writing assignments, unlike students from the Faculties of Pure and Applied Sciences and Social Sciences, who routinely say that the majority of their assignments do not involve essay-writing.

It is possible that the students' attitudes to the academic writing courses may be influenced by their perception of the practical use of the courses. One of the subscales on the questionnaire gauged students' attitudes specifically to their perception of the practical use of the academic writing courses, and a one-way ANOVA was run to investigate whether any differences existed in the means in the practical use of course subfactor according to the faculty of the students. The test revealed a significant difference among the means (F [4, 662] = 3.797; p = 0.005). Further exploration was done using the LSD post-hoc test to determine where differences existed between each Faculty. The results of the LSD revealed that:

- The Faculty of Humanities and Education (M = 3.40, SD = 0.99) had significantly higher means than the Faculty of Pure and Applied Sciences (M = 3.00, SD = 0.92)
- The Faculty of Social Sciences (M = 3.31, SD = 0.88) had significantly higher means than the Faculty of Pure and Applied Sciences (M = 3.00, SD = 0.92).

A two-way between groups ANOVA was then run to determine the impact of sex and age on the students' attitudes to the practical use of the academic writing courses. With the two recoded age group categories, the ANOVA results showed that the interaction effect between sex and age was not significant [F (1, 663) = 0.851; p = 0.357]. Sex also had no significant main effect [F (1, 663) = 0.740; p = 0.390]. Age showed a significant main effect [F (1, 663) = 7.455; p = 0.006], suggesting that students over thirty (M = 3.54, SD = 0.83) were more likely to have a more positive attitude to the academic writing courses than students under thirty (M = 3.19, SD = 0.92).

Again, these results were reflective of the opinions expressed by students in the interviews. Students in the Faculty of Pure and Applied Sciences in particular doubted the relevance of the academic writing courses to their studies. Jennifer, an under thirty student of the Faculty of Pure and Applied Sciences, said, "I haven't really used anything that I learned in the courses. You see, they teach you one thing but for Pure and Applied Sciences you are required to do something else." Carla, also an under thirty student of the Faculty of Pure and Applied Sciences, stated, "A lot of what I learned was not especially relevant to me and my major (math). I haven't had to use anything I learned yet and truthfully I don't see myself using anything I learned." Paul, an under thirty student from the same faculty, remarked, "If I'm being honest, I came out after the course the same as I went in; however, I do see how it would be helpful for some others." Carol-Ann, an under thirty student from the Faculty of Social Sciences, stated, "It [the course] was ok. Truthfully, I didn't pay much attention to it. I got a Grade 1 in CSEC English and CAPE Communication Studies, so I felt I had done it all before. I think it would be beneficial if you hadn't done those courses or had done them but not done well, but for me it was just a waste." All of these comments came from students who were under the age of thirty, supporting the instructors' insights into the impact that age can have on students' appreciation for the academic writing courses.

Generally speaking, the lecturers interviewed saw the importance of the academic writing courses. Some expressed strong disapproval of allowing students to take the academic writing courses at any point during their programs rather than making it compulsory for them to be taken at the commencement of their degree. They noted in strong terms how troubling it is to see advanced students struggling with writing simply because they had not been exposed to the courses. Dr Sealy, a lecturer from the Faculty of Pure and Applied Sciences, noted:

> The worst writing I have seen by a student this semester was by a third year student, and when I pulled up their transcript I saw that they are only now, in their final semester of UWI, taking the required academic writing course. And they are graduating this year! So it explains a lot.

Several lecturers, while not discounting the importance of attitude as a factor for students' lackluster performance in academic writing, posited another reason, discussed earlier: the starting proficiency in English of students is oftentimes not where it should be. Other reasons listed by lecturers included that students are writing how they speak, that is, they are writing in the vernacular; are using text message language in class assignments; and are not reading enough, particularly not enough academic material. Following is what three of the eight lecturers interviewed had to say:

> I would say on a scale of 1 to 10 their writing is about a 6, maybe a 7 sometimes. But one, they're not reading a lot and their vocabulary and phrases and understanding of writing conventions is not strong. They are limited because of this. Two, they tend to move more towards slang. They don't want to be challenged and therefore they look for the easiest way out. At both undergraduate and graduate level sometimes! The way we speak is being written. There are definite issues with writing and we need to get to the source of them. Is it the culture or the vernacular that are so strong they are taking over? Or maybe the students

just aren't taking the academic writing courses seriously. I'm not sure. — Dr Bascombe, Faculty of Social Sciences

Students are using text language with all the abbreviations in exams and I have told them that if they do that I won't know what they're saying! It has been getting worse; maybe technology is to blame. — Dr Brathwaite, Faculty of Pure and Applied Sciences

I find there is poor management of syntax and grammar. Poor performance is often due to a lack of knowledge. All of this really serves to stress the connection between primary school and tertiary education: if they are not learning properly at the lower levels it is difficult for them to become truly good students without that foundation. — Dr Holder, Faculty of Humanities and Education

An additional issue raised by lecturers during the interviews was that of students not transferring the skills they learn in the academic writing courses to their other courses. Many lecturers stated that the majority of students fail to apply what they learned in their academic writing courses to other courses and that many students appeared to doubt the necessity of the courses. If the students fail to see the necessity of the courses because they are satisfactory writers already, as many appeared to believe, then this failure to transfer skills would not be a noticeable phenomenon. This, therefore, suggests the possibility that either the students are overestimating their proficiency in academic writing or that the lecturers are unaware of the starting proficiency of students and are unable to tell that improvements have indeed been made. Additionally, several lecturers noted that they are able to tell when the student has not completed the academic writing courses, which indicates that at least some skills are transferred, even if not to the degree desired.

The findings here discussed reiterate the longstanding perception that students' writing overall is below the preferred standard, and more specifically that their academic writing is a cause for concern. The survey results found that where academic English and academic writing are concerned, students possessed moderate self-confidence and moderate attitudes. In terms of attitude to academic writing and the academic writing courses, differences were found relating to age of student, sex, and faculty to which students belonged. The survey findings were generally supported by qualitative data obtained from interviews with students, academic writing course instructors, and content area lecturers from the various faculties. The interviews also offered nuanced findings, giving a better understanding of the survey results, often providing explanations, agreements, and in some cases a different outlook.

Discussion

The aim of this study was to investigate the attitudes of undergraduate students of one of the campuses of The University of the West Indies to academic English as a concept and to the courses through which academic writing is taught at this institution. In addition to the questionnaire, which 667 students completed online, interviews were conducted with fifty students, eight of the twelve instructors of the academic writing courses, and twelve content area lecturers from four of the five Faculties.

The results suggest that students possessed only moderate self-confidence in their academic writing. As noted earlier, self-confidence in one's ability is a crucial component in any activity, whether physical or cognitive, and writing is no exception (Brown, 2014; Gardner & Lambert, 1972; Powell, 1984; Rushidi, 2012). The students who participated in this study possessed moderate self-confidence in their academic writing ability, which suggests they believe their writing is satisfactory. The finding of moderate self-confidence is a significant one as other studies have found a direct relationship between self-confidence and academic performance. For example, in the United States, Tavani and Losh (2003) reported a statistically significant relationship between high school students' expectations and self-confidence. The implication of this finding is that the higher the self-confidence of the students, the more likely they are to have high expectations of performance in their academic endeavors. The assumption is that high expectations can lead students to believe that the quality of their work (such as writing) is of a high standard. Naturally, high self-confidence and high expectations do not, in reality, always lead to high quality. In fact, though students reported moderate self-confidence in their academic writing ability, the lecturers generally were not in agreement. Nine of the twelve lecturers interviewed stated that they found the quality of writing submitted to them to be mediocre at best. Two expressed extreme dissatisfaction and only one believed that the inadequacy of student writing had been exaggerated. The disconnect between students' and lecturers' perceptions of student writing is not surprising. It may, in part, help to explain why so many students did not believe that they should have to take any courses in academic writing and why the effectiveness of these courses is at times called into question.

Beyond the disconnect between students and lecturers in relation to academic writing, there should also be concerns about the moderate self-confidence scores. Although not speaking directly to self-confidence, Roberts (1988) raises questions about a related construct, self-esteem. He questioned whether a link exists between self-esteem and language achievement in the Caribbean, in no small part due to the linguistic inferiority complex that he hypothesizes starts early in a Caribbean child's life and is reinforced during his/her formative years. Self-esteem and self-confidence are two related constructs: self-esteem generally refers to how a person feels about him/herself overall, whereas self-confidence relates to how a person feels about their abilities and can vary according to the ability in question. It is likely that a person with low self-esteem would possess low self-confidence. If this self-esteem/self-confidence link can be made, the question must also be asked as to whether the moderate self-confidence of the students in this study is not linked to the linguistic inferiority complex to which Roberts alluded. If this is the case, the expectation is that it will have a significant impact on the students' use of English in general, and more specifically on their writing, since research shows that the more confidence learners have in their ability to succeed at a given task, the more positive their attitude would be to it and the more effort they will put into succeeding in the task (Brown, 2014; Denzine & Brown, 2015; James, 2012; Paker & Erarslan, 2015; Rushidi, 2012; Tavani & Losh, 2003; Uckun, Tohumoglu, & Utar, 2011).

Also useful to our engagement with the findings is research conducted in Europe on the importance of writing skills in English for academic purposes (EAP) courses in an English as a foreign language (EFL) setting that found that students' attitudes improved by the end of the courses, after improvements in their writing were made (Rushidi, 2012). Rushidi's finding emphasizes the effect that self-confidence can have on attitudes. It is expected that the more students learned about writing, the more self-confident they became and, as a corollary, the more positive they became toward academic writing. In the current study, the students' moderate self-confidence was found to be mirrored by their moderate attitudes to the concept of academic English. Rushidi's study has further relevance to the one reported here as it was also found that the majority of students in her study ranked the importance of writing higher than they ranked the importance of their own performance in writing. In the current study, many students professed to see the importance of academic English and the academic writing courses but at the same time indicated that the courses were more important for other students than themselves. Based on perennial reports from lecturers, as well as the interview data of the lecturers and instructors about students' performance in academic writing, it seems reasonable to conclude that such students simply overestimate their writing ability.

Interestingly, two factors stood out as having an impact on attitudes in this study: age and faculty of student. In terms of age, students under thirty were found to have higher self-confidence in their academic writing than students over thirty, but for every other aspect of attitude observed (attitudes to academic English, to the course, and to the practical use of the courses) the students over thirty were found to be more likely to possess more positive attitudes. A large percentage of students of The University of the West Indies are part-time, many of whom may be several years removed from their last academic endeavors. Factors such as this may influence students' self-confidence, since it is possible that the younger students possessed greater self-confidence because they more recently graduated and are not as out of practice in writing as older students. Milson-Whyte (2015) notes that age may be a contributing factor to the results obtained on the UWI English Language Proficiency Test, since younger students tend to perform better on it than older students, and it may well be one of the explanations for this finding. It is also possible that the higher self-confidence possessed by younger students may cause them to feel even less need to take the academic writing courses. Conversely, the more positive attitudes towards academic English as a concept, as well as towards the academic writing courses and perceptions of the practical use of the courses, may be explained because of the maturity of older students, who may recognize the value of writing in their jobs and appreciate the impact that writing skills may have on their current and future studies. The significance between the attribution of value by both the EAP instructors and students to language learning and participants' academic achievement was also found by Uckun, Tohumoglu, and Utar (2011) in a study conducted in Europe. In that study, the students' conviction that EAP would contribute to their success affected their instrumental orientation and motivational intensity, reinforcing previous research that shows that better learning outcomes are observed once the value of a learning task is understood.

As mentioned above, in this study, the faculty in which the students were registered was also found to have a significant impact on all of the subscales here discussed: self-confidence in academic writing and attitudes to academic English as a concept, to the academic writing courses, and especially to the practical use of these courses. In all cases, students from the Faculty of Pure and Applied Sciences possessed the least positive attitudes and the lowest self-confidence. These results were supported by the interview data. Similar results were obtained by Murphree (2014) in a study in the United States. He reported that the major of the university students in his study appeared to affect the students' perception of the utility of writing exercises outside of their major. In his study, students who were science majors held the belief that their futures did not require much writing. Brockman, Taylor, Crawford, and Kreth (2010), at a Midwestern US university, also had similar findings. Their study found differences in the writing expected of humanities versus non-humanities students, particularly concerning the use of the third-person perspective, shorter paragraphs, technical jargon, and passive voice.

There is indeed a perception that science students are not as skilled in writing as students in many other disciplines. While this chapter cannot speak to this, it does suggest that many science students appear to challenge the need for the study of academic English and the relevance of a compulsory course in academic writing for their specialization. Science students were also found to possess the least positive perceptions of the practical use of the academic writing courses. The comments from science students in the interviews clearly painted a picture of students who doubted that the generic concept of academic writing applied to their fields and felt that the style of writing taught in the courses was unwanted by their lecturers and, therefore, irrelevant to their programs. Since it must be acknowledged that there is no one correct style of academic writing and that what is considered "good" academic writing will indeed vary from discipline to discipline (Brockman, Taylor, Crawford, & Kreth, 2010; Lalla, 1998), consideration must be given to the need for subject-specific writing courses, as proposed by Warrican (2012) and Milson-Whyte (2015). This would assist in reducing students' complaints about the academic writing courses not being relevant to their discipline.

Humanities students were found to possess the most positive attitudes to academic English as a concept and to the academic writing courses, and lecturers from this faculty were also the most vocal about the importance of courses that assist students in developing their skill in academic writing. This was not the case for all faculties. Some lecturers, notably in the Faculty of Social Sciences and the Faculty of Law, seemed ambivalent about the courses and their effectiveness for their students. This ambivalence may be apparent to the students of these Faculties, leading some to believe that the courses were not valuable or that the skills learned need not be transferred to their other courses, which is one point that lecturers from all faculties noted. Indeed, this is an issue that deserves special attention. Many students stated that their lecturers in their content-area courses informed them that they would not grade assignments based on what had been taught in the academic writing courses. However, lecturers from all faculties lamented that students do not appear to transfer the skills learned in the academic writing courses to other courses, in some cases leading the lecturers to doubt the efficacy of these courses. Yet, if students are under the impression that what they learn in the courses is not going to affect their grades outside of the courses, it is not inconceivable that they will not transfer the relevant skills. Also, if the lecturers are unaware of what the students' initial writing skills were, they would not be able to accurately judge whether any improvement has been made or whether the academic writing courses were beneficial for their students.

Research into the transfer of writing skills has found that while desire to transfer and positive attitudes towards transfer were observed, effort to transfer was limited, suggesting that genuine motivation to transfer was lacking (James, 2012). Where students possessed a desire to transfer or demonstrated positive attitudes towards transfer, James's study at a large, urban US research-oriented university found that it was due to how students thought transfer would benefit them (extrinsic motivation) and whether they had positive perceptions of competence (self-confidence) in their writing ability. Driscoll and Wells (2012) in their study in the United States had similar findings: certain qualities in the college-level participants affected their ability to transfer, such as a willingness to self-regulate, the value they placed on writing, and the students' self-confidence in their writing ability.

The results obtained in the present study suggest that the students were extrinsically motivated more than intrinsically motivated, but weakly so. Extrinsic motivation, as mentioned earlier, is when activities are engaged in for external reasons, such as because of an expected reward (Deci, 1975; Ryan & Deci, 2017). Traditionally, intrinsic motivation is considered a more powerful indicator of eventual success than extrinsic motivation (Brown, 1990). This may be because if people engage in an activity for no other reason than for their own personal benefit there is a higher chance that they will persist until their goal is reached. The context of the English-speaking Caribbean may be the cause of this extrinsic motivation. Since the students already speak a variety of English (despite the fact that it may not be as close to Standard English as they may think it is), academic English would constitute an additional register, as opposed to an entirely new language, and students may not perceive the benefit of performing well in the academic writing courses as improving themselves or adding to their knowledge base for their own satisfaction. Additionally, without the courses' counting towards GPAs, the motivation for devoting time and effort to these courses may be low for many students. James's (2012) study also found that some students have reservations about taking courses that they believe may not benefit them unless counted towards their GPA. Murphree (2014) noted a similar phenomenon, especially when the courses in question called for writing assignments. Subsequent to when this research was conducted, the grades earned in the academic writing courses were counted towards students' cumulative GPAs, suggesting that the university recognized the need for appealing to the extrinsic motivation of students.

Interestingly, in this study, sex was only found to have a significant impact on attitudes to academic English as a concept. Paker and Erarslan (2015) found that sex of student had a significant impact on the attitudes of university students to an English writing course in Turkey, with female students obtaining higher attitude scores than male students prior to taking the course. After students took the course, however, sex had no influence on the attitudes towards writing. Other studies have also not found a significant difference in the attitudes towards writing according to sex, such as Yong (2010) and Greene (1999), so the finding that sex did not play a significant role in the attitudes of students in the current study is supported by other research. One possibility is that the language issues affecting Caribbean people are general concerns, affecting citizens regardless of sex or age. However, it is also possible that differences may not be as prevalent in a university setting, since all students would be aware that writing is an important and unavoidable component of university work.

Similar to the findings in this study, Paker and Erarslan (2015) found that students saw the importance of an English writing course but were unenthusiastic about having to complete it. Their motivation for taking the course was not strong. While Paker and Erarslan's study was conducted in an English as a foreign language context, parallels can be made to the current study, where students accepted and agreed to the necessity of taking an academic writing course, but many were at best ambivalent about having to take it themselves. Another similarity noted in the literature was that several of the challenges affecting UWI students with the perceived effectiveness of the academic writing courses were encountered in different contexts. For example, Murphree (2014) noted the difficulties with student enthusiasm and expectations, limited capacity due to increasing enrollment, and inconsistent support university-wide in the grading of assignments.

This study aimed to shed light on one of the often-overlooked elements of academic writing: students' attitudes to writing. The views expressed in the questionnaires and interviews, as well as their comparison to wider studies, provide a deeper understanding into the complexities of how issues relating to the affective domain of academic writing are viewed by students, lecturers, and academic writing course instructors at one campus of UWI.

Conclusion

Writing is indeed a complex, demanding task, which takes years of guided instruction, quality exposure, and determined practice to master. The writing standards of students across the world are increasingly being called into question, and the Caribbean is no different. The linguistic context, sociocultural and political factors and the legacy of colonialism on language instruction (Warrican, 2015), and secondary school entrance examinations and streaming do not appear to benefit the majority of Caribbean students (Thompson, Warrican, & Leacock, 2011). It cannot be expected that one academic writing course, designed to familiarize students with the conventions of academic writing and provide opportunities for practice and feedback, would be sufficient to address the challenges that many Caribbean students face in their use of Standard English.

The moderate attitudes and extrinsic motivation observed in this study can be changed but only after establishing a general picture of the prevailing attitudes and motivational factors of students, which this study sought to provide. Research into attitude change suggests that two of the best ways to achieve change in this area are increasing the language awareness of the students and encouraging new positive experiences in the language or in writing (Petric, 2002). Several studies have shown that improving students' self-confidence and attitudes to writing is possible (Petric, 2002; Rushidi, 2012), so there is hope for what some consider an unpromising situation.

Determining the best course of action to take in the Caribbean context, however, is no small feat. The influence of the creole languages or vernaculars, which are the first language of the majority of Caribbean people, must be considered. Bryan (2010) suggested that developing language awareness would both encourage students' proficiency in standard English and also encourage confidence in the value of their mother tongue, both of which are highly desirable outcomes. In addition, if one takes the approach of first-year university students being novice writers, then one academic writing course seems insufficient. Rather, as Brockman, Taylor, Crawford, and Kreth (2010) noted, first-year students "must be mentored over the course of their undergraduate work if they are to grow into increasingly skilled writers" (p. 45). Also, as discussed earlier, the evidence seems to point to the need to consider discipline-specific writing courses, so that students can be assured that the instruction being provided is relevant to their discipline. A writing across the curriculum approach could also be considered, since this would be the most effective way to provide the support that students need as they participate in academic programs that are not confined to a single discipline. This should also address the issue reported by students that not all of their assignments are graded based on the criteria promoted in the academic writing courses.

Knowledge of student perceptions of academic writing can assist in formulating an approach to student writing that takes into account the affective factors as well as the content and targeted practice that must be offered (DeVere Wolsey, Lapp, & Fisher, 2012). The suggestions made here could contribute greatly towards improving the academic writing of students in all disciplines in the Caribbean. As Rushidi (2012) notes, "writing is the medium through which one's work, learning and intellect is [sic] judged" (p. 4) and not only in academic spheres. Every effort should therefore be made, at all educational levels, to ensure that the instruction and support provided to students is designed to address not only the language issues faced by many students but also the affective factors, without which it is unlikely that improvements can be achieved.

REFERENCES

Brockman, E., Taylor, M., Crawford, M., & Kreth, M. (2010). Helping students cross the threshold: Implications from a university writing assessment. *The English Journal, 99*(3), 42–49.

Brown, H. D. (1990). M&Ms for language classrooms? Another look at motivation. In J. E. Alatis (Ed.), *Georgetown university round table on language and linguistics* (pp. 383–393). Washington, DC: Georgetown University Press.

Brown, H. D. (2014). *Principles of language learning and teaching* (6th ed.). New York: Pearson.

Bryan, B. (2010). *Between two grammars*. Kingston: Ian Randle Publishers.

Craig, D. (2006). *Teaching language and literacy to Caribbean students: From vernacular to Standard English*. Kingston, Jamaica: Ian Randle Publishers.

Credé, M., & Kuncel, N. (2008). Study habits, skills, and attitudes: The third pillar supporting collegiate academic performance. *Perspectives on Psychological Science, 3*(6), 425–453.

Crookes, G., & Schmidt, R. W. (1991). Motivation: Reopening the research agenda. *Language Learning, 41*(4), 469–512.

Deci, E. L. (1975). *Intrinsic motivation*. New York: Plenum Press.

Denzine, G., & Brown, R. (2015). Motivation to learn and achievement. In R. Papa (Ed.), *Media rich instruction: Connecting curriculum to all learners* (19–33). New York: Springer Science and Business.

DeVere Wolsey, T., Lapp, D., & Fisher, D. (2012). Students' and teachers' perceptions: An inquiry into academic writing. *Journal of Adolescent & Adult Literacy, 55*(8), 714–724.

Driscoll, D. L., & Wells, J. (2012). Beyond knowledge and skills: Writing transfer and the role of student dispositions. *Composition Forum, 26*. Retrieved from http://compositionforum.com/issue/26/beyond-knowledge-skills.php

Ellis, R. (2008). *The study of second language acquisition* (2nd ed.). Oxford: Oxford University Press.

Gardner, R. C. (1985). *Social psychology and second language learning: The role of attitudes and motivation*. London: Edward Arnold.

Gardner, R. C. (2001). Integrative motivation and second language acquisition. In Z. Dörnyei & R. Schmidt (Eds.), *Motivation and second language acquisition* (pp. 1–20). Manoa: University of Hawaii Press.

Gardner, R.C., & Lambert, W. E. (1972). *Attitudes and motivation in second language learning*. Massachusetts: Newbury.

Greene, G. L. (1999). *Writing self-efficacy, gender, aptitude, and writing achievement among freshman university students* (Unpublished Doctoral Thesis). University of Alabama, Alabama.

James, M. (2012). An investigation of motivation to transfer second language learning. *The Modern Language Journal, 96*(1), 51–69.

Lalla, B. (1998). *English for academic purposes: Study guide*. St. Augustine (Trinidad): UWIDEC.

McIntyre, P. D. (2002). Motivation, anxiety and emotion in second language acquisition. In P. Robinson (Ed.), *Individual differences and instructed language learning*. (pp. 45–68). Amsterdam: John Benjamins.

Milson-Whyte, V. (2015). *Academic writing instruction for creole-influenced students*. Kingston, Jamaica: University of the West Indies Press.

Murphree, D. (2014). "Writing wasn't really stressed, accurate historical analysis was stressed": Student perceptions of in-class writing in the inverted, general education, university history survey course. *The History Teacher, 47*(2), 209–219.

Paker, T., & Erarslan, A. (2015). Attitudes of the preparatory class students towards the writing course and their attitude-success relationship in writing. *Journal of Language and Linguistic Studies, 11*(2), 1–11.

Petric, B. (2002). Students' attitudes towards writing and the development of academic writing skills. *Writing Centre Journal, 22*(2), 9–27. Retrieved from http://136.165.62.3/wcj22.2/WCJ22.2_Petric.pdf

Pintrich, P. R. (1999). The role of motivation in promoting and sustaining self-regulated learning. *International Journal of Educational Research, 31*, 459–470.

Pintrich, P. R., & Schunk, D. H. (2002). *Motivation in education: Theory, research and applications*. Upper Saddle River, N.J.: Merrill, Prentice-Hall International.

Popham, W. J. (2016). *Classroom assessment: What teachers need to know* (8th ed.). Boston, MA: Pearson.

Popham, W. J. (2013). *Transformative assessment*. Virginia: ASCD.

Powell, B. (1984). A comparison of students' attitudes and success in writing. *The Journal of Negro Education, 53*(2), 114–123.

Roberts, P. (1988). *Second language acquisition theory and second dialect acquisition in the Caribbean*. Nassau, Bahamas: Society for Caribbean Linguistics.

Roberts, P. (2007). *West Indians and their language* (2nd ed.). Cambridge: Cambridge University Press.

Roberts, P. (2014). Introducing policies and procedures for vernacular situations. In I. Robertson & H. Simmons-McDonald (Eds.), *Education issues in creole and creole-influenced vernacular contexts* (pp. 81–118). Kingston, Jamaica: University of the West Indies Press.

Rushidi, J. (2012). Perceptions and performance: students' attitudes towards academic English writing. *SEEU Review, 8*(2), 1–15.

Ryan, R. M., & Deci, E. L. (2017). *Self-determination theory: Basic psychological needs in motivation, development, and wellness*. New York: Guilford Press.

Tavani, C. M., & Losh, S. C. (2003). Motivation, self-confidence, and expectations as predictors of the academic performances among our high school students. *Child Study Journal, 33*(3), 141–151.

Thompson, B. P., Warrican, S. J., & Leacock, C. J. (2011). Education for the future: Shaking off the shackles of colonial times. In D. Dunkley (Ed.), *Readings in Caribbean history and culture: Breaking ground* (pp. 61–86). Lanham, MD: Lexington Books.

Tremblay, P. F., & Gardner, R. C. (1995). Expanding the motivation construct in language learning. *Modern Language Journal, 79*(4), 505–518.

Uckun, B., Tohumoglu, G., & Utar, S. (2011). The relationship between general motivation and situation-specific attitudes and beliefs related to learning English for academic purposes: Its impact on academic success. *Gaziantep University Journal of Social Sciences, 10*(1), 547–569.

Warrican, S. J. (2005). *Hard words: The challenge of reading and writing for Caribbean students and their teachers*. Kingston, Jamaica: Ian Randle Publishers.

Warrican, S. J. (2012). *Literacy: The complete Caribbean teacher*. Essex: Pearson

Warrican, S. J. (2015). Fostering true literacy in the commonwealth Caribbean: Bridging the cultures of home and school. In P. Smith & A. Kumi-Yeboah (Eds.), *Handbook of research on cross-cultural approaches to language and literacy development* (pp. 367–392). Hershey, PA: IGI Global.

Warrican, S. J., Leacock, C. J., Thompson, B. P, & Alleyne, M. L. (2014). Predictors of student success in an online learning environment in the English-speaking Caribbean: Evidence from The University of the West Indies Open Campus. *Open Praxis, 6*(4), 331–346. DOI: http://dx.doi.org/10.5944/openpraxis.6.4.158.

Yong, F. L. (2010). Attitudes toward academic writing of foundation students at an Australian-based university in Sarawak. *European Journal of Social Sciences, 13*(3), 471–477.

Section Three: Perspectives on Language and Error

Bloody English! UWI, UTech students struggle with the language
—Virtue, 2013

5 Understanding and Shifting a Marking Community's Response to Students' Writing: Lessons from Jamaican Instructors' "expression" Comments

Annife Campbell

Introduction

In the Jamaican higher education context, writing instructors have an extensive arsenal of censorious adjectives such as *unsophisticated, ineffective, imprecise,* and *informal* when they respond to students' academic essays. In commenting on students' writing nearly always in a negative manner, writing instructors play into the popular perception in Jamaica and the broader Caribbean region that postsecondary student writing skills are in a state of crisis. Milson-Whyte (2015) appropriately describes this acrimonious and disparaging, if not meanspirited, attitude towards Jamaican students' writing weaknesses as "alarmist rhetoric" (p. 19). Accordingly, to avoid promoting this sense of panic, Jamaican and other Caribbean postsecondary writing instructors should learn to appreciate the enormous power their comments wield over students' writing. As observed by Sommers (1982), in reference to North American writing instructors, "teachers' comments can take students' attention away from their own purposes in writing" (p. 149). Sommers decries the tendency of writing instructors to respond to students' work without acknowledging this problematic power dynamic between them and students; Sommers's observation on the power of instructors' comments is a caution against instructors' using their marginal and end comments to appropriate students' work by exerting dominance over students' ideas and taking ownership away from students. Although it was made decades ago and in a different educational context, Sommers' clarion call remains relevant to this day for Jamaican composition instructors—especially regarding their use of an idiosyncratic comment, *expression*, when responding to students' academic essays.

In the community of Jamaican postsecondary writing instructors, the comment *expression,* sometimes abbreviated *exp,* is written on the students' papers by instructors to bring attention to language they see as problematic, deficient, or generally unidiomatic. The *expression* comment is a unique evaluative feature used by this Caribbean marking community to guide student revision and to facilitate the assessment of students' academic writing. Interestingly, *expression* seems to be a distinctly Caribbean marginal comment, appearing on no list of revision symbols in mass-marketed North American writing handbooks (e.g., *The Brief Holt Handbook*). *Expression* comments are, like all end and marginal comments on students' essays, instructors' subjective, qualitative, and aesthetic judgements imposed on the students' text. However, what distinguishes *expression* from other marginal comments commonly made by Jamaican writing instructors (e.g., *informal, passive voice*) is the high frequency with which it appears on student papers and its general vagueness. *Expression* can be written as a marginal comment on essays to indicate a wide variety of issues, including: inaccurate diction or word choice; unidiomatic language; awkward phrasing; poor use of documentation conventions such as APA style; run-on sentences; and traditional Standard English grammatical errors—errors that may or may not stem from structures in Jamaican Creole (e.g., subject-verb agreement). Indeed, one might even go so far as to suggest that the *expression* comment functions within Jamaican grading discourse as what rhetorician Burke (1945) refers to as a *God term*—that is, a vaguely defined term such as *freedom* or *justice* to which members of a discourse community are expected to pay deference.

While the mistakes in usage that lead to the *expression* comment might be the result of students' moving from the oral codes of Jamaican Creole to the written codes of Standard Jamaican English, the nature of the errors themselves cannot be explained solely by students' movement between these languages. Rather, the errors that lead to *expression* comments seem to be primarily made because students are still building their skills as academic writers. The overapplication of *expression* comments to a variety of errors should give instructors pause not only because of how many types of errors the term is applied to but also because of the many ways that the word *expression* can be understood. To deepen our understanding of how the *expression* comment functions in the Jamaican community of academic writing instructors and their students, I will, in this chapter, first use Speech Act Theory (SAT) to interpret how *expression* comments can be perceived by students. This is important because how students interpret instructor comments affects their development as writers. Then, I will explore a sample of *expression* comments using theories from Systemic Functional Linguistics (SFL) to explain the linguistic structures in academic registers that writing instructors expect in students' essays, the absence of which can lead to the *expression* comment. Finally, I will argue for a more developmental approach to commenting that takes into consideration the sociocultural conditions of student writing. Indeed, with this chapter, I hope to encourage instructors to use marginal and end comments not just as an opportunity to impugn student writing using vague ideological terms like *expression* but to move towards seeing the "offending" linguistic structures as negotiations, inexperience, and incomplete academic socialization of developing student writers. This move can help students to appreciate academic writing as developmental, a process of nurturing and long-term growth.

Postsecondary Grading and Assessment Culture in the Caribbean

As discussed in the introduction to this volume, Anglophone Caribbean universities have inherited from the colonial education system a penchant for high-stakes end-of-semester testing, a tradition of assessment that is still common in academic writing courses in the region. (It is, for example, still possible in at least one major Caribbean university for students to fail a whole English composition class based just on their performance on the timed essay final examination, regardless of their performance on their previous out-of-class writing assignments.) While this testing culture originated from the colonial order (see, for example, Milson-Whyte, 2015), the preference for high-stakes testing has clearly been internalized over the years. Moreover, this esteem for high-stakes testing has been reinforced in recent decades by the influence of market-driven neoliberal ideology on Caribbean universities, an ideology that emphasizes the standardization of student experience and tends to treat students as customers to push through the system rather than as budding scholars in which to invest resources. In short, *testing* is easier and cheaper than *teaching*. However, if *customer service* in the realm of university education means giving students/customers convenient access to the desired final product (good grades and their end degree), then many Caribbean universities have failed in serving their "customers" — by failing them in their courses. Enduring traditional methods of assessment such as strictly graded high-stakes end-of-semester testing have served in part to push students out of or away from higher education.

Because many Caribbean institutions have traditionally privileged the rhetoric of *excellence* rather than *equity* or *access,* this has led to grading standards in academic writing and other classes that can seem punitive to faculty trained outside the Caribbean (see, for example, Oenbring, 2017). Going further with reading the Caribbean economic situation onto Anglophone Caribbean higher education practices, one might even argue that these seemingly elitist tendencies within Caribbean higher education serve to protect the small Caribbean intelligentsia class from competition for the limited resources and limited job opportunities that anemic Caribbean economies can support; it is in the best economic interest for faculty in the Caribbean intelligentsia class to *fight students off with a stick*.

Also partially inherited from the colonial education system, many Anglophone Caribbean universities utilize a hierarchical faculty structure for assessment and grading, especially for student final exams and end-of-semester papers. Student papers in many Anglophone Caribbean institutions are regularly subjected to required second grading by other faculty. Furthermore, in institutions that span more than one campus, island, or territory in the Caribbean such as The University of the West Indies, and that participate in such grading practices, it is, for example, possible for the grade a student's instructor gives the student's final exam or final essay to be changed by a higher-level faculty member on a different campus or island, who has had no contact with the student during the course, based solely on that higher-level faculty member's personal assessment of the student's essay or exam. These grading and norming protocols, which may seem involved, even byzantine, to outsiders, affect how and why Caribbean writing instructors comment on essays. Indeed, while in the American tradition of composition instruction, commenting on and assessing student papers is largely a one-way written monologue from the individual instructor to the individual student, in many Caribbean territories, conversely, commenting on student papers, especially final assignments, is a much more laborious collective activity. That is to say, while the audience of American composition instructors' marginal comments is largely the student, in many Caribbean institutions the audience of instructor comments is both the student and other instructors.

With many Anglophone Caribbean composition instructors' professional identities being based on the *greater rigor* (read: punitive grading) of their instruction, especially in comparison to American universities (Oenbring, 2017), an environment may be fostered in which instructors, in the interest of saving face during group grading and standardization meetings, potentially give students' papers lower grades than they feel the students may actually deserve. That is to say, Caribbean universities' hierarchical assessment structure and involved norming procedures may lead to posturing and/or instructors piling negative comments on essays. In such grading contexts, frequent use of the *expression* comment, among others, may be seen as a signifier of instructor toughness, with multiple *expression* comments potentially serving to induce a grading feeding frenzy among the different graders. Indeed, instructors' *expression* comments clearly play a significant role in the Jamaican writing instruction community's ingroup grading practices and in the community's ideological construction of writing failure.

Speech Act Theory

Straub and Lunsford's (1995) seminal work on teachers' responses to students' writing offers us categories that are relevant for examining instructors' comments geared towards guiding students' revision. Straub and Lunsford recommend that written comments be examined from two perspectives: *focus*, which identifies what a comment refers to, and *mode*, which looks at the degree of control the comment exerts over the student's writing. At a deeper level, Straub and Lunsford's proposal dovetails with Searle's (1969; 2010) speech act theory (SAT), which treats language performance as ultimately a public exteriorization of the contents of our private, psychological, and cognitive states of human consciousness that represent the biological and neurological foundations of human language.

However, it is important to clarify that SAT is not designed to engage in clairvoyance or metaphysical speculations on the private ephemeral thoughts of instructors when they are commenting on student papers. Instead, SAT fundamentally recognizes that language is constitutive of linguistic meaning, human consciousness, and social reality. Furthermore, SAT posits that language is primarily designed to facilitate communication about the external world. Though SAT accounts for spontaneous, face-to-face interactive exchanges and non-contemplative communication, it also recognizes that written communication, similar to speech, exteriorizes the writer's beliefs, intent, emotions, attitudes, and perceptions. Therefore, the act of responding to students' work through written marginal and end comments is fundamentally an interpretive task, involving an (at least putative) act of communication, whether the instructor's evaluative opinions as *expression* comments are geared towards students' immediate revision or not. Indeed, in responding to students' writing, the instructor is engaged in an act of communicating with an imagined interlocutor, a novice student writer affecting what they believe to be an academic voice as they learn the codes of academic writing.

METHODS

For the current study, I collected a sample corpus of academic essays written by students from across the disciplines from a number of my previously completed first-year writing courses and asked a group of experienced writing instructors at my institution (five female and one male) to reevaluate and comment on the essays in the manner that they normally would for student papers in their classes. In total, 120 different essays (20 per instructor) were assessed. Selected primarily for convenience and accessibility, the essays evaluated for this study were high-stakes, out-of-class essays written at the end of the semester; the comments provided on the essays were not directly oriented towards facilitating students' revision. Indeed, for the study, instructors' comments, including their *expression* comments, appear to reflect the marking community's general predisposition to provide comments that offer aid to their colleagues in second marking, cross-moderation, and students' anticipated requests for remarking. Although the instructors provided marginal and end comments on several areas, such as grammar, documentation, content, and paragraph development, *expression* comments were singled out for analysis in the study.

Unlike a normal end-of-semester grading session, the reevaluation of the essays for current study was not preceded by the marking community's traditional norming session in which preselected practice essays are marked and discussed to ensure consistency among instructors. Moreover, the papers did not go through second marking where previously marked essays are given to a colleague for review of comments and checking of grades. Nor were the essays subject to moderation, an activity in which a team leader helps to resolve disagreements among instructors as well as attend to fine details in anticipation of students' potentially requesting a remarking. While the absence of these routines might appear to be limitations, they were offset by the fact that all the instructors were experienced composition teachers, with four having at least fifteen years of teaching experience. All instructors agreed to and obeyed a marking period turnaround of two weeks. This marking period simulated the official marking period of the university. While in a real essay assessment situation the possibility of second marking can be face-threatening for instructors, potentially encouraging them to conform to what they believe the grading standards of their marking community are, or even to engage in posturing, the lack of planned second grading or cross-moderation activities for this study may have encouraged participating instructors to be more honest in their responses to the essays.

For the study, all instructors used a holistic marking rubric normally used at our university for scoring English Language essays that included analysis, content, organization, style, mechanics, and documentation. The essays were based on preselected general topics and carried a one-thousand-word limit. Both the students and the instructors consented to their materials being used for my PhD thesis and all related publications. In keeping with recommended protocols and ethical considerations, all identifying information has been removed for all participants. The perceived offending linguistic structures that *expression* comments targeted were identified by the graders through visual cues such as squiggly lines, circling, or underlining on the students' papers. For consistency, clarity, and accuracy in presenting samples of these *expression* targets, from different students' essays in this chapter, I put in bold the precise sequence of words that the instructors originally treated as constituting the *expression* error.

Examples of *Expression* Comments from the Corpus

Recalling Straub and Lunsford's recommendation that written comments be examined by taking into consideration their *focus*, I categorized the targets of the *expression* comments in the essays in the corpus on linguistic grounds. I identified a range of offending linguistic structures marked with *expression* comments, including: prefabricated expressions, lexical interferences, subject-verb agreement issues, and academic writing documentation conventions. What follows is a list, though not an exhaustive or ordered one, of some prototypical examples of the structures instructors targeted when writing the comment *expression*:

1. The offending structure presents no obvious syntactic, morphological, lexical, or Standard English grammatical error itself but serves as the lynchpin of a poorly formed or vague structure or sentence.

   *An example of emotional loneliness is when bullied teens feel lonely **in the sense** that no one understands them or what they are going through. (expression).*

2. The offending structure is syntactically garbled; that is, the words are jumbled.

   *There are many reports about **gay men being that were mobbed** by heterosexuals men and in most cases these gays are either beaten or shot fatally. (expression).*

3. The offending structure has missing information or a missing word necessary for complete comprehension.

   *Increasingly **it is becoming** for mothers to head the household in Jamaica due to the absenteeism of fathers (expression).*

4. The offending structure carries a word choice error based on the intended meaning of the sentence.

   *The absence of father in the household can be **very unrewarding in the upcoming of the children** in the household as this can lead to psychological effects. (expression).*

5. The offending structure contains a grammatical "error" in Standard English (in this case, a subject-verb agreement issue).

   *In the 21st century, women being barred from leadership roles **are backward ideologies** in a democratic society, therefore the barriers of socialization, gender stereotyping and female leadership styles should be ideas of the past. (expression)*

6. The offending structure is concerned with the conventional language of documentation.

   *Many of the household in Jamaica are female headed according to 2002 data from the Planning Institute of Jamaica also **as reported in the article**, children from absent father homes manifest a number of problem including aggression, delinquency and sex role difficulties. (expression)*

Locating the Source of Expression 'Errors' — Jamaican Creole or English?

It may be tempting to assume that most Standard English "errors" in papers written by Jamaican and other Caribbean students result from the interference of structures in students' home languages. However, we must exercise caution before we arrive at such a conclusion. Jamaica's language situation is complex and has been variously described by linguists. On one hand, the sociolinguistic environment in Jamaica has been characterized by Devonish (1986) as *diglossic* on the basis that "there are two separate language varieties, each with its own specific functions within the society" (p. 9). However, many linguists (e.g., Winford, 1997) prefer instead to refer to the Jamaican language situation as a *creole continuum*, involving a range of different varieties.

Milson-Whyte (2015) highlights that the Jamaican sociolinguistic context facilitates a variety of transcultural speech practices, such as code shifting, code mixing, and code switching. In the Jamaican context, a code shifter could be a monolingual Jamaican Creole speaker performing in his or her inadequately acquired L2, Jamaican Standard English, and therefore, changes into his or her L1 and continuously maintains the change to cope with the linguistic demands of the situation. A Jamaican code mixer displays an interesting psychological behavior; he or she mixes language codes, without being aware as the "mixer" that the mixed code is not Standard English, resulting in sentences such as "is English we speaking" (Morris, 1999). Code switchers in Jamaica command a series of registers through which they shift without any obvious motivation; however, some registers that are not Standard English may be psychologically perceived as such.

The shift from oral language to writing can be very daunting for Jamaican students since "the attributes of transcultural peoples, especially how creole-influenced students do language" (Milson-Whyte, 2015, p. 37) remain unacknowledged in formal writing classrooms, despite Milson-Whyte's call for the adoption of a transcultural rhetorical approach to writing development in higher education in Jamaica. However, I would cautiously suggest, that since Standard English is not technically a foreign language in Jamaica, we can connect some of these "errors" to students' academic interlanguage, which these neophyte writers have developed to help them cope with the demands of academic writing.

One of these coping strategies involves what Nero (2010) describes as "*revising* (italics mine) into edited academic English" (p.142) the alternate discourse styles from the academic interlanguage, which reflect the writer's own internalized version of a standard. Interlanguages tend to be independent of both the native language and the target language; hence, they have "items produced by the learner which reflect not the structure of the mother tongue . . . nor the target language" (Richards, 1974, p. 6). In such an interlanguage, it is quite possible that the non-idiomaticity of many of the *expression* errors could arise from:

1. Not knowing the grammatical, semantic and structural collocational restrictions placed on English subjects, verbs, and complements.
2. Assuming English prefabricated phrases to be synonymous and interchangeable with other lexical items.
3. Presenting mixed registers composed of formal written English academic structures and interactional English language structures.

However, when I evaluated the study corpus of essays, I did not find compelling patterns of syntactic, lexical, or semantic correspondence between Jamaican Creole structures and students' developing interlanguages. Moreover, attributing writing development errors primarily to Jamaican students' Creole linguistic background, without paying attention to other important factors such as context, audience, and class, may contribute to the promotion of cultural stereotypes and expectations on the ways these students may write as well as erroneous predictions and generalizations on how their writing behaviors ought to be.

Communicative Analysis — Speech Act Theory

In this section, I use speech act theory (SAT) to examine the potential communicative impacts that *expression* comments might engender on students' beliefs and attitudes towards writing. It is important to highlight that instructors' written comments on students' papers are inherently ambiguous—in the sense that, whether they were intended to facilitate revision or not, comments invite varied interpretations. What's more, instructor comments can potentially be contradictory. Reading instructors' comments is always interpretive work; therefore, in the following section I focus my analysis on the potential ways in which comments could be read by students. I will commence with an examination of *assertives*, followed by *directives*, then close with *declarations*.

Exploring Assertives

If *expression* comments are regarded as *assertives* in the SAT tradition, then they could be interpreted as being concerned with the provision of epistemically objective information, regarding the erroneous nature or accuracy of the students' vocabulary choices. In the SAT tradition, *assertives* are statements that purport to represent how things are in the real world. They are generally assessed as *true* or *false*, depending on the extent to which they do successfully represent this object–representation correspondence (Searle, 2010, p. 11). *Assertives* assume the existence of an independently, preexisting objective reality that the writer's beliefs and perceptions are matching in a transparent correspondence. Therefore, expression comments in this marking community could be interpreted by students as implied statements, descriptions, characterizations, or explanations about the inherent "correctness / incorrectness" of the vocabulary choices in their text.

Expression comments were presented unaccompanied—that is, without any direct recommendations for revision by instructors and also detached from the instructors' authorial identity as the origin of the subjective criticism being levelled at the target. Especially in an assessment context where comments on returned student essays are often written by individuals other than students' instructors and student feedback is *unauthored*, students could, therefore, potentially interpret the message of *expression* comments as an eternal truth. This suggestion heralds Russell's (2002) critique of the transparency model of language that might guide some composition instructors to be convinced that their comments are a transparent recording of reality. Milson-Whyte's (2015) summary of Russell's understanding of the transparency model indicates that a disciple of this ideology "may . . . consider writing as a neutral transparent medium for accurately and objectively recording ideas and knowledge" (p. 23).

Exploring Directives

If *expression* comments are treated as *directives*, then the underlying message could be interpreted as indirect requests to engage in some writing revision activity. In the SAT tradition, *directives* are the speech acts that are relied on to change external reality to match the speaker's (or in this case the writer's) desires. The writer's desire to change external reality invites the undertaking of an activity, changing a behavior, or demanding obedience to comply with his or her personal idealizations, preferences, or expectations. *Expression* comments, as *directives*, therefore, have the power to shift students' linguistic choices towards the instructor's romanticized ideas of Standard Written English as a stable, fixed, homogenous, and relatively unchanged linguistic code. Nero (2010) criticizes this attitude as endowed in linguistic prescriptivism since such idealizations ignore "the reality of evolving languages and discourses defying our perceptions of and desires for fixed linguistic codes" (p. 142). What Nero is pointing out is the existence of other Englishes such as African American Vernacular English, Caribbean Creole Englishes, or English as a Second Language. If Jamaican composition instructors valorize Standard Written English and its linguistic and rhetorical forms, then they may have psychological aversions and resistance towards students' use of hybrid language forms that for Jamaican students would consist of a mixture of eye-dialect versions of Jamaican Creole words, phrases, and expressions and Standard Written English school-based discourses.

For students to satisfy instructors' language and vocabulary expectations, especially if these expectations are not made visible in the instructors' own language practices, students' linguistic inventiveness will be curtailed as students become circumspect in their vocabulary choices when composing so as to ensure that their writing is not tainted with vernacular peculiarities, such as **"international top quality"** as displayed in the following example:

> "Jamaica, a tropical island, in the Caribbean once infamous for piracy, for its rum, and in recent times more so for its marijuana, has a longstanding reputation for ganja of **international top quality.**"

Disparaging this language choice as appearing stilted and unidiomatic undermines the student's attempt to "transcreate" as Flores (1993, p. 219) says of some bilingual students' efforts to exploit the resources of different languages while writing. *Expression* comments can, therefore, encourage stifling injunctions that might prompt students to write in ways that promote self-erasure from their own texts, lead them to distance themselves from their authorial identity and create prose that, in their attempts to live up to vague idealized standards and directives, might contribute to the loss of language ownership, making them feel as if they are writing in a "foreign accent" (Mao, 2010, p. 189). This sense of being estranged from one's prose can reinforce low expectations.

Exploring Declarations

If *expression* comments are treated as *declarations* in the SAT model, with no conditions of satisfaction to be fulfilled, the declared aesthetic judgements, evaluative opinions, and interpretive assessments the instructors make of the student's text represent the instructor's subjective, personally and socially constructed reality of the text itself. Searle (2010) defines *declarations* as the speech acts anchored in the psychological realm of imagination. This definition suggests that *declarations* are the speech acts that provide language users with the linguistic freedom to bring into existence sociocultural content, such as aesthetic judgements, evaluative opinions, and normative facts, because they are freed from conditions of satisfaction, such as true/false or obey/disobey distinctions being imposed on them. However, this subjective reality can be transmitted by the instructor to the students through the *expression* comments that create the impression as if this subjective version of reality was predetermined, inevitable and without a sense of history—void of the instructor's own agency, comprehension, and interpretation of the student's text. While the message that would be conveyed to students is that their linguistic choices were objectively aberrant, the students must be made aware that the atomic elements of language—prepositional phrases, embedded clauses, verbs, noun phrases, modal verbs, and sentences—were neutral.

I argue that just as instructors inscribe cultural- and social-value-laden notions onto the students' linguistic choices through grading terms such as *awkward, imprecise, incomprehensible, nonidiomatic*, students should be taught to appreciate the sociocultural appraisals of language as relative conceptualizations heavily influenced by contextual considerations. Without this awareness, students may not be able to see academic language as arbitrary conventions. In this sense, students may fail to see their linguistic choices as contributing to the realization of social contexts, an observation Halliday (1993) regards as preventing students from simultaneously recognizing the power of language in being "a part of reality, a shaper of reality, and a metaphor for reality" (p. 108).

Recall the following excerpt from a student essay that received an *expression* comment—likely due to its incorrect use of academic documentation conventions:

> *Many of the household in Jamaica are female headed according to 2002 data from the Planning Institute of Jamaica also **as reported in the article**, children from absent father homes manifest a number of problem including aggression, delinquency and sex role difficulties.*

In this case, inexperienced student writers may only superficially respond to the nudge for correction. Indeed, students' attempts to affect an academic voice with limited knowledge of the conventions of academic documentation may cause them to develop stilted linguistic habits such as flowery language, semantic fluffs—and more troubling practices such as plagiarism. In other words, without a clear understanding of the conventionalized features of academic documentation and academic language more generally, students may resort to language patterns that do not help them to use citation, facilitate debate, persuade, and avoid plagiarism (Harwood, 2008). Rather than focusing on developing these important academic writing skills, students may shift towards *hypercorrect* forms such as the passive voice (a well-known feature of legal writing and science). (Interestingly, as Roberts [2007] suggests, some Anglophone Caribbean people have a distinct esteem for stiltedly formal language, a style that he refers to as *erudite English*.)

Expression Comments from the Instructor's Perspective — A Systemic Functional Linguistics (SFL) Approach

I now turn my analysis towards instructors and their possible reasons for making *expression* comments. Within the community of Jamaican postsecondary writing instructors, what is it about the structure of the targets of the *expression* comments that makes the instructors treat the language as structurally deficient and/or inappropriate word choice?

The lens of systemic functional linguistics (SFL) offers potential clues. Years of socialization within academic discourse communities have led instructors to have certain expectations regarding what constitutes good academic writing. With regard to the social construction of academic writing registers, work in the tradition of SFL has found that academic texts make heavy and consistent reliance on technical, abstract, and specialized disciplinary jargon and have a number of distinct syntactic features (e.g., compound noun phrases). If a student's academic essay does not meet the instructor's expectations regarding academic writing registers, the text, like the essay excerpt from the study below in which the student addresses the topic "science and ageing," could be perceived negatively by instructors. In the essay excerpt, the student addresses the impacts of cosmetic surgery on women fifty years and older. One of the impacts highlighted in the student's thesis statement is the risks associated with circulatory or pulmonary problems relating to blood clots. In the student's attempt to elucidate and support this idea, the sentence containing the target for the comment *expression* was written.

Essay 1

> Broad topic: Science and Ageing
>
> Narrowed topic: Impacts of cosmetic surgery on women fifty years and older.
>
> **One day later she was found dead in her bed by her husband,** an autopsy was done and it listed the cause of death as "massive saddle pulmonary embolism." Although Embolism and Thrombosis may cause fatality another cause of fatality may due to blood loss and allergic reactions. (*expression*)

While the offending sentence as a whole contains a comma splice, it seems clear, given the fact that the instructor's indicated focus for the *expression* comment doesn't cross the clause boundary demarcated by the comma, that the comma splice isn't the targeted linguistic issue. The issue instead appears to be the fact that the clause in question isn't formal enough for the assumed scientific academic context. Moreover, the (probably unwitting) rhyme *dead in her bed* may seem unsuitable for scholarly discourse. Indeed, for this Jamaican instructor, the student clearly violates the expectations of written academic discourse, captured in the student's departure from the expected scientific/academic discourse of objectivity, and authoritativeness; *dead in her bed* seems to belong more to the discourse of the neighborhood busybody rather than a scientist/scholar.

Another way in which SFL addresses the social construction of academic language is to posit that academic writing typically shows frequent or dominant usage of declarative sentences, questions, and commands. Unfortunately, such narrow and traditional idealisms on academic writing may promote the view that effective written academic language must exhibit precision, a highly prized characteristic, originating from the skillful use of linguistic forms to make texts informationally dense in presenting information. By remaining rigidly wedded to these linguistic expectations in the language of developing academic writers, Jamaican composition instructors who admonish students not to use nontraditional linguistic forms to project authoritativeness, credibility, and knowledgeableness reinforce the belief that language choices that show imprecision, vagueness, and redundancy are always empty of any logical information.

Another pattern of usage in the academic community that we can analyze through the lens of SFL is academic discourse's use of traditional transitional words (like *however*, *furthermore*, and *nevertheless*) as discourse markers, signposts, and indicators of logical relationships between sentences. While such traditional transition words are common in academic writing, they are notably absent from most oral communication. Consider the following excerpt from a student essay in which the student examines the ways the Jamaican government can use sports to enhance tourism and build up the country's reserves of hard currency.

Essay 2

> Broad Topic: Sports and National Development
>
> Narrowed Topic: Ways in which the Government of Jamaica can use sports to enhance tourism and earn foreign exchange
>
> Therefore, not only will the country benefit economically but also it will gain global exposure. **A point in case** is the recently concluded London Olympics, where the National Broadcasting Commission in Jamaica had **to fork out** about US one billion dollars for the exclusive television rights to the hosting nation. (*expression*)

To give an example, the student relies on the phrase *a point in case*. Apart from the unidiomatic nature of the phrasing, considering SFL's perspective on expectations for written academic language appropriateness, this turn of phrase could be seen as too pedestrian, too informal, or too semantically loose to establish the valued social relationships signaled in the implied financial negotiations in the sentence above. The instructor's likely preference for discourse markers such as *however, furthermore,* and *for example* as transitional words and phrases to construct relationships of connectedness has not been satisfied. However, this idealization, if insisted on by instructors as the only appropriate means of realizing the logical and organizational structural relationships like cause and effect, problem and solution, or general to specific may push students to equate writing with formality. Canagarajah (2010) implies that rejecting a colloquial phrase can have a limiting effect on student writing given that such comments may encourage instructors to teach that "writing is formal and requires the established codes" (p. 286). A constricting notion of writing can teach students to become overly self-conscious and not take the kinds of risk necessary for their development as writers.

RE-ENVISIONING *EXPRESSION* COMMENTS — DEVIANCE VERSUS OPPORTUNITY?

To shift perspectives, instructors will have to begin to see academic language learning and development as incremental and inextricably bound to a student's personal, emotional, and cognitive development, though heavily influenced by social factors. Most importantly, learning has to be conceptualized as highly individualized and oriented towards endonormative models, the learners' own personal social construction, representation, and interpretation of academic language, not the instructor's idealization (Kohn, 2012). It is within this former conceptualization that notions like endowing learners with agency, ownership, identity, and autonomy to freely construct and experiment with language usage through approximations and adaptations are strongly encouraged. Emanating from this perspective is the suggestion for instructors to be willing to accommodate what they perceive to be "deviant" linguistic structures by appreciating the situational context of usage, the comprehensibility of the underlying message, and the communicative competence achieved by the students (see, for example, Lu, 1994; Horner, Lu, Royster & Trimbur, 2011).

To put this perspective into practical application: here are suggestions for how the instructor could re-see the student's selection of vocabulary in these previously discussed examples. Continued examination of the error above shows that the infelicitous clause *one day later she was found dead in her bed by her husband* is adrift momentarily. Admittedly, the rupturing of the scientific tenor of the academic discourse resulted in prose that became gossipy. However, here is the student demonstrating not linguistic incompetence but a challenge with maintaining an assumed academic authorial identity. I would suggest that rather than the instructor's seeing this shift as degradation in word choice/diction, the instructor could recognize instead a novice writer whose inexperience with the specialized discourse of the university and maintaining their authorial identity are still being shaped.

Indeed, as Bartholomae (2001) reminds readers, it is by "mimicking its language, finding some compromise between idiosyncrasy, a personal history, and the requirements of convention, and the history of a discipline" (p. 511) that students eventually learn to master the language requirements of the university. Therefore, instructors must ensure that *expression* comments do not contribute to students' developing a sense of linguistic insecurity. To avoid this situation, both writing instructors and content faculty should make explicit to students the rhetorical and register features of written texts and the linguistic expectations of genres in various writing assignments to achieve what Milson-Whyte (2015) designates as *visible rhetoric* through vocabulary development activities and rhetorical analyses of discipline-specific texts.

In the other example above, the failed transitional device *point in case* shows an attempt at creating connectedness and continuity across boundaries in a paper. Recall that in the sentence directly preceding, before the language that triggered the *expression* comment, the student does use a traditional academic transition word: *Therefore, the country will not only benefit economically but also gain global exposure.* However, *point in case* is both unidiomatic and too informal to be accepted by the instructor. The student's struggle exemplified in the essay captures a writer's continued learning and development through language experimentation on the boundaries of language acceptability/unacceptability in a context of shifting social practices and the continued evolution of "standards." Additionally, the apparent simplicity captured in *to fork out* might appear to be too informal and pedestrian for the expected language used in contexts of negotiation between buyers and sellers. Overall, the selection of these linguistic structures shows inexperienced writers rather than language decay. My recommendation is for instructors to re-see such sentence-level choices as attempts by students to explore the discursive practices of academic writing through experimentation, internalization, and approximation while coming to terms with the realities of language being used to rhetorically construct knowledge, language appropriateness, and language acceptability. This approach can tap into Horner's (2001) advocacy for translingualism, encouraging instructors to motivate students to question "acceptability . . . by whom, under what conditions, when written by whom in what sort of text and to challenge the shifting paradigms of language acceptability/ unacceptability" (p. 754). Such rhetorical and cultural critiques on language use and appropriateness will empower students to uncover the hidden ideologies embedded within discourses.

Conclusion

Expression comments, then, have the ability to reinforce the existing status quo that penalizes and marginalizes linguistic choices that epitomize students' negotiation and approximation of the grammatical and lexical patterns of academic writing. Jamaican academic writing instructors excessive use of *expression* comments can potentially stymie students' academic language development, promote overly conformist attitudes to writing, and dissuade students from undertaking linguistic innovations, even within the constraints imposed on school-based writing products. Furthermore, Jamaican postsecondary instructors' use of *expression* comments seem to challenge, if not undermine, broader efforts made by linguists and progressive scholars in the field(s) of writing studies internationally at changing the conversations and current social realities on linguistic prejudice, language equality, authorial identity, and vernacular language inclusion in relation to student writing and their vocabulary choices. Admittedly, many of these political confrontations have not become dominant themes in local academic writing advocacy in the Caribbean, but their non-institutionalization does not mean that Jamaican instructors and writing administrators are not keenly aware of their responsibility in embracing, affirming, and valuing students' right to their own language (Perryman-Clark, Kirkland, & Jackson, 2015).

Writing in response to the ways that African American students' oral discourse is erased in academic writing instruction, Gilyard and Richardson (2015) argue that demanding rigidity and conformity in student writing is antithetical to progressive pedagogical practices that have championed the usage of alienated African American discourse practices and rhetorical patterns such as evocative language, ethnolinguistic idioms, verbal inventiveness, and conversational tone in academic writing for the development of basic writers. Following in Gilyard and Richardson's footsteps, Jamaican instructors may need to display similar sensitivities towards students' writing and minimize the ways *expression* comments could demean students writing, especially struggling student writers in the university. It is in this vein that I offer this chapter as one way to consider how marking can influence student behavior and how reconsidering approaches to comments on student papers could assist students in finding their own authentic academic voice.

REFERENCES

Bartholomae, D. (2001). Inventing the university. In E. Cushman, E. Kingten, B. Kroll, & M. Rose (Eds.), *Literacy: A critical sourcebook* (pp. 511–524). Boston: Bedford-St. Martin's.

Burke, K. (1945). *A Grammar of motives*. London: Prentice Hall.

Canagarajah, A. S. (2010). A rhetoric of shuttling between languages. In B. Horner, M. Lu, & P. K. Matsuda (Eds.), *Cross-language relations in composition* (pp. 158–179). Carbondale, IL: Southern Illinois University Press.

Devonish, H. (1986). *Language and liberation: Creole language politics in the Caribbean*. London: Karia Press.

Flores, J. (1993). *Divided borders: Essays on Puerto Rican identity*. Houston, TX: Arte Publico Press.

Gilyard, K., & Richardson, E. (2015). Students' right to possibility: Basic writing and African American rhetoric. In S. Perryman-Clark, D. E. Kirkland, & A. Jackson (Eds.), *Student's right to their own language: A critical sourcebook* (pp. 140–149). Boston: Bedford-St. Martin's.

Halliday, M. A. K. (1993). Towards a language-based theory of learning. *Linguistics and Education, 5*(2), 93–116.

Harwood, N. (2008). An interview-based study of the functions of citations in academic writing across two disciplines. *Journal of Pragmatics, 41*(3), 497–518.

Horner, B. (2001). Students' right, English only, and reimagining the politics of language. *College English, 46*, 742–758.

Horner, B., Lu, M., Royster, J. J., & Trimbur, J. (2011). Opinion: Language difference in writing: Toward a translingual approach. *College English, 73*, 303–321.

Kohn, K. (2012). My English: Second language learning as individual and social construction. *TESOL, 4,* 28–31.

Lu, M. (1994). Professing multiculturalism: The politics of style in the contact zone. *College Composition and Communication, 45,* 442–458.

Mao, L. (2010) Why don't we speak with an accent? Practicing interdependence-in-difference. In B. Horner, M. Lu, & P. K. Matsuda (Eds.), *Cross-language relations in composition* (pp. 189–195). Carbondale, IL: Southern Illinois University Press.

Milson-Whyte, V. (2015). *Academic writing instruction for creole-influenced students.* Kingston, Jamaica: University of the West Indies Press.

Morris, M. (1999). *Is English we speaking and other essays.* Kingston, Jamaica: Ian Randle Publishers.

Nero, S. (2010). Discourse, tensions, englishes, and the composition classrooms. In B. Horner, M. Lu, & P. K. Matsuda (Eds.), *Cross-language relations in composition* (pp. 142–157). Carbondale, IL: Southern Illinois University Press.

Oenbring, R. (2017). College composition in the Anglophone Caribbean: The search for a Caribbean identity. *Journal of Global Literacies, Technology and Emerging Pedagogies, 4*(1), 533–545.

Perryman-Clark, S., Kirkland, D. & Jackson, A. (2015). Understanding the complexities associated with what it means to have the right to your own language. In S. Perryman-Clark, D. E. Kirkland, & A. Jackson (Eds.), *Student's right to their own language: A critical sourcebook* (pp. 1–6). Boston: Bedford-St. Martin's.

Richards, J. C. (1974). Error analysis and second language strategies. In J. H. Schumann & N. Stenson (Eds.), *New frontiers in second language learning* (6–32). Rowley, MA: Newbury House.

Roberts, P. (2007). *West Indians and their language.* Cambridge: Cambridge University Press.

Russell, D. (2002). *Writing in the academic disciplines: A curricular history.* Carbondale, IL: Southern Illinois University Press.

Searle, J. (1969). *Speech acts: An essay in the philosophy of language.* Cambridge: Cambridge University Press.

Searle, J. (2010). *Making the social world: The structure of human civilization.* New York: Oxford University Press.

Sommers, N. (1982). Responding to student writing. *College Composition and Communication, 33*(2): 148–156.

Straub, R. & Lunsford, R. (1995). *12 readers reading: Responding to college student writing.* New Jersey: Hampton Press.

Winford, D. (1997). Reexamining Caribbean English Creole continua. *World Englishes, 16* (2): 233–279.

6 Balancing Composition and Grammar in the UTech, Jamaica Classroom

Daidrah Smith and Michelle Stewart-McKoy

Background

Within different contexts in the Anglophone Caribbean, one often hears of how poorly secondary school students in Jamaica and other Caribbean territories perform on the regional Caribbean Secondary School Certificate (CSEC) English examination. Somehow, however, persons seem to be disappointed, shocked, and downright appalled when they realize that these same students, in their pursuit of higher education, struggle to write at the tertiary (postsecondary) level. *Poor, atrocious, substandard,* and *abominable* are only a few of the labels that have been used in reference to students' writing at this level. Such labels are usually not used because students' writing lacks cohesion or logic so much but seem to be used mainly because of the large number and wide variety of Standard English grammatical errors that students tend to make whenever they write.

In conversations surrounding Caribbean students' production of Standard English in formal written documents, many educators and researchers encounter an academic cul-de-sac, with different conversations entertaining different accusatory tones on the matter. Some dialogues speak to poor teaching styles, some to poor learner competence, some highlight inadequate curricular systems and approaches, and others point to historically entrenched misconceptions. In this chapter, we examine the discourse of academic writing in the English-speaking Caribbean tertiary-level classroom, and focus our discussion on the matter of balancing composition in English (that is postsecondary level writing strategies) and English grammar (that is, the rules regarding forms/structures and meanings of words and their arrangements in phrases, clauses, and sentences) in the University of Technology, Jamaica (UTech, Jamaica) classrooms.

STANDARD ENGLISH LANGUAGE CHALLENGES IN JAMAICA

Journalist Erica Virtue in her January 27, 2013 article "Bloody English! UWI, UTech students struggle with the language" that was published in one of Jamaica's newspapers, the *Sunday Gleaner*, highlights what she, and many others, perceive as the abominable and deteriorating Standard English language abilities of tertiary-level students at the two major universities (the University of Technology, Jamaica and The University of the West Indies, Mona [UWI, Mona]) in Jamaica. Many of these students, she points out, recurrently register for, pursue, and fail communication courses (writing and oral communication modules) during their academic tenure. The Standard English language situation at UTech, Jamaica seems to parallel that of UWI, Mona. Journalist Philip Hamilton, in his December 6, 2010 newspaper article "English test trips up university students," discloses that forty percent of students attending UTech, Jamaica fail English-based communication courses, with the majority of those passing (sixty percent) struggling to attain the passes they receive. In an academic study, Jones McKenzie and Orogun (2010) explain that UTech, Jamaica students, in their attempts to produce compositions in Standard English, make a number of errors, and as such display grave deficiencies in their ability to communicate efficiently in Standard Jamaican English (SJE). The research of Smith, Stewart-McKoy, Henry, and Hamilton (2015), which examined the performance of 2,562 UTech, Jamaica students on the university's proficiency test in English, corroborates the work of Jones McKenzie and Orugon (2010), which showed many students struggle to master Standard English in the production of their academic work.

A TRAJECTORY OF HISTORY, MYTHS, AND DENIALS

McLaren, Dyche, Altidor-Brooks, Taylor, and Devonish (2009) argue that, since the establishment of the first higher education institution in Jamaica, there have been time-honored, indelible assumptions passed down that have lasted to the present day. In their work, they explain that the British colonial authorities implemented English (via language policies) as "the subject par excellence" (p. 63). They further illustrate that "the establishment and perpetuation . . . of the dominance of an English-speaking elite, has played a key-role in entrenching English-as-a-mother-tongue mythology" (p. 63). Craig (1976) in his discussion, speaks too of the over-a-century-old fiction that "Standard English was the mother tongue of West Indian Creole-speaking or Creole-influenced children" (p. 100). Based on these ideas:

> It is still assumed that a Commonwealth Caribbean university would have a native English-speaking clientele. In addition, there is the complementary expectation that primary and secondary schools functioning monolingually in English would equip these students with the English language competence required of university entrants. There is thus no real place for the provision of English language communication skills at the university level. These have supposedly already been developed by students at the time they entered the institution. (McLaren et al., 2009, p. 64)

Although the focus of our discussion lies within the Anglophone Caribbean context, discourse surrounding or pertaining to students' language challenges is often made to seem as if these English challenges are unique to Jamaican or Caribbean tertiary-level students. However, research in the academic writing arena reveals that other tertiary-level students have struggled with writing courses, and their deteriorating writing performance and skills have overwhelmed lecturers internationally (Baden, 1974). In fact, what these writers have made clear is that learners of English tend to struggle with the same challenges and make many of the same errors in producing written work in Standard English.

CREOLE-INFLUENCED STUDENTS

In our study, we adopt the term *creole-influenced students* as utilized by Milson-Whyte (2015). In her explanation of and justification for the term, Milson-Whyte argues that although all Jamaicans do not speak Jamaican Creole (JC), all encounter and are influenced by the language. She clarifies her discussion by explaining that some Jamaicans speak only English but understand Jamaican Creole, some speak Jamaican Creole only and may or may not understand English. Some are English-dominant bilingual speakers, others are Creole-dominant bilingual speakers, some speakers remain to be named, and others express dissent based on their linguistic profiles and language behaviors. Figure 1 provides a graphical representation of Milson-Whyte's descriptions of Creole-influenced speakers.

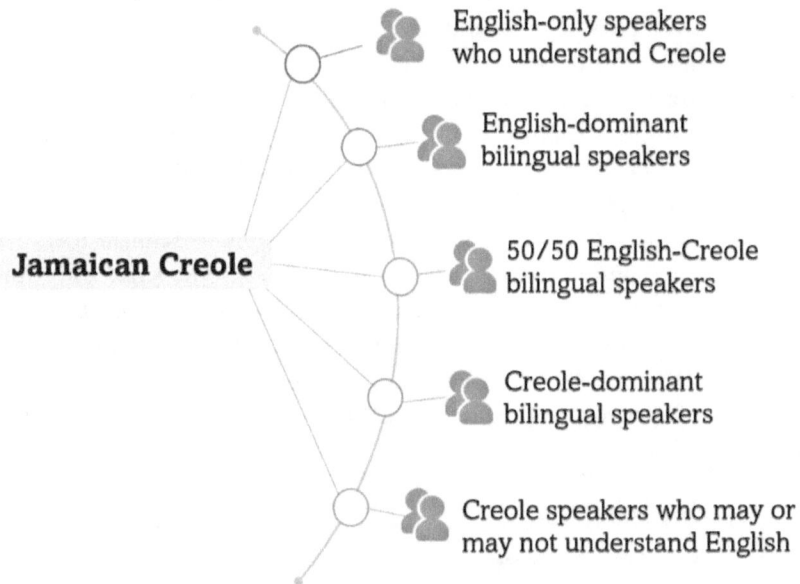

Figure 1. Descriptions of Creole-influenced speakers. Original source: Milson-Whyte (2015)

THE UTECH, JAMAICA CONTEXT

Prior to 2009, all students who matriculated into the University of Technology, Jamaica, regardless of their level of pass in the CSEC English Language examination, had to complete the same "communication" courses. Not surprisingly, this posed a challenge for both lecturers and students. Over the years, lecturers have been torn between teaching what they believe the students *should be learning* at the tertiary level and what they *need to learn* given their varying levels of competence. The two usually do not coincide.

The University of Technology, Jamaica, like many other tertiary level institutions worldwide, has attempted to implement strategies in a bid to improve the students' overall performance in writing. The School of Humanities and Social Sciences (formerly the Department of Liberal Studies), the section/department out of which writing courses are offered, has tweaked and re-tweaked its communication/writing courses based on observations made by lecturers to cater to the students' language needs. To cite an example, the curriculum for the writing course, Fundamentals of Communication taught at UTech, Jamaica, up to 2009, had specific objectives that required students to recognize and avoid common mistakes in grammar, structure, usage, and mechanics; to produce sustained writing at a level appropriate for university students; and to produce language which is grammatically and structurally coherent. However, it did not include any form of grammar instruction. In contrast, its revised, renamed counterpart *Academic Writing 1*, offered since 2010, includes a grammar review as a part of content to be covered between weeks one and five of the semester, and acknowledges learners' creole-influenced environment. The following extract in Figure 2, presents the list of topics to be covered in week one of the course:

Weeks	Topics	Reading/Teaching Aid	Out of Class Activities

Session 1 Aug 28- Sep 2	A. Overview of Module
	B. Expository Writing-Definition
	C. Effective Human Communication
	   ❖ The Communication Process
	   ❖ Factors which enhance or hinder oral and written communication
	   ❖ The inter-relatedness of language skills
	   ❖ Receptive skills (listening and reading): contribution to effective communication
	   ❖ Expressive skills (speaking and writing): contribution to effective communication
	D. Review Parts of Speech, Formal and Informal Language, and Types of Sentences
		• A Creole text preferably expository in nature will be used to discuss:
		  - communication model
		  - encoder-purpose
		  - medium-appropriateness
		  - decoder-audience
		  - feedback
		  - context-formal/informal
		  - Creole and Standard English grammar
		
		Activity
		Translate text from Creole to English then discuss formal version in context of the above
			1. Review what was done in class
			
			2. Complete Activities in the section of the workbook dealing with Jamaican Creole and Standard English
			
			3. Read up on rhetorical strategies with a focus on **cause and effect, comparison/contrast**

Figure 2. Extract from the Academic Writing 1 course outline

The Academic Writing 1 course has an accompanying student workbook (*Information Gathering, Processing, and Production*) that is aligned to and works with the course outline. Unit 2 of the workbook (pages 26 to 57) is dedicated to producing well-formed sentences in Standard English and describes language varieties in the Jamaican context as well as the features of Jamaican Creole and Jamaican Standard

English. The treatment of the creole and Standard English languages in the Academic Writing 1 workbook seems to parallel and perpetuate (albeit inadvertently) the negative, deep-rooted community attitudes towards creole. Additionally, the cursory handling of creole and Standard English languages seems to reflect and reinforce the myth that students are already accomplished learners and competent users of Standard English and merely require revision exercises to bring them to where they should be in the tertiary-level classroom. As language educators, we recommend the inclusion of a creole text in the teaching/learning process and the grammar of creole and Standard English in the students' Academic Writing 1 workbook and in the course outline.

Building off work previously presented in part in Smith and Stewart-McKoy (2017), the remainder of this chapter presents more of our error analysis study, identifying the key challenges that the creole-influenced students face in producing written work in Standard English, and the implications for tertiary-level writing courses in the UTech, Jamaica environment. We close the chapter by proposing what we consider to be practical strategies for consideration in effectively marrying the teaching of composition with grammar instruction in the Creole-influenced Anglophone Caribbean classroom.

THE ENGLISH LANGUAGE PROFICIENCY TEST

The English Language Proficiency Test (ELPT) enables the School of Humanities and Social Sciences to appraise the language competence of UTech, Jamaica entrants and to separate candidates with the lowest level of proficiency to apply corrective measures. Candidates who fail the test are required to enroll in and pass a basic writing module/course named *Foundation English* before they are allowed to select Academic Writing 1, the first compulsory writing course for all university students enrolled in degree programs at UTech, Jamaica. The candidates who take the ELPT at UTech, Jamaica complete two writing tasks: an essay of approximately 350 words and another writing task (usually a letter) of approximately 150 words. The essay carries greater weight in students' grades, which are calculated on a scale of 1–4, with 1 being highest. Students choose one of four topics, and their essays are graded using a 7-point scale (1, 1/2, 2, 2/3, 3, 3/4, 4). The grading scale is shown in Figure 3.

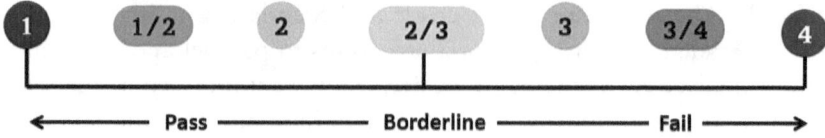

Figure 3. The 7-point grading groups used in the ELPT

For candidates to score a Grade 1 on the essay, they would have to satisfy the following criteria, according to the holistic ELPT Essay Rubric:

- Content is relevant and accurate
- Ideas are well developed and are logically organized
- English is correct and idiomatic (There are no systematic errors in sentence structure, grammar, or writing mechanics)
- Language is used effectively and economically (Tone and diction are appropriate for formal written discourse)
- A certain level of sophistication is often evident in the wording and in the control of sentence structure

This is in contrast to candidates who score a Grade 4, which is the bottom of the scale. A grade 4 essay, according to the rubric, means that a candidate's answer does not fulfill the task due to one or more of the following reasons:

- There are serious and recurrent sentence structure problems (sentence breakdown), which affect the fluency of the writing and/or the coherence of the message.
- There are recurrent and varying grammatical and/or mechanical errors at the level of individual words. These occur at a high level of frequency (i.e., they are pervasive).
- Idiomatic expression/vocabulary is generally very poor; this seriously affects the fluency of the writing and/or the comprehensibility of the message.
- Content may or may not be satisfactory. Ideas may or may not be developed and organized.

Methodology

To design an effective writing pedagogy for our specific environment, we must examine the errors that our students produce in their writing.

For the study, the systematic examination of errors was done by error analysis (EA), which is a means of identifying, describing, and classifying learner deviations from accepted standards (Brown, 2000; Corder, 1967). Language facilitators/academic writing instructors can use the results of EA research to design, develop, and advance pedagogical practices as well as to create more effective resources. For this study, we relied on computer-aided error analysis (Dagneaux, Dennes, & Granger, 1998; Thewissen, 2015). Our study employs a quantitative research approach, and its complementary procedures comprise three main components. The process, for us, began with quantitative data collection procedures, which include the collection of sample scripts (students' papers) and the creation of an electronic corpus; it ended with the analysis and presentation of the data we gathered.

Selection of Scripts

We began the data collection process with the compilation of a sample of written work (handwritten ELPT essays). From a population of 2,558 papers, we extracted for examination and analysis a total of 86 essays. This figure accounts for scripts from the three years under study (2009 to 2011). We pulled the students' papers using a random stratified sampling technique based on the grade candidates received on the writing task; that is, we made sure our sample was reflective of the relative distribution of grades. Based on this sampling strategy, the 86 students' papers account for 3% of the total scripts and represent the seven grade levels used in the coding process. To successfully create the electronic corpus of students' writing, we participated in three rigorous phases: the production of computer-ready scripts, the creation of the ELPT Error Analysis Taxonomy, and the coding of the scripts.

Phase One—Production of Computer-Ready Scripts

In phase one, we employed typists to type the handwritten student papers using Microsoft Word. This was to ensure that the scripts were computer readable. To ensure that the electronic scripts were exact replications of the handwritten versions, we disabled the spellcheck feature and deactivated the autocorrect options. Furthermore, we provided each typist with a template for inputting the data, and as a part of the research triangulation process, we randomly selected a sample of the typed scripts and checked them for consistency and accuracy.

Phase Two — Creation of the ELPT EA Taxonomy

In phase two, we created the ELPT error-analysis taxonomy. We utilized what James (2013) refers to as a bi-dimensional error analysis taxonomy, as this type of taxonomy facilitates not only the listing and description of errors but also the classification of errors. In creating this taxonomy, we were guided by the work of James and other researchers who have established documented work in linguistic error analyses. We included in our ELPT error-analysis taxonomy descriptions of lexical, grammatical, and discourse errors.

Lexical Errors

James (2013) describes lexical errors as those that relate to vocabulary used by writers and explains that lexical errors unveil "the sorts of knowledge of words that people have" (p. 144). We included lexical errors as one of the categories of the ELPT error-analysis taxonomy due to: (a.) the emergent significant role of lexis in language study; (b.) increasing significance of vocabulary to language learning; (c.) emerging research which places lexical errors as the most frequent category of errors; (d.) the significant functional load of vocabulary in early interlanguage; and (e.) the view of native speakers that lexical errors are more disrupting and irritating than the other classes of errors (James, 2013; Mohammed & Abdalhussein, 2015; Shalaby, Yahya, & El-Komi, 2009; Shormani, 2014).

Grammatical Errors

Following other research in the study of error, we define *grammatical errors* as those that have to do with morphology (word structure) and syntax (word order), which we incorporated as major categories in the ELPT EA taxonomy. We further divided morphological errors in the manner proposed by James (2013) among others. These are: (a.) *noun morphology*; (b.) *verb morphology*; and (c.) *adjective and adverb morphology*. As it relates to syntactic errors, we concentrated on the three central phrases from which errors could have been generated: (a.) *noun phrases*; (b.) *verb phrases*; and (c.) *adjective and adverb phrases*.

Discourse Errors

The third category of errors that we included in the ELPT EA taxonomy is that of discourse errors. Discourse errors refer to errors that involve syntactic units larger than the sentence level. For our study, we defined three types of discourse errors: (a.) *topical coherence* errors which incorporate discourse that is not relevant to the given topic; (b.) *relational coherence* errors which speak to propositions in the discourse that do not relate to each other; and (c.) *sequential coherence* errors which occur when propositions are not adequately organized to best reflect the information being presented. This breakdown is illustrated in Figure 4.

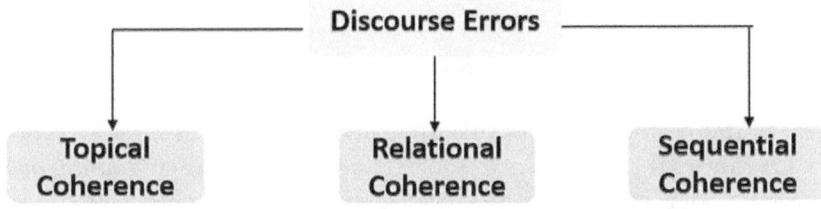

Figure 4. Discourse errors and their subcategories

Phase Three—Coding of Scripts

The third and final phase of the creation of the electronic corpus was the coding of the typed scripts using the ELPT EA taxonomy to identify and classify the errors. We applied triangulation strategies to the coding of the scripts in which coders submitted the first three scripts of each set before continuing the process. This allowed us to check for consistencies and accuracy. We then combined the coded scripts into one electronic file, thus creating the general corpus. As a means of facilitating the analysis of data by grade levels, we created seven additional mini corpora (one for each grade/ELPT scoring level) from the general corpus.

Ethical Considerations

To ensure the highest level of research integrity, the university's research committee examines all proposals and procedures for research conducted on the Utech, Jamaica campus. In following due process, we applied for and received ethical clearance from the university's research ethics committee. To ensure anonymity and to preserve the privacy of the 86 candidates whose scripts were sampled, we drafted a nondisclosure contract that was signed by each typist and coder. We also closely monitored the typing of the scripts, ensuring that typing was done only on designated university computers until the typing process was completed. We stored each completed typed set of scripts in a password-protected folder on the computers used for typing. We also ensured that the scripts assigned to the coders had only the identification numbers. We protected the identities of the typists and coders by using their initials only in our documentation processes. In referencing specific students' errors, we pulled our examples and samples from an anonymized corpus of language proficiency tests, which is different from simply taking a student's essay from a class and citing the student's writing directly.

Results

The 86 exam scripts used for this study involved a total of 1,334 sentences. Of this total, 1,216 sentences, or 91%, were coded as containing one or more errors. The remaining 118 sentences, or 9%, were found to be error-free. The data findings reveal that on average, each candidate's script comprises approximately 41 Standard English errors. The general corpus recorded a total of 3,548 errors. Of this sum, grammatical errors were the largest number of errors totaling 1,955, or 55.1%. Lexical errors, with the second highest occurrence of errors, accounted for 1,128, or 31.8%.

Out of the 1,955 grammatical errors (remember that in the study we explicitly defined grammatical errors as those specifically relating to morphology or syntax) recorded in the general corpus, the most frequently occurring were those pertaining to number marking (269), clause construction (257), tense marking (208), subject-verb agreement (163), and run-on sentences (146). These errors were followed by pronoun errors (138), referencing challenges (124), noun phrase (122), prepositional phrase (114), coordination (97), and fragment (85) errors. The aforementioned errors accounted for 1,723, or 88% of the 1,955 errors we recorded in the study. The top five recurring errors (singular/plural, clause, tense, subject-verb agreement and run-on errors) accounted for 1,043 (53%) of the grammatical errors made by the candidates. Table 2 shows the type and frequency of the errors coded in the study.

Table 2
Types and frequency of grammatical errors

GRAMMATICAL ERRORS		
Type	Freq (*f*).	Percentage (%)
Singular plural	269	13.8
Clause (omission etc.)	257	13.1
Verb Tense	208	10.6
Subject-Verb Agreement	163	8.3
Run-on	146	7.5
Pronouns	138	7.1
Referencing	124	6.3
Noun Phrase	122	6.2
Prepositional Phrase	114	5.8
Coordination	97	5.0
Fragment	85	4.3
TOTAL	1,723	88
Other Errors	232	12

As it relates to lexical errors, distortion errors (spelling errors) recorded the highest number of occurrences (604), followed by collocation errors (184), confusion of sense relations (161), and malapropisms (122). Collocation errors occur when a candidate uses a word or phrase with another word or phrase, but the combination does not sound natural to a native speaker. The number of instances of stylistic errors (47) and misformations (10) was not as high as the other types of lexical errors. Stylistic errors include instances where a candidate used verbose language, while errors of misformations represent instances where words that are produced by the candidate do not exist in the target language (Standard English) and seem to be created or adapted by the writer based on words from his/her first language. The breakdown of lexical errors is illustrated in Figure 5.

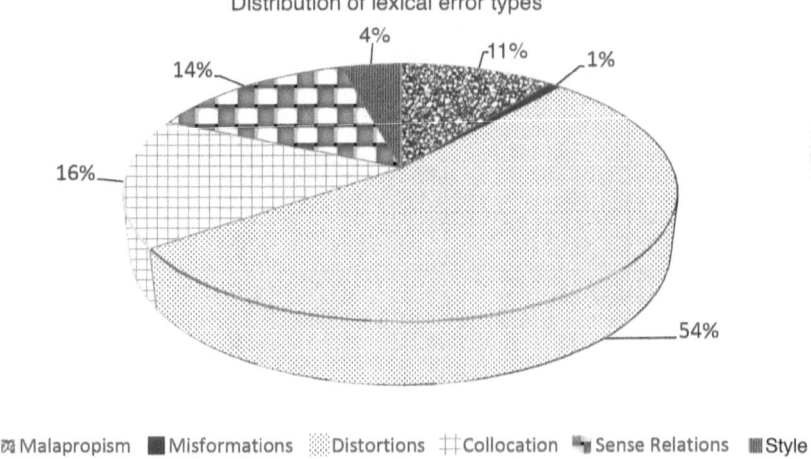

Figure 5. Percentage distribution of lexical errors by grade levels

Conversely, relatively few discourse errors were found in the corpus; in total, there were 174 discourse errors, or 4.9% of the total number. Of the three discourse error types, sequential coherence errors occurred most frequently in the students' essays (126 occurrences). For errors addressing relational coherence, we recorded 40 occurrences, while for topical coherence, we recorded a total of eight occurrences. Figure 6 shows the percentage distribution.

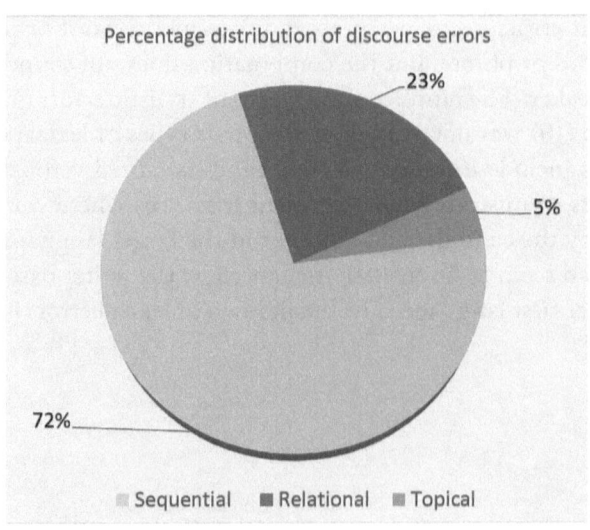

Figure 6. Percentage distribution of discourse errors by grade levels

We used the mean values of errors to determine the fifteen most common errors that students committed in their essays and the average number of errors per script. These were *spelling* (7.02), *singular/plural form* (3.12), *clausal constructions* (2.98), *verb tense form* (2.41), *collocation* (2.13), *subject-verb agreement form* (1.89), *confusion of sense relations* (1.87), *run-on sentence construction* (1.69), *pronoun referencing* (1.60), *expression* (1.59), *redundancy* (1.58), *sequential coherence* (1.46), *referencing* (1.44), *noun phrase construction* and *malapropism* (1.41), and *prepositional selection* (1.32). The remaining 17 errors are grouped under the label "Other Errors" and together account for a mean score of 6.24. See Table 3 for details.

Table 3
Frequency and mean of the most common errors committed

Error Subcategory	Frequency F	Percentage (%)	Mean
Distortion (Spelling)	604	17.0	7.02
Singular/plural	269	7.6	3.12
Clause	257	7.2	2.98
Verb Tense	208	5.9	2.41
Collocation	184	5.2	2.13
Subject/Verb Agreement	163	4.6	1.89
Confusion of Sense Relation	161	4.5	1.87
Run-on sentence	146	4.2	1.69
Pronoun	138	3.9	1.60
Expression	137	3.9	1.59
Redundancy	136	3.8	1.58
Sequential Coherence	126	3.6	1.46
Referencing	124	3.5	1.44
Noun Phrase	122	3.4	1.41
Malapropism	122	3.4	1.41
Preposition	114	3.2	1.32
Other Errors	537	15.1	6.24
TOTAL	**3548**	**100.0**	

Distortion errors, the most common error in the corpus, feature as one of the most frequent errors generally in the literature on English as a Second Language and English as a Foreign Language. (This is perhaps not surprising given the fact that Standard English spelling is not particularly phonetic.) The work of Kansir (2013), which analyzed errors in second language writing among Indian and Iranian students, noted spelling errors among the errors commonly made by these students, even though spelling errors were the minimum number of errors in the data overall. Winer (1989) found in her study of errors in Creole-speaking secondary students' writing that spelling errors accounted for 20% of the errors in her corpus. Furthermore, Pollard (1999), in her work on errors committed by Jamaican students in one of the secondary-level exit English examinations, also noted that spelling errors (what she refers to as errors associated with phonological/spelling inaccuracy) were the largest category of errors in her sample. She proposes that these errors are largely due to the influence of Creole pronunciations. While Standard English orthography is itself not particularly phonetic, and, moreover, most of the spelling errors cannot be attributed to the influence of Creole pronunciations of words, the following spelling error examples from the corpus do, however, present a clearer case of the influence of Creole phonology:

1. indispensible   "indispensable"
2. proformance   "performance"
3. respritory   "respiratory"
4. trimendous   "tremendous"
5. callapsing   "collapsing"

These kinds of errors that are due to phonological transfer from the learner's native language are common among learners of ESL (see Bardovi-Harlig & Sprouse, 2018).

Lexical errors such as collocation errors, confusion of sense relations, and malapropism point to learners' lack of knowledge of the nuances in the lexicon and semantics of the target language, which in several cases seem to be tied to those nuances being absent from the native language. Some examples of confusion of sense relations in the corpus point to a misunderstanding/lack of distinction between count and non-count nouns, a distinction that is made in the target language but not in Creole. Therefore, Creole-influenced learners often use terms such as less/fewer and amount/number interchangeably when producing English. Such usage has implications for the grammar as well, as seen when the candidate pluralizes "violence," resulting in "some violences."

Misformations represent another clear area of L1 transfer. Even though these are not among the most frequent, they are worth mentioning. Consider the following examples from the corpus:

1. ... and when they see other people their age acheiving <LF[DIS-TORT]>stuff and their parents being happy for them , they will try and badmind <LF[MISFORM]> and so they will try and convince them to join gang <GMN[SING/PLU]>and 'push' <LS[COLL]> marijuana and cocaine and influence them that its <GMN[APOS]>a quick way to get cash and school too long<A[LOG]>
2. A perfect example is Wayne Hill a born <LF[MISFORM]> jamaican working in norway.

"To *badmind* someone" and to refer to someone as a "*born* Jamaican" are both acceptable expressions in Jamaican Creole, but not in Standard English. These examples, therefore, represent a transference of a Creole structure. Interestingly though, the structure as used in example 1 above is missing the required object, making the structure incorrect in Creole as well.

Errors in grammar (that is, morphology and syntax) form the largest category of errors in the study overall, evident in the fact that 8 of the top 15 errors, in terms of frequency, belong to this category. Students make a range of grammatical errors in their writing, which is likely why markers tend to place so much focus on these errors. The ones that seem to be considered detrimental are subject-verb agreement, verb tense, and run-on and sentence fragment errors. The rubric for the argumentative essay written as the final assessment in Academic Writing 2, a writing course offered at UTech, Jamaica, identifies major grammatical errors as run-ons, fragments, errors in noun/verb agreement, and noun/pronoun agreement.

The frequency of grammatical errors in students' writing signals students' lack of command of the rules of the grammar of Standard English. Considering that students are moving from a native language that has a different grammatical structure, this lack of command is not surprising. This is particularly true in the areas of morphology, number marking, and tense marking. Pollard (1999) underscores that the errors related to tense marking, the second most frequent grammatical error in our corpus, are linked to the difference between Creole and Standard English treatments of inflection. She notes that morphological form is not used in creoles to mark a difference in tense, but instead speakers of Jamaican

Creole rely largely on the context of the situation and adverbials for such differentiation (e.g., *Mi **walk** guh a di stor yessideh* instead of *I walked to the store yesterday*). It, therefore, poses a challenge for the creole speaker who is learning Standard English to consistently use required verb endings. The following present some examples of these types of errors:

1. The overall trend shows that there were more full time students *attend* <GMV^{TENSE}> the university for the period 1996–2006.
2. This assistance that is *render* <GMV^{TENSE}> to these boys . . .
3. They may inflict bodily harm on the child or may verbally abused<GMV^{TENSE}> them.
4. My main reason to endorsed <GMV^{TENSE}> regular exercise . . .

Students and other Jamaican Creole writers may also engage in hypercorrection in their attempts at writing in Standard English by adding unnecessary inflection to verb forms that are uninflected in Standard English (see *my main reason to endorsed* in example 4); having been reminded as Creole-speaking children that *they should never forget the -ed at the end of verbs*, students may add an *-ed* when it is unnecessary.

Discussion — Implications of Findings

Almost everyone (the layperson and academic alike) in the Caribbean has an opinion about what needs to be done to improve students' writing skills, and many have put forward a number of proposals. These include ignoring the existence of creole or advocating its eradication in the teaching of Standard English, incorporating the grammar instruction more into the writing curriculum, and implementing a bilingual education program for creole-influenced learners, starting at the elementary level. While the best approach might be a combined one, we want to, in this chapter, focus on the second proposal mentioned above — the strategic incorporation of rhetorically contextualized grammar instruction in tertiary language classrooms (see, for example, Micciche, 2004).

To move forward, we have to ask certain crucial questions. Within the creole-influenced tertiary English language classroom, is there enough focus on grammar? Is there too much focus on grammar? Is the right focus being placed on grammar? Scholars at tertiary institutions within as well as beyond the Caribbean have been conflicted over whether or not to teach grammar, and if so, how much grammar to teach and on where the focus should be placed in the teaching of grammar.

This debate has been ongoing, with writers such as Kolln (1984, 1996) being sympathetic to the teaching of grammar when taught in a rhetorically contextualized way, and others suggesting that decontextualized grammar instruction is not effective, potentially even hampering native speakers' development of their writing skills (Elle, Barham, Lamb, & Willey,1979; Graham & Perrin, 2007; Hartwell, 1985).

The view of many instructors at the tertiary level, including writing instructors, has been that grammar instruction should be given at the pre-tertiary level and has no place in the tertiary-level writing classroom. The writing that learners at this level produce, however, continues to dispel this myth. Consequently, the view about the teaching of grammar at the tertiary level has been changing, with more and more persons admitting to the need to meet the students where they are. This is reflected at UTech, Jamaica in consistent changes over the years in the teaching of writing courses—the introduction of the ELPT and Foundation English, and the inclusion in the syllabi of grammar revision elements and the Creole-English distinction.

Most teachers of writing in Jamaica acknowledge that given the landscape of the Jamaican language situation, our students are largely Jamaican Creole-speakers learning English as a Second Language. Yet, this acknowledgement does not seem to translate into the development of a writing curriculum or change our expectations of what our students should be able to produce. Our research provides empirical evidence and adds to the growing body of literature that our university students dispel the underlying assumptions, which seem to steer English Language education in Jamaica. The candidates who sit the ELPT at UTech, Jamaica are definitely not English-speaking natives; rather, they are second language (L2) learners who, inevitably, are expected to make errors of a different nature that are representative of L2 learners.

Our research findings underscore what anecdotal evidence suggests—that students' written production of English comprises several types of errors, some of which severely distort the message that students are trying to produce. What our research has also made clear is that students, regardless of the grade they receive on the writing task of the ELPT, make large numbers of a wide range of Standard English errors. The results of our investigation reinforce that the majority of our students struggle to produce structures in grammatically correct Standard English. Indeed, at the university level, these high occurrences of errors legitimize the concerns of numerous stakeholders of tertiary institutions (McLaren & Webber, 2009).

However, while the concerns persist, stakeholders seem to continuously sidestep the most obvious reason for the students' challenges with the acquisition of Standard English. When we consider the academic standing of the university in general (along with its associated assumptions and implications) and the language realities of Jamaica, we find ourselves entangled in a *Catch-22*. On the one hand, there is the fallacious assumption that our students are grammatically competent in Jamaican Standard English, and as such there is no need, and certainly no accommodation, for the teaching of formal grammar in their writing courses at the tertiary level, and on the other, the writing students produce is so error-riddled and lacking rhetorical mastery that one cannot ignore the need for an intervention which emphasizes the development of skill in writing.

Balancing Composition and Grammar in The UTech, Jamaica Classroom

Undoubtedly, if we continue to do the same thing the same way, we will see the same results. If we desire different results, we, most naturally, need to incorporate different approaches. The composition/grammar balance that we seek to achieve begins with and depends on the revisiting of the assumptions about the language competence of the university's clientele, as well as the aims and objectives of the writing courses that the university offers. If we are serious about establishing realistic goals for curriculum development and revision, we must begin with *calling a spade a spade*; that is, truly acknowledging the severity of our English Language challenges within a second-language learning context. An Achilles' heel of educational policies in Caribbean countries such as Jamaica is that, as Craig (1976) outlines, "Creole or Creole-influenced language has been treated . . . as if it did not exist, or as if it should be eradicated if it existed" (p. 95). As it relates to the UTech, Jamaica context, Smith, Stewart-McKoy, Henry, and Hamilton (2015) underscore the importance of "the institutionalization of a realistic, university-wide language policy that takes a clear stance on the importance of proficiency in English and considers all the requisite factors—cultural, political, economic and socio-linguistic . . . [which] dictates a renewed and focused commitment as well as a cultural shift, moving beyond personal comfort zones and entrenched attitudes" (p. 77).

Concerning curriculum development, we must also revisit and challenge the assumptions upon which our courses are founded. One such egregious assumption is the illusion that students at the end of the secondary level cycle, and at the verge of tertiary education, have attained a high level of English proficiency. Acknowledgment is the first of a series of steps on the trajectory to addressing our challenges with English. The second, and equally important step, is an unwavering investment in and commitment to what we aim to achieve. Therefore, the university's commitment to the *total education of the individual as a social being* as expressed in its philosophy requires a greater commitment to addressing language issues.

Additionally, we believe that to bring about a change in the current attitudes, Caribbean academic writing instructors need to be adequately sensitized to the current language situation. We endorse ongoing English as a Second Language sensitization sessions for staff as well as for current and potential students. Unlike UWI, Mona, which has an active linguistics department with linguists who have been lobbying for a change in how Creole and English are treated in the education system, UTech does not have such a department and has not been very active in the dialogue regarding the acknowledgment and use of the students' native language in education. To some extent, therefore, the level of sensitization that would be expected among teachers of writing and those across the wider university is not present. This lack naturally influences the approach taken to the teaching of writing courses and other courses across the university. However, recent informal interviews with teachers of writing at UTech, Jamaica point to a greater acknowledgment of the need for teachers to use a second-language approach in the classroom and to better incorporate grammar instruction in writing courses. The sensitization of students to this approach is also necessary to avoid anticipated push-backs and to get them to buy into the aims and objectives of the approach.

Further to the aforementioned recommendations and as an integral component of the grammar/composition marriage, we endorse the development of a comprehensive learner profile that targets students' basic demographics, language behaviors, language competences, learning preferences, language-learning experiences, and attitudes. The creation of learner profiles involves the collection and analysis of learner data to better meet their needs (Powell & Kusuma-Powell, 2011). Bryan and McLean Francis in a (2011) discussion about the Jamaican language situation and its impact on achieving educational goals suggest that effectively improving students' competence in the English language requires that English-language teaching be constantly adapted to meet the needs of students (USAID/Jamaica Partners for Educational Progress, 2012). They propose the following questions to guide that process:

> What are the specific language realities of my rural or urban students? Have my students made any movement along the language continuum before or since I have begun to interact with them? Is my school in a secluded language environment? Are the language needs of my students individual or fairly uniform? What are the specific language features coming out of my students' written and verbal productions? (USAID/Jamaica Partners for Educational Progress, 2012)

These questions would enable language teachers to profile students.

Specific Strategies Which Incorporate Grammar

Given our context at UTech, Jamaica, we recommend a second-language teaching and learning holistic approach with two parts. Part one focuses on the basic writing module (as explained by Bartholomae, 1980), where the main focus is on developing students' competence in producing the English language. In this course, we propose the infusing of rhetoric within grammar teaching. As students move toward credit-bearing courses, we propose what Reece (2013) refers to as "rewriting the tradition"; that is a transition to rhetorical grammar (Kolln, 1996), which is an approach where grammar is strategically infused into rhetoric. Kolln argues for the positive infusion of grammar in writing, where the teacher strategically selects effective language structures for specific rhetorical contexts. The use of rhetorical grammar would see a shift from teaching formal traditional grammar—abstract isolated grammar rules—with a new focus on stylistic grammar, and, a change in the purpose of grammar teaching from remediation to empowerment of the student writer to effectively select correct grammatical constructions for specific purposes.

Kolln's (1996) use of the word "positive" is very important in the creole context, considering the social stigma that tends to be attached to poor grammar usage and subsequently courses that are thought to address such usage. To complement the idea of rhetorical grammar is the need to consistently have contrastive analysis while teaching grammar, which is the second part of our proposal. Without this kind of analysis, grammar teaching within the creole context will continue to be ineffective. Students need to be able to see and understand the differences between the two language codes they are juggling. Craig (1966; 2006) argues for the use of contrastive analysis in the teaching of English in the pre-tertiary level, as such analysis would help learners to better understand the similarities and differences between Jamaican Creole and Jamaican Standard English. This is a necessary precursor to producing grammatical Jamaican Standard English structures. The translation of the Creole text in Academic Writing 1, mentioned at the beginning of this chapter, is an ideal activity for such an analysis.

The approaches mentioned above would require extensive and intensive staff-training sessions. Success of the strategies, without such training, will be left to chance—the chance of instructional staff understanding Jamaican Creole grammar and the chance of staff understanding what rhetorical grammar is and how to implement such an approach. We also encourage the incorporation/rewriting of explicit goals and objectives directly related to grammar and lexicon. Further to this, we believe that the inclusion of clear descriptors within assessment rubrics is critical to balancing grammar and composition in the writing classroom.

As a strategic and complementary support system to the language classroom activities, we propose the use of grammar laboratories/writing centers (physical and/or virtual). The value of grammar laboratories/writing centers has increased in higher educational institutions worldwide. These units are a form of self-access language learning tools that are freely accessible to learners beyond their academic schedule and are known to provide writing and grammar support for learners at a pace directed by the learners themselves (Anderson & Nakahashi, 2017; LaClare & Franz, 2013). The Virtual Self-Access Learning Centre for the UTech, Jamaica context, proposed by Smith and Stewart-McKoy (2017), is a tool that can be used to assist both teachers and students.

REFERENCES

Anderson, S., & Nakahashi, M. (2017). The evolution of a SAL desk: From academic writing to language support. *Studies in Self-Access Learning Journal, 8*(4), 323–333.

Baden, R. (1974). College freshmen can't(?) write. *College Composition and Communication, 25,* 430–433.

Bardovi-Harlig, K., & Sprouse, R. (2018). Negative versus positive transfer. In J. Liontas (Ed., Volume Editor: H. Nassasji). *The TESOL Encyclopedia of English Language Teaching, Vol. I* (pp. 1–6). Oxford: John Wiley & Sons.

Bartholomae, D. (1980). The study of error. *College Composition and Communication, 31*, 253–269.

Brown, H. (2000). *Principles of language learning and teaching.* New Jersey: Prentice-Hall.

Corder, S. P. (1967). The significance of learner's errors. *International Review of Applied Linguistics, 5*, 160–170.

Craig, D. (1966). Teaching English to Jamaican creole speakers: A model of a multi-dialect situation. *Language Learning, 16*, 49–61.

Craig, D. (1976). Bidialectal education: Creole and standard in the West Indies. *International Journal of the Sociology of Language, 8*, 93–134.

Craig, D. (2006). *Teaching language and literacy to Caribbean students: From vernacular to Standard English.* Kingston, Jamaica: Ian Randle Publishers.

Dagneaux, E., Denness, S., & Granger, S. (1998). Computer-aided error analysis. *System, 26*(2), 163–174.

Elley, W. B., Barham, I. H., Lamb, H., & Wyllie, M. (1979). *The role of grammar in a secondary school curriculum. Educational Research Series No 60.* Wellington: New Zealand Council for Educational Research.

Graham, S., & Perin, D. (2007). A meta-analysis of writing instruction for adolescent students. *Journal of Educational Psychology, 99*, 445–476.

Hamilton, P. (2010, December 6). English test trips up university students. *The Gleaner.* Retrieved from http://jamaica-gleaner.com/gleaner/20101206/lead/leAD5.html

Hartwell, P. (1985). Grammar, grammars, and the teaching of grammar. *College English, 47*(2), 105–127.

James, C. (2013). *Errors in language learning and use: Exploring error analysis* (2nd ed.). New York: Routledge.

Jones McKenzie, C., & Orogun, J. (2010). *Transferability of English language skills from the secondary to the tertiary level context* (Unpublished report). University of Technology, Jamaica.

Kolln, M. (1984). *Language and composition: A handbook and rhetoric.* New York: MacMillan Publishing Company.

Kolln, M. (1996). Rhetorical grammar: A modification lesson. *The English Journal, 85*(7), 25–31.

LaClare, E., & Franz, T. (2013). Writing centers: Who are they for? What are they for? *Studies in Self-Access Learning Journal, 4*(1), 5–16.

McLaren, I., Dyche, C., Altidor-Brooks, A., Taylor, R., & Devonish, H. (2009). Reversing power relations and curricular reform: English language education activism in the academy. *The UWI Quality Education Forum, 15*, 61–82.

McLaren, I., & Webber, D. (2009). Writing right: Enhancing student engagement and performance in an ecology course. *International Journal of Environmental and Science Education, 4*(4), 365–380.

Micciche, L. (2004). Making a case for rhetorical grammar. *College Composition and Communication, 55*, 716–737.

Milson-Whyte, V. (2015). *Academic writing instruction for creole-influenced students*. Kingston, Jamaica: University of the West Indies Press.

Mohammed, M., & Abdalhussein, H. (2015). Grammatical error analysis of Iraqi postgraduate students' academic writing: The case of Iraqi students in UKM. *International Journal of Education and Research, 3*(6), 283–294.

Pollard, V. (1999). Beyond grammar: Teaching English in an Anglophone Creole environment. In J. Rickford & S. Romaine (Eds.), *Creole genesis, attitudes and discourse: Studies celebrating Charlene J. Sato* (pp. 323–336). Philadelphia: John Benjamins.

Powell, W., & Kusuma-Powell, O. (2011). *How to teach now: Five keys to personalized learning in the global classroom*. Alexandria, VA: ASCD.

Reece, D. (2013). Grammar in the composition classroom: Rewriting the tradition (Unpublished master's thesis). Brigham Young University, Provo, Utah. Retrieved from http://scholarsarchive.byu.edu/etd/3887

Shalaby, N., Yahya, N., & El-Komi, M. (2009). Analysis of lexical errors in Saudi college students' compositions. *Journal of the Saudi Association of Languages and Translation, 2*(3), 65–93.

Shormani, Q. (2014). Lexical choice difficulties: A psycholinguistic study towards Solution. *Journal of Literature, Languages and Linguistics, 4*, 43–53.

Smith, D., Stewart-McKoy, M., Henry, A., & Hamilton, G. (2015). Performance on the Proficiency Test in English at the University of Technology Jamaica: A university-wide problem and implications for teaching and learning. *Journal of Arts, Science and Technology, 8*, 60–80.

Smith, D., & Stewart-McKoy, M. (2017). "Under examination": An analysis of students' writing errors at UTech, Ja and implications for the teaching of English. *Journal of Arts, Science and Technology, 10*, 156–178.

Thewissen, J. (2015). *Accuracy across proficiency levels: A learner corpus approach*. Louvain, Belgium: Presses Universitaires de Louvain.

USAID/Jamaica Partners for Educational Progress. (2012). Collaboration or collision: A tale of two languages—Jamaican Creole and Jamaican Standard English. Retrieved from https://www.mona.uwi.edu/cop/sites/default/files/consolidated_reply_files/EduExchange%20Summary%205_0.pdf

Virtue, E. (2013, January). Bloody English! UWI, UTech students struggle with language. *The Gleaner*. Retrieved from *http://jamaica-gleaner.com/gleaner/20130127/lead/leAD71.html*

Winer, L. (1989). Variation and transfer in English Creole—Standard English language learning. In M. Eisenstein (Ed.), *The dynamic interlanguage: Topics in language and linguistics* (pp. 155–173). Boston, MA: Springer.

7 "African American" Anglophone Caribbean Writers in a Historically Black University Writing Center

Kendra Mitchell

Introduction

African American rhetorics and knowledges can be understood through a rhetorical method that is concerned with what circulates as Black, but is not limited to Black bodies, while avoiding becoming mired in the quicksand of authenticity.

—Nunley, 2011, p. 27

It is important to note that Ebonics is not just an 'American thing.' Ebonics is diaspora in language.

—Williams-Farrier, 2017, p. 219

I begin this chapter with two polemic quotations that echo similar sentiments concerning the vitality and necessity of black language. Williams-Farrier's (2017) claim makes room for considering African American Language (AAL) as a lingua franca that is constantly changing and being changed by its users, particularly for black people throughout the diaspora. Nunley's (2011) statement strikes a balance and rescues Williams-Farrier's statement from the clutches of essentialist ideologies or the "quicksand of authenticity." In other words, not all black people play by AAL's rules, and it is possible for those outside of black member groups to be fluent in it. Both writers' positions on AAL provide a common sentiment of participants in my study of self-identified African American students in a historically black university writing center, and they more broadly provide a framework for the needed discussions of AAL speakers as multilingual, multiliterate writers. Taken together, Nunley and Williams-Farrier point us to a place beyond fixed language identities for black student writers born in the US and in the Caribbean.

Accordingly, in this essay, I focus on two Anglophone Caribbean participants, Jessica and Sherry (these names, like all in the study, are fictitious), who self-identify as African American, in a case study of African American student speakers of African American Language. By extension, I include their African American male tutor, Matthius. Although their linguistic patterns did not follow the grammar of AAL—use of the invariant *be*, etc.—their discourse pattern modalities mirror African American Verbal Traditions (AVT) (Williams-Farrier, 2017; Williams, 2013), a subset of AAL (Smitherman, 1998; Williams-Farrier, 2017). Using select features of Williams-Farrier's AVT tool and Denise Troutman's African American Women's Language (AAWL) features, I identify patterns of languaging, noted as patterns of linguistic push-pull (LPP), as the reconstruction of identities in these women's oscillation between subject positions. Although the original study on which this chapter is based included three patterns of LPP—*reticence as amotivation, resistance as amotivation,* and *diversions as amotivation*—in this chapter I highlight resistance and reticence as amotivation. Moreover, I use the manifestations of AVT as markers of this linguistic push-pull in Sherry's verbal language interactions and verbal and written tutor-tutee language interactions, noting the points of convergence and divergence that unify and disrupt communication between her and Matthius. This work has implications for understanding the relationship between amotivation, culture, and language among black student writers. Another aim of this chapter is to understand the methodologies used within this ethnic-specific writing center as well as to probe the fluid identity constructions of the participants despite diasporic differences.

The results of shifting linguistic identities among the two Anglophone Caribbean participants reveal new perspectives in language studies and writing center practices. The results of locating these students in the larger study of self-identified African Americans using AAL and Edited American English (EAE) show their (a)motivation as resistance to be the beginning of an agentic turning point in their sessions. Therefore, they negotiated AAL and EAE for similar ends: to work using AAWL features, such as capping and latching. Reflecting on these writing-center language interactions through Bhabha's (1994) work affords us the opportunity to understand the language negotiations at the fissures of our binaries and nudges us toward a better understanding of the interstitial spaces of students beyond the purview of the academic lens. Specifically, by including Anglophone Caribbean students who self-identify as African Americans in the writing studies and writing-center scholarship, writing-center practitioners and compositionists can understand the fluid linguistic identity constructs of these students in historically black universities where discrete language systems converge and diverge, making naturalized double-consciousness (Milson-Whyte, 2013) an act of translanguaging that has yet to be explored.

Naming a Thing a Thing

The exigence for this chapter stems from my recognition of my unique participant pool. I mistakenly assumed using "African American" as a descriptor targeted the persons I aimed to study in the historically black university writing center. However, I had a range of students who willingly engaged in the prolonged observation of their languaging patterns in various situations while occupying a range of racial and ethnic monikers. While maintaining their position as "African American," they also maintained other markers ranging from Nigerian to Jamaican. My instinct was to omit these participants from this "African American" study of language but soon recognized how problematic it would be to erase my participants' identity construction as a researcher. Who am I to say they were not African American? What did that mean, anyway? The collective decision for black people to self-identify as African American occurred in the latter part of the twentieth century and signified a dual connection between an American identity and an African ancestry (Smitherman, 1998). In my study, I projected, like some scholars, that participants would choose to ascribe "Black" as a moniker that includes the diaspora (Bryce-Laporte, 1972; E. Richardson, 2003) and African American as an indicator of US-born black people. On the contrary, participants colored outside of the research lines, especially my second-generation Caribbean participant, Jessica, and foreign-born participant, Sherry.

Although the original study focused on the fluid language interactions as manifestations of multilingualism, translingualism proves to be a more productive label for these language interactions in that it "enables a consideration of communicative competence as not restricted to predefined meanings of individual languages, but the ability to merge different language resources in situated interactions for new meaning construction" (Canagarajah, 2013, pp. 1–2). Therefore, examining their translanguaging practices within the context of an Historically Black University (HBU) proved salient for this chapter. My choice to shift to a translingual approach—I use translingual and translanguaging interchangeably—is supported by Canagarajah's assessment of the stiff linguistic borders in multilingualism. Jessica and Sherry move in and out of LPP in their separate sessions with Matthius, and it is at those moments that they are negotiating more than their embracing and distancing of AAL. In a similar way, Matthius's session with graduate student Sherry reveals another iteration of translanguaging through latching.

Translanguaging in the US

Williams-Farrier's (2017) case for viewing AAL as the diaspora in language is a potentially controversial perspective for some Anglophone Caribbean scholars. Afro-Caribbean scholars have varying views about the identity formation of black Caribbean natives and American-born blacks. The politics of identity for foreign-born blacks in the US reveal a need to assimilate to an African American identity that is often invisible (Bryce-Laporte, 1972). Their subject position constitutes its own liminality for, as Bryce-Laporte writes, they "are perhaps the least visible but most articulate and active of America's ethnic constituencies . . . their cultural impact as foreigners has generally been ignored or has merely been given lip service in the larger spheres of American life" (p. 31). These various subject positions make a case for translanguaging that converges with and diverges from African Americans. Nero (2001) points towards this fluidity more broadly as she analyzes the shifts in language boundaries. Nero suggests that the decentering of language boundaries points towards a greater shift in "linguistic identities of speakers" (p. 146). Mc-Gill (2005) posits that Afro-Caribbean scholars, such as "Portes, Zhou, Waters, and others warn that the cultural practices of hip hop might prove inimical to the class aspirations of post-1965 immigrant parents, but they never consider what these cultural practices afford Caribbean American youth who try to locate themselves ethnically and racially in African America, American society, and even immigrant enclaves" (pp. 2–3). This practice is rooted in cultural experiences shaped by their liminality, and such determinist boundaries between African Americans and Afro-Caribbean people, inclusive of Anglophone Caribbean immigrants and their descendants, miss the interstitial spaces created by these groups.

This notion becomes important when considering all stigmatized languages because it exposes the racial and class politics surrounding the attitudes towards the languages in society as well as the academy, an ongoing "interaction of the mind/body and social world and language/mind/culture mosaic" (Morgan, 2002, p. 37). Just as Morgan situates this ambivalence in the dynamism of language ideologies as "mirrors and tools that probe, reflect, refract, subvert and exalt social and cultural production, reproduction and representation" (p. 37), Bhabha's (1994) notion of hybridity as an articulation beyond binaries provides the agentic framework for these students' choices. Bhabha refers to this phenomenon as "the act of cultural enunciation—the place of utterance—[that is] crossed by différance of writing . . . It is the difference in the process of language that is crucial to the production of meaning and ensures, at the same time, that meaning is never simply mimetic and transparent" (p. 52). Milson-Whyte (2013) investigates the benefits of code-meshing as a translingual approach for Jamaican Creole speakers, positing a "translingual approach, as a philosophy on languaging, could prove useful for both educator and student—foregrounding student writers' agency, allowing for discussion and negotiations on what is written, and increasing learning for both parties" (p. 118). Similarly, I use the participants' fluid identification as articulations beyond stringent labels of solely being Anglophone Caribbean or African American during a speech or written act, allowing me to explore continuity and discontinuity with other black participants in the study as an expression of a deeper ideology, one moving beyond the shores of morphology (Green, 2002) toward broader discussions and negotiations of a more equitable writing conference.

In addition to AAL's external challenges, the continuum of beliefs among AAL proponents pose internal challenges. To define AAL is to take a position on its validity, and a central part of defining AAL is naming AAL. For instance, Perryman-Clark (2013) uses *Ebonics*, the most highly criticized term gaining public recognition during the Oakland School Board decision in 1996, synonymously with AAL. Perryman-Clark's definition of *Ebonics*, "the language derived from Africans' transport during the African Holocaust" (p. 14), anchors the definition of this chapter. For this study, I acknowledge the various names for this language. A long-standing argument surrounding the nature of AAL is based on whether it is an independent language or a dialect of English. From a purely linguistic perspective, the question of the autonomy of AAVE poses the same difficulties that concepts like *language* and *dialect* have always posed (Winford, 2003, p. 28; Horn, 1993; Rafoth, 2015). Editors of *Black Linguistics: Language, Society, and Politics in Africa and the Americas*, Makoni, Smitherman, Ball, and Spears (2003) borrow Childs's term *Black Languages*, which is a construction of the "pidgins and creoles in Africa and the Caribbean; African American (Vernacular) English [AAVE] in the US (also known as US Ebonics, African American Language, Black English); standardized and non-standardized African languages; and 'vehicular' languages emerging in urban African centers" (p. 2). Many AAL users may not even have a name to describe their language, but this absence of naming is typical of communities (p. 3).

Translanguaging and Racism

Although I frame translanguaging through an agentic lens, it stems from the systemic racism of black people, forging a conflated sense of blackness onto a diverse population. Ibrahim (1999) argues that second language learners are constantly appropriating cultures due to the mediated identity formations presented to them. More importantly, his argument that a part of this identity formation includes "becoming Black" (p. 350), which "is deployed to talk about the subject-formation project (i.e., the process and the space within which subjectivity is formed) that is produced in and simultaneously is produced by the process of language learning, namely learning BESL [Black English as a second language]" (p. 350), resonates with historically black colleges and their writing centers. For these students and others, HBCUs are a first choice because African American students expect to receive more personal care at HBCUs than at predominantly white institutions (Jordan, 2012, p. 100), yet the HBCUs still "want their students to produce in speech and writing the Edited American English valued in academe and business settings ... The HBCU composition classroom with its mixture of black southern, midwestern, and northern dialects, as well as Afro-Latino, Jamaican, West African, and other influences, is undeniably diverse, but largely overlooked in the scholarship on language diversity and writing assessment" (p. 101).

Ibrahim's (1999) study of BESL becomes important for this case study because Jessica and Sherry exhibit patterns of this identity formation as a result of the appropriation of African American culture. Further, Ibrahim's questions about what it means for non-African Americans to identify with African American Language has not fully been discussed in writing-center studies. These are questions of interest wherever African American and non-African American groups interact, but these questions are heightened at HBCUs given their historical investment in students of color from various parts of the world. Not only are these questions of identity essential for broader institutional audiences, but also these identity constructions remain relevant in ethnic-specific learning environments where marginalized groups are systemically overlooked and riddled as homogenous and static (M. Young, 2013). The essence of Students Right to Their Own Language (SRTOL) is already at play in the instructional practices of these unique institutions.

HBCU Background

Issues concerning diversity in writing-center scholarship have been and continue to be explored in university settings where the demographic has shifted to include more marginalized races (Cook-Gumperz, 1993; DiPardo, 2011; Grimm, 2011), but none of the recent studies include HBCUs. However, these HBCUs share a similar history as that of writing centers, in the sense that, by their mere existence, they are counterculture; yet this shared history is often overlooked in writing-center studies. These constructed educational communities were oftentimes forged together to spite discriminatory laws, such as Jim Crow, which were intended to ensure blacks as a permanent underclass. With the assistance of local churches, some governmental assistance, and community fundraising, HBCUs became the epicenter for the academic and social development of blacks. Earl S. Richardson, president emeritus and distinguished university professor of Morgan State, notes that "few academic administrators and an even smaller segment of the general population understand the significance of the distinction between HBCUs and TWIs [traditionally white institutions] as well as those individuals who have had experiences at HBCUs either as a student, professional, employee, parent, and/or past president" (E. S. Richardson, 2013, p. xi). Though other institutional types have distinguished themselves, Kynard and Eddy (2009) define HBCUs in terms of Perry, Steele, and Hilliard's definition, stating that these sites are "'intentional educational communities' that have served as 'counterhegemonic figured communities' on the American educational landscape" (p. 25). HBCU supporters, graduates, and other constituents will attest to distinct, observable patterns of behavior at the heart of any given historically black campus because these schools carry the legacy of the uplifting of the African American community as a whole.

These institutions received this designation as a result of the amended Higher Education Act of 1965, which defines them as "any accredited institution of higher education founded prior to 1964 whose primary mission was, and continues to be, the education of Black Americans" (Brown II & Freeman, 2004, p. 5). While HBCUs vary in many ways, they share "their historic responsibility as the primary providers of post-secondary education for Black Americans in a social environment of racial discrimination" (p. 5) with the hopes of upholding and instilling cultural traditions. Moss (2003) posits that "shared cultural knowledge (or understanding, including norms, ideology, and artifacts) contributes significantly to the roles and expectations of participants, intertextual relations, and just about everything else in this [African American churches] institution. That is, there are expectations and shared experiences that dictate 'the way we act' and 'what we recognize as acceptable behavior'" (pp. 8–9), an aspect often overlooked in composition classrooms and writing centers alike.

In terms of writing studies specifically, when HBCU administrators and professors have a proclivity for code-switching, especially those in the classroom (V. Young, 2009, p. 50), language and composition scholars posit an alternative, that is a more strategies-inclusive approach to academic writing (Perryman-Clark, 2013; Williams-Farrier, 2017; V. Young, 2009). Young proffers code-meshing, or the "blending dos idiomas or copping enough Standard English to really make yo' AAE be Da Bomb" (p. 50). Young's example of AAE does not fully illustrate the typical meshing of AAL learners in many college composition courses. AAL learners use the language on a continuum based on their socialization with the language. Some AAL features are evident in the sentence structure, but other features are evident in how the user makes meaning.

Diversity of the HBCU Classroom

This diversity of the HBCU classroom can be traced to the founding of HBCUs during the post-Civil War as a result of the second Morrill Act of 1890 (Gasman, Lundy-Wagner, Ransom, & Bowman III, 2010, p. 6). Even during the Reconstruction era, African Americans were the forerunners of education for all people. During this time, "many post-slavery developments provided ex-slaves with compelling reasons to become literate. The uses and abuses of written labor contracts made it worthwhile to be able to read, write, and cipher. Frequently, planters designed labor contracts in ways that would confuse and entrap the ex-slaves" (Anderson, 1988, p. 18). Despite adversity, they initiated the first campaign among the native southerners for universal education (p. 18). This context of the HBCUs' emergence has resulted in "the express purpose of educating African Americans" (Gasman et al., 2010, p. 2) despite funding constraints, instability in university administration, and traditional—sometimes caustic—curricular views concerning the historically black colleges or universities. A byproduct of this purpose of educating African Americans has been the long-overlooked collisions of language varieties that this chapter is exploring as AAL and EAE are negotiated within these intentional educational communities. In other words:

> [t]he racial and ethnic makeups of our classrooms and institutions have not resulted from historical or contemporary political coincidences, and, as such, HWCUs and HBCUs, even after accounting for the varied institution types . . . varieties that run across both HWCUs and HBCUs, have considerably different histories in how they have defined who the college student is, should be, and can be. (Kynard & Eddy, 2009, p. 26)

HBCUs have historically provided educational opportunities to students of color, as well as other marginalized populations, based on their learning potential and not solely on ability to masterfully navigate academic literacies. This consideration is evidenced in the "African American Diaspor[ic]" (Fort, 2013, p. 15) lens by which teaching and learning occur in these spaces.

The Study

Linguistic push-pull is not restricted to African American students attending any particular institution. Both the SRTOL Resolution and the Background Statement to the Resolution use *dialect* and *language* interchangeably, but they do so not to challenge the distinctions between language and dialects but because their focus is strictly on dialect differences within English: that is, by *language*, they by and large mean *dialect* and, more specifically, refer to dialects of English. This elision of other languages, and the speakers of other languages, is evident even in their attempt to account for the different levels of prestige associated with particular language varieties. The statement presents a history and account of language use in the United States that denies this nation's longstanding and continuing multilingual tradition and the diverse national origins of its immigrants (Horner, Donahue, & NeCamp, 2011, pp. 742–43).

This study situates itself not only in the exigencies of SRTOL but also in my personal experiences as a former student, tutor, and administrator in the selected site. This study includes participants, those who self-identify as African American, who recognize the expectation to navigate the varying terrains of academic discourse and the cost of misunderstanding these expectations. The data for this study were collected over the period of seven months. The initial interviews were scheduled during the beginning of Spring 2015. During this time, participants had a chance to read, review, and sign their informed consent and video release forms. At the conclusion of the brief interview, the participants scheduled their hour-long session. In the second step in the study, I negotiated with the participants in varying degrees, but mainly the third phase, the stimulated recall interview, proved to be our most collaborative moment. The tools I used to answer the questions were direct observation, videotaping, examining student texts, and interviews.

Anglophone Caribbean Participants

Jessica, a Jamaican-American first-year, nineteen-year-old female student majoring in political science/pre-law at the time of the study, had aspirations of attending a top law school. For Jessica, there is a clear distinction between *home* languages and *academic* languages. Her lines of demarcation between home and professional language correlate to EAE being associated with *profitability* and AAL being associated with *family*, and for her both were valuable. It is only after asking about her home languages that I learned that she cannot speak Jamaican Creole, but she understands her mother and grandmothers when they speak to her. Sherry, a 27-year-old Jamaican immigrant and mother, was earning her master's degree in public health and leading several organizations at the time of the study. She immigrated to the US when she was seven, speaks fluent Jamaican Creole, and still identifies with the rigorous language standards of her early British-influenced schooling.

Analysis

Though each phase provided important information, I draw most of the information from the second and third phases of the study. In response to my research questions, "How is AAL and EAE used in the session? How do the uses of AAL and EAE reflect linguistic push-pull?" I identify one of Williams-Farrier's AVT tools, *signifying*, as evidence of linguistic push pull (LPP). The AVT marker, however, covers a linguistic ecosystem of enunciations (Bhabha, 1994) of identity interruptions: a place where the writers are not completely Anglophone Caribbean or African American. Bhabha explains this "unconscious relation" as the introduction of "ambivalence in the act of interpretation" (p. 54). Put differently, the unspoken agreement in the languaging act between tutor and tutee is often passively constructing an identity beyond the framework provided by theoretical frameworks.

Resistance as (A)motivation

Although the essays that Jessica brought to her session had previously been graded by her professors (and she had received above average grads for them), Jessica, nonetheless, experienced moments in her session when LPP produced tutee amotivation through African American verbal traditions. Matthius challenged her self-perception of her writing, oftentimes missing her initial, nonverbal resistance as a result of AAWL. I argue that Troutman's (2001) AAWL provides a fine-grained definition of *signifying* and *indirection*, terms usually defined in relation to men, which broadens the interstitial space already existing between the tutor/tutee's unrecognized languaging identities. Building upon Stanback's claims, Troutman determines this assertiveness results from "African American women's work in public spheres," which explains they "must curtail their outspokenness as a result of community standards, which only allow assertiveness to a certain point for women" (p. 219). Specifically, Troutman's definition of capping, a part of her taxonomy of assertiveness, is a highly skilled "verbal weapon" that uses a "formal manner of speaking" (p. 221). As Troutman posits, this form of AAWL is best understood when interpreted because of its reliance on tonal semantics. This instance of AAWL, an extension of AAL, becomes particularly noticeable when Jessica interrupts Matthius after he spends over seven minutes reading and marking her essay. It is his line of questioning about pronouns that triggers Jessica's assertiveness (p. 219). Instead of remaining on the receiving end of the questions, she takes control of the session by asking Matthius pointed questions about how she actually used pronouns in her essay in contrast to the broad, circular questions he asked her regarding her knowledge of pronouns. Matthius, in turn, maintains a "stoic" look to "evoke neutrality." Repeating this example signifies the importance of verbal resistance as an aspect of amotivation in this writing center because resistance, at the onset, counters the tutor's goal to assist the student and the tutee's goal to receive help. I posit that resistance as amotivation is a common, though temporary, feature within a tutor/tutee relationship negotiating LPP, such as Matthius's sessions with Jessica.

Jessica noted that she was surprised that he marked so much on her essay even though she earned an A on it. Nevertheless, she remained in the session; Jessica even noted, "I was kinda surprised of all the stuff I was doing that I didn't know . . . like misusing pronouns." Her response is unexpected because her session with Matthius deviates from the welcoming strategies DeCheck (2016) offers. Jessica resists the learning of pronouns initially because Matthius begins *narrativizing*, teaching her about pronouns broadly while she does not see the benefit of the lesson. However, Matthius intensifies his approach with tonal semantics, or the artful variation of vocal tones to make meaning, instead of folding into her frustration. In her reflection, Jessica explained: "He was just underlining a lot. I was like, 'What did I do?' I thought it was a bad essay for a minute." Despite the cultural dissonance between them (evidenced by when Matthius began reading quietly to Jessica's dismay and Matthius's performance of AAL), Jessica, nonetheless, left the session feeling informed and supported, which provides another example of how her resistance as amotivation subsided once she negotiated LPP in her verbal interaction with Matthius.

Though Jessica shared other markers that signaled as errors, such as the use of vague pronouns, which are common to all writers from time to time, Jessica demonstrates a pattern of narrativizing in her writing that seems to support her learning goals. For example, Jessica uses narrativizing in her plot summary in a way that allows her to minimize LPP in terms of frustration in translation: "Alternately, Othello will listen to Iago; when Iago tells Othello that he sees Cassio wiping his beard with the handkerchief Othello gave to his wife Desdomona in act three." As Jessica employs competent academic literacies, she does so through African American verbal traditions. Jessica, in the end, was successful in achieving the learning goals of the writing center, as well as her own by permitting the tutor to teach her lessons about writing she did not recognize on her own.

Analysis: Jessica's Essay

Below is an analysis of Jessica's essay. The essay includes AAL in ways the student and tutee do not recognize but that demonstrate successful uses of AAL to manage LPP and support their learning. I posit that focusing on these features in a systematic way better supports motivation even in the face of LPP, which potentially leads to resistance as amotivation.

Jessica's character analysis of Othello opens with markers of signifying in the first sentence: "Ancient Iago, *that master mind* of Othello, tricks everyone into believing he is honest and true, little do the characters know that their world is about to be flipped upside down." The underlined portions represent the markers of signifying, which requires the reader to *read between the lines*. It often works in tandem with indirection, and, in this case, Jessica uses that to signal how effective he was at deceiving others. In addition, Jessica uses *master mind* to describe Iago when she could have simply stated that Iago was a trickster, but she emphasized with an appositive that boasts of Iago's craftiness. Another example of signifying in Jessica's writing occurs in her topic sentence of the second paragraph on her second page: "Iago's use of props and perfect timing are essential in Othello, because without these thoughtful schemes and use of words Othello wouldn't be a tragedy." Again, Jessica uses subject-verb agreement standard to EAE usage, but her arrangement of the sentence suggests a "matter-of-fact" tone that is not explicitly stated. Though her lesson pronouns represented an instance of frustration with EAE, a marker of LPP in this study, her vague use of pronouns in her oral session did not overshadow her nuanced use of AAL features, such as signifying and narrativizing. This is not to say that her use of vague pronouns is not a feature of AAL and thus a potential marker of LPP; the tutor did not discuss her use of vague pronouns in terms of AAL and its features but in terms of EAE and its grammatical structure. Of interest for future study is the fact that he delivers this lesson using AAL rhetorical strategies.

Although Anglophone Caribbean writers may not perceive themselves as "native" English speakers, they expect to be understood in that manner (Nero, 2000, p. 489). For this chapter, the participants' linguistic identities align more closely with Edited American English, confirming their assumptions as indicated in their interviews. It is necessary to acknowledge this shift in composition pedagogy to reflect this change in the academic landscape.

Reticence as (A)motivation

When Sherry exhibited resistance as (a)motivation, she did so through her silences and paralingual responses during the writing conference. As a referred student, Sherry had to complete a number of hours in the writing center following tutor-guided instructions geared towards the professor's suggested focus. For the study, Sherry was supposed to bring a writing sample or assignment for her tutor to work on with her. Since she did not have a writing sample or assignment, Matthius assigned a standard post-test, using the results as the focus for the structure of the session. Although Sherry agreed to this modification, her body language suggested that she wasn't convinced the change would be beneficial, and this was confirmed during the stimulated recall step. During the introduction phase of the session (Mackiewicz & Thompson, 2015), Matthius opened with a question about her purpose asking what she wanted to accomplish during the session. Using Edited American English, a modicum of AAL phonology, and a straightened back and hands placed squarely on the table, Sherry carefully articulates the following: "I kind of wanted you to give me a bit of guidance on how to formulate the body; like, what are some common mistakes thatchu, and writing errors that [moving her left hand] that people neglect to incorporate or should incorporate in their paper." In response, Matthius leans back in his chair before drilling her on basic grammar skills:

> M: Um, give me some action—give me some examples of a verb.
>
> S: Juuump [slowly]. Kiiiicked. [shrugs shoulders. Locks eyes with him]

M: Is *is* an example of a verb?

S: [moves eyes back and forth, shakes head] No.

M: Okay, um, anythin' else thatch you know you need to have a complete sentence?

S: [after 14 seconds of silence] No.

Although Sherry enunciated almost all of her words in EAE, an intentional strategy to avoid revealing her Jamaican accent, she signified through her silent, ocular paralinguistic responses such as eyeballing and cutting her eyes in disapproval (Hudson, 2001). Her emphatic "no" exhibited Troutman's (2001) clapping, as well. The session progressed to the learning phase, but Sherry had not settled on the grammar instruction. In fact, she continued to look for a writing sample for an extended period of time. This suggests her resistance to the tutoring process. After a closer examination of her resistance in terms of her language choices and her body language, it became apparent that steps could have been made to understand the reasons for her resistance and make her feel more comfortable and open to the situation.

Conclusion

This chapter points us towards a rhetorical argument for translanguaging as a byproduct of the linguistic push-pull among African American Language and Caribbean Creole English writers, as evidenced by the Anglophone Caribbean writers highlighted in this chapter. This argument moves beyond standardized varieties and their attendant prescriptive grammars and pushes us towards thinking about the languaging of the Anglophone Caribbean student writer in the midst of diverse identity constructions within an HBU writing center. Acknowledging translanguaging in these ways affords writing center studies the opportunity to nuance the impact of race, racism, and the transnational students' experience. Liminality in the context of LPP as translanguaging is the place where chiasmic play creates creases of freedom of expression or linguistic cyphers. LPP is as American as the racism that caused it, but it moves beyond the pristineness that racism can't tame. The translanguaging in my study bops to its own rhythm, always *signifyin'* beyond the Atlantic and back again.

References

Anderson, J. D. (1988). *The education of blacks in the south, 1860–1935*. Chapel Hill, NC: University of North Carolina Press.

Bhabha, H. (1994). *The location of culture*. New York: Routledge.

Brown II, M. C., & Freeman, K. (2004). The state of research on black colleges: An introduction. In M. C. Brown II & K. Freeman (Eds.), *Black Colleges: New Perspectives on Policy and Practice* (pp. xi-xiv). Westport, CT: Praeger.

Bryce-Laporte, R. (1972). Black immigrants: The experience of invisibility and inequality. *Journal of Black Studies, 3*, 29–56.

Canagarajah, S. (2013). Introduction. In S. Canagarajah, (Ed.) *Literacy as translingual approach: Between communities and classrooms* (pp. 1–10). New York: Routledge.

Cook-Gumperz, J. (1993). Dilemmas of identity: Oral and written literacies in the making of a basic writing student. *Anthropology and Education Quarterly, 24*, 336–356.

DeCheck, N. (2016). The power for common interest for motivating writers: A case study. In L. Fitzgerald & M. Ianetta (Eds.), *The Oxford guide for writing tutors: Practice and research* (pp. 336–342). Oxford: Oxford University Press.

DiPardo, A. (2011). 'Whispers of coming and going': Lessons from Fannie. In C. Murphy & S. Sherwood (Eds.), *The St. Martin's sourcebook for writing tutors* (pp. 233–249). Boston: Bedford-St. Martin's.

Fort, E. (2013). *Survival of the historically black colleges and universities: Making it happen*. Lanham, MD: Lexington Books.

Gasman, M., Lundy-Wagner, V., Ransom, T., & Bowman III, N. (2010). *Unearthing promise and potential: Our nation's historically black colleges and universities*. Las Vegas, NV: Association for the Study of Higher Education.

Green, L. J. (2002). *African American English: A linguistic introduction*. Cambridge: Cambridge University Press.

Grimm, N. M. (2011). Retheorizing writing center work to transform a system of advantage based on race. In L. Greenfield & K. Rowan (Eds.), *Writing centers and the new racism: A call for sustainable dialogue and change* (pp. 75–100). Logan, UT: Utah State University Press.

Horn, S. (1993). Fostering spontaneous dialect shift in the writing of African-American students. In T. Flynn & M. King (Eds.), *Dynamics of the writing conference: Social and cognitive interaction* (pp. 103–110). Urbana, IL: NCTE.

Horner, B., Donahue, C., & NeCamp, S. (2011). Toward a multilingual composition scholarship: From English only to a translingual norm. *College Composition and Communication, 63*, 269–300.

Hudson, B. H. (2001). *African American female speech communities: Varieties of talk*. Westport, CT: Bergin & Garvey.

Ibrahim, A. (1999). Becoming black: Rap and hip-hop, race, gender, identity, and the politics of ESL learning. *TESOL Quarterly, 33,* 349–369.

Jordan, Z. L. (2012). Students' right, African American English, and writing assessment: Considering the HBCU. In A. Inoue & M. Poe (Eds.), *Race and writing assessment* (pp. 97–110). New York: Peter Lang.

Kynard, C., & R. Eddy. (2009). Toward a new critical framework: Color-conscious political morality and pedagogy at historically black and historically white colleges and universities." *College Composition and Communication, 61,* 24–42.

Mackiewicz, J., & Thompson, I. K. (2015). *Talk about writing: The tutoring strategies of experienced writing center tutors.* New York: Routledge.

Makoni, S., Smitherman, G., Ball, A., & Spear, A. (2003). Introduction. In S. Makoni, G. Smitherman, A. Ball, & A. Spear, (Eds.), *Black linguistics: Language, society, and politics in Africa and the Americas* (pp. 1–18). New York: Routledge.

McGill, L. G. (2005). *Constructing black selves: Caribbean American narratives and the second generation.* New York: New York University Press.

Milson-Whyte, V. (2013). Pedagogical and socio-political implications of code-meshing in classrooms: Some considerations for a translingual orientation to writing. In S. Canagarajah (Ed.), *Literacy as translingual practice: Between communities and classrooms* (pp. 115–127). New York: Routledge.

Morgan, M. (2002). *Language, discourse, and power in African American culture.* Cambridge: Cambridge University Press.

Moss, B. J. (2003). *A community text arises: A literate text and a literacy tradition in African American churches.* Cresskill, NJ: Hampton Press.

Nero, S. (2000). The changing faces of English: A Caribbean perspective. *TESOL Quarterly 34,* 483–510.

Nero, S. (2001). *Englishes in contact: Anglophone Caribbean students in an urban college.* Cresskill, NJ: Hampton Press.

Nunley, V. (2011). *Keepin' it hushed: The barbershop and African American hush harbor rhetoric.* Detroit, MI: Wayne State University Press.

Perryman-Clark, S. M. (2013). *Afrocentric teacher-research: Rethinking appropriateness and inclusion.* New York: Peter Lang.

Rafoth, B. (2015). *Multilingual writers and writing centers.* Logan, UT: Utah State University Press.

Richardson, E. S. (2013). Foreword. In E. Fort, *Survival of the historically black colleges and universities: Making it happen* (pp. xi-xii). Lanham, MD: Lexington Books.

Richardson, E. (2003). *African American literacies.* New York: Routledge.

Smitherman, G. (1998). Black English/Ebonics: What it be like? In L. Delpit (Ed.), *The real Ebonics debate: Power, language, and the education of African-American children* (pp. 29–37). Boston: Beacon Press.

Troutman, D. (2001). African American women: Talking that talk. In S. Lanehart (Ed.), *Sociocultural and historical contexts of African American English* (pp. 211–37). Amsterdam: John Benjamins.

Williams, B. J. (2013). Students' 'write' to their own language: Teaching the African American verbal tradition as a rhetorically effective writing skill. *Equity & Excellence in Education, 46*, 411–429.

Williams-Farrier, B. J. (2017). Signifying, narrativizing, and repetition: Radical approaches to theorizing African American language. *Meridians, 15*, 218–242.

Winford, D. (2003). Ideologies of language and socially realistic linguistics. In S. Makoni, G. Smitherman, A. Ball, & A. K. Spears (Eds.), *Black linguistics: Language, society, and politics in Africa and the Americas* (pp. 21–39). London: Routledge.

Young, M. (2013). Neither Asian nor American: The creolization of Asian American rhetoric. In S. Canagarajah, (Ed.). *Literacy as translingual approach: Between communities and classrooms* (pp. 59–69). New York: Routledge.

Young, V. A. (2009). "Nah, we straight": An argument against code switching. *JAC, 29*(1–2), 49–76.

Section Four: Institutional Contexts

> *In most Creole language situations, education policy is seldom chosen by explicit and rational processes; rather, communities tend to drift into policy positions under the force of historical and emotional commitments.*
>
> —Craig, 1980, p. 246

8 Administrators' and Lecturers' Perceptions of English Language-Mediated Academic Literacy Skills Development at a Jamaican University

Clover Jones McKenzie and Beverley Josephs

Introduction

Some Jamaican tertiary-level students, despite meeting the English Language matriculation requirements of the institutions they attend, continue to face serious problems coping with the reading and writing needs of their respective programs (McKenzie & Orogun, 2013; McLaren & Webber, 2009). Standard English is a second language for many Jamaican students, and very often they suffer from a lack of adequate exposure to and competence in using the language (Devonish & Carpenter, 2007; Feraria, 2008). Since "education is mediated through language," as Weideman (2014) notes, this problem can seriously impact tertiary students' success (p. ii). Information is frequently passed on in lectures and course material through the use of Standard English, the official language of education in Jamaica, and students have to use this medium to produce responses, especially in writing, to display their understanding of concepts. To further complicate the situation, students have to contend with the conventions of academic literacy, the norms associated with reading and writing at the postsecondary level.

The difficulties some students face prompt various institutions to undertake initiatives to assist the learners with meeting the language demands. These strategies include introducing English Language proficiency tests and general academic writing courses focused on exposition and argumentation, as well as the creation of writing centers. The various initiatives, however, often seem not to be achieving the intended objectives. As McLaren and Webber (2009) and McKenzie and Josephs (2016) note, some Jamaican university students' reading skills and written output are still unacceptable even after completing required general education academic writing courses. This situation frequently sparks discussions regarding what or who is to be blamed, with fingers generally pointed at the writing instructors or the courses (Rose, 2016). At our institution, the University of Technology, Jamaica (UTech, Ja.), in various meetings and within informal discussions, there are comments that question the value of the academic writing courses and the strategies used in their delivery. Similar to the situation discussed in Milson-Whyte (2015) in relation to The University of the West Indies, Mona (UWI, Mona), the suggestion is that the writing courses should *fix* the problems seen in the students' written output, and they are failing at this task. These comments ignore the fact that students worldwide struggle with academic writing (Doolan & Miller, 2012) and that efficient academic literacy (AL) development demands collaboration from all stakeholders, including policy makers and content lecturers (Hallett, 2013; Lillis & Scott, 2007; Tapp, 2015). One may deduce, however, that some of the persons making these comments are not aware of the demands of language learning and would need to be assisted in understanding this phenomenon.

Representatives from the English Language and Linguistics sections at UWI, Mona, on recognizing that the general writing courses cannot by themselves adequately prepare students for writing in the disciplines, added a writing across the curriculum (WAC) element to at least two content-area courses. In this approach, the writing facilitators/instructors and content specialists collaborate within the discipline-specific course to assist the students in developing the requisite skills. Although this effort is small-scale, McLaren and Webber's (2009) description of the results of the initial WAC project suggests that it is a possible means of mitigating the issues in disciplinary writing. Other postsecondary institutions, including UTech, Ja., need to also examine their academic literacy (AL) offerings and find means of better assisting the students to acquire mastery of required reading and writing skills. We believe, however, that this task should not just involve the academic writing instructors; all stakeholders within the institution must play a role.

This paper reports on the first step in a much larger project seeking to engage other stakeholders within the university regarding the discovery of more effective methods of catering to the AL needs of the UTech, Ja. students. This initial stage examined the views of some consenting administrators and content-area lecturers as to their perceived role in the development of students' AL skills. In order for us to not just depend on anecdotal evidence and assumptions in seeking to understand the current situation in relation to the improvement of these skills, the analysis of stakeholders' perceptions was a necessary step. The focus on perception, "a way of seeing or understanding a thing, phenomenon or process" (Garg, 2011, p. 102), is important as it is a significant factor in determining how people behave (Sulphey, 2014). Thus, if the administrators or content lecturers do not view AL skills development as significant or being their concern, then it would be difficult to garner their participation in identifying more successful strategies for improving these skills. Analysis of the collected data revealed that while the administrators and content lecturers predominantly saw academic literacy skills development as being crucial and had some degree of dissatisfaction with the current efforts being made to improve students' reading and writing skills, the overriding view was that academic writing lecturers are mainly responsible for engendering progress.

Why Academic Literacy?

Although UTech, Ja. offers only two general writing courses, labeled Academic Writing 1 and 2, we chose the concept *academic literacy* since the skills involved in the courses cover much more than the mere production of written text. For example, there is an emphasis in the courses on information literacy—the ability to know when there is an information void and to locate, critique, synthesize, and use these details effectively (United Nations Educational, Scientific and Cultural Organization, 2008). These skills are not only useful in writing. We believe that courses in academic literacy must move beyond just essay writing, as they should seek to prepare students to "use language to meet the demands of tertiary education" (Weideman, 2014, p. ii), and we wish to add: professional practice. The focus on a range of language-related skills within the investigation would, we hope, serve as a subtle means of highlighting the many skills involved in understanding and producing information and alert the participants to the fact that these skills are relevant to their courses as well.

METHODOLOGY

Site. The University of Technology, Jamaica (UTech, Ja.), a predominantly technical university in Kingston with two colleges and five faculties on the main campus, chiefly requires passes in Caribbean Secondary Education Certificate (CSEC) subjects for admission. Thus, matriculating students have mainly completed Grade 11, although they can go up to Grade 13, where they sit the Caribbean Advanced Proficiency Examination (CAPE). Due to historical data on students' performance in the production of written texts in English, incoming students, despite having a pass in the CSEC English A or an equivalent examination, have to sit an English Language Proficiency Test (ELPT). This test determines whether they must complete a one-semester pre-university course or begin the first of the two three-credit bearing general education writing courses offered through a unit dedicated to the teaching of English Language-mediated writing skills. Each course is a semester or thirteen weeks long and focuses on academic reading and writing skills geared towards preparing students for the production of formal expository and argumentative essays.

In spite of various modifications to the courses, most of the students consistently score within the "C" range, which is 50–59% at UTech, Ja. (McKenzie & Josephs, 2016), and some content-area lecturers consistently lament their students' inability to transfer what should have been learnt in the writing modules/courses. In addition, employers, as seen in the last survey commissioned by UTech, Ja., continue to complain about the graduates' failure to think critically and effectively communicate in English. Clearly, something has to be done to better assist the students to cultivate the required skills, and the answer cannot just come from the writing facilitators/instructors within two thirteen-week courses.

Participants. Similar to other universities, UTech, Ja. has a hierarchical structure. The ranking at UTech, Ja. moves from president, deputy president, vice-presidents, deans, vice-deans, heads of school, program directors, course coordinators (referred to as module coordinators at UTech, Ja.) and lecturers. There are also influential individuals, such as the curriculum and teaching and learning officers, who play key roles in the creation and delivery of academic content. For the purpose of this study, all ranks above the lecturer were classified as administrators, including the curriculum and teaching and learning officers. Administrators above the deans are responsible for institution-wide policy and overall management of the university. Therefore, if there are to be drastic shifts in how academic literacy is treated, their involvement is crucial. The other categories of administrators are the managers within the colleges and faculties who lead program and curriculum development; some of them also regularly interact closely with top management. We initially selected a convenience sample of thirty administrators, but only twenty participated. Thirty-two of the fifty content-area lecturers from across the colleges and faculties responded. The academic writing facilitators/instructors were not involved in this phase of the project.

Ethical Considerations

Prior to starting the investigation, we submitted a proposal document, questionnaires, and informed consent forms to the university's research ethics committee for approval. In addition, participants registered their willingness to participate by signing the consent form, which outlined the purpose of the research, plans to publish the results, and measures to ensure confidentiality. Respondents were also told not to include their names or other identifying features on the questionnaires.

Research Questions

There were two major questions in this investigation:

1. How do administrators view academic literacy (AL) skills development within the university?
2. What are content-area lecturers' views of academic literacy skills development within the university?

However, to gather more specific data, we divided the questions into the following sub-questions, as indicated in Table 1.

Table 1
Major Questions and their Sub-Questions

Major Questions	Sub-questions
1. How do administrators view academic literacy (AL) skills development within the university?	1 (a) What do policy documents reveal about the administrators' perceptions of academic literacy skills? 1 (b) What do the administrators' expressed opinions reveal about their views of academic literacy skills development within the university?
2. What are content-area lecturers' views of academic literacy skills development within the university?	2 (a) What value do content-area lecturers place on academic literacy skills development? 2 (b) How do content-area lecturers define their role in academic literacy skills development? 2 (c) How are content-area lecturers' perceptions of their roles translated into action?

Data Collection

According to Mulendema, Ndhlovu, and Mulenga (2016), "perception is a cognitive process" that determines how persons view objects and events (p. 15). This implies that perceptions are internal and may not be easily measured. However, Garg (2011), as well as Robbins and Judge (2013), suggest that analyses of individuals' expressed opinions or behavior can assist in this effort. In line with these suggestions, we sought access to the views of the participants through an analysis of relevant documents—the university's philosophy, vision, and teaching and learning policies—and via the administration of survey instruments. We expected that the act of creating policy statements that spoke to particular skills and concepts would point to the administrators' perceptions, while the questionnaires would flesh out respondents' beliefs about writing instruction.

The administrators and content-area lecturers received two different questionnaires although they contained some similar questions and made use of open-ended and Likert scale-type closed questions to provide both qualitative and quantitative data. Both instruments explored the participants' knowledge of the academic writing courses, types of skills they would want to be included, and the adequacy of provisions made by the institution to support academic literacy (AL) skills development. Where they differed was in the reference to the policy documents of the university, since the administrators, based on their responsibilities, would be more involved in crafting these. The administrators are less involved in teaching; thus, more of their time can be spent on developing policies. Furthermore, although representatives from the academic, administrative, and technical staff sit on many of the decision-making bodies at the university, final decisions on policies are made by committee members comprising chiefly of top executive and middle management teams.

ANALYSIS

The documents and open-ended questions yielded qualitative data in verbal form, which were analyzed using a type of discourse analysis (Mayring, 2014). In this procedure, the investigator decides on a method by segmenting the text, whether by words, phrases, or clauses based on the phenomenon under study. We examined the policy statements for references to components of academic literacy and the open-ended responses for themes related to the participants' attitude to the topic. The closed Likert scale-type questions provided quantitative data, which we analyzed based on the percentage of participants who selected various options, and significance established, where appropriate. Tools within Microsoft Excel proved useful in calculating percentages and frequency of language-related text. Both types of data were compared to yield overall assumptions about the perceptions of the participants.

RESULTS

Sub-Question 1(a): What do policy documents reveal about the administrators' perceptions of academic literacy skills?

The university's philosophy and vision, as well as the teaching and learning policy were combed for words and phrases that could be aligned to academic literacy (AL) skills. The frequency of these language segments was used as a signal of the importance that administrators ascribed to these skills. All the documents showed a high occurrence of literacy-related terms. This signaled that great significance was placed on graduates of UTech, Ja. displaying competence in the use of AL skills. The results of the perusal of each document are discussed below.

Philosophy

There are no overt language or literacy-focused terms within the philosophy statement; however, the italicized concepts shown here allude to these skills:

> The university is committed to the *total education* of the individual as a *social being* and seeks to develop the *whole person* in terms of personal well-being and *social and intellectual competence*. It promotes *life-long learning*, personal development and service to the community.

Implicit in the notions of "total education" and "social being," and "intellectual competence," for instance, are issues related to effective communication and critical reasoning, as well as the critical consumption and application of information. Olson and McCaslin (2008), for example, point to the ability to interact and live with others, as integral to our social being. This ability demands effective language use in building relationships and coping with conflict. The other UTech documents confirm the view that the attributes named in the philosophy are aligned to academic literacy. Normally, an entity's philosophy guides what it does; therefore, all other policy documents should mirror the values named in the philosophy. This is exactly what we saw in the analysis of the vision and teaching and learning policy.

The Vision Statement

The vision statement includes concepts that implicitly relate to literacy skill development. It refers to the training of "globally competent, versatile, innovative, entrepreneurial graduates." This training cannot be achieved without focusing on the ability to communicate ideas, think logically, and use effective tools in problem solving. These are all a part of literacy skill development.

The Teaching and Learning Policy

This document details what students should be able to do after successfully completing their program and speaks most clearly to literacy skill improvement. Table 2 highlights the fact that a significant number of the sections of the policy refer directly to aspects of literacy development.

Table 2
Extract from UTech's Teaching and Learning Policy

Segments of Policy All graduates of UTech will be able to:	Occurrence of Literacy Attribute
6.1 communicate effectively, both orally and in writing, in their professional practice and as members of their communities.	Communicate
They should also communicate in a manner which reduces the possibility of conflict.	Communicate
6.2 apply logical, critical, and creative thinking when solving problems	Logical, creative, and critical thinking
Assess, evaluate, and synthesize information from a range of sources utilizing appropriate methods and technologies	Access, evaluate, and synthesize information
6.3 utilize lifelong learning skills in their pursuit of personal development and to achieve excellence in professional practice	Utilize lifelong learning skills
6.7 utilize research skills to solve problems and inform decision making	Utilize research skills
6.8 demonstrate intercultural awareness and understanding by thinking globally and considering issues from a variety of perspectives	Demonstrate critical thinking

The policy documents demonstrate, either implicitly or explicitly, that literacy skills are valued by the leadership of the university, based on the attributes identified for its graduates. The highlighted skills, which detail what students should be able to do when they complete their program of study, appear to be central to the work of the university. Hence, the focus should be on more than just the creation of academic essays within two 13-week general education writing courses. With this level of regard for the development of these skills should come action that includes: (a) ensuring that all facets of the institution have measures in place to cater to the nurturing of the skills; (b) calling for greater collaboration with literacy facilitators/writing instructors; and (c) providing necessary resources, such as adequately equipped literacy resource centers. The absence of the required actions, we believe, points to individuals' perceptions of how academic literacy skills development occurs. As Rose (2016) suggests, they may see this activity as easy, once the writing classes accomplish what they should. The responses from the survey instruments were instructive in providing details on the participants' expressed views of the importance of AL skills at the postsecondary level and the role of the institution in their development.

Analysis of Administrators' Closed-Question Responses

Sub-question 1(b): What do the administrators' expressed opinions reveal about their views of academic literacy skills development within the university?

Most administrators, especially those at and below the rank of dean, are involved in teaching; however, they are also involved in policy development and implementation. Thus, their questions were more heavily weighted towards policy, despite there being some overlap with the content lecturers' questionnaires. We analyzed survey questions 3, 4, and 10 together since they provided data in relation to policy:

Survey Questions 3, 4 and 10

> 3. UTech's philosophy refers to the "total education of the individual as a social being." To what extent does this descriptor include attention to language-related skills?
> 4. To what extent do you agree with the inclusion of language-related characteristics in the document on the attributes of the UTech graduate?
> 10. How important is a university implemented language-related policy framework to the effort to assist students in developing their literacy skills?

Analysis of the three questions implied a strong relationship between policy guidelines of the institution and literacy skills. In the case of survey question 3, there is no word overtly mentioning language skills in the philosophy; however, 15 of the 20 administrators, or 75%, claimed that they see a relationship between the content of this document and language skills. One of the remaining five respondents was not sure. Survey question 4 had 18, or 90%, of the participants strongly agreeing with the inclusion of literacy skills in the attributes of the ideal graduate. In relation to the importance of a university implemented language skill-related policy framework, the responses of 90% of the participants ranged between very important and important.

The next set of questions related to literacy skill development at the tertiary level in general. We wanted to get some indication of what administrators believe should occur within the actual literacy skills development process at the postsecondary stage. The data helped us to get an idea of how they viewed the movement from policy statement to implementation of action. They responded to the following questions:

Survey Questions 5 and 6

> 5. To what extent do you agree with the view that Jamaican secondary school graduates need to complete reading and writing modules (label for course at UTech, Ja.) at the tertiary level?
> 6. (a) Which of the following literacy skills should be focused on at the tertiary level? Rank your selections, based on their order of importance.
>
> (b) Please identify any skills you would wish to add.

The results show that the majority of the administrators felt that tertiary-level reading and writing courses were necessary. In fact, 17, or 85%, of them stated that they strongly agreed with the view that the students should complete these courses. As far as the types of skills that should be developed are concerned, from the given options, critical thinking and reading topped the list, with the construction of various types of texts placed at the bottom. Figure 1 displays the selected skills and their rank based on the frequency of selection.

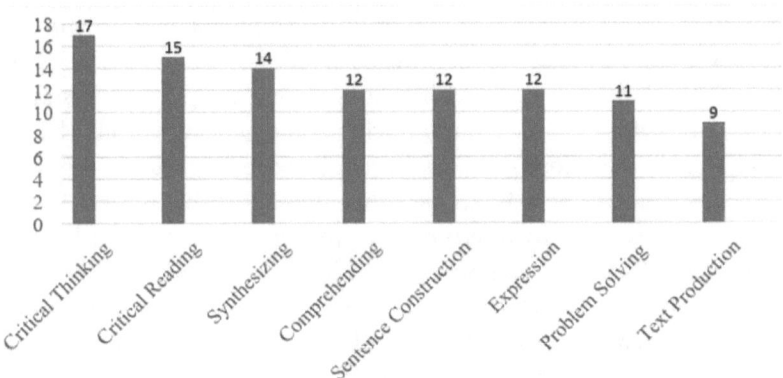

Figure 1. Frequency of Selected Skills

The fact that text production received the lowest ranking was interesting in a context where the actual courses offered to students were in the area of academic writing. Within these writing courses, the focus is predominantly on the production of formal academic expository and argumentative essays. The literacy facilitators/instructors take the students through a writing process that involves the other skills, such as problem solving, comprehending texts, and summarizing and synthesizing information. However, the ultimate aim is to have the students construct essays at the end of the semester. Based on the position of this skill in the responses, we began to wonder whether there was a mismatch between what the academic writing courses emphasized and the perceptions of the administrators. On reflection, we should not have been surprised, since anecdotal evidence suggests that many of the complaints about the writing modules tend to center on their emphasis on essay writing specifically (rather than other genres). Nevertheless, these responses warrant further investigation during the next phase of the project, which will see us conducting interviews, based on some of the responses we received on the survey instruments. For example, we did not specify what we meant by *text production*; thus, the respondents may have had varying interpretations of this concept.

For question 6(b), which asked the respondents to name any other skills they would add to the list of given options, the eight participants who responded provided some interesting feedback. One administrator wanted the interpretation of questions to be a part of the reading and writing courses. Another two participants listed technical report and letter writing, while four named oral skills development as requiring focus. We saw these responses as significant since they seem to suggest that these skills should be dealt with in a literacy class. The understanding of questions, for example, while having some general aspects that may be applicable to various disciplines, requires specific attention based on the subject area. There is no way that literacy specialists could effectively teach students to interpret all types of questions. Similar to the views of Jacobs (2007), we believe that literacy practitioners/writing instructors are not equipped to take on the responsibilities of facilitating the development of all the literacy skills students require for successfully manipulating the academic and professional contexts (see, for example, Oenbring and Jaquette, 2018). In addition, given the difficulties students still face in coping with reading and writing within the discipline despite completing generic writing courses, it is clear that transfer of skills is not effectively taking place. At UTech, Ja., for example, APA documentation is required for academic writing courses, yet some content-area lecturers consistently complain about the absence of even basic competence in this area.

The remaining questions on the survey instrument turned the spotlight on the administrators' perceptions of the provisions made for academic literacy skills development at the institution. Given the importance that most administrators appear to place on literacy skills development, we were curious to ascertain their level of familiarity and satisfaction with the opportunities provided. Survey questions 7–11, minus question 10, offered some useful data.

Survey Question 7

> 7. (a) Are you familiar with the content of the academic writing modules offered through the School of Humanities and Social Sciences?
> (b) Based on your level of familiarity, how satisfied are you with the content of the modules?

The responses to survey question 7 suggest that administrators' knowledge of the content of the writing courses is not very high. Only 35% of the administrators said they were very familiar with the writing courses being done by their students, as only seven selected this option. Another four (20%), stated that they were slightly familiar with the content, while two persons declared that they had fair knowledge of the content. The declared low level of familiarity seems odd within a context where the philosophy, vision, and intended attributes of the graduates of the institution appear to heavily emphasize literacy skills. In some cases, the writing courses are prerequisites for content-area courses. Academic managers should be knowledgeable about the content of these courses in order to assist in determining the appropriateness of the content and possibly fulfilling resource needs.

Of the thirteen respondents who claimed to have some knowledge of the courses, nine took a position in relation to their degree of satisfaction. Figure 2 reveals that there was almost a balance between those who said they were moderately satisfied and the moderately dissatisfied group.

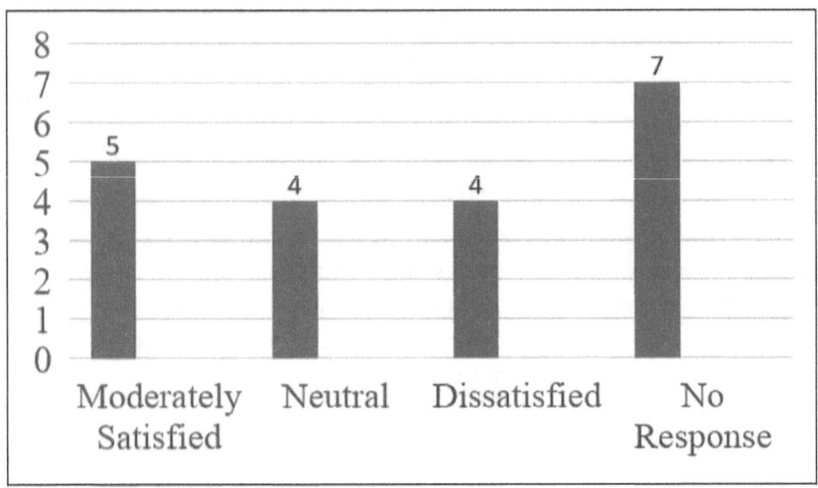

Figure 2. Satisfaction Level with Academic Writing Courses at UTech, Ja.

The fact that only four participants chose the *dissatisfied* rating is not very comforting, but it is difficult to draw a definitive conclusion about the degree of satisfaction in relation to the writing courses based on the responses given. With the four respondents also remaining neutral and seven offering no response, a total of eleven, 55% of the sample, did not provide a definite answer. Yet, the fact that nobody chose *satisfied* and the only responses on the positive side were four selections of *moderately satisfied* could suggest that the satisfaction level is not very high. Once again, though, further probing is necessary before we voice precise conclusions. The ratings for survey question 8 will be interesting when compared to those for this question.

Survey Questions 8 and 9

8. Based on your knowledge of the English Language proficiency level of students entering UTech, Ja., how satisfied are you with the opportunities being offered for literacy development?
9. In your views who needs to do more to better facilitate students' academic literacy skills development?

The frequency of selected options in answer to survey question 8 is shown in Figure 3.

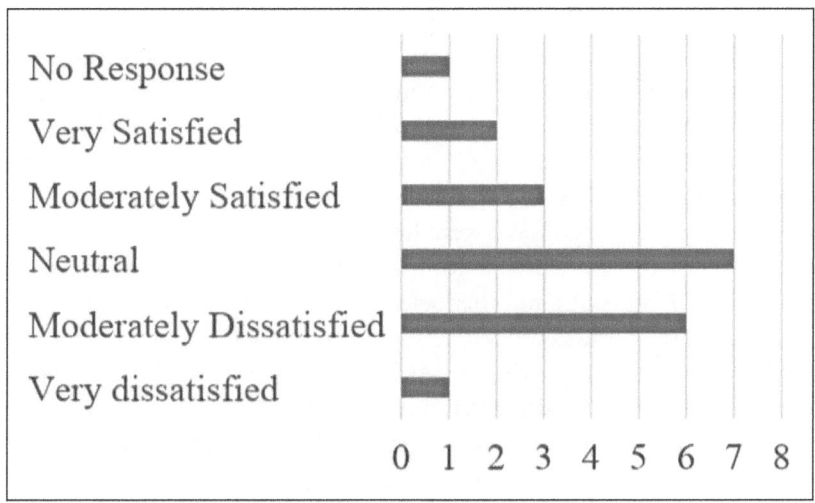

Figure 3. Responses Rating Degree of Satisfaction with General Opportunities

The responses to survey question 8 revealed some concerns. While a larger number of persons responded, when the seven *neutral* selections are added to the one person who did not respond, it gives a total of eight (40%) not providing a definitive response. The reason for this occurrence may be an unwillingness to commit to a particular response, uncertainty as to what is required, or inadequate knowledge of provisions made for AL development. Only further probing can provide the answer. Despite the reason, the situation is troubling as administrators are the group that would need to bring matters impacting students and staff into discussions with top management, including the president. We believe that administrators should have an opinion on areas that impact teaching and learning. It was also interesting that although no participant selected *very satisfied* or even *satisfied* in relation to question 7(b), which focused on satisfaction with the writing courses, two respondents selected *very satisfied* with the opportunities provided by the institution. Additionally, 6 of the 7 respondents who claimed not to have much knowledge of the writing courses offered opinions on the opportunities provided. If one has little or no knowledge of the main means of focusing on AL skills development at UTech, Ja., how can one effectively voice an opinion on this matter?

Survey question 9 was meant to be a follow-up to the previous one. Based on the complaints about some students' inability to meet the reading and writing demands of their programs, we anticipated that there would be a high degree of dissatisfaction with the available opportunities. This question aimed at revealing whether the respondents would blame a specific entity. We, therefore, wanted the respondents to select one option from the list; however, most of the respondents supplied more than one. On careful analysis, we acknowledge that the question was poorly worded if this was our objective. The given responses, nevertheless, still proved helpful. We were heartened to see that only three persons selected the academic writing lecturers as the entity that needed to do more. The same number selected the students only, with seven selecting all the options offered: academic writing lecturers, content-area specialists, the students, the university administration. No respondent selected the university administration as the sole entity that needed to do more. The majority seem to be suggesting that it is a joint responsibility. This notion was further explored in survey question 11.

Survey Question 11

> 11. How would you rate the university's provision of resources to facilitate literacy development?

Although no administrator selected the university administration as the sole entity that should do more to facilitate the development of literacy skills, the option with the highest frequency of selection—all the above—implies that all the mentioned stakeholders need to act. A part of the university administration's action would be to provide resources needed for literacy skills development (such as providing more writing courses or expanding the writing center). The offered responses to survey question 11 showed a recognition of the fact that while some resources, such as writing courses and a small writing center are provided, there are deficiencies in this area. As Figure 4 shows, 40% of the respondents selected the moderately adequate option.

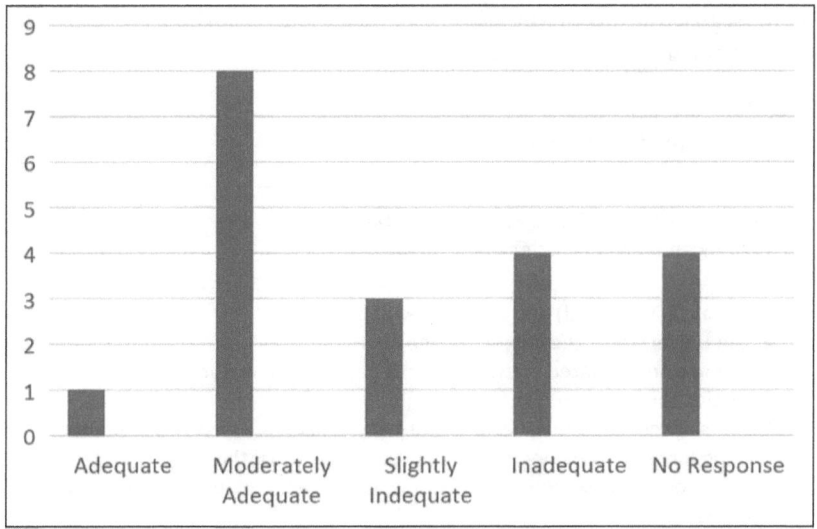

Figure 4. Rating of the University's Provision of Resources

When the 40% *moderately adequate* option is added to the 20% who selected *inadequate*, there is a total of a 60% negative rating of the resources. Only 15% of the respondents selected *slightly inadequate*, suggesting that there are only minor issues with the provision of resources. This result is interesting given the fact that only one respondent reported being dissatisfied with the provision of opportunities for the development of academic literacy skills. The administrators appear to be separating resources from opportunities, but can the opportunities for advancement be adequate if the resources are insufficient? Further exploration of how the administrators view the provision of opportunities and resources by the administration occurred during the analysis of the open-ended survey responses.

Analysis of Administrators' Open-Ended Responses

Both the administrators and content lecturers' questionnaires contained an open-ended question that asked for other suggestions in relation to academic literacy development. The responses from each set of participants were analyzed based on the principles of critical content analysis with the help of Excel tools. The responses were first examined for words and phrases that indicated themes aligned to the respondents' attitude. The focus of the responses appeared to be the taking of some type of action. The verbs (stated and unstated) that indicated actions were used in the segmentation of the data. Each segment was then coded for the agent of the action, based on the coding scheme in Table 3.

Table 3
Coding Scheme for Qualitative Data

> Coding Dimensions: Code action as the performance/execution of the main verb by an individual or entity.
>
> 1. Code as *university* (U) any clause in which
>   a. the university is the subject of the sentence.
>   b. the action is related to policy or the general operations of the institution.
> 2. Code as *academic writing lecturer* (AL) any clause in which the academic writing lecturer is named or implied as the agent of the action, there is reference to course content, teaching strategies, and learning outcomes in the classroom.
> 3. Code as *content lecturer* (CL) any clause in which the content lecturer is named or implied as the agent of the action.
> 4. Code as *student* any clause in which the student is named or implied as the agent of the action.
> 5. Code as *unstated* any clause that has no clear subject and the possible agents could be one of many.

To achieve greater reliability in this process, we asked a second rater to complete the process without being aware of the first coding outcome. The study had an interrater reliability of 76%. Table 4 presents some of the responses the administrators gave.

Table 4
Sample of Administrator Statements and the Stated or Implied Agent

Language Segment.	**Agent**
Develop a true writing center.	AL
Aim at full collaboration of the administrators, faculties, and language unit.	AL
Interface with lecturers, through professional development involving AL development.	AL
Reading and writing labs for special needs of students.	AL
Provide assistance for students.	AL

Language Segment.	Agent
Academic Literacy development at the university should *consider* the literacy needs of the students, relevance to the area of academic specialization, and subsequent career.	Unstated
Regular *review* of our literacy development practices.	Unstated
The university needs to *encourage* reading in the modules.	U
Establish a policy regarding writing standards across faculties and colleges.	U
University needs to *see* the gaps in literacy in students and devise a strategy to fill.	U
Lecturers/academics should *enforce* the need for academic writing.	CL

Analysis of the data shows that although many of the administrators were involved in teaching or were managers of the curriculum process, many of the identified actions related to the university in general or the academic literacy facilitators/instructors. Even in the scenario involving the unstated agents, one could argue that the academic literacy facilitators/instructors were the intended agents. In addition, the use of *university* could mean that the individuals wanted to embrace all stakeholders including or, the reverse, excluding themselves. We were not sure. The attested segment "we need to organize" is a possible indicator of the desire to include themselves.

Analysis of Content-Area Lecturers' Closed-Question Responses

Similar to the situation with the administrators, there was one major research question for the content lecturers study: *What are content-area lecturers' views of academic literacy skills?* This question was then subdivided. To facilitate analysis, the survey questions were grouped based on their relevance to the sub-question. Thirty-two lecturers from across the various colleges and faculties completed the questionnaires. The findings are presented in relation to the sub-questions.

Research Sub-questions:

2(a) What value do content-area lecturers place on academic literacy skills development?

2(b) How do content-area lecturers define their role in academic literacy skills development?

2(c) How are content-area lecturers' perceptions of their roles translated into action?

Survey Questions 1—4 provided data for research sub-question 2(a). These were:

1. How would you rate your knowledge of the content and requirements of the academic writing modules?
2. How would you rate the importance of the Academic Writing modules to students' development and progress at the tertiary level?
3. How do you rate the relevance of the Academic Writing modules to students' performance in your area of specialization?
4. Are the Academic Writing modules prerequisites for students in any of your modules?

The responses to this survey's question 1 were very surprising. Of the 32 participants, 19, or approximately 59%, stated that they had inadequate or no knowledge of what their students were being offered in the academic writing classes. This could be interpreted as a suggestion that, for these lecturers, literacy skills development was of little importance; thus, the lecturers would be less likely to reinforce them in the classes. With this low knowledge base, we expected that the other responses related to the importance of the development of the skills would be negatively impacted.

However, in contrast to what we expected about the significance of the courses, answers to survey question 2 showed that almost 94% of the content lecturers reported that the courses were either "extremely important" or "important." Some participants who claimed to have insufficient or no knowledge of what was involved in the writing courses now saw them as being "extremely important." This anomaly may suggest that, although they saw the significance of the skills, the content lecturers who claimed ignorance of the content of the academic writing courses did not feel that it was necessary to have in-depth knowledge of them. After all, they were not the ones teaching these courses.

In relation to question 3, regarding the relevance of the writing modules to their areas of specialization, the responses were chiefly positive. Twenty-six persons selected either extremely relevant or relevant. Only four respondents chose little relevance, with two selecting irrelevant. We noted some shift in the percentage of responses for each option when compared to question 2, which focused on importance of the courses to students' development and progress at the tertiary level. The top positive response decreased in selection by almost 43%, while the middle band widened. For relevance to performance at the university in general, 21, almost 66%, selected "extremely important," while only 12, 37.5%, chose "extremely relevant" in respect to the specialization. The downward movement in the assessment of relevance could be interpreted as a shifting away from personal engagement with the skills. This interpretation coincides with the possible covert message in the responses to survey question one: *Yes, the writing modules are important but not for me specifically.*

Survey question 4 focused on the use of the modules as prerequisites for any of the modules within the courses taught by the content lecturers. We noted that the same number of persons who saw the courses as being extremely relevant to their specialization also indicated that they were prerequisites for some of their courses. Tables 5A and 5B highlight this comparison.

Table 5A and Table 5B
Degree of Relevance to Specialization   Academic Writing as Prerequisite

Degree	**Num**	**%**		**Prereq**	**Num**	**%**
Extremely Relevant	12	37.5		Yes	12	37.5
Relevant	14	43.7		No	15	47
Little Relevance	4	12.5		Not sure	4	12.5
Irrelevant	2	6.25		No response	1	3

Sub-Questions 2 and 3

  2. How do they define their role in the process of academic literacy skill development?
  3. How are their values and perceptions of their roles translated into action?

Survey questions 5 to 8, which focused on the types of academic literacy skills and their integration in the content-area classes, provided data in response to the above sub-questions. Survey question 5 asked the content lecturers to indicate which skills students have to master to successfully complete their modules. The responses showed an overlap with those given by the administrators. Both sets of respondents, for example, gave prominence to critical thinking skills. Of the 32 respondents, 87.5% named it as the number one skill to be mastered by students. One dominant difference is in the labeling of the least favored skill. Whereas the administrators placed *text production*, based on their interpretation of this concept, at the bottom of the scale, the content lecturers had *summary skills* in this position.

The responses to the survey question 6 required the lectures to indicate which of the skills they identified in survey question five were emphasized in their classes. The data here further confirm the belief that content-area lecturers may not see academic literacy skill development as their concern. Figure 5 highlights the disparity in the number of persons who selected the skill as being important and those who said they actually focused on these skills in class.

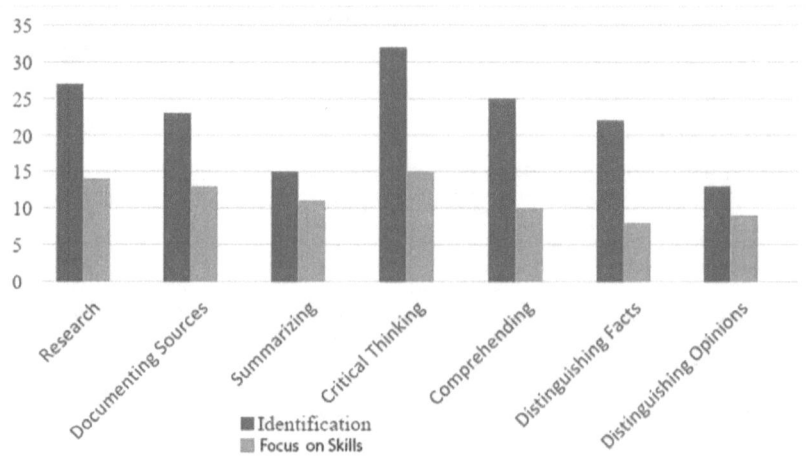

Figure 5. Comparison of Identification of Versus Focus on Skills

To get an indication of how the content lecturers apply their beliefs to the teaching process, we asked them to indicate the ways in which they sought to reinforce the skills. They could choose more than one option from the list. The majority of them said that they included these in the rubrics for written and spoken presentations, as well as emphasized their necessity in lecture and tutorials. The least selected option was the encouragement to self-monitor. Figure 6 displays the distribution of the responses.

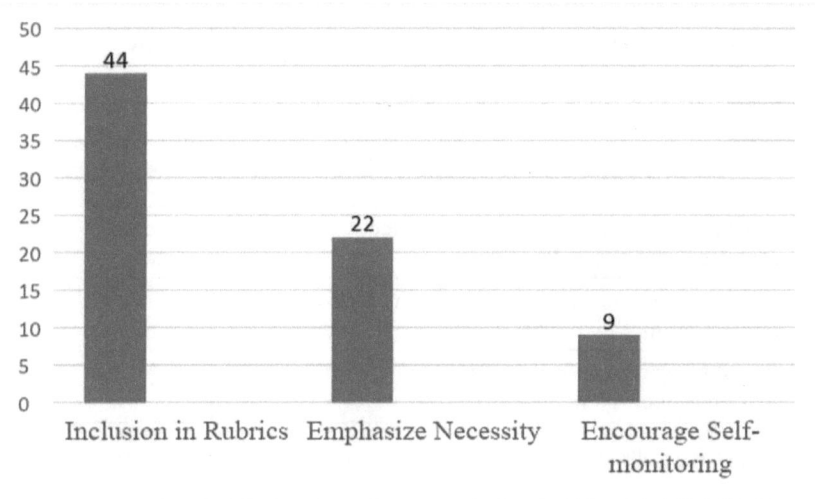

Figure 6. Frequency of Selected Method Used to Emphasize Skills

Analysis of Content-Area Lecturers' Open-Ended Responses

Using a similar procedure as for the administrators' opinions, we examined the content lecturers' texts for possible themes related to the value placed on the academic writing courses, or the means by which the students can receive assistance. The analysis showed that these participants also focused on the fact that the students are facing difficulties handling the demands of academic writing even after completing the writing courses. Some of their comments suggest that much of the blame rests with the wrong methodology used by the academic writing lecturers. Just as the administrators did, some of the content-area lecturers singled out the academic writing lecturers as the ones who should act, even when the difficulty related to the content area. The sample segments in Table 6 illustrate this.

Table 6
Language Segments and the Associated Agents

Language Segment	Agent
Academic writing should be offered at every year of study, students complete and can't write a sentence . . . Students seem to have basic flaw in grammar and knowledge of APA formatting is mostly poor.	student/ unstated
Written and oral assignments do not reflect that students acquired the skills.	student/ unstated
Standards . . . not seeing in the classroom. Delivery and assessment methodologies?	AL
Skills not being transferred to disciplines . . . some intervention is necessary.	unstated
How to have skills learnt applicable to other modules.	unstated
Students should apply principles of academic writing, but many do not effectively do so.	student
More accommodating lecturers.	AL
Give students real life experiences.	AL
Use specialized area cases for practice in class activity.	AL
Give students from each faculty assignments and projects relevant to their field.	AL
. . . know how . . . knowledge is beneficial to other courses. More consultation with other lecturers in other modules would help.	AL
Requisite for several courses . . . however, ill-equipped . . . do not display critical thinking expected after passing Academic Writing . . .	student/ unstated

Conclusion

The findings of this investigation reveal that a high degree of value is placed on academic literacy (AL) skills by both the university administration and content-area lecturers. However, the expression of inadequate knowledge of the content of the writing courses on the part of both sets of participants and the seeming unwillingness to take a stance, evidenced in either no responses or the selection of the neutral option, hint at some amount of personal detachment from the development of the skills. This detachment is further seen in the content-area lecturers' admission of the lack of focus on AL skills in their courses, expecting perhaps, that AL facilitators/writing instructors should take sole responsibility. These content lecturers fit Williamson and Goldsmith's (2011) description of not being aware of their role in AL development, as even when content-area lecturers made reference to activities related to the disciplines, they often named the AL facilitator/writing instructor as the agent. Jacobs (2007) puts it more bluntly when he declares that they "abdicate their role" (p. 875) and expect AL facilitators/writing instructors in a limited time span to adequately prepare students for mastery of academic literacy requirements in all contexts across the university. These problems with AL skills development are not unique to UTech, Ja. Thaiss (2012) in his overview of comments made by academic writing facilitators from various countries identifies issues related to the "lack of care" about academic writing development as evidenced by inadequately resourced writing centers and insufficient time and funding (p. 15).

The advice the participants in this study gave made it seem as if difficulties with AL skills development were quite easy to fix if the writing facilitators just did the right thing. However, students cannot just transfer generic skills to other areas; they have to be taught to do so (Gunn, Hearne & Sibthorpe, 2011). Students will never by themselves *get it right*. As the responses from some administrators within this investigation suggest, there has to be a partnership among stakeholders. However, engendering partnerships as the solution for UTech, Ja. is not so straightforward, given the manner in which the university operates in relation to lecturers' teaching load and budgeting. Thus, this ongoing project will, based on the findings of this study, further engage the various stakeholders in building awareness of the demands of AL skills development. Furthermore, with the deficit in AL skills development research in Jamaica and the broader Caribbean, we, like Butler (2013) in referring to the South African context, call for more empirical research to guide the decision-making process and more collaborative research among different institutional stakeholders.

References

Butler, G. (2013). Discipline-specific versus generic academic literacy intervention for university education: An issue of impact? *Journal for Language Teaching, 47*(2), 71–88.

Devonish, H., & Carpenter, K. (2007). *Full bilingual education in a Creole language situation: Jamaican bilingual primary education project.* St. Augustine, Trinidad and Tobago: Society for Caribbean Linguistics.

Doolan, S., & Miller, D. (2012). Generation 1.5 written error patterns: A comparative study. *Journal of Second Language Writing, 21*(1), 1–22.

Feraria, P. J. (2008). Language hurdles and the race for literacy: Implications for Caribbean classrooms. *Journal of the University College of the Cayman Islands: Grand Cayman,* 126–148.

Garg, M. (2011). Peeping into the learning world of secondary teacher trainees: Can their academic success be predicted? *Australian Journal of Teacher Education, 36*(12), 97–116.

Gunn, C., Hearne, S., & Sibthorpe, J. (2011). Right from the start: A rationale for embedding academic literacy skills in university courses. *Journal of University Teaching & Learning Practice, 8*(1). Retrieved from http://ro.uow.edu.au/cgi/viewcontent.cgi?article=1159&context=jutlp.

Hallett, R. E. (2013). Undocumented student success: Navigating constraints related to retention. *Journal of Latino-Latin American Studies (JOLLAS), 5*(2), 99–112.

Jacobs, C. (2007). Mainstreaming academic literacy teaching: Implications for how academic development understands its work in higher education. *South African Journal of Higher Education, 21*(7), 870–881.

Lillis, T., & Scott, M. (2007). Defining academic literacies research: Issues of epistemology, ideology and strategy. *Journal of Applied Linguistics, 4*(1), 5–32.

Mayring, P. (2014). *Qualitative content analysis: Theoretical foundation, basic procedures and software solutions.* Retrieved from http://nbn-reading.de/um:nbn de:0168-ssoar-39513.

McKenzie, C., & Josephs, B. (2016). A Jamaican university's experiences with academic literacy development: Meandering paths to the same destination. Paper presented at the 21st Biennial Conference of the Society for Caribbean Linguistics (SCL), UWI Mona, August 2–6, 2016.

McKenzie, C., & Orogun, J. (2013). Investigating the transferability of English Language skills from the secondary to the tertiary level. *Journal of Arts, Science and Technology, 6,* 53–73.

McLaren, I., & Webber, D. (2009). Writing right: Enhancing student engagement and performance in an ecology course. *International Journal of Environmental & Science Education, 4*(4), 365–380.

Milson-Whyte, V. (2015). *Academic writing instruction for creole-influenced students*. Kingston, Jamaica: University of the West Indies Press.

Mulendema, P., Ndhlovu, Z. & Mulenga, H. (2016). Perceptions and attitudes of student teachers and their cognitive-metacognitive awareness in mathematics in colleges of education in Zambia. *Journal of Education and Practice*, 7(27), 15–25.

Oenbring, R., & Jaquette, B. (2018). It takes an island: A survey of writing instruction across the curriculum at the University of The Bahamas. *Caribbean Journal of Education*, 40, 28–52.

Olson, A., & McCaslin, M. (2008). Students as social beings. In T. L. Good, (Ed.), *21st century education: A reference handbook* (pp. 87–96). Thousand Oaks, CA: Sage Publications.

Robbins, S., & Judge, T. (2013). *Organizational behaviour*. Delhi, India: Pearson.

Rose, P. (2016). A case for academic literacies: Informed needs analysis. *UWI Quality Education Forum*, 21, 42–62.

Sulphey, M. (2014). *Behaviour finance*. Delhi, India: PHI Learning Private.

Tapp, J. (2015). Framing the curriculum for participation: A Bernsteinian perspective on academic literacies. *Teaching in Higher Education*, 20(7), 711–722.

Thaiss, C. (2012). Origins, aims, and uses of writing programs worldwide: Profiles of academic writing in many places. In C. Thaiss, G. Bräuer, P. Carlino, L. Ganobcsik-Williams, & A. Sinha (Eds.), *Writing programs worldwide: Profiles of academic writing in many places* (pp. 5–22). Anderson, SC: Parlor Press.

United Nations Educational, Scientific and Cultural Organization (UNESCO). (2008). *The global literacy challenge: A profile of youth and adult literacy at the mid-point of the United Nations literacy decade* 2003–2012. Retrieved from http://unesdoc.unesco.org/images/0016/001631/163170e.pdf

Weideman, A. (2014). Introduction. In A. Weideman & T. van Dyk, (Eds.), *Academic literacy: Test your competence (pp. ii–ix)*. Bloemfontein: Geronimo Distribution.

Williamson, F., & Goldsmith, R. (2013). Passwrite: Recalibrating student academic literacies development. *Journal of University Teaching and Learning Practice*, 10(2). Retrieved from http://ro.uow.edu.au/cgi/viewcontent.cgi?article=1353&context=jutlp

9 Solving Problems and Signaling Potential in Writing Program Administration at The University of The West Indies, St. Augustine Campus (UWISTA)

Tyrone Ali

Introduction

Let the main ingredient be an Anglophone Caribbean-based tongue. Allow student writers of the creole-language continuum to begin initial preparations of the dish using their secondary or postsecondary education communicative competencies. Marinate from the basket of seven academic writing courses and three language workshops. Flavor with the standardized input of nine full-time and twenty part-time instructional staff, three clerical staff, and a research assistant. Sprinkle with three sittings of an English Language Proficiency Test (ELPT) annually. Simmer consistently over a period of fourteen years using a web-enabled blending learning educational framework. Attempt to settle in the face of pointed and noticeable changes in the incoming student body's oral and written communication skills over the years. Cool down with the limited services of The Writing Centre (TWC). Decorate against the backdrop of a campus that sparingly allocates resources towards the evolution and continuous development of its academic writing program. Now, have this convoluted dish served by an individual with a full teaching load along with the responsibility for coordination of the entire process and ultimate oversight of four thousand students from five large faculties annually. The end result? A concoction of a Writing Program (WP) continually garnished with diverse problems yet predicated on the promise and potential of a campus and wider university slowly moving forward. This chapter addresses how I, as the current coordinator of the academic program at The University of the West Indies, St. Augustine (UWISTA), have inherited, approached, and resolved writing program administration problems over the last decade and a half. As Writing Program Coordinator (WPC), I aim to maximize appreciation for the linguistic and educational evolution of the writing program, with a view to ensuring quality, while securing upper management's financial investment in the program for years to come.

Operational Context of UWISTA's Academic Writing Program

WPA is the cornerstone for the structure and solid implementation of visionary tertiary academic writing programs. To deny this is to court chaos in the writing instructional process with disparate perspectives, theories, and approaches given free reign. Writing program administration at UWISTA, the premier research university in Trinidad and Tobago, ensures a shared philosophy, a streamlined approach, and a unified set of goals for both instructional staff and students. As WPC, I have overseen two major waves of transition in the writing program over the past fourteen years. The initial sought to update the program's aims, pedagogy, and assessment practices, seeking harmonization with sister campuses in The UWI system. The other was characterized by two elements: first, a phased adoption of a blended learning technique characterized by increased use of educational technology; and, second, an adaptation to the noticeable shift in written communicative competencies of the incoming student body. Through it all, writing program administration has not been a simple nor all-time rewarding endeavor; rather, it has been a continuous exercise with various superficial and deep-seated problems. Yet, the WP at UWISTA remains steadfast to its mandate regarding the tertiary-level academic writing experiences of its student body. As Baldwin (2009) notes, "to succeed in the face of challenges, we should not forget what we are 'administering' for—the advancement of learning and knowledge by teaching and research and the provision of a University education" (p. 93). This has certainly been a continuous mantra at UWISTA where existing instructional staff are reminded of the dynamic nature of writing instruction that must be cultivated by related research, while incoming instructional staff are taught the overarching goals of the writing program with regard to students' needs.

Significantly, the sheer size of UWISTA's student body makes WPA a difficult task. Coupled with limited faculty and staff, the WP has to grapple with the major problems of resource allocation, language competencies, and students' and faculty members' perception of writing courses. Moreover, the WP is granted limited instructional time to focus on students' writing skills. Coordinating St. Augustine's program has become a mammoth exercise, with one WPC having ultimate responsibility for academic planning and preparation throughout the institution. Through it all, the WP's offerings aim to be grounded on best practices for teaching tertiary-level students in the Anglophone Caribbean, students whose mother tongues, as indicated in the introduction to this volume, are usually not Caribbean Standard Englishes but, rather, varieties of English-based creoles. Complicating the situation is the fact that many students, whose first love is anything other than English, writing, or rhetoric, remain unconvinced of the value of writing courses and workshops. Moreover, the prevailing attitude of some content-area faculty in non-language disciplines, exacerbates the situation. As Milson-Whyte (2008) writes about her experience at UWI, Mona, "academics . . . have perpetuated a certain tacit assumption that writing is a natural process" (p. 12). Indeed, content-area faculty seem largely of the view that their students will either miraculously develop a proportionate increase in written competencies as they grow in their own disciplines or that having students take a solitary writing course at the beginning of their undergraduate degree will furnish them with the requisite communication skills for success throughout their degree program.

Tradition and Change in Academic Writing and the Role of Writing Program Administration at UWISTA

As writing instruction has not always been valued at UWISTA and at other Caribbean postsecondary institutions the way it is now, it is critical to understand the historical development of tertiary writing instruction at UWISTA and the broader region. Initially, in 1963, UWISTA began to offer one Foundation English course titled "Use of English" (U/E). This course was patterned after a related British course of the same name that was taken by incoming university students across Britain who were unsuccessful in a related U/E examination set by the Thames-estuary universities of Cambridge, Oxford, and London. The primary aim of the early U/E course was to stimulate a general appreciation for and receptiveness to language and, specifically, to develop students' linguistic sensibilities. This course had a different focus from American rhetoric and composition courses that center explicitly on building students' academic writing skills. Success in the U/E approach was relatively low as students were made to operate within an adopted discourse that held little root in their individual and collective linguistic competencies (for more on the U/E course, see Milson-Whyte [2015]).

The 1970s saw the infusion, by the then WPC, of a module designed to develop students' awareness of the role that creole languages play in Caribbean societies. However, there remained an increasing number of students whose writing in Caribbean Standard English was deemed to be less than satisfactory, due in part to students' inability to bridge the gap between their native language and the standard target language. As a result of the continuing student writing problems, the course content was changed fundamentally in 1980 to focus more specifically on the production of writing. At the same time, the course changed its title to Language, Logic, and Composition (LLC). Its content indicated that the aim was to develop skills of critical thinking, research, and writing in English. While competence in Standard English was readily taken for granted in the previous U/E course, LLC included explicit grammar instruction, such as modules on the mechanics of writing, spelling, punctuation, and sentence construction. LLC, like its predecessor U/E, was a year-long course. A session lasted for three hours per week with one of those hours set aside for students to consult with instructors. Course components included critical analysis of a piece of writing, summary, production of argument, exposition, description (imaginative and technical), and a research paper. The student support offered in the course revolved around lecturing, discussion of writing tasks in actual writing mini-sessions, provision of reading materials, and one-on-one consultations. Assessment took the form of in-course tests of the different writing modes and a research paper. The class size was thirty students.

When UWISTA moved to the semester system in 1996, the WPC developed two semester-long courses to replace the year-long course under the overarching label *Academic Writing for Different Purposes*. This umbrella label subsumed three individual courses based on students' respective disciplines, and came on stream to supplement the primary English for Academic Purposes (EAP) course that had emerged as the final variant of the initial U/E. Under the new system, all students took the one general EAP course and then branched into discipline-specific courses. Such course growth occurred as a direct response to feedback from other faculty members who were complaining about students' weak academic language skills. This reality was not UWISTA-specific but, rather, a UWI-wide phenomenon. Indeed, McLaren and Webber (2009) note persistent complaints from UWI, Mona faculty about undergraduate students' poor academic language skills, and Rose & Sookraj (2015) discuss UWI, Cave Hill's undergraduates' weak attainment of skills in Foundation English/composition courses there despite students' exposure to Caribbean Standard English in secondary school courses and examinations.

Apart from semesterization, other factors that shaped the WP were a lack of funding and the increases in the yearly intake of students. In the late 1990s, the University required that UC010, a remedial course, stop being offered as stakeholders believed that remediation was not the task of UWI. Instead, it was offered as a course by an outside body and with extra fees attached. At the same time, the English Language Proficiency Test was introduced as mandatory on entering the university for those students not having examination results deemed worthy (a Grade 1 or 2 in CXC English Language or an A or B in General Paper). Because there was no free remedial course, few of the students who had failed ELPT took any course; students simply sat the ELPT repeatedly until they passed. (Milson-Whyte, 2015, describes a similar situation on the Mona campus.)

Since the initial academic writing course had been introduced in 1963 until 2004, writing courses at UWISTA followed a fairly traditional mode of operation as obtained in other courses. Therefore, issues complicating the delivery of the writing courses included the utilization of a dated face-to-face lecture-style approach by all instructors and assessment dominated by single-sitting, in-course examinations devoid of research elements. There were no support services other than a single weekly office hour with the coordinator who, until 2004, was the sole full-time instructional staff member attached to the program, which was as largely delivered by a bevy of part-time instructors. More recently, from 2001 to 2004, the then WPC at UWISTA implemented a number of changes, including full screening and subsequent training of all incoming part-time faculty and increasing assessment standardization through the preparation and distribution of answer frames for standardized tests and group grading.

Current Issues and Solutions of Writing Program Administration at UWISTA

In addition to offering courses and providing support to the main campus, UWISTA's WP services five on-site instructors at three tertiary-level institutions (TLIs) in other territories—specifically, in St. Lucia, St. Kitts and Nevis, and St. Vincent and the Grenadines. While the difficulties faced by Caribbean students around the region are alike in theory, they are often divergent in particulars since there are no linguistic features shared by all Caribbean creole languages (see, for example, Mufwene, 1999, p. 4). To attempt to deal with this issue, I introduced a number of formal training sessions in writing instruction done either at UWISTA with the staff of the TLIs in attendance, or via Skype with identified TLI staff. Supplementing this is a number of ongoing weekly email dialogues that are meant to ensure that all TLI staff are fully inducted members of a shared community regarding the goals, approaches, philosophy, and implementation of the writing courses. This approach has been useful given the cultural, social, and political backgrounds of all students, particularly as the specificities of the TLIs' student bodies are different from those in Trinidad and Tobago.

Horner (2007) acknowledges that "often writing programs fail simply on the basis of budget and ideology" (p. 170). So, what is the pertinent ideology that must be acknowledged in language instruction for Anglophone Caribbean students? Fundamentally, it is two-pronged; on one hand, an appreciation of the native creoles is paramount and, on the other, writing programs must apply theory that emerges from linguistics and other disciplines relevant to the broader cultural and socio-political background. Craig (1971) underpins this assertion when he speaks to the problem of a general deficiency in English Language competence displayed by students at all levels of education in Barbados. He notes that this problem is found throughout the English-speaking Caribbean and can be attributed to the fact that various forms of English-Creole speech are the everyday language of the majority of their populations (p. 371). This phenomenon ripples out to teachers themselves, who are schooled to deliver the target language without being certain of accurate constructions due to their own native language interference. Alleyne (2010) points to this difficulty faced by students in the Anglophone Caribbean when she writes "input from teachers is not guaranteed to be Standard English, as many Caribbean creole or creole-influenced vernacular speakers (teachers included) have difficulty distinguishing between standard and non-standard English" (p. 4).

As one can easily see from Table 1 presenting the results of UWISTA's main academic writing course, FOUN 1001: English for Academic Purposes, UWISTA students, even well into the 2000s, failed the class at a notably high rate.

Table 1
Student performance in FOUN 1001 from 2003–2008

Year	Number of students	Number of students passing	Pass Rate
2003–2004	1465	762	52%
2004–2005	1457	803	55%
2005–2006	1480	863	58%
2006–2007	2254	1330	59%
2007–2008	1668	1219	73%

Against the backdrop of these statistics, it is worth noting that UWISTA saw an annual rate of 13.3% more students (presumably mostly English-based Creole speakers) entering its gates each year between 2002 and 2005 with little change in measures adopted to address their language needs. In 2012, the problem became exacerbated as the Trinidad and Tobago government articulated a vision of gradually increasing tertiary participation from 15% (2004) to 60% (2015). The goal, therefore, was to increase access to university education. However, the government did not articulate the accompanying need for an increase in resources or shifts in paradigms to accommodate these new students. Accordingly, mediocrity in student performance in general, and writing competence in particular, continues for students who benefited from the government's decision to increase access to university education and training without the necessary support for students' writing development.

In a study in St. Lucia, Simmons-McDonald (1996) notes that once students acquire a lect that is considered acceptable for use in the wider community (for example, the acquisition of St. Lucian Creole English by St. Lucian French Creole Speakers), they tend to remain at that level rather than moving to Standard English; students remain "fossilized" at the intermediate level. In the Barbadian context, since most children would already possess a lect that is both understood and used in a wide variety of communicative contexts, they may not be sufficiently motivated to acquire Standard English, especially if they have not received explicit instruction in the differences that exist between Bajan dialect and Standard English. Writing program adminstration at UWISTA has experienced much of the same given the Trini dialect and Standard English.

In an effort to harness empirical evidence of the challenges facing the WP at UWISTA regarding this ever-growing number of Caribbean English-based Creole speakers, I developed a study involving a number of qualitative and quantitative measures. For the study, I used a sample of 452 students across five territories in the Anglophone Caribbean, and across faculties, majors, genders, age ranges, and years of study. Moreover, I conducted a series of interviews with course administrators, writers, examiners, and lecturers to flesh out the quantitative data. I, then, analyzed and classified the data according to a variety of categories of problems. Of these areas of concern, the top three are identified and discussed here: the university student, the writing instructor, and the course curriculum.

The University Student

The idea that the Anglophone Caribbean is truly "English-speaking" presents serious WPA repercussions in academic writing ideologies, course construction, program delivery, and assessment practices regarding the teaching and learning of Caribbean Standard English (CSE). There is a false idea that since we are "English-speaking," no clear arrangements need to be made for the systematic teaching of CSE and for Creole interference. Milson-Whyte (2008) argues:

> When administrators chose to use English as the medium of instruction in a land where the majority spoke Creole, and when teachers did not teach English but only taught *through* it, they

> conveyed the sense of transparency in language use. In other words, the belief was that students arrived at school prepared to use English and would therefore not need to be taught English. It is this same discourse of transparency that would emerge in the university setting: only that there the view was that after much "repetitive" writing and being educated, students did not require explicit instruction in disciplinary discourse. (p. 144)

Milson-Whyte's perspective is in-line with noted language critic, Hodge (2001), who declares, "our children will breathe SE in the air, we assume, or they will absorb it through osmosis." The reality is that the Anglophone Caribbean is characterized by multiple creoles and emerging out of this are two major challenges faced in the teaching of formal CSE to university students.

To begin to resolve these issues, as WPC, I have encouraged the full recognition of Caribbean English Creoles as the first language of many students and the teaching of formal CSE as a mix of elements of both second language acquisition and foreign language acquisition. Rather than ignore the linguistic identity of students, I and other colleagues display an open acceptance of creoles as students come to appreciate the importance, place, and value of these languages. In our courses, we draw parallels between their mother tongues and CSE to reveal the capacity to express the nuances of a people in a manner that CSE may not be able to. At the same time, exposure is made to the obvious strengths of CSE as the suitable language of education, law, international trade, and commerce in a globalized environment, which can assist graduates in achieving a competitive edge. The program's instructional staff also draw attention to code-switching, audience, situation, and context in language use.

Another significant WPA problem relates to the feeling of some university students that their native tongues are being attacked by the homogenizing linguistic forces of globalization. The fact that students' respective creoles already allow—even celebrate—effective oral communication adds impetus to students' openly challenging the adoption of CSE. This cognitive dissonance causes many intelligent students to strive for bare passes in their courses as they focus not on learning and utilizing formal English but rather on exiting the courses; students have a tendency to view English composition courses as *speed bump* courses. Indeed, Foundation-English/composition students feel disempowered as they do not believe in their potential to learn because they have not been provided with models to bridge the gap between their own communicative competencies and the desired ones in Standard English. However, I have found incorporating a wide range of topical issues reflecting students' needs, interests, and majors—in an effort to make learning CSE meaningful, relevant, and interesting—reduces student disillusionment. Additionally, I have partnered with other faculties to develop additional discipline-specific writing courses that address students' strengths and specific purposes.

One of the pressing concerns, when I first took over as WPC in 2004, was a recalibration of the program to meet the needs, interests, and skill set of the incoming millennial student body. Working together with other stakeholders, I crafted a vision and mission for the writing program, aligned with the various UWI strategic plans from 2005 to the present day. I also streamlined all our course offerings through a painstaking application of the university's requirements, in conjunction with the Centre for Excellence in Teaching and Learning (CETL, then known as the Instructional Development Unit), in terms of the course outlines, pedagogical considerations, currency in assessment, and adherence to the operational spiral curriculum that characterizes educational reform in Trinidad and Tobago. Moreover, we infused the courses with appropriate educational technology with the assistance of the Campus Information Technology System Unit, and we fostered the use of technological tools that transformed the WP from a traditional lecture-style approach to a web-enabled blended learning offering. In fact, the WP at UWISTA was the first academic unit on campus to adopt the university's Moodle electronic platform.

Multiple opportunities now exist for students' linguistic development in CSE at UWISTA through an adoption of the new technologies. Catering to a large student body at the tertiary level today begs the utilization of cutting-edge technology that reaches everyone in a comprehensive yet individual manner. Composition courses at UWISTA now use blended learning techniques encompassing online tutorial groups, self-assessment tasks, and written models presented through the university's myeLearning system. As Leech (1997) points out, using model examples and self-assessment exercises has many benefits, including promoting a learner-centered approach while allowing students to profit from tailored learning. Indeed, the internet has proven to be an invaluable resource as students are able to view and listen to a variety of media, including video recordings of lectures, and, what's more, students are able to access a network of websites that provide assistance in the learning of CSE by English-Creole speakers. Such an integrated approach in the academic writing classroom lends credence to Morgan (2000), who contends that the implementation of a judicious mix of face-to-face and distance learning strategies has the capability to reduce the gulf between these modes and to create measurable enhancement in students' writing performance. The success of these ventures may be seen in current course completion statistics as well as in the written testimony of students who all evaluate lectures and tutorials every semester—the latter being another measure created and sustained by the current coordinator as part of his WP quality assurance.

The Writing Instructor

The current practices of the WP are designed to ensure that incoming instructional staff are adequately screened and trained. Considering that UWISTA's WP is now staffed by nine full-time and twenty part-time instructional staff, as opposed to the pre-2006 staffing level of a single full-time lecturer and a bevy of part-time instructors, the issues with the previous system are obvious: training and development opportunities became difficult as part-timers had other time commitments. There was no extrinsic motivation for part-time instructors to do much more than be prepared for their classes and deliver them. Students, therefore, experienced a lack of standardized approaches and even interpretation of instructional content in the classroom.

Resolution of these problems became a major professional goal for me. Accordingly, I have endeavored over the years to make sure that all instructors are fully standardized in aims, goals, and objectives of the courses, pedagogy, assessment practices, script-marking standards, and university policies. In fact, part-time instructors are now required to participate in these critical team-building, professional, and developmental exercises. And the completion of all related tasks does not end when the semester ends. Rather, all staff attend and participate in a post-mortem review exercise at the end of the semester with a view to ascertaining strengths and limitations to be addressed in the forthcoming semester. Full-time instructional staff are tasked with the additional staff development exercise in a weekly two-hour session held to discuss teaching strategies, time-management concerns, and means of improving and shaping the academic writing curriculum. In this regard, instructional staff development and curriculum review remain a pertinent pillar of UWISTA's WP.

A seemingly simple measure that had not been adopted until recently was the issuance of bona fide UWI email addresses to all part-time instructional staff, a move that facilitates timely and relevant communication such that all instructional staff remain updated on all aspects of program delivery. Furthermore, I lobbied UWISTA management to provide payment to part-time instructional staff for the conduct of a weekly office hour with students; this was successfully implemented in 2010. These measures generated significant gains since, apart from interfacing with their tutors in classes and via email, students had an additional opportunity to benefit from one-on-one consultations, clarify expectations, erase doubts, and glean personal motivation during these scheduled contact times. I sincerely hope that the 2019 Quality Assurance exercise of the WP at UWISTA will reveal the need for additional full-time positions and so supplement annual requests to management for same.

Against the backdrop of a growing student body over the years was the directly proportionate problem of an alarmingly increasing number of coursework and final examination scripts for faculty assessment. Rather than simply transfer this problem to existing instructional staff, I implemented a more potent and effective writing program administration strategy. I delivered to management a plan, complete with rationale and budgetary concerns, for hiring script-markers for student final papers and timed essay examinations. This plan was approved, and in 2010, the first public call for script-markers was issued. Successful candidates underwent a six-month training exercise in all dimensions of UWISTA's academic writing courses and were eventually contracted to assist in the script-marking exercises of final examination scripts. In 2013 and 2017, the training of additional script-markers was undertaken, and there exists today a cadre of trained script-makers who may be called upon at any time to assist in the assessment of students' work without dramatically increasing the workload of full-time and part-time instructional staff.

The investment in both full-time and part-time instructional staff as well as trained script-markers has borne considerable fruit in the academic writing classroom and facilitates a more effective WP. Instructional staff are more motivated and willing to engage in team-building exercises for the benefit of the student body as well as for their own professional development. There is closer adherence to program stipulations and attention to matters among instructional staff, and standardization script-marking sessions have allowed for far fewer disparities in marking and the expectation that a sound rationale must be provided for the assignment of each and every grade. Not only has the utilization of varied teaching techniques, including cooperative learning, individual research and reporting, and blended learning, offered opportunities to expand faculty's instructional repertoire, but faculty have also testified to the many gains for the English-based Creole speakers under their charge, as documented in the WP's semesterly post-mortem meeting notes.

THE COURSE CURRICULUM

Several of the challenges I have faced as WPC are embedded in the course curriculum itself. Some of the major complaints that previous WPCs have had to grapple with over the years include: extensive focus on assessment for credit without offering sufficient practice in writing, the assessment rubrics not always reflecting instructional content, and limited assessment sittings underpinned by high-stakes testing. Coupled with these are aspects of an old instructional paradigm characterizing course delivery and a heavy focus on the ideal *product* with little regard for the *process* involved in English-based Creole speakers' achieving the objectives of the courses. At the other end of the spectrum, high achievers claim that the courses offer minimal challenges, which negatively affect student throughput. Further, students' awareness of a comparative lack of focus in writing skills in their other faculty courses, particularly after Year 1, does little to encourage more than passing interest in the academic writing course curricula in particular and in CSE in general.

These challenges are not insurmountable, and the remedy has had far-reaching benefits for such students. Accordingly, I began the process of course assessment and curriculum overhaul by first analyzing the existing curricula against the backdrop of what is offered in UWISTA's sister campuses and in other local, regional, and global institutions. The potential of related measures was examined given the specificities of the socio-cultural and linguistic background of UWISTA's student body. This was done initially via consultation with WP instructional staff, other faculty personnel, and staff at the CETL. And, secondly, emergent ideas from the various conversations were then implemented as pilot projects to determine aspects of writing program instruction. Results were generated and discussed among instructional staff to determine what was likely to be effective on a large scale and what was not. For instance, one idea that was put into place was the publishing of PowerPoint presentations and lecture notes for students. One idea that failed in the pilot was the adoption of a full 36-contact-hour course done online with no face-to-face interaction. Opportunities were created for students to develop an appreciation for writing without the accompanying stress of assessment for credit. This has been achieved, in part, through the provision of opportunities for the submission and non-credit assessment of practice writing. A focus on formative evaluation in addition to summative evaluation of students' work forms part of an overhaul of the spiral curriculum linking the courses' objectives, content, instructional strategies, and evaluation tasks.

In light of student performance in the classes and student feedback regarding the courses' assessment practices, I ensured that I gave consideration to multiple assessment sittings and continuous assessment, and the utilization of portfolio assessment techniques with students' input in the planning stage. Traditional pencil-and-paper, single-sitting assessments were replaced by multiple assessment practices inclusive of sit-down tests, online quizzes, collaborative projects and reports, portfolio work, reflective writing practices, and application of report writing to real-life scenarios and problems that are usually encountered in the world of work. Such a re-orientation of the curriculum to incorporate current trends and practices in language courses has been made more practical with the involvement of what employers have deemed as desirable communicative competencies in their potential workers, as well as what the impending world of graduate studies requires for advanced studies, regarding academic writing skills. This partnership certainly involves the inclusion of content matter and assessment strategies that provide opportunities for high achievers to develop critical thinking, problem solving and other higher order thinking skills.

Altogether, the changes I have implemented during my tenure as WPC have been accompanied by a progressively increasing pass rate in the WP's seven undergraduate courses across both semesters (see Table 2). These courses are as listed.

1. FDMU 0005 — Preparatory Academic Writing
2. FOUN 1001 — English for Academic Purposes
3. FOUN 1103 — Argument and Report Writing
4. FOUN 1104 — Writing About Literature
5. FOUN 1105 — Scientific and Technical Writing

6. FOUN 1106—Academic English for Research Purposes
7. FOUN 1107—Writing in the Visual, Performing and Carnival Arts

Table 2
Student performance in academic writing courses

2016/2017					
SEMESTER 1			SEMESTER 2		
COURSE	% Passed	% Failed	COURSE	% Passed	% Failed
FDMU 0005	81.2	18.8	FOUN 1001	92.3	7.7
FOUN 1001	91.6	8.4	FOUN 1103	62.1	37.9
FOUN 1103	70.4	29.6	FOUN 1105	73.4	26.6
FOUN 1106	80.1	19.9	FOUN 1107	69.2	30.8

2015/2016					
SEMESTER 1			SEMESTER 2		
COURSE	% Passed	% Failed	COURSE	% Passed	% Failed
FDMU 0005	76.7	23.3	FOUN 1001	76.2	23.8
FOUN 1001	71.9	28.1	FOUN 1103	83.7	16.3
FOUN 1104	78	22	FOUN 1105	77.5	22.5
FOUN 1106	61.8	38.2	FOUN 1107	75.3	24.7

The Potential to Build

Despite those successes, the academic writing program at UWISTA still has significant potential for growth and evolution. The current 2017–2022 university-wide strategic plan is anchored in the tripartite *Ac-*

cess-Agility-Alignment paradigm that issues a clarion call for an upward recalibration of all dimensions of operations that will ensure development across the campuses. UWISTA's WP embraces this strategy as a vehicle to carry it forward in terms of plans and proposals that will see an even more developed and all-encompassing academic writing program at the institution. For example, plans are afoot to introduce additional relevant writing courses such as *Business Communication in the Workplace* and *Writing Skills for the Entrepreneur* that speak directly to the needs of the student body going forward. Such students will have the increased opportunities to gain access to the world of work where jobs are aligned with their communicative competencies in very real and substantial ways.

Given the campus-wide interest in promoting academic writing skills, the writing program is also planning to partner with other faculties to implement writing across the curriculum strategies, including adding scaffolding and infusing language use in the assessment rubric of their courses. This proposal received the strong support from the 2011 Quality Assurance Review team, which reported that the campus management should promote the efforts of WPA by having UWISTA "make a university commitment to a writing across the curriculum program. Resources should be provided for developing workshops and offering incentives (faculty development grants, stipends) to encourage all faculty in all disciplines to design and teach courses integrating writing into the learning of course content" (Quality Assurance Unit, 2011, p. 14). Structuring a related program also holds the promise of content faculty becoming sensitized to the tensions, contentions, and collisions in language teaching and learning and may just be the vehicle needed to have them understand and appreciate what have been the social realities experienced in the instructional process in language teaching at UWISTA. As Milson-Whyte (2008) writes:

> Indeed, there is a need for recognition of probable weaknesses in students' English language acquisition without faculty's abdication of their responsibilities for students' writing development, especially as regards helping students to navigate the situational contingencies that are inherent in writing in different disciplines. If our concern is widening participation, then we have to be prepared to use the resources that those invited bring to the learning situation. If we desire knowledge production (rather than merely reproduction), and by extension personal, institu-

tional, and national development, then all stakeholders have to be involved in students' writing development. (p. 366)

As WPC, I have been able to successfully lobby management at UWISTA for increased resources over time, and while the current scenario is not optimal, at least there is the benefit of open discussion between management and the WP. Despite the economic difficulties being experienced at UWISTA and other Caribbean postsecondary institutions, management still ensures that funding is adequate to continue the operations of the WP.

Conclusion

Writing program administration, in all dimensions of operations concerning Anglophone Caribbean Creole speakers at UWISTA, has been characterized by myriad challenges that the current coordinator has had to confront and grapple with in terms of the university student, prevailing language philosophies, the writing instructor, curriculum, assessment practices, and instructional strategies. There are, however, multiple techniques that have been utilized over time that have the capacity to assist in the mitigation of these very problems while building on the potential for growth and development. These techniques have been gradually tested and tried in the academic writing program at UWISTA. Those that generate success are capitalized on. Indeed, one may even (incorrectly) surmise that it has only been a success story. Far from it. Perhaps what may account for this is the ready acceptance of related problems and my genuine desire to effect positive change. With continued reflection and critical thinking, I intend to continue along a trajectory of growth that is grounded on sound linguistic and pedagogical theories, consideration of financial and human resource sustainability, and relevant systems thinking and design. Indeed, considering where the Writing Program at The University of the West Indies, St. Augustine, was fourteen years ago and where it has journeyed to today, the program has much to be proud of and much to look forward to.

References

Alleyne, M. L. (2010). *Academic English: An attitude and motivation study* (Unpublished Ph.D. dissertation). University of the West Indies, Cave Hill, Barbados.

Baldwin, J. F. (2009). Current challenges in higher education administration and management. *Perspectives, 13*(4), 93–97.

Craig, D. (1971). Education and Creole English in the West Indies. In D. Hymes (Ed.), *Pidginization and creolization of languages* (pp. 371–391). Cambridge: Cambridge University Press.

Hodge. M. (2001). Feature address: 14th annual Easter workshop of the Trinidad and Tobago Reading Association, Port of Spain, April 19, 2001.

Horner, B. (2007). Redefining work and value for writing program administration. *JAC, 27*(1/2), 163–184.

Leech, G. (1997). Teaching and language corpora: A convergence. In A. Wichmann, S. Fligelstone, T. McEnery & G. Knowles (Eds.), *Teaching and language corpora* (pp. 1–23). London: Longman.

McLaren, I. & Webber, D. (2009). Writing right: Enhancing student engagement and performance in an ecology course. *International Journal of Environmental & Science Education, 4*(4), 365–380.

Milson-Whyte, V. R. (2008). *A history of writing instruction for Jamaican university students: A case for moving beyond the rhetoric of transparent disciplinarity at The University of the West Indies, Mona.* (Unpublished doctoral dissertation). The University of Arizona, Tucson, Arizona. Retrieved from http://arizona.openrepository.com/arizona/

Milson-Whyte, V. (2015). *Academic writing instruction for creole-influenced students.* Kingston, Jamaica: University of the West Indies Press.

Morgan, P. (2000). Strengthening the stakes: Combining distance and face-to-face teaching strategies—Preliminary discussion issues. *Caribbean Curriculum.* Cave Hill: University of the West Indies Press.

Mufwene, S. (2009). Creolization is a social, not a structural, process. Retrieved from http://humanities.uchicago.edu/faculty/mufwene/mufw_creo.html

Quality Assurance Unit. (2011). *Report of the review of the English Language Foundation Programme, Faculty of Humanities and Education*, St. Augustine Campus, Trinidad and Tobago.

Rose, P. V., & Sookraj, R. (2015). Needs analysis: Undergraduates' evaluation of a university-wide English language course. *Caribbean Educational Research Journal, 3*(1), 62–75.

Simmons-McDonald, H. (1996). Language education policy (2): The case for Creole in formal education in St. Lucia. In P. Christie (Ed.), *Caribbean language issues old and new* (pp. 120–142). Kingston, Jamaica: University of the West Indies Press.

Section Five: Regional Perspectives: Archipelagic Thinking

> *The use of creole languages, the mass vernaculars of the Caribbean, is now a vital factor in the democratization of national life and institutions and in the accessibility of these institutions to the mass of the population. Only in this way will the region be able to exploit the full potential of its human resources, break down traditional elitist structures, and remove the alienation that exists in the region.*
>
> —Alleyne, 1994, p. 14

10 THE SMALL ISLAND *POLIS*: RHETORICAL PEDAGOGY IN THE CARIBBEAN

Raymond Oenbring

INTRODUCTION

> *One of the comforts of the traditional model of humanist agent was its close link between the mission of rhetoric and the concept of the rhetorical agent. Specifically, a rhetorical agent seen to make choices among the available means of persuasion is an agent rhetoricians can educate to make the best choices. The post-modern agent is not so obviously educable and, if not educable, what agency do we as rhetoricians have?*
>
> —Geisler, 2004, p. 15

Although not explicitly theorized by ancient Greek rhetoricians as an integral element of their theories of rhetoric, the concept of the *polis* (or the ancient Greek city-state) has proven an alluring model to contemporary rhetoricians looking for a theoretical concept to describe an ideal discourse community (see, for example, Flemming, 2009). Contemporary rhetoricians have construed the *polis* as an ancient ideal to recover, analogous to contemporary theories of ideal communicative situations, such as the *ideal speech situation* and/or the *public sphere* described in the work of Habermas (e.g., Habermas, 1974). Indeed, noted rhetoric and composition scholar Carolyn Miller argues that the concept of the *polis* is an "unarticulated presupposition" (Miller, 1993, p. 212) operating behind the scenes in most ancient Greek theories of rhetoric. In another publication, Miller (1994) describes the ancient

Greek *polis* as the "ur-rhetorical community" (p. 62). This means, Miller construes the *polis* as an operative model for democratic discourse within a diverse community as it is "a site of political debate between citizens, a locus of self-defining communal action" (Miller, 1993, p. 239); Miller understands the *polis* as a place where citizens can meaningfully confront issues of local importance using discourse.

As defined by Aristotle (2004, although outside of his rhetorical treatise *Rhetoric*), one of the most salient features of the *polis* is that it can only exist in communities with small populations—thereby allowing all citizens genuine participation in democratic discourse. Quoting Aristotle's *Politics*, Miller (1993) observes that "another feature of the ideal Aristotelian *polis* is that it is participatory. This means that it cannot be too large, for 'in order to give decisions on matters of justice and . . . merit, it is necessary that the citizens should know each other and know what kind of people they are'" (p. 232). Accordingly, it may be no coincidence that the polis/city-state model of antiquity developed within the marine archipelagic environment of the Mediterranean basin, where the physical geography of small islands played a role in limiting and building group identity in each of the ancient Greek city-states—a physical environment analogous to the Caribbean basin.

Although scholars in the fields of linguistics, anthropology, and folklore have long been interested in the language practices of the peoples of the Caribbean, rhetorical scholars have actually had—despite the unique cultures of oral persuasion in the Caribbean—relatively little to say on the topic of Caribbean rhetoric. (Indeed, the most extensive study of Caribbean language practices within the rhetorical tradition is Browne [2013].) Furthermore, rhetoricians seem to have failed to notice the alluring geographic and socio-geographic similarities between the Greek islands and the Caribbean basin: both are marine archipelagic environments where the very geography has the potential to create a greater sense of community identity and place in each locale. Accordingly, in this chapter I argue that, given Caribbean nations' cultural proclivities to oratory and orality, the ancient Greek *polis* can function as an alluring ideal for elevating discourse both inside and outside the classroom in small island Caribbean states.

Before I reach that argument, however, I acknowledge the significant problems that exist in applying the contemporary vocabulary of rhetorical studies to predominately oral societies such as those that exist in the Anglophone Caribbean. Indeed, while ancient Greek and Roman rhetorical lexicons developed largely for the purposes of instructing rhetors in the production of persuasive speech, in contemporary rhetoric and composition studies, *rhetoric* is largely written in its application. (Nonetheless, American composition scholars have demonstrated increasing interest in the relationship between oral and written persuasion in recent years. Indeed, in his 2012 book *Vernacular Eloquence: What Speech Can Bring to Writing*, seminal rhetoric and composition scholar Peter Elbow explores in great detail the ways oral language can be used to inform and produce more effective writing.) In this chapter, I focus on problems and potentials involved in importing the American English-department-based tradition of rhetoric and composition's understanding of *rhetoric*, at present a largely text-based concept, into the postsecondary writing classroom in the Anglophone Caribbean, a region where oral and oratorical culture dominates. That is to say, while the contemporary discipline of rhetoric and composition is indeed a product of material, cultural, and historical relations that govern the United States, its pedagogical strategies may be better tuned for the uniquely oral and oratorical cultures of the Anglophone Caribbean, potentially guiding Caribbean peoples further toward the ideal of the *small island polis*.

Of course, one might argue that to apply the ancient Greek concept of the *polis* to the Caribbean is, like any other attempt to apply ancient Greek and Roman rhetorical vocabulary to contemporary discourse communities, to get caught up in an overly sentimental narrative of return. Furthermore, one might argue that as the vocabulary of the rhetorical tradition is so entwined with its historical development in classical European antiquity that any attempt to apply the terminology of rhetorical studies to non-European peoples may constitute a form of cultural imperialism. In spite of these concerns, I argue that the notion of the *small island polis* can serve as a powerful *mythos* around which to organize postsecondary writing courses in the Anglophone Caribbean.

Orality and Rhetoric in African American and Afro-Caribbean Culture

Like the African American community in the United States, the peoples of the Bahamas and the broader Anglophone Caribbean have a long tradition of respect for oratory (e.g., that of the politician, the lawyer, and the pastor). Moreover, Bahamians and other Caribbean peoples are familiar, even comfortable, with the notion that their revered leaders may practice differently on Sunday afternoon and outside the House of Parliament from what they preach on Sunday morning and/or pronounce in the House of Assembly. In other words, many Caribbean people, even young adults, are comfortable with the notion of oratory as *a game that one plays*. This appreciation for the game of oratory is supported by the practice of "speechifying" at community events such as tea meetings and weddings (Abrahams, 1983, p. 116) and by a solid tradition of debate and public speaking in Anglophone Caribbean secondary schools and by the maintenance of the traditional divide into rhetorical modes in secondary education, with argumentation viewed by many educators in the Anglophone Caribbean as a special mode of discourse. Furthermore, it is common for Anglophone Caribbean universities (for example, The University of the West Indies, Mona, Jamaica) to have public speaking courses that draw heavily on rhetorical terminology.

Many scholars have noted the special place that oratorical performance holds in the black community in the English-speaking Caribbean and in the African American community in the United States (see, for example, Abrahams, 1976, 1983; Gates, 1988; Rickford & Rickford, 2000; Nunley, 2011; Browne, 2013; Bailey, 2014). Discussing African American discourse from a sociolinguistic perspective, Whatley (1981) notes that "black preaching styles, verbal games, and ritual insults of black children, and vivid and allusive styles of street talk among adults have long been a part of black community life" (p. 95). Whatley further suggests that in black oratory "both performer and audience know that it is the performance and not the content of the language that counts" (p. 94). These language games are commonly referred to in the tradition of black rhetorical theory and literary criticism as *signifyin'* (see, for example, Gates, 1988; and Rickford & Rickford, 2000). In the pulpit, this linguistic proclivity manifests itself in the uniquely black style of preaching described by numerous scholars (e.g., Niles, 1984; Gates, 1988; Banks, 2011). The unique features of the black style of preaching are familiar to rhetoricians and other scholars, and include the strategic deployment of alliteration, anaphora, stammering syncopation, crescendo, and intonation.

Similarly, a noted Caribbean linguist observes that one of the most striking features of Afro-Caribbean culture "is the competitive and performative use of words. One of the salient factors of 'talking sweet' is that the communicative function of language is not paramount. In fact, it is very often absent, and the sole intention of the speaker is to impress by sound, length or unusual combinations of words" (Roberts, 2007, p. 31). Working within the traditions of anthropology and folklore studies, Abrahams (1976) argues, moreover, that oral contests "are so central to the sense of entertainment in the West Indies that they are observable whenever people congregate, whether for a special event or in the marketplace or rum shop" (Abrahams, 1976, p. xvii). Indeed, language games are an important element of the daily lived experience of many Caribbean people, occurring commonly in myriad Caribbean forms of expression, including deejaying, poetry *clashes*, dancehall, reggae, calypso, and soca (see, for example, Browne, 2013).

RHETORICAL AGENCY AND THE NORTH/SOUTH DIVIDE

As is well-known within the field of rhetorical theory, for most of the history of the systematic study of rhetoric, rhetoric was a field focused primarily on instructing public orators on the most effective use of language; from ancient Greece until the nineteenth century, rhetoric was primarily a discipline focused on the production of persuasive speech. However, driven in part by a desire to provide historical backing for their nascent field, a field given impetus by the underprepared cohorts of postsecondary student writers that entered American universities in the postwar period and the decades after, rhetoric and composition scholars have in recent decades imported traditionally orally-focused rhetorical vocabulary into pedagogical discussions and classrooms where writing is much more common than public speaking (e.g., *You think there's nothing to composition studies, eh? Ever heard of Aristotle??!*).

In the twentieth and twenty-first centuries, rhetoric and rhetorical theory have, furthermore, taken a turn away from the *production* of persuasive speech toward the *hermeneutic*; scholars have increasingly used rhetorical terminology to *interpret* the persuasive moves made by texts both written and non-written, even for texts where persuasion in the traditional sense isn't clearly the central goal (e.g., scientific writing). This use of rhetorical terminology to interpret texts has become a solidified tradition in contemporary postsecondary composition courses. For example, a common activity in contemporary first-year writing courses in the United States is to have students analyze a text's use of the Aristotelian appeals of *ethos, pathos,* and *logos*. While one still finds the use of rhetorical terminology to teach the production of effective oral presentation in communication departments, in English departments, where most North American college composition instructors find their homes, *rhetoric* is at present largely a written activity.

Another element of the rhetorical tradition that has been deemphasized within certain strains of the contemporary American discipline of rhetoric and composition is the concept of *rhetorical agency*—that is, the notion that rhetors move audiences based on their active choice of language to meet the needs of their specific rhetorical situation. Developing in part as a response to earlier process composition theories that placed emphasis on dubious constructs like the student writer's *authentic voice*, this recent concern by rhetoric and composition scholars regarding the topic of rhetorical agency has largely been motivated by postmodern and post-process theories' problematizing of the autonomous author-subject (see, for example, Bizzell, 1992).

Indeed, the rhetorical vocabulary as a whole has been challenged by post-process composition theorists due to its overt focus on authorial agency. Quoting fellow rhetorician Gaonkar, Geisler (2004) notes, for example, that "recent concern with the question of rhetorical agency arises from the post-modern critique of the autonomous agent . . . fault[ing] traditional rhetoric for an 'ideology of agency,' viewing 'the speaker as origin rather than articulation, strategy as intentional, discourse as constitutive of character and community'" (p. 10). Describing the post-process critique of the autonomous rhetorical agent, Ewald (1999), furthermore, notes that "the postmodern subject, inscribed by language, is caught in a web of dominant discourses even as she or he tries to operate within and perhaps resist those discourses" (p. 118). In place of the student writer's search for their *authentic voice*, post-process composition theorists have, in addition to their critiques of the notions of a single, unified author-driven composing process, advocated assignments and pedagogies that work to build students' critical consciousness of how culture, media, and discourse construct their experience.

While building students' critical consciousness of how language operates on and through them is indeed a laudable goal in every teaching environment, I would like to suggest that post-process compositionists' attendant challenge of the notion of rhetorical agency is a critique more useful and more relevant to large western nations, where students are unlikely to have substantial effects on their national cultural discourse and institutional structures than a small Caribbean nation like the Bahamas, a country with a current population of approximately 370,000, a number comparable, in fact, to the population of the ancient Athenian *polis* (cf. Thorley, 2005, p. 74). In short, one has a greater potential to actually effect cultural and institutional change through discourse in a small island nation such as the Bahamas and other Caribbean nations. Indeed, if a primary concern of post-process compositionists in the United States is that we need to take off the blinders of ideology and show to students how they are constructed by language and media, should this apply equally to small, still developing countries that are in many ways outside of the hegemonic culture?

A Productive Synthesis: Embracing the Oral in the Caribbean Composition Classroom

Without fail in every college composition course I teach at the University of The Bahamas (UB), the same illuminating moment occurs: on the first day of class, after having spent some forty-five minutes overviewing the syllabus and my expectations for the class using a traditional didactic lecture style, I then ask that each student introduce herself/himself to the student next to herself/himself so that the second student can then introduce the original student, hopefully previously unknown to them, to the class as a whole. Immediately the students' glum and sober faces — unchanged since the beginning of the class, and undoubtedly expecting the same lecture style to continue — change to smiles, their eyes brightening, as they begin to converse; my students respond positively to this simple display of respect to them as thinking individuals, putting their cultural oral proclivities to use, beginning a dialogue rather than what must seem a droning inculcating monologue. Surprisingly, this simple turn of classroom discourse structure and classroom authority changes the mood and tone of the class until the end of that period, the positive mood seemingly remaining in the classroom for the next several sessions.

I believe that the above simple anecdote is symbolic of a larger cultural proclivity waiting to be harnessed by Caribbean university writing instructors. In other words, an effective way to engage Bahamian and other Caribbean students in the university writing classroom is through harnessing their cultural taste for oratory and orality. (This is not, however, to essentialize or to suggest that *all* Anglophone Caribbean students are better at oral conversation than at written compositions; many Anglophone Caribbean students are much better at written communication. Indeed, it is often striking how wide the gap between students' communicative efficacy in one medium versus the other may be.) Given this cultural proclivity, and given the didactic *sit-down-shut-up* pedagogical style that dominates in the classroom in much of the English-speaking Caribbean from the primary up to the postsecondary level, I have found students to be quite receptive to assignments and tasks where they can engage in dialogue and oratorical performance, rather than be silenced and alienated by a didactic monologue—a monologue in a language (Standard English) that is a different language from their home languages (Caribbean English Creoles).

Accordingly, I routinely design classroom activities that involve small or large group discussions and/or oral presentations, with students becoming active participants in potentially transformative classroom discourse. For instance, I often have students make individual and group oral presentations, both as independent assignments and as scaffolding assignments for the major papers, with the goal of both improving students' oratorical abilities and helping them build ideas for their written assignments. For example, in UB's 300-level English composition class, a class with a focus on disciplinary modes of writing and discourse, I routinely break up students into groups based on their fields of study, with each group producing an oral presentation critically analyzing the features of one or more salient genres of writing in their fields of study (e.g., the IMRaD research article for science majors and corporate annual reports for business majors). After the group oral presentation, students then draw upon the arguments and points of analysis that they originally developed for the group oral presentation, honing their portion of the oral presentation into a developed, focused genre analysis essay on an important genre of writing used in their field of study.

I also use classroom debates as a teaching strategy in my composition classrooms. Specifically, I break up students into two groups, one for and one against a proposition, then give them time to strategize the arguments that they will make and the ways they will attempt to refute the opposing sides' counterarguments. The debate proper begins with a nominated speaker from each side presenting both their group's arguments for their proposition as well as their arguments against the opposing proposition. After each group's appointed speaker has made their initial case, the debate becomes a more unstructured point-counterpoint in which any member of the class can participate. Inevitably, the discussion at this point becomes raucous, but nonetheless quite productive. Indeed, on more than one occasion the laughter and callbacks that have been engendered by these debates have been so loud that instructors in nearby rooms have poked their heads in our class to tell us to quiet down. After the debate is complete, I end the day's session with a meta-critical discussion of the argumentative techniques that the students used during the oral debate, listing the various arguments, as well as the strategies the students' used to make each argument, on the board, with the goal that students could draw upon these strategies in their written compositions. (While not all students are able to successfully transform their strategies of oral debate into successful Standard English written arguments, I find that many do.)

This use of oral argumentative strategies as developmental and conceptual scaffolding in the teaching of argument has a long history in the rhetorical tradition. For example, in ancient Greece, young students were introduced to the study of rhetoric through the *progymnasmata*: a series of preliminary written and oral rhetorical exercises students were taught before learning more involved forms of declamation (see, for example, Kennedy, 2003). Classical rhetoric scholar Kennedy notes that "a major feature of [progymnasmata] was stress on learning refutation or rebuttal: how to take traditional tale, narrative, or thesis and argue against it. If anything, the exercises may have tended to encourage the idea that there was an equal amount to be said on two sides of any issue, a skill practiced at a later stage of education in dialectical debate" (p. x). That is to say, progymnasmata exercises placed special emphasis on honing students' powers of critical thinking and analysis in an oral medium.

Although not part of the cannon of progymnasmata exercises, an oral activity/game that draws upon the principles of the progymnasmata that I have found works quite well in the Caribbean composition classroom involves the ancient Greek rhetorical text "Dissoi Logoi," or *opposing arguments*, a sophistic relativistic treatise that consists largely of a series statements recognizing that seemingly convincing arguments can be found in support of most propositions, even seemingly preposterous ones. The unknown sophist author of the "Dissoi Logoi" (2000) notes, for example, that "illness is bad for the sick but good for the doctors. And death is bad for those who die, but good for the undertakers" (p. 45). For the exercise, I first have students read a fragment of the "Dissoi Logoi" text. After we read the excerpt, I break students up into groups, asking them to develop a short speech with a preposterous thesis, such as *crime is good for the Bahamas* or *the Bahamas Power and Light is the greatest utility in the world* (the electricity in the Bahamas is notoriously unreliable, and the subject of many jokes in Bahamian popular discourse). Once the groups are done strategizing, a member of the group then regales the class with the group's outlandish arguments.

Interestingly, when students engage in these oral activities from the rhetorical tradition in the classroom, much of the original oral focus of rhetorical vocabulary seemingly returns. For example, our classroom discussions of common ancient rhetorical figures and tropes such as those articulated in the ancient Roman rhetorical treatise *Rhetorica Ad Herennium* (e.g., *hyperbole*) often turn toward examples found in everyday Bahamian conversation (e.g., *Bey, it too hot. I ga die if da curren and A/C een come back on* [Standard English: *Man, it's too hot. I'm going to die if the electricity and A/C don't come back on*]), with students both analyzing and producing examples.

Of course, the most obvious concern that some Caribbean composition instructors might have with an orally-focused approach to teaching composition is that it potentially takes away from students' important time-on-task in the classroom doing other activities such as in-class writing or listening to lecture. Furthermore, highlighting the oral and oratorical might be construed as *teaching students how to do something they already know how to do* (read: be black) or as deemphasizing the importance of students' learning to write in error-free Standard English. Nonetheless, in the United States, a number of black educators have similarly advocated classroom strategies that draw upon black oral cultural knowledge in order to facilitate black students' development in traditional classroom learning environments. Dalji (1998), for example, has advocated using African and African American folktales and folk songs as a way to build students' awareness of the differences between Standard English and African American Vernacular English, with the goal of assisting students' learning of Standard English (p. 111).

While my proposal to use oral vernacular language as scaffolding for writing activities does indeed mirror those made by Elbow (1999; 2012), I do not advocate the vernacular, as Elbow does, as merely something that should occur *upstream* from the "polished" Standard English final draft, thereby—as those critics of Elbow charge—privileging Standard English over nonstandard varieties (Green, 2016; Robinson, this volume). Although I welcome code-meshing and oral performance at all stages of the writing process, I do so as a composition instructor (and, recently, as a writing program administrator) who, despite living in the Caribbean for a nearly a decade, remains, as a white American/Canadian man, linguistically and racially privileged in a country and region where most locally raised and trained English instructors retain much more traditional attitudes to standard and nonstandard English (see, for example, Oenbring, 2017). That is to say, following the charge of Milson-Whyte (2014), I advocate code-meshing in the Caribbean with a deep respect for the complex linguistic and material realities on the ground in the Caribbean. Indeed, as Milson-Whyte argues, "although deliberate code-meshing seems a useful strategy to help teachers attend to students who use various language varieties, considerations of its application should include the complex realities in which individuals work and are worked by English. Chief among these realities is that languages used by the marginalized are often denigrated" (pp. 104–5).

Conclusion

The story is familiar to rhetoricians: *as an oral society, ancient Greek law and statecraft were largely the products of oral recitation and deliberation* (see, for example, Thomas, 1992). *In poleis with democratic traditions, male citizens were called to participate in public assemblies to persuade others and to vote on matters of substance to the state. As a citizen's influence and success depended heavily upon his oratorical abilities in such societies, the first schools devoted to the practice of rhetoric soon developed. These schools taught citizens to choose from the available means of persuasion in order to persuade their audience in order to achieve their desired goals within the polis.* While the above story is undoubtedly mythologized, I argue that treating students as active rhetorical agents that select language to meet the needs of their audience within their local *polis* can serve as a powerful myth to organize composition classrooms and elevate the level of classroom discourse—especially in small, orally-driven societies such as those found in the Caribbean region.

Of course, designing classroom activities that draw from Caribbean students' cultural proclivities to oratory and orality and using rhetorical vocabulary in the classroom does not, in and of itself, a *small island polis* make. While orally-focused in-class activities can serve to enhance student engagement and critical thinking, to truly advance the transformative effects of the *small island polis* in the Caribbean composition classroom and Caribbean societies at large, Caribbean postsecondary writing instructors must build students' rhetorical and meta-critical awareness of the potentials of discourse in Caribbean oral societies.

As the quote by the rhetorician Geisler (2004) that serves as the epigraph of this chapter suggests, the mission of rhetorical education is indeed deeply entwined with the notion of students having authorial and rhetorical agency. While placing emphasis on the way language constrains and constructs our experience may indeed be best practice in university writing classrooms in large, mass market countries such as the United States, to deny Caribbean students rhetorical agency would seem to preclude them from participating meaningfully in the cultural and social development of their countries—something that Caribbean postsecondary students and future Caribbean professionals can, for certain, engage in.

Moreover, although composing in written Standard English is for certain an important skill for Bahamian and other Caribbean college and university students to master—and it is, indeed, a skill toward which I focus the majority of my efforts in the composition classes I teach at the University of The Bahamas—it is arguable that Caribbean young adults and future Caribbean professionals are more likely to effect important change in their countries through participation in dialogue and oratory rather than through writing. Indeed, if the reason the American rhetoric and composition tradition has focused so heavily on building students' written skills is to empower them during their college life, in the workforce, and in the marketplace of ideas, in the Caribbean the same could be emphasized with orality, with students' oral efficacy playing an arguably greater role in determining their communicative prowess and their general success in life. In a word, rhetoric and composition scholars working with Caribbean students should, unabashedly, embrace the oral and the oratorical in their classrooms.

REFERENCES

Abrahams, R. (1976). *Talking black*. New York: Newbury House.
Abrahams, R. (1983). *The man-of-words in the West Indies*. Baltimore: Johns Hopkins University Press.
Aristotle. (2004). *Rhetoric* (W. R. Roberts, Trans.). New York: Dover Publications.
Bailey, C. (2014). *The poetics of performance: The oral-scribal aesthetic in Anglophone Caribbean fiction*. Kingston, Jamaica: University of the West Indies Press.
Banks, A. (2011). *Digital griots: African American rhetoric in a digital age*. Carbondale, IL: NCTE/Southern Illinois University Press.

Bizzell, P. (1992). *Academic discourse and critical consciousness*. Pittsburgh, PA: University of Pittsburgh Press.

Browne, K. (2013). *Tropic tendencies: Rhetoric, popular culture, and the Anglophone Caribbean*. Pittsburgh: University of Pittsburgh Press.

Dalji, H. (1998). Listen to your students. In T. Perry & L. Delpit (Eds.), *The real ebonics debate: Power, language, and the education of African-American children* (pp. 105–116). Boston: Beacon Press.

"Dissoi Logoi." (2000). In. P. Bizzell & B. Herzberg (Eds.), *The rhetorical tradition: Readings from classical times to present* (pp. 45–55). Boston: Bedford/St. Martin's.

Elbow, P. (1999). Inviting the mother tongue: Beyond 'mistakes,' 'bad English,' and 'wrong language.' *JAC, 19*, 359–388.

Elbow, P. (2012). *Vernacular eloquence: What speech can bring to writing*. Oxford: Oxford University Press.

Ewald, H. R. (1999). A tangled web of discourses: A post-process pedagogy and communicative interaction. In T. Kent (Ed.), *Post-process theory: Beyond the writing process paradigm* (pp. 116–131). Carbondale, IL: Southern Illinois University Press.

Flemming, D. (2009). *City of rhetoric: Revitalizing the public sphere in modern America*. Albany, NY: SUNY Press.

Gates, Jr., H. L. (1988). *The signifying monkey: A theory of African-American literary criticism*. Oxford: Oxford University Press.

Geisler, C. (2004). How ought we to understand the concept of rhetorical agency? Report from ARS. *Rhetoric Society Quarterly, 9*, 9–16.

Green, N. A. S. (2016). The re-education of Neisha-Anne S Green: A close look at the damaging effect of "a standard approach," the benefits of codemeshing, and the role allies play in this work. *Praxis: A Writing Center Journal, 14*(1), 72–82.

Habermas, J. (1974). *Theory and practice*. Portsmouth, NH: Heinemann.

Kennedy, G. A. (2003). *Progymnasmata: Greek textbooks of prose composition and rhetoric*. Boston, MA: Brill.

Miller, C. (1993). The *polis* as rhetorical community. *Rhetorica: A Journal of the History of Rhetoric, 11*, 211–240.

Miller, C. (1994). Rhetorical community: The cultural basis of genre. In A. Freedman, & P. Medway (Eds.), *Genre and the new rhetoric* (pp. 67–78). London: Taylor and Francis.

Milson-Whyte, V. (2014). Working English through code-meshing: Implications for denigrated language varieties and their users. In B. Horner & K. Kopelson (Eds.), *Reworking English in rhetoric and composition* (pp. 103–115). Carbondale, IL: Southern Illinois University Press.

Niles, L. (1984). Rhetorical characteristics of traditional black preaching. *Journal of Black Studies, 15*, 41–52.

Nunley, V. (2011). *Keepin' it hushed: The barbershop and African American hush harbor rhetoric*. Detroit: Wayne State University Press.

Oenbring, R. (2017). College composition in the Anglophone Caribbean: The search for a Caribbean identity. *Journal of Global Literacies, Technologies, and Emerging Pedagogies, 4*, 533–545.

Rickford, J., & Rickford, R. (2000). *Spoken soul: The story of black English*. New York: John Wiley & Sons.

Roberts, P. (2007). *West Indians and their language*. Cambridge, England: Cambridge University Press.

Thomas, R. (1992). *Literacy and orality in ancient Greece*. Cambridge, England: Cambridge University Press.

Thorley, J. (2005). *Athenian democracy*. New York: Routledge.

Whatley, E. (1981). Language among black Americans. In C. A. Ferguson & S. B. Heath (Eds.), *Language in the USA* (pp. 92–107). Cambridge: Cambridge University Press.

11 Transnational and Translingual Perspectives on Creoles in Education: Casting a Wider Net into the Caribbean Sea

Valerie Combie

Introduction: A Lack of Progress

Teaching literacy and promoting education in local creole languages in the Caribbean has been a point of formal discussion for over sixty years. The discussion began formally in 1953 when the United Nations issued a report on the cognitive value of teaching literacy in the mother tongue. The report emphasized the importance of learning a second language and offered recommendations for the smooth transition from the vernacular to Standard languages (United Nations Educational, Scientific and Cultural Organization [UNESCO], 1953). Additionally, it listed practical limitations that would delay the implementation of such a program. Some of those limitations were insufficient materials, a shortage of well-trained teachers, and the general public's opposition to the plan.

Fast forward to 1993, when, at the Caribbean Community (CARICOM) Ministers of Education conference, members formulated three language goals for the region's schools: first, by the age of ten, children should be competent in the official language of their country at a level appropriate to their age and experience; second, bilingualism/multilingualism or multidialectalism should be seen as a positive attribute; and finally, by the end of high school, all Caribbean children should know an orthography (that is a codified set of spellings) for the representation of their creole (Ministry of Education, Youth and Culture [MOEYC], Jamaica, 2001, p. 9). Although little progress had been made in any of these CARICOM ministers' proposals, the issue of creole languages in education was once again revisited in 2011 at the conference (facilitated by the International Center for Caribbean Language Research) on the Charter for Language Policy and Language Rights in the Creole-Speaking Caribbean, which was endorsed by "linguists, educators, and government officials from at least 15 territories" (Wilkinson, 2015, p. 153).

The reports issuing from the United Nations, the CARICOM education ministers meeting, and the International Center for Caribbean Language Research may be considered mandates, but it seems that no significant actions have been taken by governments and educational policymakers in the Anglophone Caribbean. This provokes the question: why haven't the recommendations made by these bodies been broadly implemented? It is easy to assume, as some stakeholders in educational policy discussions in the Caribbean do, that the lack of sweeping change in educational policy in the region is simply due to the fact that teachers and administrators remain hesitant to change colonial era language policies and practices because of their ingrained belief that creole languages are somehow inferior to others, and while they may be acceptable for use as a source of entertainment, they are considered inappropriate for formal interactions and for educational situations. Others may point to the importance of clear and effective communication with outsiders who speak and write in standard varieties (read tourists) to the economies of Caribbean countries as putting the brakes on these reforms. Finally, others may assume that Anglophone Caribbean countries simply do not have the financial or human resources to engage in such an ambitious reprogramming of educational policies and practices in their territories, against the tide of history, economic brain drain, and the continuing flood of outside media. Although these perspectives on the failure to institutionalize sweeping language education reform in the English-speaking Caribbean have merit, in this study I focus instead on how the persistence of *one nation, one language* ideology in territories of the Commonwealth Anglophone Caribbean (that is, the former and current colonies of Britain), an ideology supported by a lack truly of regional, transnational, and translingual scholarly perspectives informing

English (and Creole English) language instruction in the region, has stifled efforts to reform language and writing instruction here.

ON A DIFFERENT BEACH: THINKING OUTSIDE THE COMMONWEALTH CARIBBEAN SANDBOX

While the policy statements issued by the UNESCO in the 1950s, the CARICOM ministers in 1990s, and the International Center for Caribbean Language Research in the 2010s were *multinational* statements, they were all based on an ideology of the nation state rather than being *transnational* or *translingual* in their perspective. That is to say, in spirit they encouraged budding small postcolonial states to attempt to build local esteem for their own national creole languages, despite the fact that these budding states clearly lacked the educational resources to broadly implement such ambitious policy changes. The policy statements, in their effect, called upon the budding nation states of the Anglophone Caribbean to build their own educational cultures and materials (including, for example, orthographies, teaching materials, teacher training, and mass education programs) despite the fact that the territories were ill-prepared individually to tackle these challenges. What's more, the policy statements, because they did not encourage Caribbean nations to look sufficiently outside their boundaries into other political and linguistic environments, did little to undermine the ideology of *one nation, one language*.

While organizations such as the Society for Caribbean Linguistics (formed originally by scholars from The University of West Indies campuses in Jamaica and Trinidad, and formally established in 1972) have developed in the Commonwealth Caribbean, with the goal to facilitate and to coordinate research from scholars around the region, these organizations have had limited success in building wide-ranging and lasting connections with scholars in the Spanish-speaking, French-speaking, French-Creole-speaking, and *other Caribbeans* in the region. Although the Society for Caribbean Linguistics (SCL) encourages participation from scholars around the Caribbean region and internationally (and offers versions of the organization's website in Spanish, French, Dutch, and Haitian Creole), participation by scholars from these other non-Anglophone regions in the Caribbean at the organization's meetings is often limited. Indeed, to the extent that scholarly discourses around teaching in creole languages in the Anglophone Caribbean have developed, these discourses have been largely between and within larger Commonwealth Caribbean countries, such as Jamaica and Trinidad & Tobago — with other meaningful participation from scholars of Caribbean languages working in western nations, such as the United States, the UK, Canada, and Germany.

In this chapter, I encourage compositionists and other scholars in the traditional Commonwealth Anglophone Caribbean (including Jamaica, Trinidad & Tobago, Barbados, and the Bahamas, etc.) to cast a broader net into the Caribbean sea and to look outside their region order for both examples of successful language policy experiments and examples of other creole language educational policy situations, both for examples of what to do, and for examples of what not to do (see, for example, Siegel's [2007] overview of the state of use of creole languages and minority dialects in education both within and outside the Caribbean). This approach will allow scholars to deepen their perspective on creole-language educational policy. One interesting, largely negative, case is the language situation in the United States Virgin Islands (USVI), which, as it is a territory of the United States, is not a part of the Commonwealth Caribbean. Moreover, while it may seem that no progress has been made in institutionalizing meaningful change in building respect for creole languages in the *Anglophone* Caribbean, many of the more ambitious efforts to accommodate local creole languages in education have taken place in regions where an English-lexifier creole isn't the major language (for example, Haiti, where the dominant language is Haitian Creole, a French-lexifier creole; and Curaçao where the Portuguese-based Creole language, Papiamentu, is the medium of instruction). These efforts, while largely focused on primary and secondary education, can serve as inspiration for postsecondary composition instructors and educational policymakers in the region.

Drawing on my own experience working at the University of the Virgin Islands in the United States Virgin Islands and research from pilot studies from around the Caribbean region outside the Commonwealth Caribbean, I argue that regional, transnational, and translingual perspectives should be the foundation of all attempts to build esteem for local marginalized languages, including creole languages (for important background information see Alleyne, 1994). Moreover, I argue, following calls made by Oenbring (2017) and Jones McKenzie & Campbell-Dawes (this volume), that, in the absence of clear national or regional discourses on best practices in teaching writing at the postsecondary level in the region, we should call scholars, educators, and policymakers from across the Caribbean region into action to share resources and provide material support for one another to build the field of writing studies in the region.

To achieve these aims, I shall first, after some theoretical explication, outline the situation in the USVI, particularly the situation regarding writing instruction at my home institution, the University of the Virgin Islands, focusing specifically on how, as a territory of the United States, and thus subject to American educational discourses and policies, language and writing instruction have been framed in USVI through the American understanding of national languages (and second languages), a framework that puts the local English creole, Virgin Islands Creole, doubly under erasure. I present the situation in the USVI as an example for faculty in the Commonwealth Caribbean of how the discourses of nationhood—manifest severely in the USVI due to the territory's position of linguistic and political subjugation to the United States—stand in the way of meaningful reform in building respect for local creole languages. In other words, the inward focus of the discourses of nation states by their very nature leads to *one nation, one language* ideology. Next in the chapter, I overview a few successful pilot projects that have been implemented, largely at the primary and secondary level, from around the Caribbean region. Finally, I end with a discussion of transnationalism and translingualism in composition theory, outlining the possible way forward for compositionists in the region.

In challenging the prevailing *one nation, one language* ideology and advocating translanguaging and a transnational perspective, my proposal calls for stakeholders around the region to confront their attitudes to language, thereby enabling them to embrace students' home languages and use those languages as teachable moments (Nero, 2000) with the intent of ultimately maximizing learners' potential for academic and social development, instead of leaving it to stagnate, which has too often been the case under the language policies that have prevailed in the educational systems of the region since the colonial era. Indeed, the rich variety of languages in the Caribbean region must no longer be regarded as a barrier to students' progress but instead as a "resource for producing meaning in writing, speaking, reading, and listening" (Horner, Lu, Royster, & Trimbur, 2011, p. 303). This new understanding of linguistic diversity concurs with linguists such as Nero (2006), and Canagarajah (2006) as well as with the 1974 resolution of the Conference on College Composition and Communication (CCCC) that recognizes and honors the "Students' Right to their Own Language"—a resolution that was put forward to embrace and accommodate students' multilingualism, while simultaneously affirming their worth as people (Horner, Lu, Royster, & Trimbur, 2011).

"English as Mother Tongue" (EMT) Traditions

I argue that the most significant hurdles preventing meaningful progress in building respect for English creoles in education in the English-speaking Caribbean are "English mother tongue (EMT) traditions" and "confusion of objectives in language and literacy education" (Wilkinson, 2015, p. 156). It is no secret that the medium of instruction in the Anglophone Caribbean is English although most children entering school do not speak it or develop literacy in their creole language/s. This disconnect is linked to the promotion of English or the erroneous assumption that all citizens speak English (see Milson-Whyte, 2015). Despite students' challenges in various written examinations in English, instruction in the Anglophone Caribbean has continued to be in the "mother tongue," English (see, for example, Robertson & Simmons-McDonald, 2014). In Guyana, for example, Guyanese Creole receives no "educational value in the assessment of students' speech and writing" (Wilkinson, 2015, p. 154). To rectify the current situation, stakeholders should view writing in the academic classroom as a recursive process that is intricately connected to knowledge making, which Russell (2002) describes as "a process of socialization or acculturation, analogous to a young child learning to speak" (p. 15, cited in Milson-Whyte 2015, p. 27). This concept ties in with Vygotsky's theory of first language acquisition, which is embedded in the community and depends on a step-by-step process that uses what the students already know (their home language) to introduce what they do not yet know (the standard variety used in school). The student's home language is the first line of defense. It is the language in which the student thinks and responds. It is Vygotsky's "internal language" that enables the student to function competently in the community (cited in Milson-Whyte, 2015, p. 28).

Caribbean students' difficulties with writing stem in part from their inability to code switch from their Caribbean lexifier Creole language that is primarily oral to an "academic register" such as the standard variety used in schools. Linguists have introduced strategies such as "instrumental, accommodation, and awareness programs" (Nero, 2000) to bridge the gap and improve students' facility with the standard variety of the English language. Proponents of these programs have reported a significant measure of success in applying various aspects of such programs (Faraclas, Kester, & Mijts, 2013; Aceto & Williams, 2003).

THE SITUATION IN THE USVI: CREOLE AS A THIRD LANGUAGE

Situated fifty miles east of Puerto Rico, St. Croix, where the main campus of the University of the Virgin Islands (UVI) is located, is the biggest of the four major islands of the United States Virgin Islands, with St. Thomas, St. John, and Water Island being the others. The United States Virgin Islands (USVI) has a history of colonial rule by several different western powers, including: Britain, France, Spain, the Netherlands, Denmark, and, finally, the United States, which purchased the territory from Denmark in 1917. Accordingly, the US Virgin Islands' educational system has been, since 1917, governed by the educational principles, policies, and practices of the United States. Furthermore, since 1917 American English has served as the "standard administrative, educational, and economic language" (Highfield, 2009, p. 131) in the territory.

USVI's history has been a dynamic one in terms of population flows. While decimated in their numbers by their first contacts with European explorers and colonizers, a number of indigenous groups (including Arawaks, Caribs, and Tainos) survived well into the colonial era, coexisting with Europeans and African slaves. Eventually, the English Creole-speaking descendents of African slaves became the largest demographic group in the country, presently constituting approximately 75% of the territory's population. More recently, people have migrated from other Caribbean islands and Puerto Rico, bringing their distinct cultures and languages with them. Due to the influence of these groups, a very strong and dynamic Spanish-speaking culture has developed on the USVI, which is the main reason why the territory is popularly identified as bilingual, with English being the official language of commerce.

While the majority Afro-Caribbean population in the USVI shares linguistic and cultural similarities with the rest of the Anglophone Caribbean, the USVI's distinct experience as a territory of the United States with a Spanish-speaking minority has made it a unique situation for (dis)accommodating the local creole tongue. That is to say, although, like the rest of the Anglophone Caribbean, the majority of the population speak an English Creole as a first language, the fact that USVI's educational discourses stem from the United States has meant a near complete erasure of the place of creole in USVI society; English as a Second Language (ESL) in American educational discourse refers to Spanish. The average UVI student is English/English creole bilingual, but institutionally this term *bilingual* is normally only associated with Spanish-speaking students (see, for example, Government of the USVI, 2008). Those who speak creole as a home language in USVI are assumed by the educational establishment, including many English professors, to simply speak English. That is to say, despite being the mother tongue of the majority of the people, in the USVI, Virgin Islands Creole isn't a first language or second language—it is a third language.

There are many signs that the prevailing educational policies in the USVI, stemming from American educational discourse, are failing students. Firstly, in the 2014–2015 student assessment administered by the Virgin Islands Department of Education, only some 17% of students from all grades met or exceeded the English and Language Arts standard, while only an average of 7% met or exceeded standards in math (cited in Community Foundation of the Virgin Islands, 2016). Overall, the low number of passes indicates serious problems in education in the United States Virgin Islands, which may to some degree be related to a form of "Linguistic Imperialism," designed to control and segregate people through their language (Phillipson, 1992, p. 47).

Secondly, approximately 88% of incoming freshmen at UVI are deemed to need remediation, which requires them to register for basic writing and other developmental classes; consequently, their graduation is delayed. Another facet of this complex situation is the fact that a passing grade for the English Proficiency Examination (EPE) is a requirement for graduation. The UVI website states that the "purpose of the English proficiency requirement is to ensure that all UVI graduates have demonstrated a required level of proficiency in using English as an effective means of written communication" (University of the Virgin Islands, para. 1). Empirical data from the EPE results (2010–2016) indicate that students are deficient in major areas of English competence, especially sentence structure and the use of English, two of the criteria by which the EPE is evaluated. Results of students' performance on the EPE from 2010 to 2016 show an average passing rate of 69%. While this is up from the 40% pass rate reported by Irvine and Elsasser (1988) at the then College of the Virgin Islands (now UVI), it does not allow for rejoicing. In the EPE, students are evaluated on the following criteria: focus, support, organization, use of English, sentence structure, and mechanics. They consistently perform well on the first three criteria and a little better on mechanics, but they experience great difficulty in Standard English writing and sentence structure.

Students—and the broader population in the USVI—furthermore, lack awareness of the fact that they speak a creole language. Indeed, the average student at the University of the Virgin Islands fails to understand the differences in the full spectrum of language varieties (including creoles) spoken in the territory. Of 35 respondents to an informal questionnaire, when asked: *How many languages do you speak fluently?*, sixty-eight percent (68%) said one. When asked *Do you speak a Creole language?*, only twenty-two percent (22%) responded positively. Fifty-four percent (54%) defined *Creole* as an English *dialect*, and *Patois* as a French *dialect*. Indeed, at UVI, even many professors of English composition assume that students are monolingual, even when there are clear signs to the contrary.

Case Studies: Around the Caribbean Region

In this section, I overview a handful of promising case studies that have been conducted by scholars and language policymakers around the Caribbean region, with the goal of deepening the perspective of composition scholars and educational policy makers in the region. The scope of my overview is truly transnational and translingual, in that it includes pilot studies both beyond and within the Commonwealth Anglophone Caribbean. Although empirical data proving the efficacy of these practices are not available for all of these studies, in some cases the authors have been able to present empirical data suggesting positive results from these programs.

One major difference in language policy that distinguishes Haiti from Anglophone Caribbean nations is that Haitian Creole, unlike Anglophone creoles, has a codified orthography (that is, a set of spellings) that has actually had some traction in terms of its implementation. While scholars have attempted to promote orthographies for Anglophone creoles (e.g., the Cassidy & LePage [1967] orthography for Jamaican Creole that has had a few on-again-off-again attempts to spread its use [Devonish, 1986; Adams, 1991]), few have had any lasting traction. Since 2014, Haitian Creole orthography has been officially governed by the Haitian Creole Academy (Akademi Kreyòl Ayisyen) located in Port-au-Prince.

One noteworthy project promoting reading and writing in Haitian Creole orthography is the MIT-Haiti Initiative, a project led by MIT creolist Michel DeGraff. DeGraff (2013) argues that, as 95% of the Haitian population is fluent in Haitian Creole/Kreyòl, using the language with which Haitian students are most comfortable and in which they are most fluent is the most inclusive method to provide "quality and access for education for all" (p. 4). Beginning in 2010 as a series of workshops, and eventually leading to the establishment of a center for pedagogy, the MIT-Haiti Initiative provides access to Kreyòl-based STEM textbooks and other materials for Haitian students at both the high school and postsecondary level. Per the organization's website, the goal of the MIT-Haiti Initiative, is "to promote technology-enhanced active learning and the use of Kreyòl in science, technology, engineering, and math (STEM) disciplines, to help Haitians learn in the language most of them speak at home" (MIT-Haiti Initiative). As an additional benefit, the Initiative has been "contributing to the glossary of technical terms in the language" (Miller, 2016, p. 4). Furthermore, as Miller states, "one of the outcomes of these workshops is a convincing demonstration that there is no real obstacle to conducting technical discussions in Kreyòl." That is to say, the MIT-Haiti Initiative has found that one of the primary hurdles to accommodating creoles in education is, at least in Haiti, a mental hurdle. (Of course, having material support and funding from one of the world's premier research universities and a large grant from the United States National Science Foundation helps too.)

In the Dutch territories of Aruba, Bonaire, and Curaçao (the ABC islands), Papiamentu, a Portuguese-based creole that is the native language of the majority of students, is widely used in primary schools (Dijkhoff & Pereira, 2010). Scholars such as Nicholas Faraclas encourage the use of Papiamentu to teach students initial literacy skills, which will help them to acquire other languages as well, such as English, Dutch, and Spanish. In an interview on language and education, Faraclas (2012) reminds us that "language is the basis of culture and identity; when children learn in their own language," it enhances "their confidence as learners and individuals"; it thus enables them to build a solid foundation for academic success, including the eventual mastery of the academic standard varieties of language. Faraclas believes that one's native language possesses a rich history, and it transmits aspects of students' culture and tradition. Therefore, when students are allowed to use their native languages, they will feel proud of themselves and their culture, which will be transferred to other learning experiences. Faraclas clearly affirms that acknowledging and valorizing students' native languages reinforces their confidence and enhances their competence in other languages. This approach, he claims, will result in "pluricultural multilinguals" who will be prepared to function in a "globalized world." Elsewhere, Faraclas and his collaborators drew on a case study of teaching in the local English creole variety in the Dutch colony of Sint Eusaticus to provide empirical data showing that students who are allowed to use their home languages/creoles to learn other languages perform better on standardized tests than their peers who are forced to do all of their learning in the standard language (Faraclas, Kester, & Mijts, 2013).

Although several of the more sustained projects in accommodating local creole have come from outside the Commonwealth Anglophone Caribbean, I would be remiss not to mention the most significant pilot study to date in the Anglophone Caribbean, a study initiated in 2004 in Jamaica by Hubert Devonish and the Jamaican Language Unit (Devonish & Carpenter, 2010). Devonish and his team introduced the Bilingual Education Project (BEP) in 2004 by using Jamaican Creole English (usually referred to locally as Patwa) to "improve [student] performance and competence in the content subject areas as well as improving linguistic fluency in both Jamaican Creole and English" (cited in Le Compte Zambrana, 2017, p. 37). As part of the overarching BEP, a pilot study was conducted whereby students at the kindergarten to third grade level were taught primary literacy in Jamaican Creole in bilingual Jamaican Creole/Standard Jamaican English classrooms. Devonish clarifies that the BEP was introduced primarily to demonstrate the possibility of achieving bilingualism while valorizing Patwa (cited in LeCompte Zambrana, 2017, p. 43). He argues that for the successful implementation of the program, there should be "recognition of English and Jamaican Creole as distinct varieties and shedding long-held misconceptions that regarded bilingualism as a source of psychological harm to children" (cited in LeCompte Zambrana, 2017, p. 43). Accordingly, a mental shift from "broken English to Jamaican Creole or Patwa enabled residents to embrace Jamaican Creole as a distinct variety" (Devonish & Carpenter, 2007). Notably, at the end of the program, in 2008, the BEP students "took the National Grade Four Literacy Test and their performance . . . in English literacy skills was better than that of those who were taught in the traditional manner" (UWI Notebook, 2010).

Deepening/Widening Reach: Translanguaging/ Code-Meshing

How, then, can the students' native language be fruitfully accommodated in postsecondary composition classes? Should language requirements be dichotomized into home and school, formal and informal discourses? While code-switching, practiced in educational environments, is a widely established method for accommodating home languages, linguists and other scholars have more recently introduced *code-meshing* as a more deliberate method for students to navigate their way between formal and informal languages (Canagarajah, 2006; Young, Barrett, Young-Rivera, & Lovejoy, 2014). *Code-meshing* involves the blending of languages and styles in creating and communicating meaning. Milson-Whyte (2013) proposes that code-meshing is one manifestation of a translingual orientation to writing. This approach "treats standardized rules as historical codifications of language that inevitably change through dynamic processes of use" (Horner, Lu, Royster, & Trimbur, 2011, p. 305). Given that each new communication situation has its specific requirements, advocates of translingualism argue that "writers can, do, and must negotiate standardized rules in light of the contexts of specific instances of writing" (p. 305). With specific regard to code-meshing, Canagarajah (2006) claims that when it is applied in the classroom, it enhances students' expectations and generates the sense of "contact zone textualities" (p. 601). In essence, code-meshing enables the students to connect both facets of their lives, thus creating a productive environment through self-acceptance. Indeed, Canagarajah believes that the time has come for a pedagogical shift, which will involve educators and policymakers, as well as communities of parents and students over what could be an extensive period of time (p. 612). To be literate in the twenty-first century, students should be multilingual, a fact that can be used to help pave the way for the validation and use of creole languages in education. It is essential that we change the paradigm from the "traditional" English curriculum to more inclusive approaches that will accommodate the multilingual practices that the students bring from home — even while bearing in mind challenges in implementing proposals from other shores (see Milson-Whyte, 2013; 2014).

In the Caribbean, as in most countries, education is a means of upward mobility. If some members of the community, primarily creole speakers, are denied that opportunity, they will be excluded from the wider community and opportunities for academic, social, and economic progress. In an attempt at demonstrating social equity and simultaneously promoting academic egalitarianism, the academy should embrace the considerable knowledge that all students bring to the classroom, especially their linguistic knowledge. Instead of marginalizing them, educators should give students the opportunity to excel by using the home language as the foundation from which they can be taught Standard English or any other language. Conforming to such principle would help to eliminate what Milson-Whyte (2015) refers to as "linguistic prejudice" (p. 45).

Furthermore, paradigm shifts in the global landscape have had a great impact on the traditional *one language, one nation* ideology, which will require extensive modification to accommodate the realities of the twenty-first century. Canagarajah (2006) believes that these realities require "us to develop in our students a multilingual and polyliterate orientation to writing" (p. 587). Indeed, the recursive nature of writing necessitates more than a one-semester or two-semester course in the use of English; writing is a process that requires consistent practice from developmental to advanced stages. By the same token, consistent practice of the home languages with appropriate guidance will equip students for academic success (Faraclas, 2012; Milson-Whyte, 2015). When students are encouraged to write in elementary school, they develop an affinity for writing, and by the time they advance to junior high school the fear of writing would have diminished to the extent that they anticipate writing in high school. When that writing is evaluated and students receive timely feedback and are given the opportunity to revise their writing, they will be better equipped to handle college writing. Creole-influenced students can attain success if careful and consistent consideration is given to their situation and to their languages, as has been done in some institutional cases, such as The University of the West Indies.

In moving from one generic writing course to adding four new Faculty-specific courses and one developmental course to its offerings, The University of the West Indies, Mona, Jamaica (2013–2014), has demonstrated an interest in accommodating creole-influenced students, but there's a need for greater accommodation in institutions in the region (Milson-Whyte, 2015, p. 191). Milson-Whyte has identified five conditions that need to be met in order to satisfy this need:

1. The reach of transculturation, especially as concerns how creole-influenced students *do language*;

2. Writing in disciplines as *visible rhetoric*;
3. Writing instruction in the academy as developmental and necessary across the years of a student's degree program;
4. The academy as plural, having multiple tongues in its many disciplines, but which creole-influenced students—by their very linguistic/cultural experiences—are advantageously poised to manipulate;
5. The goal of writing development as social equity in an atmosphere of excellence. (p. 191)

While these five conditions may not be considered various points on a continuum, they do offer guidelines that demonstrate a sensitivity to the needs of the students. They also contribute to the process by training teachers to understand their roles in addressing the needs of creole-influenced students and equipping them for success in academia. Teachers' sensitivity will help them to look more favorably at creole languages, which should be recognized on their own merit instead of being considered "broken" forms of standard European languages. It is my hope that the issues faced by creole speakers in the Caribbean will be discussed more frequently and given more attention, especially regarding best practices and successful case studies from within and beyond the region, as part of an effort to move language education in the Caribbean and for Caribbean-origin students to a more equitable perspective.

References

Aceto, M., & Williams, J. P. (Eds.). (2003). *Contact Englishes of the eastern Caribbean*. Amsterdam: John Benjamins.

Adams, E. (1991). *Understanding Jamaican Patois*. Kingston, Jamaica: Kingston Publishers Limited.

Alleyne, M. C. (1994). Problems of standardization of Creole languages. In M. Morgan (Ed.), *Language and the social construction of identity in Creole situations* (pp. 7–18). Los Angeles: Center for Afro-American Studies, UCLA.

Canagarajah, S. (2006). The place of world Englishes in composition: Pluralization continued. *College Composition and Communication, 57,* 586–619.

Cassidy, F., & LePage, R. (1967). *Dictionary of Jamaican English*. Cambridge: Cambridge University Press.

Community Foundation of the Virgin Islands. (2016). *USVI kids count data book*. Retrieved from https://cfvi.files.wordpress.com/2018/12/2016-data-book-final-12-14-18.pdf

Devonish, H. (1986). *Language and liberation: Creole language politics in the Caribbean.* London: Karia Press.

Devonish, H., & Carpenter, K. (2007). *Full bilingual education in a creole language situation: Jamaican bilingual primary education project.* St. Augustine, Trinidad and Tobago: Society for Caribbean Linguistics.

Devonish, H., & Carpenter, K. (2010). Swimming against the tide: Jamaican Creole in education. In B. Migge, I. Leglise & A. Bartens (Eds.), *Creoles in education: An appraisal of current programs and projects* (pp. 167–182). Amsterdam: John Benjamins.

DeGraff, M. (2013). MIT-Haiti Initiative uses Haitian Creole to make learning truly active, constructive, and interactive. Retrieved from https://haiti.mit.edu/mit-haiti-initiative-uses-haitian-creole-to-make-learning-truly-active-constructive-and-interactive/

Dijkhoff, M., & Pereira, J. (2010). Language and education in Aruba, Bonaire and Curaçao. In B. Migge, I. Léglise, & A. Bartens (Eds.), *Creoles in education: An appraisal of current programs and projects* (pp. 237–272). Amsterdam: John Benjamins.

Faraclas, N. (2012, February). Interview. *Native Language/Idioma Materno.* Retrieved from https://www.youtube.com/watch?v=lqz7zORze2M&fbclid=IwAR3BBi1S0L-dnzOuHZRTxDQ614r8UXdLFx-htylUVX6r80fJpPunQMI0_w4

Faraclas, N., Kester, E. P., & Mijts, E. (2013). Language in instruction in Sint Eustatius: Report of the 2013 research group on language of instruction in Sint Eustatius. Ministry for the Caribbean Netherlands. Retrieved from https://zoek.officielebekendmakingen.nl/blg-348672.pdf

Government of the USVI. (2008). State Office of English Language Acquisition Bilingual/ESL Educational Program. Retrieved from http://www.stx.k12.vi/state%20page/bilingual/index.htm.

Highfield, A. R. (2009). *Time longa dan twine: Notes on the culture, history, & people of the USVI.* Christiansted, USVI: Antilles Press.

Horner, B. Lu, M., Royster, J. J., & Trimbur, J. (2011). Opinion: Language difference in writing: Toward a translingual approach. *College English, 73*, 302–321.

Irvine, P., & Elsasser, N. (1988). The ecology of literacy: Negotiating standards in a Caribbean setting. In B. Rafoth & D. Rubin (Eds.), *The social construction of written communication,* (pp. 304–320). Norwood, NJ: Ablex.

Le Compte Zambrana, P. A. (2017). *Creole languages in education and their role in shaping Caribbean identities: Models for integrating English lexifier Creoles into school Curricula in the Eastern Caribbean.* (Unpublished doctoral dissertation). University of Puerto Rico, Rio Piedras, Puerto Rico.

Miller, H. (2016). The MIT-Haiti Initiative: An international engagement. *MIT Faculty Newsletter, 29.* Retrieved from http://web.mit.edu/fnl/volume/291/miller.html

Milson-Whyte, V. (2013). Pedagogical and socio-political implications of code-meshing in classrooms: Some considerations for a translingual orientation to writing. In A. Suresh Canagarajah (Ed.), *Literacy as translingual practice: Between communities and classrooms* (pp. 115–127). New York: Routledge.

Milson-Whyte, V. (2014). Working English through code-meshing: Implications for denigrated language varieties and their users. In B. Horner and K. Kopelson (Eds.), *Reworking English in Rhetoric and Composition: Global Interrogations, Local Interventions* (103–115). Carbondale, IL: Southern Illinois University Press.

Milson-Whyte, V. (2015). *Academic writing instruction for creole-influenced students*. Kingston, Jamaica: University of the West Indies Press.

Ministry of Education, Youth, and Culture (MOEYC) [Jamaica]. (2001). Language education policy. Retrieved from http://dlpalmer.weebly.com/uploads/3/5/8/7/3587856/language_education_policy.pdf

MIT-Haiti Initiative. (2017). About. Retrieved from https://haiti.mit.edu/about/

Nero, S. J. (2000). The changing faces of English: A Caribbean perspective. *TESOL Quarterly, 34*(3), 483–510.

Nero, S. J. (2006). *Dialects, Englishes, creoles & education*. Mahwah, NJ: Lawrence Erlbaum Associates.

Oenbring, R. (2017). College composition in the Anglophone Caribbean: The search for Caribbean identity. *Journal of Global Literacies, Technologies, and Emerging Pedagogies, 4*, 533–545.

Phillipson, R. (1992). *Linguistic imperialism*. Oxford: Oxford University Press.

Robertson, I., & Simmons-McDonald, H. (Eds.). (2014). *Education issues in Creole and Creole-influenced vernacular contexts*. Kingston, Jamaica: University of the West Indies Press.

Siegel, J. (2007). Creoles and minority dialects in education: An update. *Language and Education, 21*(1), 66–86.

United Nations Educational, Scientific and Cultural Organization (UNESCO). (1953). *The use of vernacular languages in education: Monographs on fundamental education*. Paris: Author.

University of the Virgin Islands. (2019). English Proficiency Examination. Retrieved from https://www.uvi.edu/enrollment/registrar/testing/registrar-epe.aspx

UWI Notebook—Researchers: Bilingual education yields better results. (2010, June 27). *The Gleaner*. Retrieved from http://jamaica-gleaner.com/gleaner/20100627/arts/arts3.html

Wilkinson, C. (2015). Teachers' language attitudes in Guyana: Preliminary inquiries in the primary schools. *Caribbean Journal of Education, 37*(1–2), 152–175.

Young, V. A., Barrett, R., Young-Rivera, Y., & Lovejoy, K. (2014). *Other people's English: Code-meshing, code-switching, and African American literacy*. New York: Teachers College Press.

Section Six: A Way Forward

It is not language, but people, who make revolutions.
—Brathwaite, 1984, p. 13

12 ACADEMIC LITERACIES: LITERACY FACILITATORS' FRAMEWORK FOR SELF-EMPOWERMENT IN THE ANGLOPHONE CARIBBEAN POSTSECONDARY CONTEXT

Clover Jones McKenzie and Tresecka Campbell-Dawes

Within the Anglophone Caribbean, misconceptions exist regarding the purpose of tertiary-level reading and writing courses. As recounted in Milson-Whyte (2015), the wider society in the region generally believes that academic writing courses should *fix* grammar problems that occur in students' writing. Indeed, research conducted at the University of Technology, Jamaica (UTech, Ja.) in 2017 found that some content-area specialists also share this view (McKenzie & Josephs, 2017). In addition, the UTech, Ja. study established that—similar to Rose's (2016) description of the history of writing course development at the University of Guyana—no clear philosophy has guided changes to the institution's writing program over the years. While there have been uneven attempts to infuse some of the principles of current writing development theories made popular under the banner of composition studies within the United States, such as the *process* approach, into programs at Anglophone Caribbean postsecondary institutions (see, Milson-Whyte, 2015), a deliberate effort toward the creation of an overarching philosophy to guide practice across the region is still absent.

This chapter argues that what is needed in Anglophone Caribbean tertiary institutions in the context of academic writing is for instructors/

facilitators to develop professional identities. This will allow instructors to develop a deeper understanding of the specific problems and potentials of teaching writing in the Caribbean context and to carve out individual teaching philosophies that will collectively drive the advancement of the field of writing studies across the region. This demands critical action, including the literacy facilitators' becoming more vocal about matters related to literacy skills development. In order to achieve these aims, we first overview the academic literacies approach, an influential philosophy governing postsecondary writing, particularly in the United Kingdom, which is a promising framework within which this "critical reflexivity" (Street, 2004, p. 14) and "professionalization" (Matsuda, 2012, p. 147) can take place.

The Academic Literacies Approach

For postsecondary academic writing instructors who wish to forge ahead with the creation of a professional identity, the academic literacies approach, with its strong emphasis on transformation or going against conventions (Lillis, Harrington, Lea, & Mitchell, 2015), is a useful framework. As Hamilton (2013) argues, the development of our identity is highly dependent on our reaction to factors within the social environment; we can either accept the identity imposed on us by our environment or we can develop our own counter-identity. Especially within a professional context within which one has very little power (as is the case for many Caribbean academic writing instructors bound by restrictive course outlines and involved norming procedures [often referred to in Caribbean contexts as cross moderation]), this task of self-identity creation will become easier if a clear framework, such as that explored in this chapter, is available. Although the academic literacies (ALs) framework has been developed to improve student writing, we wish to offer it as a means of assisting writing instructors/facilitators towards better preparing themselves for the task of helping the students. To show how the ALs approach could possibly assist in this endeavor, we use the following section to provide a brief description of this philosophy, after which we attempt to align it with the situation in the Anglophone Caribbean postsecondary context.

Academic Literacy/Literacies as a Label for Knowledge and Skills

Writing instructors and theorists both inside and outside the Caribbean may be more familiar with the singular version *academic literacy*, since, according to Lillis and Scott (2007), it is becoming a popular label for courses focusing on the development of required reading and writing skills at the tertiary level at institutions around the world. Topics covered in academic literacy courses include: critical thinking, logical reasoning, problem solving, production of various types of texts, and information literacy (Gunn, Hearne, & Sibthorpe, 2011; Weideman & van Dyk, 2014); courses labeled *academic literacy* tend to be general or generic in nature, predominantly focusing on formal English sentence construction and the composition of expository, reflective, and argumentative essays.

However, the plural version, *academic literacies*, is the preferred term for proponents who renounce the view of there being one form of literacy and wish to indicate that reading and writing processes differ across disciplines and academic institutions (Lillis & Scott, 2007; Paxton & Frith, 2014). According to this view, there are differences in how knowledge is arrived at and disseminated within each field or profession, and these specific behaviors serve to identify the members of a particular profession or specialization (Jacobs, 2007; Sacre & Nash, 2010). Thus, *academic literacies* is a label signaling awareness of the variation in the means through which varied groups compose and share knowledge. This awareness of the differences in writing in diverse areas of study and professions mirrors the concerns of the fields of Writing Across the Curriculum (WAC) and Writing in the Disciplines (WID) within the American tradition of rhetoric and composition.

Academic Literacies as an Ideology

Yet, there is another more complex, ideological meaning attached to the concept of academic literacies that, based on Street (2004), goes beyond the mere recognition that literacy practices differ based on the context or discipline. *Academic literacies* in this interpretation represents a philosophy that seeks to contest the "skills-based, deficit model of student writing and to consider the complexity of writing practices" within the university context (Lea & Street, 1998, p. 157). While it may be argued that explicit skills-based models still exist, and are even foregrounded, within certain strands of American-style composition instruction — particularly in the field of writing in the disciplines (WID) in the form of traditional formal models repackaged in different names (like the concept of *genre*) — under the academic literacies approach, writing practices are, conversely, not merely designed to facilitate skill acquisition and are not merely focused on what writers do when composing texts. Instead, writing in the academic literacies tradition encompasses the students' culture, knowledge, and experiences, which vary given the diversity in the student population as access to tertiary-level education increases. This interpretation of writing development, which began within the United Kingdom and has benefitted extensively from the work of Brian Street (Lillis & Scott, 2007; Lea & Street, 1998; 2006; Wingate & Tribble, 2012) and denounces the heavy focus on *the student as the problem*, depicts a link between literacy skills development and issues of identity and power (Street, 2004; Lea & Street, 2006; Lillis & Scott, 2007).

The institution is the provider of the required qualification that students seek; therefore, it has the power to determine what is suitable as knowledge (Tapp, 2015) and how this knowledge should be communicated. The suggestion here is that the institution can hold back the students' progress by determining that what they know or can do is not up to standard. The academic literacies ideology invites recognition of who students are and the literacy practices that they may bring to the learning contexts and calls for a rejection of the notion that there is only one strict way of expressing meaning within a given context (Horner, 2013). To ensure that students are not unfairly judged because they display literacy proficiency in different ways from the expected norm, for instance, the institution would need to adopt Street's (2004) suggestion that all aspects of the writing program, including assessment strategies, undergo careful scrutiny, through a process of critical reflexivity. The institution here appears to suggest an entity, not just the administrators of the universities, or the course managers, such as heads of schools or program leaders; literacy skills and content-area educators should also play integral roles. For this to occur, all participants should have a common understanding of the literacy needs of the students and how to fulfill them. The literacy skills development facilitators must lead this process, since they are the ones with the in-depth knowledge of this field. However, they first have to know what their roles are and establish a clear path to achieving their goals.

Applicability of Principles of Academic Literacies to the Anglophone Caribbean

While academic writing instruction in the Anglophone Caribbean could benefit from aspects of both the rhetoric and composition and the academic literacies approaches, we lean towards ALs, for good reasons. As we note, the academic literacies approach explicitly calls for strong critical action and advocacy; this call to action is a crucial aspect of the ALs approach, which focuses very heavily on activism on the part of facilitators in the quest to assist their students. Many of the situations we reference, in presenting our arguments, will come from the Jamaican context, particularly our home institution, the University of Technology, Jamaica (UTech, Ja.). However, we contend that with the shared linguistic history, issues related to resources, and, as Oenbring (2017) states, the absence of a unique national or regional approach to education, there is value in calling the entire Anglophone Caribbean into action. Greater benefits are likely to accrue from a larger community of practitioners who can offer support to one another, and policy makers tend to pay more attention when the voices are many.

The Status of Academic Literacy Development in the Anglophone Caribbean

Lack of Professional Development

Literacy skills development within the Anglophone Caribbean is suffering from underdevelopment and lack of professional vigor. This is seen in the absence of a unique Caribbean philosophy of postsecondary literacy skills development despite decades of literacy offerings at this level and the scarcity of available empirical research (Oenbring, 2017; Oenbring, Jaquette, Kozikowski, & Higgins, 2016). The explanation Oenbring et al. (2016) provide for this predicament at the University of The Bahamas is applicable to other institutions; it is that most of the facilitators' effort is devoted to teaching. The seeming lack of voice on the part of Caribbean facilitators, who unlike their counterparts in the United States and the United Kingdom have not been seriously engaged in carving out a philosophy of academic writing appropriate for their context, feeds the obscurity surrounding academic literacy skills improvement. It also robs academic writing instructors of the chance to claim that what they do is of the caliber of content-area offerings and should be ascribed higher status. Accordingly, literacy facilitators need to carve out their own sense of identity before taking on the required advocacy role demanded by the academic literacies' ideology.

Searching for the Identity of Postsecondary Literacy Facilitators

The *near silence* of Caribbean literacy facilitators can add to the false perceptions of the public, whose members tend to see the role of postsecondary writing instructors as an extension of that of teachers of English at the pre-tertiary levels. Indeed, in contrast to earlier levels of the education system, at the tertiary stage there is sometimes confusion as to the identity and true purpose of academic literacy specialists within Caribbean institutions. Are these facilitators also teachers of the grammatical structures of English? The belief of persons who indicate that these courses should focus on students' weaknesses in grammar, as well as the students' view that the academic literacy courses merely continue what was done at high school (McKenzie, 2014) would seem to suggest that they are. The use of the word *English* in the names of courses and departments or units under which these courses fall can serve to reinforce the notion that tertiary-level writing is synonymous with the teaching of English-language skills. The labels *Use of English* and *English for Academic Purposes*, for example, can imply a focus on language structure.

The name or label given to an entity or person can serve as an indication of what that entity or individual does or represents. In the case of Jamaica, for instance, names ascribed to persons or objects are highly descriptive of their characteristics. When the very thin plastic bags for use at supermarkets were first introduced to the island, they took on the moniker *scandal bags* because they clearly revealed their contents, thus scandalizing the owner of the goods. Another example from the educational sphere is the use of the word *Communication* in the literacy courses offered through a unit referred to as the *Communication Division* at the UTech, Ja. (hereon referred to as UTech) during 1995–2006. Advertisements placed by the human resources department requiring "lecturers in communication" led to persons trained in mass communication applying and being employed to deliver these courses. Clearly, there was a mismatch between their training and what they were asked to do—teach academic literacy skills. This misalliance occurred partly because of the labels used.

In 2007, administrators at UTech decided to employ more persons with qualifications in the field of linguistics to teach academic writing courses; however, like Rose (2016) in her discussion on the situation in a Guyanese university, we are uncertain of the real rationale. Perhaps, the reasoning did not go beyond the thought that these individuals were exposed to the structure of language and maybe principles affecting its teaching and learning. When the literacy offerings were modified due to institutional requirements in 2009, the names of the courses were changed to *academic writing*. This action had no impact on the philosophy of or orientation towards teaching. The names changed because the number of credits decreased from eight to six and some of the content of the earlier literacy offerings were removed. Oral and Business Communication were cut, and the focus placed only on expository and argumentative writing. At UTech, we are only now trying to introduce the concept of academic literacies to the members of the teaching staff and seeking to include this concept in discussions of the curriculum and other related matters. This is one indication of the Caribbean facilitators' not keeping abreast of advancements in the field.

The name changes also had little influence on content-area lecturers and students' views. The renamed courses, like similar ones delivered at The University of the West Indies and University of Guyana, are being offered through the *English Language Section* and *English Language and Linguistics* units. Thus, content-area lecturers and employers continue to expect that fixing problems with the grammatical use of Standard English is the remit of these classes. However, some of the academic writing lecturers at UTech refuse to accept that they operate out of an English Language unit, since they do not teach English Language; their mandate is to facilitate the development of academic writing skills. This could be mediated through the use of any language, including creole, if this were the official language. This dispute remains unresolved since there has been no further discussion on the issue. While the academic writing lecturers remain under a single unit, some persons just avoid the use of this label.

If the writing lecturers are not teachers of English although they operate out of Departments of English, then who are they? Is there a more suitable term, and does it make any difference? These are questions that may seem trivial but could assist in the clarification of the general misconceptions. Clarence and McKenna (2017) put forward the label *academic literacies practitioners* to refer "to faculty members who work in academic development or teaching and learning units, or within faculties, whose particular role is to work with lecturers and students to develop students' academic literacy practices, most specifically for writing in the disciplines" (p. 38). Indeed, could *writing in the disciplines*, a label that is still not widespread in the Anglophone Caribbean, be a more appropriate organizing label and set of principles for postsecondary writing classes? Or, following the dominant influence of the United States, should the label *composition* be adopted? For some persons, the latter label may not be so acceptable within Caribbean contexts since the term *composition* is often associated with essay writing at primary school. Again, there could be a link to the pre-tertiary level and possible misrepresentation as to what the courses involve. If the label *composition* is used, the literacy facilitators would have to be responsible for highlighting the fact that composition is more than just writing; it can also depict oral and visual creations at various levels. However, this issue of what academic literacy facilitators call themselves or the units from which they operate may become insignificant once they are actively engaged in public discussions and research publication.

Institutional Issues Impacting Academic Literacy Skills Development

General Status of Academic Writing Courses

Changing the names of courses does not improve students' writing skills nor does it change the environment in which these crucial academic literacies are taught; the institutional context within which students learn these skills also requires scrutiny. Indeed, the role of the institution is identified as an important feature in the academic literacies model, as literacy development is not seen as an isolated entity. It operates within a social and cultural context (Pineteh, 2013), which impacts the overall attitude towards and treatment of literacy issues.

Similar to the state of affairs in the United States, the situation in some Caribbean institutions showcases a system of marginalization of writing courses that operate as part of the general education offerings. The courses are sometimes seen by stakeholders as a waste of time, money, and other resources as they seem not to be achieving their desired objectives. Fueling this belief is the fact that—despite recent changes to the writing courses and overarching writing programs at the UTech (McKenzie & Josephs, 2016), University of the West Indies (Milson-Whyte, 2015), and University of Guyana (Rose, 2016)—students still perform in the mid-range on writing assignments, and content area lecturers and employers continue to comment on deficits in the formal English Language output of students who pass these courses. Lecturers or students are often blamed for the lack of sufficient improvement in students' reading and writing skills; lecturers and their students are, according to proponents of this argument, not doing what they should. However, these detractors often ignore the impact of various other factors, most of which are out of the control of writing instructors and their students (for example, the institution having limited resources).

Indeed, many Caribbean institutions—despite being aware of the difficulties some students face in relation to competence in the use of Standard English—do not provide students with adequate support for the upgrading of their literacy skills. Students, based on the global drive to widen access to tertiary education, come from diverse types of experiences and with different qualifications. Their varied experiences at school and home may lead to variations in their level of proficiency in the use of Standard English. This code is the official language and medium of education in the Anglophone Caribbean; it, thus, serves as a gatekeeper. Creole speakers who are not able to pass an external English Language examination will have problems. However, research has shown that the writing proficiency of even those candidates who were successful in external examinations shows varying degrees of writing deficits (McKenzie & Orogun, 2013; McLaren & Webber, 2009; Rose, 2016; Smith, Stewart-McKoy, Henry, & Hamilton, 2015), whether they completed grade 11 or grade 13 at secondary institutions. The institutions signal their awareness of these issues through actions, such as the imposition of English Language proficiency tests, the implementation of writing centers, and the offering of general education academic literacy courses, predominantly in writing.

Inadequacy in the provisions institutions make to assist students' writing development is most obvious in the amount of time they allocate. Ferris (2008) argues, for example, that "it takes years to acquire competence in a second language approaching that of native speakers," but "when the standard of 'competence' is academic literacy tasks required in higher education, the timeline is even longer" (p. 92). Many Caribbean students, after completing classes focusing on the structure and use of formal English between the ages of eleven and thirteen years, do not enter tertiary-level institutions being able to effectively use this language. However, institutions expect that within one or two semesters of exposure to predominantly generic writing classes, students will be adequately prepared for effective communication within other subject areas and then the world of work. The expectation is that the skills acquired in the general classes will be transferred to other courses (Gunn, Hearne & Sibthorpe, 2011). Unfortunately, this does not happen, and if the students still seem to struggle with skills they should have attained at the pre-tertiary level after approximately eleven to thirteen years at that stage, how then can they master the expected academic skills in one or two thirteen-week periods, for instance? Indeed, disappointing results after the completion of the two required first-year writing courses by students at the University of The Bahamas led to the addition of a third course taken in the third year (Oenbring et al., 2016).

Added to the issue of inadequate time are problems associated with numbers to a class and variation in the types of difficulties faced by students. At UTech, a class usually comprises twenty to twenty-five students who meet once for three hours per week in a tutorial setting, or twice with one of the hours being devoted to a lecturer session. As might be expected, classes contain students with varying levels of proficiency. An analysis of candidates' performance on the English Language Proficiency Test for the period 2009–2011 at UTech showed that performance varied based on the faculty to which candidates belonged and the skill being tested (Smith, Stewart-McKoy, Henry, & Hamilton, 2015). Each academic writing class at UTech contains students from different faculties, and according to the research project, some students may be struggling in different ways with reading comprehension, mastery of the English language in general or basic essay writing skills in particular. Yet, in two or three hours, the facilitator is expected to assist each student in achieving competence in academic writing skills over thirteen weeks. This scenario is repeated across the Anglophone Caribbean, as the students share some similar experiences.

In the case of the second of the two academic writing courses offered at UTech, the three-hour slot was changed in 2014 to two sessions: a one-hour lecture session and a two-hour tutorial. A team of academic writing lecturers that was tasked with the mission of reviewing the course recommended this modification because the students felt that the three-hour sessions were too long. The compromise was that the number of students for the tutorial session would move from twenty-five to twenty, and a process approach be used in the production of the students' final essays. This arrangement necessitates a greater degree of interaction between individual students and the facilitator; but, with twenty students in a two-hour slot, it does not seem feasible that the needs of each student will be met. Two of the cited motivating factors for changes made to the course were students' discontent with the three-hour timeline and unsatisfactory student performance. We are not quite sure how instituting a lecture session assists with the issue of performance and note that there was no theoretical rationale for this action. Certainly, the lecture hour made it easier and less costly for the institution to place students from varying faculties and programs into a given slot. Nevertheless, the question is, was this the best thing for the students?

However, if, according to Street (2004), transfer of generic skills does not happen naturally, just allocating more time to general writing classes—and adding more required general education writing classes—will not be fruitful. If literacy is to be seen as social action, as Street proposes, with diverse practices across various settings, then, as prescribed by the advocates of the academic literacies model, what students truly need is a deeper understanding of how to access and generate information within their disciplines of study. Indeed, Hutchins (2015) warns that this exposure cannot just be provided by literacy practitioners, who may know very little about the particular disciplines. What would be needed is similar to the project done at The University of the West Indies, Mona, by McLaren and Webber (2009). This intervention followed a writing across the curriculum (WAC) approach that involved a partnership between McLaren, the literacy specialist and Webber, the content specialist, within an ecology course. This project sought to assist students who successfully completed the first-year general writing courses but struggled with producing laboratory reports and other documents required for the science course. McLaren and Webber worked as partners at using the process approach in assisting the students. While there were issues with student compliance with the production of drafts, the researchers noted positive results from this engagement.

Unfortunately, the type of partnership that existed between McLaren and Webber does not occur commonly within Anglophone Caribbean postsecondary institutions. McLaren and Webber's (2009) project was just that, a research investigation, and while others at UWI, Mona, may be considering this strategy, the researchers acknowledge that it is not an institution-wide endeavor. Like many other institutions across the world, the Caribbean tertiary-level system predominantly subscribes to the situation in which there is a separation of generic and content knowledge, as Jacobs (2007), speaking in relation to the South African context, states.

Jacobs argues that when there is a reliance on generic courses only, "content lecturers abdicate their role in making discourse practices of their discipline explicit to students" (p. 876).

Moreover, the way in which the institutions view literacy specialists as part of the general education framework may impact the attempt to establish partnerships with content-area specialists. In some instances, general education units are not accorded the same type of rating as program offering entities. Since general education literacy specialists do not operate within a program of study, they do not "own" students (and their *full-time equivalents*); therefore, they are not seen as generating income for the university. This means that another unit brings in the students for writing instructors to teach. Furthermore, at technical universities such as UTech, lecturers within general education may not be viewed as specialists because they do not focus on practical skill development.

Added to the above issues is the problem of dissimilar benefits for writing instructors and content faculty. At a prominent Jamaican university, which shall remain unnamed at the request of the respondent, writing facilitators on short term renewable contracts do not receive some benefits enjoyed by other faculty, including duty concession on motor vehicles (Personal Interview, January 7, 2018). They also have more contact hours than content specialists, despite the demands of their courses. These writing facilitators are expected to complete fourteen hours, while content specialists complete ten. One explanation for this disparity has to do with the qualifications of the staff members and the terms of their contracts. Some of these less privileged faculty members may be those with only master's degrees, who are employed as instructors, or assistant lecturers. They may, therefore, teach and grade papers but not be expected to conduct research, a needed action for the growth of the field. This situation, while understandable in parts, still points to the question of value placed on literacy skills development. Our question here is whether this is the same scenario for content-area lecturers.

Of course, the operationalization of these partnerships will also be difficult, especially in relation to how hours are allocated, and in the case of institutions such as UTech, who will pay. The necessary overlap in the hours carried by the content-area and literacy facilitators will be problematic since they belong to different faculties and each faculty, as a budget unit, deals with expenditures from income it generates. Resolving these issues may seem insurmountable; however, some of them can be worked out through engagement involving administrators, literacy specialists, and content-area lecturers.

Articulating a Professional Identity

However, before the academic literacy skills development facilitators can impact how the academic literacy skills improvement programs are viewed within the institutions, they must first carve out their own identities. Individuals have a part to play in how they are viewed; therefore, if the facilitators portray themselves as just service givers, then they will continue to work "largely from the fringes of universities" (Williamson & Goldsmith, 2013, p. 1). For others to see what they do as valuable and to respect the contribution they make to the preparation of students for entry into society and the workplace, the literacy skills development facilitators must critically reflect on their portrayal of themselves and how their field is represented. Thus, they are responsible for creating a professional identity, which according to Neary (2014), is "how we perceive ourselves within our occupational context and how we communicate this to others" (p. 14).

The means of professionalizing a subject area were outlined many years ago; according to Shermis (1962), moving "marginal areas into full-fledged disciplines" involves the development of a "process of inquiry" (p. 85). Shermis advocates that persons seeking to professionalize their subject must see available theories as tools, rather than dogma. Professionalization of the field of rhetoric and composition within the American context during the 1950s and 1960s, according to Matsuda (2012) and McLemee (2003), was largely achieved through the questioning of theory or practice and the development of scholarship surrounding writing skills development. This critical analysis of current theory during that time led to a movement away from the heavy dependence on the teaching of grammar and the development of recent principles focusing on writing skills development. We, as Caribbean academic writing instructors, must lift the profile of the field by becoming our own advocates and engaging in public discourse on areas of significance in the field.

Another important facet of professionalization is the creation of a community of practitioners. Currently, apart from individual discussions between facilitators at UWI, Mona, and UTech, for instance, there is no partnership across institutions in the region; facilitators at each institution tend to discuss issues within their own silos. Noticeably absent is the type of robust engagement of issues out of which shared principles evolve, especially within the framework of organizations, such as the Conference on College Composition and Communication (CCCC) in the United States of America. Organizations such as the National Association of Teachers of English (NATE) in Jamaica, and the Society for Caribbean Linguistics exist; however, the former caters to the teaching of English at the secondary level, while the latter, as the name suggests, focuses on linguistic matters. Academic writing instructors require a platform from which they can articulate concerns related to their field and share possible answers for overcoming some of the difficulties faced. This may require the formation of a professional organization and research caucuses across the Anglophone Caribbean region. Without this dynamic, there will continue to be an absence of effective advocacy that could affect policy decisions across the region and better move the literacy courses towards their goals. Facilitators within the Anglophone Caribbean should not just attend international conferences and rely on principles practiced elsewhere; they need to interrogate available theories and articulate their own versions.

Conclusion

Academic literacy skills development at the tertiary level continues to face a number of challenges in institutions worldwide. The Anglophone Caribbean, while sharing some of these problems, has its unique set of issues. One of the most prominent difficulties is the perception that writing skills development is peripheral in relation to content-area subjects. Academic writing instructors can assume some of the blame for this situation. This is so as the necessary professional community engagement among practitioners and the vigorous scholarship associated with academic disciplines are absent. Therefore, the associated degree of advocacy required in situations involving lack of status and power is absent from practitioners who are supposed to be preparing students to engage in critical discourse. We invite these practitioners to adopt the stance promoted through the academic literacies' ideology, not as a teaching methodology, since it is not a teaching strategy, but as a philosophy engendering the spirit of critique and advocacy.

References

Clarence, S., & McKenna, S. (2017). Developing academic literacies through understanding the nature of disciplinary knowledge. *London Review of Education, 15*(1), 38–48.

Ferris, D. (2008). Students must learn to correct all their writing errors. In J. Reid (Ed.), *Writing myths: applying second language research to classroom teaching* (pp. 90–144). Ann Arbor, MI: University of Michigan Press.

Gunn, C., Hearne, S., & Sibthorpe, J. (2011). Right from the start: A rationale for embedding academic literacy skills in university courses. *Journal of University Teaching & Learning Practice, 8*(1). Retrieved from http://ro.uow.edu.au/cgi/viewcontent.cgi?article=1159&context=jutlp

Hamilton, S. E. (2013). Exploring professional identity: The perceptions of chartered accountant students. *The British Accounting Review, 45*(1), 37–49.

Horner, B. (2013). Ideologies of literacy, "academic literacies," and composition studies. *Literacy in Composition Studies, 1*(1), 1–9.

Hutchins, T. D. (2015). A new approach to teaching business writing: writing across the core—a document-based curriculum. *American Journal of Business Education, 8*(2), 131–138.

Jacobs, C. (2007). Mainstreaming academic literacy: Implications for how academic development understands its work in higher education. *South African Journal of Higher Education, 21*(7), 868–879.

Lea, M. R., & Street, B. (1998). Student writing in higher education: An academic literacies approach. *Studies in Higher Education, 23*(2), 157–172.

Lea, M. R., & Street, B. (2006). The 'academic literacies' model: theory and applications. *Theory into Practice, 45*(4), 368–377.

Lillis, T., Harrington, K., Lea, M. R., & Mitchell, S. (Eds.). (2015). *Working with academic literacies: Case studies towards transformative practice*. Anderson, SC: Parlor Press.

Lillis, T., & Scott, M. (2007). Defining academic literacies research: Issues of epistemology, ideology and strategy. *Journal of Applied Linguistics, 4*(1), 5–32.

Matsuda, P. (2012). Let's face it: Language issues and the writing program administrator. *WPA: Writing Program Administration, 36*(1), 141–163.

McKenzie, C. (2014). A set of Jamaican students' experience with the consciousness-raising strategy in a second language writing class (Unpublished PhD thesis), University of the West Indies, Mona, Jamaica.

McKenzie, C., & Josephs, B. (2016, August 3). A Jamaican university's experiences with academic literacy development: Meandering paths to the same destination. Paper presented at the Society for Caribbean Linguistics Conference, University of the West Indies, Mona. Kingston, Jamaica.

McKenzie, C., & Josephs, B. (2017). Academic Writing at UTech, Ja.: Views of content-area lecturers (Unpublished research project). University of Technology, Jamaica.

McKenzie, C., & Orogun, J. (2013). Investigating the transferability of English Language skills from the secondary to the tertiary level. *Journal of Arts, Science and Technology, 6*, 53–73.

McLaren, I., & Webber, D. (2009). Writing right: Enhancing student engagement and performance in an ecology course. *International Journal of Environmental and Science Education, 4*(4), 365–380.

McLemee, S. (2003). Deconstructing composition. *Chronicle of Higher Education, 49*(28), A16.

Milson-Whyte, V. (2015). *Academic writing instruction for creole-influenced students*. Kingston, Jamaica: University of the West Indies Press.

Neary, S. (2014) Professional identity: What I call myself defines who I am. *Career Matters, 2*(3), 14–15.

Oenbring, R. (2017). College composition in the Anglophone Caribbean: The search for a Caribbean identity. *Journal of Global Literacies, Technologies and Emerging Pedagogies, 4*(1), 533–545.

Oenbring, R., Jaquette, B., Kozikowski, C. E., & Higgins, I. (2016). First-year English at the College of the Bahamas: Student perceptions. *The International Journal of Bahamian Studies, 22*, 43–53.

Paxton, M., & Frith, V. (2014). Implications of academic literacies research for knowledge making and curriculum design. *Higher Education, 67*, 171–182.

Pineteh, E. A. (2014). The academic challenges of undergraduate students: A South African case study. *International Journal of Higher Education, 3*(1), 12–22.

Rose, P. (2016). A case for academic literacies: Informed needs analysis. *UWI Quality Education Forum, 21*, 42–62.

Sacre, S., & Nash, R. (2010). Assessing and developing academic literacy in first year health undergraduates. *The International Journal of Learning, 17*(19), 189–196.

Shermis, S. S. (1962). What makes a subject respectable? On becoming an intellectual discipline. *Phi Delta Kappon*, 84–86.

Smith, D., Stewart-McKoy, M., Henry, A., & Hamilton, G. (2015). Performance on the proficiency test in English at the University of Technology, Jamaica: A university-wide problem and implications for teaching and learning. *The Journal of Arts, Science and Technology, 8*, 60–80.

Street, B. (2004). Academic literacies and the "new orders": Implications for research and practice in student writing in higher education. *Learning and Teaching in the Social Sciences, 1*(1), 9–20.

Tapp, J. (2015). Framing the curriculum for participation: A Bernsteinian perspective on academic literacies. *Teaching in Higher Education, 20*(7), 711–722.

Weideman, A., & van Dyk, T. (Eds.). (2014). *Academic literacy: Test your competence*. Bloemfontein: Geronimo Distribution.
Williamson, F., & Goldsmith, R. (2013). Passwrite: Recalibrating student academic literacies development. *Journal of University Teaching and Learning Practice, 10*(2). Retrieved from http://ro.uow.edu.au/cgi/viewcontent.cgi?article=1353&context=jutlp
Wingate, U., & Tribble, C. (2012). The best of both worlds? Towards an English for Academic Purposes/Academic Literacies writing pedagogy. *Studies in Higher Education, 37*(4), 481–495.

13 Postcolonial Composition: Appropriation and Abrogation in the Composition Classroom

Heather M. Robinson

This chapter starts from the premise that composition instruction in the post-colonies serves students best when taught as *postcolonial composition*. For composition to avoid perpetuating the imperialistic language practices that extend from the colonial period, it is necessary to take an explicitly postcolonial stance about language and the teaching of writing in our classrooms. A postcolonial approach requires consciously making space for all students' language affiliations (Rampton, 1990) in formal writing assignments, and teaching students and teachers a vocabulary of resistance to monolingualist writing pedagogies, practices, and policies. And, moreover, it requires an orientation towards history that contextualizes writing with respect to the linguistic legacy of colonization. A postcolonial approach to the teaching of writing is particularly appropriate in a Caribbean context, although the strategies that apply in the West Indies could be equally valuable in composition and academic English as taught in the "metropolitan centres" of the United Kingdom and the United States (Ashcroft, Griffiths, & and Tiffin, 2002; Canagarajah, 2006a), as well as countries in Kachru's (1985) "inner circle," such as Australia and New Zealand.

Postcolonial writing spaces strengthen students' academic Englishes because they foreground the context in which any language form is used. They are spaces where students can write their plural and pluralized Englishes, and where students consider their motivations behind how they write while they consider *what* they are writing, and where they practice writing for particular linguistic audiences. Teaching postcolonially, however, does not necessarily require complete rejection of standardized American and standardized British English. For many tertiary students with creole language inheritances (Rampton, 1990), standardized (or acrolectal) forms are also among the varieties of English that they use and understand every day, alongside more mesolectal, creolized, or "local" forms. I, therefore, consider how to reorient writing instruction to a postcolonial perspective while incorporating the legacy of colonial linguistic markers in student speech and writing and recognizing the fact that speakers' language practices in the Caribbean move about on the creole continuum (Alleyne, 1980; DeCamp, 1971). Although it is important to maintain a skepticism about the ability of the Englishes of the colonial centers to effectively represent the lived experiences of postcolonial subjects, as Brathwaite (1984) and Glissant (cited in Britton, 1999, pp. 4–5) caution us, it is nonetheless important to teach students, through methods discussed by sociolinguists and composition specialists, how to include some forms from standardized English and globalized academic writing in their written academic discourse. I hope to extend the discussion by considering what students can do, at the level of the sentence, to engage more critically with the context(s) in which they are writing, and to incorporate a plural, postcolonial subject position into what they write, so as to bring together the many facets of the linguistic identities which, in a colonial space, are often split, by force.

The first step in taking a postcolonial approach to teaching writing is to have instructors recognize and express to their students the need to do so. Ashcroft, Griffiths, and Tiffin (2002) describe the process of reshaping language to a postcolonial sensibility as one of taking the imperial language and making it "bear the burden of one's cultural experience" (p. 38). Academic writing spaces are often, however, portrayed as decontextualized from lived experiences and local communities, and instead are contextualized only in terms of a disciplinary community, and often not explicitly. Indeed, in academic spaces, the very "communicative efficiency" of "fairly local or substandard varieties of the language, and whose language is hardly intelligible for speakers of other varieties of English" (Moussu & Llurda, 2008, p. 318) is called into question, because of a perceived incompatibility between English as a global(ized) language and English as a language of local communities in real physical and social spaces. The stance described by Moussu and Llurda assumes that English is most efficient when it is decontextualized and standardized. This stance, moreover, puts the burden of assuring comprehension squarely on the writer, rather than considering what the audience might be asked to do in understanding what they are reading or hearing. These assumptions are dangerous because they perpetuate unequal linguistic hierarchies, where metropolitan (Canagarajah, 2006a) speakers of a language are always those whose comprehension needs should be primary. It also places the maintenance of the standardized form of the language in a position of more importance than that of non-standardized varieties of English that do, indeed, "bear the burden of cultural experience."

At the heart of this postcolonial approach to teaching student writing, I propose, lies engagement with a linguistic tension best expressed through two specific terms offered by Ashcroft, Griffiths, and Tiffin (2002): "Abrogation, . . . the refusal of the categories of the imperial culture, its aesthetic, its illusory standard of normative or 'correct' usage and its assumption of a traditional or 'fixed' meaning 'inscribed' in the words" (p. 37) and "Appropriation, . . . the process by which the [imperial] language is made to bear the burden of one's own cultural experience" (p. 38). These terms contextualize the language of speakers and writers in the West Indies—or any other postcolonial place—with respect to the languages of the colonial center and periphery, placing a writer's linguistic agency at the heart of this nexus. Importantly for student writers, *abrogation* and *appropriation* emphasize that speakers of World Englishes—even those who are assigned the identity of "student"—can (are capable of and should be allowed to) make choices whether to embrace, reject, or adapt the language of empire. Abrogation and appropriation take postcolonial resistance to the level of the sentence and the word.

In the West Indian context, the need for a shift in attitudes towards language, and specifically towards the relationship between standardized English and creole-influenced vernaculars, is urgent. For instance, Milson-Whyte (2015) describes the widespread assumption that students at The University of the West Indies (UWI), should be able to write in a standardized English that showed no "interference" at all from Jamaican Creole (p. 5). The fact that English comprehension and production issues arose for many students at UWI, she writes, should not be shocking (though, as she details, it is often perceived as such), due to the "imposed language problem that has plagued generations of Jamaicans" (p. 12); that is, the language of instruction and the language in which students are expected to be proficient as they enter university is not the language of the majority of the population. Nero (2014) explains the situation in Jamaica further: "given that [Standard Jamaican English] SJE is the official language in Jamaica, the language of power, and education, the goal is to lessen the use of [Jamaican Creole] (JC) through educational structures—essentially an ideology of linguicism and an implicit policy of eradicationism" (p. 239). Here, Nero shows the legacy of colonialism in full play. My argument in this chapter stems from a contention that, if we do not make the classroom an explicitly postcolonial space, only this "ideology of linguicism and eradicationism" can prevail. My proposal, in terms of implementation, might have a lot in common with Milson-Whyte's proposals for a philosophy and pedagogy for composition for "creole-influenced" students in the West Indies (chapter 6), whereby she suggests that institutional attitudes must shift to embrace:

> a progressive way to view (1) the reach of transculturation, especially as it concerns how Creole-influenced students *do language*; (2) writing in disciplines as visible rhetoric, (3) writing instruction in the academy as developmental and necessary across the years of a student's degree programme; (4) the academy as plural, having many tongues in its many disciplines . . . ; and (5) the goal of writing development as social equity in an atmosphere of excellence. (p. 191)

What differentiates the present proposal, however, is that it asks students and instructors to locate themselves specifically within the historical context of colonialism, and from this location, to resist the discourses that have arisen due to colonialism. Without such a location, negative attitudes towards creole-influenced languages can be naturalized, in that, without a postcolonial approach, speakers can maintain an attitude that Creole and other non-standardized varieties of English are just "bad English," rather than separate language systems that have emerged out of a particular social and linguistic context that held—and still holds—racism and white supremacy at its core.

Postcoloniality and Composition

This chapter builds on many years of work in composition studies drawing connections between that field and postcolonial theory. As Bahri (2004) writes, "the concept of the 'subaltern' has been well adapted to composition spaces . . . to identify marginal student populations, to describe resistive modes of agency, and to tackle the difficulty of locating agency in the subaltern" (p. 73). In fact, the entire volume in which

Bahri's abovementioned essay appears articulates the relationship between postcolonial theory and composition studies (Lunsford & Ouzgane, 2004). However, the essays included in the latter collection, while conducting important theoretical explorations, generally do not suggest classroom practices whereby students can learn to write postcolonially; they stop short of putting theory into practice and having students "write back" to postcolonial theory, as Lu (2004) suggests is a necessary step in the development of the relationship between literary theories and composition. Furthermore, there is only one essay in this anthology—David Dzaka's reflection on his own education in postcolonial Ghana—in which the author explores a postcolonial space like the Caribbean, situated in the global Anglophone "periphery" (Dzaka, 2004). Other texts (such as Huddart, 2015) reflect skeptical attitudes among people in the post-colonies to the broadening of what counts as acceptable academic English, reflecting the language attitudes in the West Indies that Milson-Whyte (2015) and Nero (2014) describe.

Postcolonial composition requires us, as Jarratt (2004) describes it, to "imagin[e] students capable of inscribing multiple selves" (p. 122), rather than restricting them to exploring only one side of their linguistic identity in the writing classroom. Teaching composition postcolonially means teaching students to take a postcolonial position when they write. For instructors, this will mean not just teaching students writing skills that function at the level of the sentence or the paragraph, but also helping students recognize and articulate the context(s) in which they are writing, and teaching student writers to theorize their own subject positions when they are writing.

The West Indies is a special postcolonial space, even as, as the essays in Lunsford and Ouzgane (2004) show, the concept of *postcolonial* has been embraced enthusiastically and appropriately as a framework in which to understand the experiences of minoritized students in "metropolitan" educational contexts. Bahri (2004) reminds her reader that the literal post-colonies—those nations that were colonized by the European imperial powers and are still impacted every day by the legacy of that colonization, such as white supremacy and slavery, must occupy an important place in any discussion and application of the ideas of postcolonial theory. Moreover, the Caribbean is special linguistically, too. Left out of Kachru's (1985) original formulation of the concentric "Inner," "Outer," and "Expanding" Circles because of the complexity of language affiliations, expertises, and histories in the West Indies, this bi- or multi-lingual space offers the potential to be at the forefront of linguistic decolonization. Perhaps a focus on the agency and writing practice of students in writing classrooms can build an educational culture of resistance, rather than perpetuation of colonial attitudes.

Colonial Composition

As Milson-Whyte (2015) details, higher education in the West Indies was initially created in the image of higher education in the United Kingdom, and the expectations for students' language and writing within this system were founded on linguistic elitism and racism. She writes, "for a long time, higher education was reserved for a few for whom proficiency in English was considered a mark of distinction. Students considered literate in English could write without interference from Jamaican Creole" (pp. 5–6). Nero (1997) reinforces this description of the relationship between proficiency in English and access to education:

> British colonization also left a legacy of socially stratified societies where one's public identity was marked, among other things, by the degree to which one's speech approximated or deviated from the acrolect. This phenomenon was reinforced by an educational system whose sole medium of instruction was standard English and that flatly denied any validity to Creoles. Colonial education, therefore, reflected and reinforced the rigid social stratification of Caribbean societies, and language was its most palpable manifestation. (p. 587)

The structures and attitudes that govern academic writing in the Caribbean, which Milson-Whyte (2015) describes in detail, can be seen clearly as a legacy of British colonialism, especially in the sense that writing courses are not always adapted to specific local linguistic and cultural contexts, but instead show "universalist" tendencies—i.e., a focus on formalism, and generic writing topics. They can also be seen as part of the "soft colonialism" (Oenbring, 2017, p. 538) of the United States, specifically via the impact of research in composition studies coming out of that country. These pedagogies and attitudes have the following results in terms of expectations of students' language use:

- Maintaining and perpetuating a single language goal: standardized British/American English. Standardized English is the language of instruction and the expectation for all written work.
- Many writing instructors in the Caribbean tend to prefer "traditional," product-focused pedagogies over more process-based ones (Oenbring, 2017).
- Writers as people with connections to various and diverse language communities are invisible; writers are permitted only a singular linguistic subjectivity. Language is decontextualized; or, rather, the standardized form is seen as appropriate for all contexts; or, rather, contexts where the standardized form is seen as appropriate are the only important ones.
- Non-standardized voices are relegated to works of fiction or poetry; analysis and discussion of such texts must be in standardized English (see Nero, 2014).
- Other varieties of English are embraced outside the classroom, and fetishized and marginalized within (See Soliday, 1994).
- There is a mono-directional trajectory of "improvement," away from vernaculars, towards standardized forms.

These facets of composition have been discussed in various other locations, under other names—Matsuda (2006); Horner and Trimbur (2002); Horner, Lu, Trimbur, and Royster (2011); and many more, within the context of the composition classroom in the United States. Even the most apparently progressive scholars in composition, in their pedagogical approaches to linguistic variation in the composition classroom, reinforce such colonial attitudes. We find such reinforcement in, for instance, Elbow (2012). Elbow, a long-time advocate for the inclusion of students' spoken vernaculars in the composition classroom, still limits their role in students' formal writing. His advocacy focuses on the use of spoken vernaculars for drafting and free-writing; his advice to students for their final work, however, is that they limit the presence of vernacular formations to those that are "invisible" and that do not challenge the linguistic expectations borne out of colonialism and white supremacy.

Elbow (2012) argues, for example, that "Young [2009] and Canagarajah [2011] are right to pursue the value and importance of what might be called 'in your face' code-meshing, but writers at this very cultural moment will have a much easier time writing for conventional readers . . . if they learn how to 'fix' the few features of their vernacular that set off error alarms" (p. 332). By conventional readers, he means white, middle-class readers who hold the linguistic capital in US society. Green (2016) problematizes this approach effectively in the following quotation:

> If part of the purpose of code-meshing, as Young [2009] puts it, is to present "an alternative vision of language to teachers, one that offers the 'disempowered' a more egalitarian path into Standard English, a route that integrates academic English with their own dialects and that simultaneously seeks to end discrimination," then if we instruct students to use their vernaculars only for free writing or brainstorming aren't we still upholding that some languages are equal but separate? If I tell them to code-mesh only with some of the words in their vocabulary, the words I know are right but others will see as wrong, am I not upholding linguistic racism still? Aren't we still saying to them that only some parts of them have merit?—especially if the rationale is that they should do it so others don't think that they're wrong or so that they aren't judged? Doing that unfairly places the responsibility that educators should carry directly onto students. (p. 79)

In other words, even such seemingly progressive approaches as Elbow's do nothing to challenge or change the status quo of linguistic racism in the college classroom; they still place the responsibility for making audiences "comfortable" squarely on the students, rather than implicating the linguistic attitudes of their teachers and their broader audiences and asking them to reconsider their own stances with respect to non-standardized forms.

Whether or not creole-influenced students are in the West Indies or in the United States, they are afflicted by these colonial attitudes to language, or colonial pedagogies. But in a context, such as the West Indies, where the majority of the population is very much influenced by English-based creoles, the imperative to decolonize composition is even more acute. As Milson-Whyte (2015) and Oenbring (2017) show, the tertiary education system in the West Indies is a doubly-colonized space, still recovering from the legacy of British linguistic and social imperialism and the influence of the United States in terms of cultural and educational effects. Oenbring writes, "while the former British colonies of the Anglophone Caribbean have received the bulk of their political and educational structures from Britain, we must, nevertheless, take into account the ever increasing 'soft colonial' influence of American media, language, and educational culture" (p. 538). The influence, too, of the large transnational Caribbean populations in the major cities of the United States, who maintain close ties with the West Indies even over multiple generations of immigration within families, must have a significant impact on language use in the Caribbean, as does the embrace—and sometimes adaptation—at The University of the West Indies of the US models of college composition, either current, or more traditional ones.

Postcolonial Composition

In opposition to a colonial approach to composition, a postcolonial approach to language considers linguistic plurality as a resource. Further, the composition classroom is a place where we can encourage students to develop a plural linguistic subjectivity, rather than a split one; that is, complete code-switching does not have to be necessary in academic contexts. Juhasz (2003) argues, for example, that "writing can form connections between subject positions, including those which have been split off or denied because of culturally induced ambivalence, to establish a subjectivity that is multiple rather than split" (p. 395). My argument here, following Juhasz, is that, not only is the composition classroom an appropriate place to help students find a plural, postcolonial subjectivity, but that the act(s) and process(es) of writing are mechanisms by which students can approach such a subjectivity. According to the perspective described by Juhasz above, writing can be used not only to *reflect* a postcolonial perspective but is also vital in *constructing* a postcolonial student subjectivity, where students integrate their multiple linguistic identities while building strategies of resistance towards white supremacy and the privileging of standardized metropolitan Englishes over the English-based creoles that the students speak, often alongside a standardized form of their national or regional variety of English (e.g., Standard Jamaican English).

I suggest that this split linguistic subjectivity is even more prevalent among students in tertiary institutions, because successful university students have often achieved this success at least in part by keeping their creole or creolized language forms out of the classroom. But even though it has been fruitful for some students, there is still a need to create strategies that help more students to achieve their academic goals, as well as create a space where using creole-influenced forms is part of their success. Thus, I am arguing that postcolonial composition is a necessary part of creating these strategies, and part of the process must be, as Jarratt (2004) puts it, "enabling our students to write multiple versions of themselves informed by a knowledge of rhetoric in its political and figurative functions, [so] we may give them access to their own experiences of conjunction and disjunction, of association and substitution" (p. 128).

Persistent "colonial" attitudes to Caribbean Englishes can also be seen in the linguistic affiliations claimed by students from the West Indies. For example, at least one student in my World Englishes class claimed a linguistic affiliation with British English. Such a claim is, I suggest, a claim of the privilege associated with high levels of literacy in the literature of the metropolis, of knowing the "mother tongue" as a good colonial does. We colonials—and I as an Australian share this perspective—know, the language, the forms, the spaces of England; those of us with educational capital will claim them, too. Ashcroft, Griffiths, and Tiffin (2002) describe this connection as follows, with respect to writers in the (former) British colonies: "a mimicry of the center proceeding from a desire not only to be accepted but to be adopted and absorbed. It caused those from the periphery to immerse themselves in the imported culture, denying their origins in an attempt to become 'more English than the English'" (p. 4). In taking a postcolonial stance in the composition classroom, we try to move away from this "desire . . . to be adopted and absorbed" towards establishing a new linguistic center that reflects the current space, as well as its history.

From my experience, claiming a position as an outsider can help in the establishment of a new linguistic center. For me, it has meant embracing, highlighting, and using my own linguistic difference as a teaching tool. My racial and educational privilege—I am white and highly educated and stand at the front of the classroom—helps my audience to see my language use as "different," rather than as "incorrect," and my language itself helps me to form a bridge with my students from the Caribbean. We share a vocabulary and discourse that is foreign in the United States; we live and speak on the same linguistic continuum. At York, this continuum is a space that most students in the classroom can place themselves upon somewhere: as I have mentioned above, they have strong, multigenerational ties to the Caribbean, even if they themselves identify as being from New York City, and as speakers of that city's varieties of English. So, it is my responsibility to shift these colonial similarities into a feeling of postcolonial solidarity in my classroom; I do it by working with my students to examine the contexts and the ways in which our languages have been and continue to be marginalized in the US college context and by writing about and in our vernaculars.

Of course, beyond arguing for an attitudinal shift among instructors in postcolonial contexts of writing instruction, there are specific pedagogical strategies that have been shown to be effective for students whose dominant language is a minoritized one in the context in which they are being educated, whether it is minoritized because it is creole-influenced, because it is not the local "national" language, or because it is a vernacular that does not have social prestige. Successful approaches with students who are speakers of minoritized languages and varieties make a positive space for vernaculars in the classroom. Siegel (2007), basing his discussion on a review of scholarship concerning pedagogies that are effective for students whose dominant languages or varieties are marginalized, writes of the importance of contrastive approaches, where the linguistic properties of vernaculars and dominant community languages are contrasted with standardized English(es), and where instructors contextualize all languages not only linguistically, but also socially and ethnically, even when recognizing that a goal of education might and probably will be at some level training students to use the standardized variety of English effectively.

The Language Identity Awareness and Development (*LIAD*) approach, articulated in Nero (2005), proposes a set of strategies for teaching students with West Indian language inheritances in New York City classrooms and affirms the importance of the contrastive approach to incorporating non-standardized varieties of English, and other national languages, in the classroom. Nero encourages instructors to "validate the multiplicity of Englishes" by reading many varieties of English in class texts and "allowing" them in class discussions; and by conducting repeated contrastive analyses at levels of grammar and of rhetorical style (p. 509). She also suggests a number of action points for instructors, in terms of how they engage with creole-influenced and minority-dialect-influenced students, such as having the instructors ask the students to clarify meaning when it is unclear, rather than assuming that students have made errors in the way that they have tried to express a concept or idea, and discussing the features of various dialects and their appropriateness for various genres of writing and speech.

Nero's (2005) approach is of particular interest here because it foregrounds writing in the classroom as a way to help students and instructors attain their language goals. Having students produce a lot of writing, as well as asking students to read and analyze writing in different varieties and languages with respect to these texts' linguistic features, their audience, and the authors' apparent purposes in writing in vernaculars, reinforces the social and context-driven nature of all language use. Importantly for the present project, Nero also places reading and writing at the center of building a more equal and affirming pedagogical practice for multilingual and multidialectal students: providing more opportunities to write, and treating writing as a process, offers students opportunities to make rhetorical choices about their language use, and to change their usage according to guided feedback from instructors and peers, in a negotiation with a real rather than an imagined audience, so allowing them to see writing as a process of negotiation with an audience, in which the student can, too, exert power.

Resistance To → Resistance From

There are several sites of resistance to postcolonial approaches to writing in English, coming from both students and instructors, whose attitudes reflect those of the larger society. Huddart (2015), writing about students at the Chinese University of Hong Kong, describes resistance coming from the students, who expect that being university students will entail being taught, and being expected to use standardized, British-like English in their university writing. In the multilingual society of Hong Kong, there is a local variety of English that is, according to Huddart, strongly inflected by the linguistic influence of the Chinese languages to which most of the population have primary affiliations; Huddart argues that his students see the university space as one from which hybridized varieties of English should be banned—sometimes in contrast to the approach to English language and writing instruction that the teachers prefer to take. He writes, "postcolonial linguists ought to be rather disconcerted if and when (some of) the people their teachings have (in theory) empowered to use their own Englishes demand (in practice) what they perceive as the native speaker standard" (p. 71). While authors such as Rampton (1990); Leung, Harris, and Rampton (1997); Moussu and Llurda (2008); Faez (2011); and many others have effectively problematized the definition of, and reliance upon, the idea of the native speaker in English-language classrooms, and researchers in the TESOL community have suggested that so-called native speakers of English may not be the most effective English instructors to students with other primary language affiliations (e.g., the essays in Braine, 1999), the "native-speaker standard" is still a powerful force, especially in "Expanding Circle" contexts such as Huddart describes.

Attitudes in which the native-speaker standard is held as being more valuable than hybridized or creole-influenced forms in educational contexts are prevalent in the West Indies, where standardized English is associated with success, both academic and professional. Nero (2014) writes, "many teachers' experiences, attitudes, and practices are strongly influenced by the aforementioned classism, which ultimately reinforces social stratification and outcomes in the classroom. Thus, there appears to be a strong link among socioeconomic class, language, education, and academic achievement" (p. 225). Such attitudes, residues of colonization, demonstrate a very limited imagining of what students can and should do. They are based on a presumption of deficit—that students' non-standardized, or non-acrolectal, languages are a problem, rather than a resource—and, to paraphrase Lu (2004), thus limit what students are *allowed* to do by their instructors, based on the assumption that students are not *able* to write in ways that are acceptable in an educational context (p. 21).

A postcolonial stance challenges these attitudes: it admits a desire for hybridity, for linguistic difference in educational contexts. As Nero (2014) and Milson-Whyte (2015) show, the acceptance of creole-influenced language forms in the classroom—especially classrooms in which students are expected to show high academic achievement—will be exceptionally slow to come down from the top in the West Indies. As Milson-Whyte (2015) writes, "[the] focus on 'grammatical English' [at UWI] is an unfortunate colonial legacy that reflects a language policy that many stakeholders have uncritically accepted" (p. 17). My position in this chapter is, thus, change might instead come from the "bottom," that is, from the students whose linguistic identities have been forcibly split for so long. But making the embrace of linguistic variation in the classroom desirable for students must come with rewards designed by instructors. The postcolonial pedagogy and stance that I am describing shifts language practice in the post-colonies from a "resistance to" creole, hybridity, and the stigma associated with the meso- and basilect, to "resistance from" the students, and to a different kind of imagining, from instructors, of what all students can do. A postcolonial approach to academic writing, I suggest, helps students integrate their linguistic identities — and helps instructors support such integration in classroom practices and evaluation measures. To define what a postcolonial classroom philosophy might involve, we turn to postcolonial literary scholars, who have described the work that carving out spaces for local vernaculars in the literary canon entails.

Postcolonialism in the Writing Classroom

Bahri (2004) writes, "a post-colonial inquiry is built upon the premise that *difference and marginality are produced in particular contexts rather than being inherent by virtue of category*" (p. 77). For students in composition classes in the West Indies and other postcolonial spaces, this postcolonial inquiry would take place in their active investigation of where their attitudes to creolized languages and standardized languages come from, in a consideration of the contexts in which the margins of creole and of standard might be blurred, and in a deliberate extension of the margins of where creole "should" be in their academic writing. As I suggested in the introduction to this essay, postcolonial composition describes a stance that students and instructors take towards the learning and teaching of writing in the composition classroom. What this stance looks like, in implementation, depends on the instructor, and the students. It might include code-meshing and other explorations of marginalized language varieties, including creoles and creole-influenced varieties of English, in formal writing (Young, 2009; Canagarajah, 2011, and contra Elbow, 2012); it might include adopting a translingual positioning towards students' language identities and language practices (Horner, Lu, Royster & Trimbur, 2011; Canagarajah, 2006b), even as an instructor explicitly teaches the forms of standardized English in contrast to creole-influenced forms (e.g., Nero, 2005; Siegel, 2007); it might involve a historical analysis of how English came to be what it is, in its many iterations, in the Caribbean. It would certainly involve overt discussion of and play with language and language variation, alongside discussion of rhetorical context, in class.

Milson-Whyte (2015) puts forward a detailed proposal of what effective writing courses might look like in the Caribbean, the "transcultural rhetorical perspective on writing," which builds on the types of approaches discussed by Siegel (2007) and Nero (2005), which I describe above. But in this essay, I am perhaps less interested in the specific curriculum of our writing courses, and more interested in thinking through how to create a context in which students approach their own writing differently because of a new/re-articulation of their subject position with respect to their languages and also with respect to the history of the places in which they speak them—and where students can write their own lived experience in an academic context. Doing so acknowledges and engages with the intense linguistic stigma and personal trauma (as relayed by Jones and by Dyer Spiegel in this volume) that has prevailed in the West Indies since the beginning of the colonial period. A postcolonial approach to composition is, most accurately, considered as a strategy to "legitimize Creole varieties, . . . help Creole-influenced students develop metacognitive awareness of their linguistic resources, and encourage educators to engage in the attendant reflective teaching for these students' academic writing development," the terms in which Milson-Whyte describes the purposes of her own proposed "transcultural approach" (p. 204). Whatever the many specific implementations of this strategy might look like, taking a postcolonial stance requires that instructors actively interrogate their own positionality with respect to colonialism, either historical or present-day, and center the facets of students' linguistic identity that have traditionally been marginalized in the composition classroom.

In this discussion also, I want to foreground the potentialities for postcolonialism that student writing holds, to carefully consider what we are asking students to produce affords us and them, and to ask how students in the West Indies can create their own postcolonialism in their writing classes. Thus, we turn to the two terms that I introduced at the beginning of this essay, which I place at the heart of postcolonial composition: *appropriation* and *abrogation*, both as a means of resisting historically-imposed prejudices against creole-influenced forms of English, and of resisting pressures from the neoliberal language economy to decontextualize language in order to accommodate the imagined language needs of a supposed globalized audience.

Abrogation, again, as Ashcroft, Griffiths, and Tiffin (2002) describe it, is "the refusal of the categories of the imperial culture, its aesthetic, its illusory standard of normative or 'correct' usage and its assumption of a traditional or 'fixed' meaning inscribed in the words" (p. 37). In specifically linguistic terms, it amounts to a refusal to translate or to otherwise accommodate audiences who expect standardized, decontextualized English; in fact, it challenges the category of "standard" language as a construct of the colonizers' culture. Appropriation, on the other hand, is "the process by which the [imperial] language is made to bear the burden of one's own cultural experience" (p. 38); it is a remaking or an adaptation of the language of empire so that it will express ideas that are particular to the local environment. Crucially, both abrogation and appropriation require not just an awareness of, but a negotiation with, an audience: a decision on the part of the writer about when to work to help the reader understand and when to put the burden of doing that work onto the reader.

To show what a student text written from a postcolonial subject position might look like, I turn to a paper written by a student in the World Englishes class that I mentioned earlier. This student, V, is an immigrant from Jamaica to New York City. They completed their secondary education in Jamaica and worked as a primary school teacher there. Upon moving to New York, they enrolled in a Childhood Teacher Education program at my institution. The paper from which I will share an excerpt is V's exploration of how Louise Bennett-Coverley resisted linguistic imperialism in her poetry and also in her public persona as Jamaican poet. V interweaves postcolonial theories; theories of translingualism; and stories of Louise Bennett's life, poetry, and performances with descriptions of and reflections on their own experiences, as a teacher and as an immigrant. In the passage below, we see V mixing genres and languages as they tell and analyze "Ms. Lou's" story:

> Now back to de story, a who tell de heroine fi go tell de story in which har Aunt guh compare de origin of Jamaica Patois and "standard" English, a yah so she mek wan a har biggest mistake. Because little afta de story pap, Miss Lou, get international attention—yuh hear dat, yes mi dear: INTERNATIONAL attention, Suddenly!!! X 2. As har fame grow, har vice became stronga and stronga—nuh pla pla, fenky fenky vice mi a chat bout no maasa mi a chat bout the real deal. Miss Lou—one woman against de nation begging de people of Jamaica to dethrone the language of the Empire, and to accept *the nation language* (Brathwaite 459) as de language of POWER. Yuh think people woulda listen rite; eh-eh poopa Jesus. Mi dear, instead a listen, all H*** bruk loose, and just like dat, de heroine suddenly fall from grace and was given a new social title—piawk-ka by the handful of "highly educated" people who controlled de

> education system and a portion of de media. Nevatheless, Ms. Lou neva mek dat frighten har sah nor stop har from publicly denouncing English as superior to de good ole Jamaican Patois.

In this passage, V does two important things. Firstly, they give their narrator a voice and an accent, making the writer into a person with a linguistic history. The narrator can be "heard" telling a story. Secondly, they construct an ideal reader who exists within a *local*—rather than a decontextualized—linguistic community: someone who can draw all the levels of meaning from this text. In doing so, V appropriates the forms and structures of academic discourse, as we see in their reference to Kamau Brathwaite's *nation language*, cited in MLA format; however, they also abrogate the imperialist forms of academic discourse, as in the passage in the first paragraph: "As har fame grow, har vice became stronga and stronga—nuh pla pla, fenky fenky vice mi a chat bout no maasa mi a chat bout the real deal." This moment in the passage is in eye dialect Jamaican Creole (a.k.a., *patwa*) and is perhaps untranslatable into standardized English, and as such is inaccessible to a reader from outside a Jamaican linguistic community. I suggest that using language that is inaccessible to a "globalized" audience is very important in student writing, because it helps students learn to position themselves as writers, rather than as students: they control the discourse. While V is using all the possibilities of code-meshing, as described in Canagarajah (2011), in this portion of their essay—typographical embellishments, phonetic spelling, conversational asides (*Mi dear*)—they also show control of academic discourse, using MLA citation format, coordinating adverbs (*Nevatheless*), and academically-appropriate vocabulary (*publicly denouncing*). This passage, in short, shows V navigating the space between appropriation, mimicry, and abrogation in their writing.

We see V take a turn towards a stronger form of appropriation two paragraphs later. Much of this excerpt seems to be standardized Jamaican English rendered with a Jamaican accent, rather than a rendering in the eye-dialect Jamaican Creole we saw earlier: it uses more academic vocabulary and argumentative forms, but still with a fully voiced narrator, as we see below:

> Dis was a big blow to Ms. Lou because she really used to enjoy both seeing and hearing Jamaican children reciting fi har as well as other local poems or retelling Brer Anansi stories especially since it provided opportunities for de children to synchronous-

ly learn about their *linguistic inheritance* (Leung, Harris, and Rampton 557) as well as to develop a positive attitude towards other languages dubbed vernaculars/ dialects because these languages are dubbed inferior because their rhythm of speech, intonation, and flow of words differs from "propa" English. Ms. Lou attempt to develop a *culturally relevant* (Gabriel Okara 41) language failed miserably and so did har spirit, but soon after our heroine had har second epiphany. Abruptly, she memba wey ole tyme people use to sey: "a butcha is neva recognized inna him own parish." Dis put a big smile pan har face and de next ting yuh know, Ms. Lou "flyout."

In this passage, V "follows the rules" of academic discourse: they use (mostly) correct citation format as they quote from scholarly and literary sources; they take an example and summarize it in such a way as to highlight its significance to their own larger point, and they also use technical vocabulary to explain specialized linguistic content, for example: "since it provided opportunities for de children to synchronously learn about their *linguistic inheritance* (Leung, Harris, and Rampton 557)." But V also gestures towards Jamaican Creole, particularly in their use of eye-dialect, a representation of Patwa vocabulary, pronunciation, and syntax through strategic but not comprehensive inclusions of creole markers, for example, "'propa' English," "Ms. Lou attempt," "Dis put a big smile pan her face." We note that the syntax in this passage mostly belongs to standardized, rather than creole, English, reinforcing the idea that V is working *with* the standardized form rather than rejecting it. Additionally, in their rendering of this primarily spoken language into its written form, V seems to be approaching the task of writing down Jamaican Creole from a stance similar to that which other writers-down-of-creoles take, as described in Sebba (cited in Deuber & Hinrichs, 2007). That is, the spelling that V chooses renders their language as an "anti-standard," constructed to be visibly in opposition to the local standardized variety.

V wrote the paper from which these excerpts are taken in a course at a four-year college in New York City. As such, V is not necessarily typical of students in tertiary education contexts in the Caribbean, in that V has been linguistically othered not by whether they are creole- or English-dominant, but because V is "foreign" in a US educational context. Therefore, because of their "foreignness," V has had to build a subjectivity that is multiple: student, Jamaican, immigrant, teacher-in-training—all of which have specific linguistic manifestations. V was the only student in this course who wrote a completely code-meshed essay: many students who wrote in the vernacular also used their standardized English extensively, either as the voice of the narrator or as the voice in which they conducted metacognitive reflection on their use of their own "nation languages" in their classroom writing. But rather than representing the vernacular, as these other students did, using it as a symbol of their cultures, V wrote from the vernacular, placing themselves in the culture of the Englishes of Jamaica. V's refusal to detach themselves from Jamaican English and Jamaican creole in this academic context suggests a way forward, where, in the composition classroom, we make space for students to find out what their creole-influenced academic voices are, so they can write themselves into multiple subject positions, rather than split ones. Once students can reflect on the set of choices and responses to context that helped them craft their creole-influenced academic writing, in the context of other writers who discuss or use creole-influenced and other vernacular languages in academic contexts, they might be on their way to their own contrastive analyses of their language competences.

Students in this World Englishes class who chose to write in their vernaculars did so eagerly: they saw the assignment, and the course more generally, as an opportunity to express their multiple linguistic identities in a context in which they were usually limited to the performance of a singular one. Indeed, the course did important work in legitimizing linguistic identities that students had experienced as being marginalized in an academic context. One student, D, who wrote a story that included standardized English and Guyanese Creole, wrote, "my writing in both Standard English and Guyanese Creole was to represent my linguistic identity in the fullest and most prideful way I could—to say that I accept both Englishes as part of my identity and that one language is most certainly not more legitimate than another." Of course, several students in each of the semesters in which I have taught the World Englishes course have chosen to write a more traditional academic paper, responding in standardized English to prompts that I have assigned. So, the students who have written in their vernaculars so far are a self-selecting group. However, in teaching the course I have adopted a postcolonial stance, and I have found that even students who do not feel comfortable with or interested in writing in their vernaculars still embrace, in their final papers, a pluralistic attitude to language and to their own linguistic identities. Furthermore, it is possible that vernacular writing such as this might be particularly popular among students in composition classrooms in the West Indies, due to the direct connections that such writing makes with what Oenbring (2017) refers to as "the largely oral nature of Caribbean culture, and/or the Caribbean esteem for public oratory" (p. 541). While I would argue that the writing that I discuss above is planned and strongly connected with written modes of thought (in contrast with the unplanned, informal vernacular writing that Elbow [2012] advocates for), the assignment to which students were responding could be seen as drawing upon "Caribbean students' cultural proclivities to oratory and orality" (Oenbring, 2017, p. 542). I believe the students enjoyed the connection between speech and writing that the vernacular writing assignment created space for them to make.

Conclusion

For there to be a postcolonial stance in the composition classroom, certain points must be brought to the fore as the standardized form of the language is interrogated. For instructors to take up a postcolonial pedagogical position, they first might acknowledge that language is never decontextualized. It is always for a community of speakers or readers, whether those communities are face-to-face, virtual, social, or disciplinary (for instance). This fundamental repositioning is a particularly difficult one in academic writing spaces, and not just those in the Caribbean, because we have come to consider standardized English—whether British or American-inflected—as being, in fact, decontextualized: the language that "everyone" can understand the most easily. But before starting on a consideration of standardized and other Englishes, instructors might stay within the academy and consider—and show their students—how academic discourse changes from discipline to discipline. Even the choice between passive and active voice in sentences is governed by disciplinary norms. Understanding context and how writers position themselves is at the core of writing in the disciplines, and, furthermore, Milson-Whyte (2015) argues that "Creole-influenced students—by their very linguistic/cultural experiences—are advantageously poised to manipulate" the "multiple tongues" of the university's many disciplines (p. 191). So, what if postcolonial composition, and teaching students to theorize their subject positions, is the first step in training students to write in their disciplines? That is, by exploring their multifaceted subjectivity with particular relation to language, and by having space to perform many parts of their linguistic identity depending on the context, students are learning a sensitivity to what a context will bear, how language reflects the context of use, and how to engage in a two-way conversation with a reader, rather than the writer constructing themselves as an invisible deliverer-of-content.

In this chapter, I am advocating for a pedagogy of resistance—of teaching students that they, too, have linguistic agency, even in an education system stratified and bound by the legacy of British linguistic imperialism. A composition course does not have to be a Sociolinguistics course to teach the kind of linguistic resistance that I am advocating for here. Abrogation and appropriation, two terms of postcolonial literary theory, instead describe agentive decisions that a student writer can make about the language that they use, from the level of the word right up to the level of syntax; they reconstruct writing as a set of decisions that the author can make, rather than a response to a set of assumptions imposed from outside.

Teaching this kind of resistance, moreover, requires sharing with students the tools of theorizing one's subject position, and helping them discover an awareness of what they have to offer in academic discourse. It also recognizes what students have to contend with in the residually colonial classroom, in the West Indies, and also in the metropolitan centers of empire. Specifically, a postcolonial pedagogy would be based around reading of texts that use various varieties of English for a variety of purposes. It would include regular analysis of rhetorical use of variation, of structural qualities of English variants, and create many opportunities for students to explore their linguistic repertoire in writing, for different purposes, while imagining different audiences. For, while it is not necessarily difficult to get students to perform different language identities, or multiple language identities, in the classroom, the instructor needs to make the performance meaningful, to discuss how it might be connected to other kinds of academic writing, and to value the writing that these students produce as central to students' marks in a course.

References

Alleyne, M. (1980). *Comparative Afro-American*. Ann Arbor, MI: Karoma Publishers.

Ashcroft, B., Griffiths, G., & Tiffin, H. (2002). *The empire writes back: Theory and practice in post-colonial literatures* (2nd ed.). Abingdon, England: Routledge.

Bahri, D. (2004). Terms of engagement: Post-colonialism, transnationalism, and composition studies. In A. Lunsford & L. Ouzgane (Eds.), *Crossing borderlands: Composition and post-colonial theory* (pp. 67–83). Pittsburgh, PA: University of Pittsburgh Press.

Brathwaite, K. (1984). *The history of the voice.* London: New Beacon Books.

Braine, G. (1999). *Non-native educators in English language teaching.* Abingdon, England: Routledge.

Britton, C. (1999). *Edouard Glissant and post-colonial theory.* Charlottesville, VA: Virginia University Press.

Canagarajah, A. S. (2011). Codemeshing in academic writing: Identifying teachable strategies of translanguaging. *Modern Language Journal, 95*(3), 401–417.

Canagarajah, A. S. (2006a). The place of world Englishes in composition: Pluralization continued. *College Composition and Communication, 57,* 586–619.

Canagarajah, A. S. (2006b). Toward a writing pedagogy of shuttling between languages: Learning from multilingual writers. *College English, 68,* 589–604.

DeCamp, D. (1971). Introduction: The study of pidgin and creole languages. In D. Hymes (Ed.), *Pidginization and creolization of languages* (pp. 13–39). Cambridge: Cambridge University Press.

Deuber, D., & Hinrichs, L. (2007). Dynamics of orthographic standardization in Jamaican Creole and Nigerian Pidgin. *World Englishes, 26*(1), 22–47.

Dzaka, D. (2004). Resisting writing: Reflections on the post-colonial factor in the writing class. In A. Lunsford & L. Ouzgane (Eds.), *Crossing borderlands: Composition and post-colonial theory* (pp. 84–94). Pittsburgh, PA: University of Pittsburgh Press.

Elbow, P. (2012). *Vernacular eloquence: What speech can bring to writing.* Oxford: Oxford University Press.

Faez, F. (2011). Reconceptualizing the native/nonnative speaker dichotomy. *Journal of Language, Identity and Education, 10*(4), 231–249.

Green, N. A. S. (2016). The re-education of Neisha-Anne S Green: A close look at the damaging effect of "a standard approach," the benefits of codemeshing, and the role allies play in this work. *Praxis: A Writing Center Journal, 14*(1), 72–82.

Horner, B., Lu, M., Royster, J. J., & Trimbur, J. (2011). Opinion: Language difference in writing: Toward a translingual approach. *College English, 73,* 303–321.

Horner, B., & Trimbur, J. (2002). English only and U. S. college composition. *College Composition and Communication, 53,* 594–630.

Huddart, D. (2015). Error and innovation in post-colonial composition: The implications of world Englishes. In T. D'haen, I. Goerlandt, & R. Sell (Eds.), *Major vs. minor: Languages and literatures in a globalized world* (pp. 67–80). Amsterdam: John Benjamins.

Jarratt, S. (2004). Beside ourselves: Rhetoric and representation in post-colonial feminist writing. In A. Lunsford & L. Ouzgane (Eds.), *Crossing borderlands:*

Composition and post-colonial theory (pp. 110–128). Pittsburgh, PA: University of Pittsburgh Press.

Juhasz, S. (2003). Mother-writing and the narrative of maternal subjectivity. *Studies in Gender and Sexuality, 4*(4), 395–425.

Kachru, B. B. (1985). Standards, codification and sociolinguistic realism: The English language in the outer circle. In R. Quirk & H. Widdowson (Eds.), *English in the world: Teaching and learning the language and literatures* (pp. 11–36). Cambridge: Cambridge University Press.

Leung, C., Harris, R., & Rampton, B. (1997). The idealised native speaker, reified ethnicities and classroom realities. *TESOL Quarterly, 31*(3), 543–560.

Lu, M. (2004). The vitality of the ungrateful receiver: Making giving mutual between composition and post-colonial studies. In A. Lunsford & L. Ouzgane (Eds.), *Crossing borderlands: Composition and post-colonial theory* (pp. 3–32). Pittsburgh, PA: University of Pittsburgh Press.

Lunsford, A., & Ouzgane, L. (Eds.) (2004). *Crossing borderlands: Composition and post-colonial theory.* Pittsburgh, PA: University of Pittsburgh Press.

Matsuda, P. K. (2006). The myth of linguistic homogeneity in U. S. college composition. *College English, 68*, 637–651.

Milson-Whyte, V. (2015). *Academic writing instruction for creole-influenced students.* Kingston, Jamaica: University of the West Indies Press.

Moussu, L., & Llurda, E. (2008). Nonnative English speaking English language teachers: History and research. *Language Teaching, 41*(3), 315–348.

Nero, S. J. (1997). English is my native language . . . or so I believe. *TESOL quarterly, 31*(3), 585–593.

Nero, S. J. (2005). Language, identities, and ESL pedagogy. *Language and Education, 19*(3), 194–211.

Nero, S. J. (2014). De facto language education policy through teachers' attitudes and practices: A critical ethnographic study in three Jamaican schools. *Language Policy, 13*(3), 221–242.

Oenbring, R. (2017). College composition in the Anglophone Caribbean: The search for a Caribbean identity. *Journal of Global Literacies, Technologies, and Emerging Pedagogies, 4*(1), 553–545.

Rampton, B. (1990). Displacing the "native speaker": Expertise, affiliation and inheritance. *ELT Journal, 44*, 97–101.

Siegel, J. (2007). Creoles and minority dialects in education: An update. *Language and Education, 21*(1), 66–86.

Soliday, M. (1994). Translating self and difference through literacy narratives. *College English, 56*, 511–526.

Young, V. (2009). "Nah, we straight": An argument against code switching. *JAC, 29*(1–2), 49–76.

AFTERWORD: *CREOLE COMPOSITION?*

A START

This collection, with its alliterative title, accomplishes much. First, through its composition, it allowed academic writing teacher-researchers connected to the Anglophone Caribbean to engage in reflective inquiry and write about their practices (and the theories that inform them) as well as their aspirations for *liv(e)able* Caribbean situations. Second, it provides scholars in the Caribbean and elsewhere with knowledge about teaching academic writing in the Caribbean and an axis from which to build scholarship and professional engagement regarding (teaching) academic writing in the Caribbean. Third, it enables academic writing teacher-researchers in North America and the UK to contemplate the reach of their scholarship as well as areas of their work that could be strengthened when considered from transnational perspectives or in light of use with students of Caribbean origin or students with experiences similar to students in/from the Caribbean. However, as the preface acknowledges, the collection is but "part of the start" of discussions on what would constitute effective praxis regarding Anglophone Caribbean students' academic writing development. As practicing academic writing teacher-researchers in the Caribbean with experience teaching and studying composition in the US and Europe, we proffer here strands for expanding the discussion and reach of the scholarship in the Caribbean and other countries where academic writing is taught.

WRITING OUR WAY IN

In her trenchant critique of narrow thinking and questionable operations in *a small place*—Antigua—in the Anglophone Caribbean, Kincaid (1988) asks readers to contemplate the mirror that natives and tourists are for each other:

> That the native does not like the tourist is not hard to explain. For every native of every place is a potential tourist, and every tourist is a native of somewhere. Every native everywhere lives a life of overwhelming and crushing banality and boredom and desperation and depression, and every deed, good and bad, is an attempt to forget this. Every native would like *to find a way out*, every native would like a rest, every native would like a tour. But some natives — most natives in the world — cannot go anywhere. They are too poor. They are too poor to go anywhere. They are too poor to escape the reality of their lives; and they are too poor to live properly in the place they live, which is the very place you, the tourist, want to go — so when the natives see you, the tourist, they envy you, they envy your ability to leave your own banality and boredom, they envy your ability to turn their own banality and boredom into a source of pleasure for yourself. (pp. 18–19, emphasis added)

Each reflection that Kincaid (1988) presents reminds of a desire to "find a way out" (p. 18); however, this collection begs for a critical turn inwards, and for Caribbean scholars to build the discipline of writing studies and engage with international scholarship on best practices in the teaching of writing from within the Caribbean space. Natives, citizens of the small Caribbean island space, seem, due to their material surrounding, to lack agency to contemplate and act in ways that would lead to self- and state improvement. However, agency emerges as an important concern for students and instructional staff in the chapters by Campbell, Mitchell, Jones McKenzie and Campbell-Dawes, Oenbring, and Robinson in this volume. Oenbring even claims that residents of the *small island polis* are uniquely equipped to claim agency and use language strategically to persuade other members of their community and, ultimately, improve their lives. Given the challenging material conditions in universities in the Anglophone Caribbean, instructors and students find themselves in an intriguing situation in which they must use the language (of the tourist) that some may feel has oppressed them to claim the agency that would allow them to engage with language in rhetorically beneficial ways. A call to *write our way in* is not, however, a call to turn away from the international scholarship in writing studies but to recognize that real change has to engage with these theories while valuing and understanding the specific circumstances of the Caribbean.

Our suggestion is that colleagues inside and outside the Caribbean pattern Hamilton in Miranda's (2016) musical and "write everything down"—document reflections, plumb teaching situations, investigate new and old practices/strategies—as a way not only to claim and ascribe agency in Caribbean national contexts but also to continue to participate in broadening international discussions regarding rhetoric and composition/writing studies/academic literacies. For example, Campbell has started to investigate his marking community's practice regarding feedback with his work on *expression*—a popular, seemingly indigenous, marginal comment in the region. However, the kind of consistent engagement with research that we envision is no small order, for as Ali and the introduction indicate, teaching loads are heavy in Caribbean institutions, and course or program coordinators do not get adequate release time for the demands of course or program administration.

How we encourage academic writing colleagues in the Caribbean to invest in both teaching *and* research, therefore, remains a challenge, but one with which we must grapple. It seems ironic that postsecondary institutions would (as many in the Caribbean and elsewhere do) hire facilitators to teach writing but not to do research and publish their work. The very act of doing research is a necessary political one akin to teaching composition/academic literacies. To suggest that the scholarly engagement that researching and writing allow is not necessary is to strip writing instructors of the very kinds of civic and other engagement their courses are supposed to encourage. Caribbean colleagues have to become aware, in Murray's (2004) words, that *a writer teaches writing* and lobby for administrators to facilitate writing instructors' ongoing career/professional development. We may also have to rely on scholarship on writing program administration elsewhere to lobby for institutional recognition of writing program administration as scholarship deserving of the benefits, such as substantial course releases, associated with it in other jurisdictions.

The Oral Claim

Of course, culture and customs, besides unsatisfactory working conditions, can militate against teacher-researchers' attempts to *write their way in*. Kozikowski shows how beliefs about Caribbean/*island time*, along with students' resultant "no harm meant" unpunctuality, negatively affect how much an instructional staff member is able to accomplish in a given class session. Additionally, as Oenbring's chapter indicates, Caribbean societies are highly oral, and Caribbean students' oral penchant is a good resource for rhetorical engagement in academic writing classrooms. A challenge, however, is that most citizens in every Anglophone Caribbean country speak a creole language that, for the most part, has no standardized orthography. This means that writing done in such languages is very recent and limited—mostly occurring in informal environments, such as social media and other forms of electronic communication, and usually written in eye dialect creole. Additionally, with avenues like libraries being under-resourced, as Kincaid (1988) describes them, and with English-as-mother-tongue traditions prevailing in the education system, many citizens are not literate in their Creole or in English and some, as Jones and Dyer Spiegel demonstrate, cannot banish memories of the traumatic experiences they faced since their early years of schooling. Caribbean colleagues in academic writing stand, therefore, to gain by drawing on multi-modal forms of engagement (especially those that privilege the oral and aural) for teaching and research.

Increased Knowledge/Theoretical Engagements

While this collection means more knowledge about academic writing in the Caribbean and for teacher-researchers in rhetoric and composition/writing studies/academic literacies, the traditional perspectives regarding language and error presented by Smith and Stewart-McKoy, for example, may seem potentially *passé* to scholars outside the region, especially in comparison to the translingualist and poststructuralist perspective on language expressed by Mitchell. While it may be easy to dismiss traditional perspectives on language and error, common throughout the region, as old fashioned or theoretically uninformed, the *back to basics* approaches to literacy instruction suggested by these studies do evoke concerns expressed by noted African American educator Delpit (1995) among others. The perspectives Smith and Stewart-McKoy present also suggest that academic writing instructors must walk a tightrope. Is the issue one of more grammar instruction, more teaching of contrastive analysis, or more acceptance of ignoring the supposed boundaries of each language? That nearly every contributor to the collection addresses *language* suggests that it may be the single most critical factor in the teaching of academic writing in the Anglophone Caribbean, influencing not only critical thinking, logical writing, and stylistically pleasing expression but also the identities that students assume in the face of demands to produce (in) a standard language that many do not speak or write in confidently.

Robinson proposes that instructional staff need to adopt a postcolonial orientation that would see them shedding past linguistic trappings and restrictions regarding what is language or which language is useful for writing in/about. Her radical proposal suggests that instructors of students from non-traditional backgrounds stand to gain by engaging, as Combie argues, with current scholarship on code-meshing and translanguaging or academic literacies in fields such as applied linguistics, rhetoric and composition, or New Literacy Studies. Translingualism, specifically, according to Horner, Lu, Royster and Trimbur (2011) "proclaims that writers can, do, and must negotiate standardized rules in light of the contexts of specific instances of writing" (p. 305) and "teaches language users to assume and expect that each new instance of language use brings the need and opportunity to develop new ways of using language, and to draw on a range of language resources" (p. 312). This approach would see teacher-researchers shifting their perspectives on "error," for example. However, teacher-researchers in the Anglophone Caribbean and elsewhere cannot forget the importance of grounding theorizing in reality. As Milson-Whyte (2013; 2014) cautions, proposals about how to do language cannot ignore how speakers of marginalized/minoritized languages value the languages in their repertoire. Teacher-researchers (whether local or expatriate) who use/invite vernaculars in the academic writing classroom could be seen by students to be just *funny*, downright condescending, or outright suspect as Dyer Spiegel and Jones intimate. Of course, the ultimate aim would be not only to engage carefully with theories developed elsewhere but also to deepen the local theory base to make decisions based on theory and scholarship rather than on the *this is the way we've always done it* approach that Ali and Jones McKenzie and Josephs critique.

Professional Engagements

Mere engagement with theory might not yield decisions about language policy or writing that are theoretically grounded. An urgently needed regional professional body dedicated to the teaching of academic literacies, as Jones McKenzie and Campbell-Dawes advocate, may be a significant route to addressing unsatisfactory working conditions and labor relations and to being the voice of teacher-researchers in interactions with top level administrators. Existing regional professional organizations such as the Society for Caribbean Linguistics or the Caribbean Studies Association, while being avenues through which teacher-researchers have sporadically disseminated their ideas on teaching writing in postsecondary contexts, do not have a clearly defined *academic writing* arm. Teacher-researchers of academic writing could attempt to find ways to propose committees or standing groups within these organizations; however, they could get lost within these already broad organizations that could themselves lose disciplinary focus. Given that there are inadequate numbers of scholars/researchers in academic literacies in any one institution or in most Anglophone Caribbean countries, forming a related organization means working across institutions as well as geopolitical boundaries (as Combie advocates). Increased agency that a powerful regional professional body focused on academic literacies can assist teacher-researchers in accessing would also augur well for the agency of students too. Alleyne demonstrates that student performance in academic writing classes is affected by students' feelings and attitudes regarding those classes. Students taught by an instructor whose professional identity is not uncertain (that is, not just teaching academic writing to pay the bills) or students who know that their program or instructor is aligned with a powerful organization or that the work their instructor encourages them to engage with is empowering are likely to exhibit attitudes other than negative to academic writing classes.

CREOLE COMPOSITION

By this, it would be clear that beyond the alliteration in the title, *Creole Composition* is a multiplicity of perspectives regarding language, approaches to teaching, administration, and research that, while informed by Caribbean sensibilities, have implications for colleagues involved in increasing literate practices via academic writing education. In addition to the connections already presented implicitly or explicitly, several of the contributors (including Jones, Dyer Spiegel, Mitchell, Robinson, and Campbell) demonstrate unquestioningly the importance of acknowledging multiple systems of knowledge and of tapping into and valuing students' knowledge. These orientations are instructive not only for colleagues who teach Creole-speaking students but also for colleagues who find themselves in classrooms they may feel contain homogenous groups of speakers of a standard language only (be that language English, Spanish, French, Dutch, or other). The pictures the contributors have painted underscore the presence of multiple areas/systems of knowledge rather than any one path/answer to teaching academic writing. Engaging students' knowledge, values, habits of mind, or customs can mean more reward for students who will feel valued and for instructors as we learn from students.

Indeed, the scholarship this collection contains indicates fertile ground for colleagues in rhetoric and composition/writing studies/academic literacies elsewhere to partner with those of us who teach and research academic writing in the Anglophone Caribbean. The grim descriptions of the material conditions correctly hint at remuneration that is (often) hardly comparable to remuneration in, say, North America or the UK; however, the fledgling academic writing research tradition hails opportunities to share scholarship, to assemble hybrid voices—inherent in the term *creole*—in the name of fostering students' academic writing education and advancing the broader field of writing studies beyond national or regional boundaries.

REFERENCES

Delpit, L. (1995). *Other people's children: Cultural conflict in the classroom.* New York: The New Press.

Horner, B., Lu, M., Royster, J. J., & Trimbur, J. (2011). Opinion: Language difference in writing: Toward a translingual approach. *College English, 73,* 303–321.

Kincaid, J. (1988). *A small place.* New York: Farrar, Straus and Giroux.

Milson-Whyte, V. (2013). Pedagogical and socio-political implications of code-meshing in classrooms: Some considerations for a translingual orientation to writing. In S. Canagarajah (Ed.), *Literacy as translingual practice: Between communities and classrooms* (pp. 115–127). New York: Routledge.

Milson-Whyte, V. (2014). Working English through code-meshing: Implications for denigrated language varieties and their users. In B. Horner & K. Kopelson (Eds.), *Reworking English in rhetoric and composition: Global interrogations, local interventions* (103–115). Carbondale, IL: Southern Illinois University Press.

Miranda, L. (2016). Hamilton: An American musical. In J. McCarter (Ed.), *Hamilton: The revolution* (pp. 23–26). New York: Grand Central Publishing.

Murray, D. (2004). *A writer teaches writing* (Rev. 2nd ed.). Boston: Heinle, Cengage Learning.

Contributors

Tyrone Ali is a lecturer (assistant professor) and coordinator of the Academic Writing Program at The University of the West Indies, St. Augustine in Trinidad and Tobago. His research interests include tertiary-level writing, Caribbean literatures in English, and masculinity studies.

Melissa L. Alleyne is a planning officer in the department of Planning and Institutional Research for The University of the West Indies, Open Campus, located in Barbados. Among her research interests are applied linguistics, literacy, online and distance education, and institutional research.

Annife Campbell is an instructor in Academic Writing at The University of the West Indies at Mona, in Jamaica, where he teaches Critical Reading and Writing to first-year students in the social sciences. He is currently pursuing a PhD in applied linguistics and rhetoric, exploring the ideologies, values, beliefs, and scoring decisions of markers through their comments and marking rubric.

Tresecka Campbell-Dawes is a lecturer (assistant professor) of English at the University of Technology, Jamaica where she teaches academic writing with a focus on exposition and argument. She has presented papers at conferences on the literary genres of ecocriticism, travel narrative and poetry, specifically the postcolonial appropriation of language to establish national identity by women writers in the Caribbean.

Valerie Combie is an associate professor of English at the University of the Virgin Islands in the United States Virgin Islands. She is also the director of the writing center at the Albert A. Sheen Campus on St. Croix and the director of the Virgin Islands Writing Project.

Jacob Dyer Spiegel is an assistant professor of English Studies at the University of The Bahamas, where he also serves as campus director of

Global Studies. His work focuses on traditional Yoruba religious systems in the literary and visual arts of the African diaspora with a focus on Brazil, Cuba, and the Anglophone Caribbean.

Brianne Jaquette is an associate professor of English literature and culture at Western Norway University of Applied Sciences (Høgskulen på Vestlandet) in Bergen, Norway. Her work on composition and literature can be found in the *Journal of the Midwest Modern Language Association, The International Journal of Bahamian Studies, Tulsa Studies in Women's Literature,* and *Pedagogy*.

Carmeneta Jones is a lecturer (assistant professor) in the Department of Language, Linguistics, and Philosophy at The University of the West Indies, Mona in Jamaica, where she teaches a variety of academic writing courses. Her essays have appeared in *International Advances in Writing Research: Cultures, Places, Measures* and *the Caribbean Journal of Education*.

Clover Jones McKenzie is a senior lecturer (associate professor) of Academic Writing at the University of Technology, Jamaica, where she teaches courses in academic literacy with emphasis on writing development at the graduate and undergraduate levels, as well as reading in the content area. Her book chapters and articles have appeared in *Applied Linguistics and Language Teacher Education, Readings in Language Studies* and *Journal of Arts, Science and Technology*.

Beverley Josephs is a lecturer in the School of Humanities and Social Sciences, Faculty of Education and Liberal Studies (FELS), University of Technology, Jamaica, where she facilitates a number of modules including Academic Writing I and II, Public Relations, Marketing Communication, and Corporate Communication.

Christine E. Kozikowski is an assistant professor in English Studies at the University of The Bahamas. She has published several articles on nineteenth century medievalism including, "Mary Shelley and Romantic Medievalism" and "Historical Fiction: A Comparative Analysis of Medieval Romance and Scott's *Ivanhoe*" and co-authored an exit study of first year composition studies published in the *International Journal of Bahamian Studies*.

Vivette Milson-Whyte is a senior lecturer (associate professor) at The University of the West Indies, Mona in Jamaica, where she serves as the coordinator of the Language Section that offers courses in academic writing and technical and professional communication in the Department of Language, Linguistics, and Philosophy. Her essays have appeared in *JAC: A Journal of Composition Theory*, *Caribbean Journal of Education*, and various edited collections; and her book *Academic Writing Instruction for Creole-Influenced Students* was named a finalist in the education/academic (non-fiction) category of the 2017 Next Generation Indie Book Awards.

Kendra L. Mitchell recently completed a nine-month Fulbright fellowship at the University of Pretoria, Groenkloof Campus (South Africa) where she taught hundreds of multilingual preservice undergraduates and postgraduates and served as a cultural ambassador. She earned her doctorate in English with a concentration in rhetoric and composition studies from the Florida State University (FSU).

Raymond Oenbring is an assistant professor in English Studies at the University of The Bahamas, where he serves as writing program coordinator. His work has appeared in a variety of academic fora, including *English World-wide*, and *Language, Discourse & Society*, the latter article receiving in 2014 the Academic Excellence Award from the Language and Society research committee of the International Sociological Association.

Heather M. Robinson is an associate professor at York College of the City University of New York, where she currently serves as English department chairperson and teaches courses in World Englishes, Critical Methods, English grammar and syntax, and first-year composition. Her publications have appeared in the *Journal of Basic Writing*, *American Speech*, the *WAC Journal*, and *Composition Studies*.

Daidrah Smith is a lecturer (assistant professor) of language and linguistics at the University of Technology, Jamaica, where she lectures Academic Writing and Language Development. Her essays have appeared in the *Journal of Arts, Science and Technology* (*JAST*).

Michelle Stewart-McKoy is a lecturer (assistant professor) of languages and digital literacies at the University of Technology, Jamaica, where she lectures Spanish, Academic Writing, and Web 2.0 interactions. Her essays have appeared in *the Journal of Arts, Science and Technology* (*JAST*), *Studies in Self Access Learning* (*SISAL*), *the Caribbean Journal of Education* (*CJE*), and *the Journal of Educators Online* (*JEO*).

INDEX

abrogation, 322, 334–336
academic discourse, 171–172, 174, 211, 321, 336–337, 339–340
academic English, 22, 29, 125–126, 129–131, 133–138, 143–147, 149, 153, 166, 320, 324, 327
academic literacies, 3, 6–7, 23, 28, 33–34, 210, 214, 223–225, 227–232, 235–236, 232, 239, 240–244, 246–249, 304–311, 313, 315–319, 345–349
academic writing: see writing
access, 5–6, 32, 84, 97, 160, 199, 228, 256, 259, 265, 294, 306, 311, 313, 325, 329
acrolect/al, 10, 11, 41, 58, 321, 325, 332
adult learners, 9
African American English, 217–219
African American Verbal Traditions (AVT), 203, 212
African American Vernacular English (AAVE), 8, 9, 168, 207, 280
African American Women's Language (AAWL), 203–204, 212, 213
African Americans, 24, 203–206, 208, 210
Afro-Caribbean scholars, 205

agency, 29, 33, 73, 112, 169, 173, 206, 271, 276, 282–283, 322–323, 325, 340, 344–345, 348
agent: rhetorical, 271, 276, 281
American English, vii, 10, 273, 291, 326
Amerindian language, 79
Anansi: see Brer Anansi
Anguilla, ix, 12
ANOVA (analysis of variance), 133–141
Anson, Chris, 22, 31
Antigua, 8, 11, 26, 343
Antigua & Barbuda, 8, 11
Anzaldúa, Gloria, 84, 103
appropriation, 85, 208, 322, 334–336, 340
archipelagic thinking, 27
argument, xii, 29, 35, 93, 207, 216, 219, 224, 253, 272, 274, 279, 311, 323, 328, 342
Aristotle, 272, 275, 282
art, 40, 45, 49, 58, 73, 80, 99–101, 123
Aruba, 294, 299
assertives, 167
assessment, vii, xi, 13, 20–21, 130, 138, 152, 153, 158–161, 163, 167, 193, 199, 205, 208, 218, 243, 246, 251, 254–255, 257, 259–263, 265–266, 290, 292, 306; self-assessment, 259

355

assignments, 30, 46, 66, 76, 86, 87, 88, 91, 92, 98, 107, 108, 109, 110, 111, 112, 114, 116, 117, 118, 119, 120, 121, 122, 123, 139, 140, 142, 148, 150, 151, 161, 215, 246, 262, 276, 278, 338, 339; course assignments, 14; low-stakes assignments, 108; major assignments, 117
attitudes, 50, 64, 122, 126, 131–136, 138–139, 141–143, 145–146, 149, 151, 153, 157, 168, 229, 239, 252, 266, 310, 323, 337–338
audience, xi, 30, 58–59, 76, 86, 98–99, 161, 166, 258, 274, 281, 322, 329, 331, 334–336

Bahamas: The Bahamas, vii–viii, xii, xiii, 4, 8, 11, 18, 20, 27, 34, 76, 79, 81–82, 89, 90, 101–103, 109–110, 112, 124, 153, 273, 276–277, 279, 288, 318
Bahamian Creole English, 76, 80, 82, 87, 101–103
Banks, Adam, 274, 282
Barbados, 4, 8, 11, 18, 130, 255, 266, 288
Bartholomae, David, 22, 31, 174, 176, 198, 200
basilect, 10, 332
Bazerman, Charles, 3, 7, 31
Belize, 8, 12
Bennett-Coverley, Louise, 49–50, 335
Berlin, James, 25, 31
Bermuda, 12
best practices, xi, 7, 24, 28, 44, 252, 288, 298, 344
Bhabha, Homi, 204, 206, 212, 217
Bilingual Education Project (BEP), 295
Bizzell, Patricia, 32, 276, 283

Black English, 207, 218
Black English as a second language (BESL), 207–208
body, xii, 7, 13, 61, 88, 195, 206, 215, 216, 250–252, 254, 259, 261–262, 265, 347, 348
Bonaire, 294, 299
Brathwaite, Kamau, 20, 77–80, 87, 93, 96–97, 99, 100–103, 143, 301, 321, 335–336, 341
Brer Anansi, 49–51, 70, 72, 336
British English, vii, 10, 329
Browne, Kevin, 272, 274, 275, 283
Bryan, Beverley, 40, 41, 44–46, 50–52, 70, 151, 152, 198
Burke, Kenneth, 158, 176
business writing, 109, 317
Butler, Ruth, 247–248

calypso, 275
Canada, 16, 35, 288
Canagarajah, Suresh, 3–4, 7, 23, 29, 31, 103, 173, 176, 205, 217–219, 289, 296–298, 300, 320, 322, 326, 333, 336, 341, 349
capping, 204, 213
Caribbean: Anglophone, 4–8, 10–12, 14–18, 22–24, 28, 34, 45, 63, 68–69, 79–81, 99, 103, 107, 110, 159–161, 170, 177–178, 180, 183, 202–206, 211–212, 215–216, 218, 250, 252, 255–258, 266, 272–274, 277, 282–284, 286–288, 290–291, 293, 295, 300, 303–304, 307, 310–313, 316, 318, 327, 342–344, 346–349; creoles, 9, 11, 15, see creoles
Caribbean Advanced Proficiency Examination (CAPE), 13, 30, 130, 226
Caribbean Examinations Council (CXC), 13, 254

Caribbean region, vii–viii, 7, 12, 16, 27, 79, 110, 157, 281, 287–289, 293
Caribbean Secondary Education Certificate (CSEC), 13, 30, 130, 133, 141, 178, 181, 226
Caribbean Standard English, 10–11, 15, 252
Carrington, Lawrence, 11, 31
Cayman Islands, 12, 248
class politics, 206
classwork, 111
Cleary, Beverly, 49
code-switching, 35, 40, 58, 62, 165, 219, 342
code-meshing, 23, 103, 206, 209, 218, 280–281, 283, 296, 300, 326–327, 333, 336, 341, 347, 349
collaboration, 224, 231, 240
College Composition and Communication, 289, 316
colonialism, viii–xi, 4–6, 8, 10, 12, 20, 26, 32, 76–79, 81–82, 85, 88, 97, 99–101, 150, 154, 159–160, 180, 286, 289, 291, 320–323, 325, 326–329, 332–334, 340–342
communication, 4, 6, 8, 10, 12, 39, 46, 51, 78, 84, 122, 127, 162, 179, 180–182, 203, 230, 250, 252, 261, 275, 277, 286, 292, 296, 299, 308, 312, 346
Communication Studies in the Caribbean Advanced Proficiency Examination (CAPE), 13, 30, 130, 141, 226
communicative competence, 41, 173, 205
competence, 4, 130, 148, 178, 180–181, 183, 196, 198, 223, 229–230, 235, 249, 253, 255–256, 292, 295, 311–312, 319

composition: colonial, 341; composition class, 6, 20, 29, 31, 73, 107–108, 112–113, 117– 118, 121, 159, 177, 201, 207, 209, 278–279, 281, 282, 296, 326, 328–329, 333–334, 338–339; courses, 25, 88, 92, 96, 98–99, 101, 107–108, 113, 209, 254, 258, 275, 277, 340; composition instructors, 6, 15, 6, 25, 97, 158, 161, 167, 168, 172, 276, 280, 288; composition pedagogy, 109, 215; composition program, 5; composition scholar, 3, 6, 19–20, 33, 209, 217, 273, 276, 282, 293; composition studies, xii, 3–4, 7, 18, 20–21, 22, 24–25, 29, 32, 35, 108, 275, 303, 317, 323–325, 341; composition theory, 6, 289; first-year composition, 76, 109; transnational, x, xii, 27, 109, 216, 286– 289, 293, 328, 343
Composition Forum, 152
composition studies, xii, 3–4, 7, 18, 20–22, 24, 25, 29, 32, 35, 108, 275, 303, 317, 323–325, 341
computers and composition, 16, 51, 187–188
Conference on College Composition and Communication (CCCC), 19, 31, 289, 316
Connors, Robert, 22, 32
content-area lecturers, 132, 225–228, 235, 241–242, 244, 246–247, 309, 314–315, 318
continuum, 10, 32, 34, 64, 111, 165, 198, 206, 209, 250, 298, 321, 329
conventions, 15, 58, 126, 150, 158, 164, 170, 223, 304

coordinator, 17, 30, 251, 254, 260, 266
craft, 4, 90, 259, 338
Craig, Dennis, 14, 32, 41, 45, 53, 70, 125, 152, 180, 196, 199, 200, 221, 255, 267
Creole: continuum, 10, 32, 34, 165, 198, 250, 321
creole: languages, 8–10, 13–14, 19, 20, 27–28, 34, 151, 253, 255, 269, 285–290, 293, 296, 298–299, 321, 341, 346
Creole: Jamaican, 8, 12, 18–19, 20, 35, 39–48, 50, 52–59, 61–64, 68–69, 71–72, 158, 165–166, 168, 180, 182, 193–195, 199, 201, 206, 212, 293, 295, 299, 322–323, 325, 336–337, 341
Creole English, ix, 168
creoles, 5–6, 8–15, 19, 20, 22, 24, 27–28, 31–34, 66, 73, 81, 89, 103, 151, 153, 165–166, 177, 180, 182–183, 193–194, 198–201, 207, 249–250, 252–253, 255–256, 258, 267, 269, 285–300, 309, 318, 321–323, 327–330, 332–334, 337–338, 341–342, 346, 349
critical reflexivity, 304, 306
critical thinking, 39, 51, 67, 92, 231, 233, 244, 246, 253, 263, 266, 279, 281, 305, 346
cultural consciousness, 122
Curaçao, 288, 294, 299
curriculum development, 196–197, 227

dancehall (music), 51–53, 55–56, 72, 275
deadlines, 21, 107, 108–109, 111–124

DEAL (Drop everything and listen), 49
DEAR (Drop everything and read), 49, 72
debate, x, 34, 80, 170, 195, 218, 272, 274, 278–279, 283
declarations, 167, 169
decolonization, 4, 325
Delpit, Lisa, 7, 34, 41, 70, 218, 283, 346, 349
Devonish, Hubert, 5, 32, 45, 48, 51–53, 63, 70–71, 165, 176, 179, 200, 223, 248, 293, 295, 299
deficit models, 247, 305, 332
dialect, 8, 20, 76, 77–88, 91–102, 153, 168, 200, 207, 211, 217, 257, 293, 330, 336–337, 346
dialectic, 18, 112
dialects: nonstandardized, 11
directives, 167–169
discourse communities, 27, 158, 271, 273
diversity, 17, 35, 76, 79, 208, 210, 306; linguistic, 3, 289
Dominica, 11–12
Donahue, Christiane, 4, 7, 32, 33, 211, 217

Ebonics, 202, 206–207, 218
ecology, 33, 201, 248, 267, 299, 313, 318
economics, vii, 32
Edited American English (EAE), 203–204, 207, 210–212, 214–216
education: postsecondary, xi, 5–7, 13–15, 17–23, 25–28, 30, 57, 107, 130, 157–158, 170, 175, 178–179, 209, 223–224, 232–233, 250, 252, 266, 273, 275, 278, 281–282, 288, 294, 296, 303–304, 307–308, 310, 313,

345, 348; secondary, 12–13, 57, 274, 288, 335; universal, 210
educational policy, 286, 288, 293
Elbow, Peter, 19, 22, 29, 32, 35, 53, 71, 93, 103, 273, 280, 283, 326–327, 333, 339, 341
empathy, 67–69, 74
empirical research, 18, 20–21, 23, 25, 31, 108, 195, 247, 257, 293, 295, 307
English as a foreign language (EFL), 145, 150
English as a Second Language (ESL), 34, 40, 68, 168, 191–192, 195, 197, 218, 292, 299, 342
English Creoles: Caribbean, 6, 7, 9–10, 12, 14, 258, 278, 290
English for academic purposes (EAP), 128, 138, 145, 153–154
English Language Proficiency Test (ELPT), 13, 130, 146, 183–187, 195, 226, 250, 254, 312
epistemology, 248, 317
equity: social, 6, 297–298, 323
errors, 16, 163–164, 174, 183, 185–186, 188, 190–193, 196, 200–201, 248, 280, 326, 346–347; discourse, 186–187, 190; ethics and, 32, 163, 187; grammatical, 158, 178, 186, 188–189, 193; lexical, 186, 189–190, 201
ethos, 275
excellence: and/vs equity, 160, 219, 298, 323
exploration, 20, 88, 90, 92, 94, 100, 129, 134–136, 139, 141, 239, 335
expression, 15, 22, 53, 74, 76, 78–80, 82, 84, 85, 92, 97–99, 102, 109, 157, 158–159, 161–172, 174–176, 184, 191, 206, 216, 246, 275, 345, 347
expression (comment), 15, 22, 53, 74, 76, 78–80, 82, 84–85, 92, 97–99, 102, 109, 157–159, 161–172, 174–176, 184, 191, 206, 216, 246, 275, 345, 347

Facebook, 112
feedback, 32, 110, 120, 127, 150, 167, 234, 254, 263, 297, 331, 345
first-year composition, 5, 12, 13, 25, 30, 34, 76, 108–109, 133, 162, 275, 312
folktales, 280
French 8, 9, 48, 90, 131, 287, 349
French Creole, 12, 257, 287, 288, 293
French West Indies, 8

Gardner, Robert, 44, 71, 126–128, 131, 144, 152, 154
Geisler, Cheryl, 271, 276, 282–283
gender, 29, 110, 122, 152, 164, 218
General Certificate of Education (GCE), 13, 130
General Certificate of Secondary Education (GCSE), 12, 30
genre, 31, 53, 58, 278, 283, 306
Gilyard, Keith, 19, 32, 175–176
Glissant, Édouard, 27, 32, 111–112, 123, 321, 341
globalization, ix, 4, 30, 64, 122, 172, 174, 201, 249, 258, 262, 295, 297, 311, 321, 324, 334, 336, 341
grades, 12–13, 92, 117–118, 126–127, 148–149, 160–161, 163, 183, 185, 292
grading, 6, 22, 29, 30, 90, 111, 120, 150, 158, 160–163, 169, 183, 184, 255
grammar, 13–14, 22–24, 57, 67, 86, 88, 91, 143, 162, 179, 182–

184, 192–201, 203, 215–216, 246, 253, 303, 308, 315, 330, 346; rhetorical, 198–199, 201
Great Britain, 4–5, 27, 120, 253, 286, 291, 327
Grenada, 8, 11
Guardian, The (UK), ix, xii
Gullah, 8
Guyana, 8, 12, 70, 290, 300, 303, 309–310
Guyanese Creole, 8, 290, 338

Habermas, Jürgen, 271, 283
habits of mind, 349
Haiti, 9, 77, 88–90, 287, 288, 293–294, 299–300
Haitian Creole, 9, 287, 288, 293, 294, 299
Halliday, M. A. K., 40, 71, 170, 176
Hamilton (play), ix–x, xii, 179, 196, 200–201, 304, 311–312, 317–318, 345, 349
Hamilton, Philip, 179
Harris, Joseph, 101, 103, 331, 337, 342
HBCUs (Historically Black Colleges and Universities), 24, 33, 202–205, 207–210, 218
hegemony, viii
heuristic, 40
Higher Education Act of 1965, 209
Historically Black Colleges and Universities (HBCUs), 24, 33, 202–205, 207–210, 218
Høgskulen på Vestlandet, xiii, xiv
holistic assessment, 44, 163, 184, 198
Honeyghan, Glasceta, 41, 47, 49, 72
Hope, Donna, 55, 72

Horner, Bruce, 3, 4, 7, 23, 25, 33, 73, 100, 103, 173, 175–177, 211, 217, 255, 267, 283, 289–290, 296, 299, 300, 306, 317, 326, 333, 341, 347, 349
Hurricane Irma, vii, ix–xii, 87
Hurricane Maria, ix
hurricanes, ix
hypercorrection, 11, 194

identity, x, 4, 8, 24–25, 29, 33, 53, 83, 87, 99, 167, 169, 173–176, 203–205, 207–208, 212, 216–218, 272, 294, 298, 304, 306, 308, 318, 322, 325, 338; Caribbean, x, 34, 177, 284, 300, 318, 342; linguistic, ix, 23–24, 81, 204, 258, 324, 334, 338–339; linguistic identities, 4, 203, 205, 215, 321, 328, 332–333, 338; professional, 6, 25, 161, 304, 315, 317, 348
ideology, 48, 97, 159, 167, 206, 209, 248, 255–277, 286, 287, 289, 297, 306, 308, 316–317, 323
immersion, 40, 44, 46
immigrants, 89, 205–206, 212, 335, 337
imperialism, x, 4, 98, 102, 321–322, 324, 334–336
information literacy, 225, 305
Inoue, Asao B., 218
inquiry, 119, 152, 315, 333, 343
instructors: academic writing, 22, 159, 175, 185, 197, 224, 304, 307, 315, 316, 346; composition, 6, 15, 6, 25, 97, 158, 161, 167, 168, 172, 276, 280, 288; writing, 23, 26, 27, 28, 65, 115, 119, 157, 158, 159, 160, 162, 170, 174, 195, 224, 231, 234, 247,

257, 260, 266, 277, 281, 304, 305, 308, 311, 314, 326, 345
interference: language, 15, 32, 165, 257, 322, 325
International Center for Caribbean Language Research, 286–287
island time, 21, 109, 345

Jamaica, xii, 8, 11, 17–18, 20, 25, 27–28, 39, 41, 44–45, 48–49, 55, 57–59, 61–63, 68–69, 77, 86, 88, 94, 130, 157, 164–166, 168, 170, 172, 178–179, 196, 198, 223, 247, 287–288, 295, 308, 316, 322–323, 335, 338
Jamaican Creole, 8, 12, 18–19, 20, 35, 39–48, 50, 52–59, 61–64, 68–69, 71–72, 158, 165–166, 168, 180, 182, 193–195, 199, 201, 206, 212, 293, 295, 299, 322–323, 325, 336–337, 341
Jamaican Language Unit, 57, 295
Jaquette, Brianne, vii, 3, 109, 124, 234, 249, 307, 318
Jarratt, Susan, 324, 329, 341
Jim Crow, 208

Kennedy, George, 279, 283
Kennedy, Michele, 41, 57, 58, 72
Kincaid, Jamaica, 26, 33, 343–344, 346, 349
knowledge: content knowledge, 313
Kolln, Martha, 195, 198, 200

Language Identity Awareness and Development (LIAD), 330
languages: substrate, 9; superstrate, 9
lecturers, 82, 132–134, 140, 142–148, 150, 180–182, 224–228, 232, 235, 238–247, 257, 308–309, 311–315, 318

lexicon, 9, 32, 86, 192, 199
linguistic push-pull (LPP), 203, 205, 212–216
listening, 14, 39, 45, 51, 53, 57, 63, 280, 289
literacies, 7, 14, 28, 31, 51, 53, 69, 71–73, 217–218, 304–307, 310, 318, 348; academic, 3, 6–7, 23, 28, 33–34, 210, 214, 248–249, 304–310, 313, 316–319, 345–349
literacy, xii, 19, 32, 33, 39–49, 51–57, 63, 68–75, 152, 154, 200, 218, 225, 229–236, 238, 241, 242, 248–249, 285, 290, 294–295, 299, 300, 304–317, 319, 329, 342, 346; information, 225, 305; literacy courses, 305, 308, 316; literacy education, 40, 44, 46, 48–49, 290; literacy narratives, 342
literacy skills, 39–40, 45, 51, 54, 56–57, 69, 231–235, 238, 242, 294–295, 304, 306–307, 311, 314–316
literature, 7, 25, 46, 49–50, 59, 81, 108–109, 123, 134, 140, 150, 191, 195, 329
logos, 275
Lu, Min-Zhan, 4, 23, 33, 73, 173, 176, 177, 289, 290, 296, 299, 324, 326, 332, 333, 341, 342, 347, 349
Lunsford, Andrea, 15, 22, 31–33, 161, 163, 177, 324, 341–342

malapropisms, 191–192
marginalized languages, 288
mechanics, 22, 163, 182, 184, 253, 293
media, 20, 66, 69, 259, 276, 277, 286, 328, 336; social media, vii, 346

memory, 41, 61, 62, 84, 87, 97
mesolect, 10
metacognitive awareness, 249, 334
metaphor, 170
Miller, Carolyn, 271
Milson-Whyte, Vivette, vii, 3, 6, 9, 13–14, 25, 33, 58, 73, 91, 94, 103, 146–147, 153, 157, 159, 165–167, 174, 177, 180–181, 201, 204, 206, 218, 224, 249, 252–254, 257–258, 265, 267, 281, 283, 290, 296–297, 300, 303, 310, 318, 322–325, 327, 332–334, 339, 342, 347, 349
Miranda, Lin-Manuel, x, xii, 345, 349
moderation: cross-moderation, 30, 162, 163, 304,
Montserrat, 12
morphology, 8–9, 186, 188, 193, 206
Morrill Act, 210
mother tongue, 7–8, 19, 32, 47, 70, 74, 77, 96–97, 100, 151, 166, 180, 252, 258, 283, 285, 290, 292, 329
motivation, 21, 110, 123, 126–129, 131, 134, 148–149, 150, 152–154, 165, 203, 212, 214–215, 260, 261, 266
multilingualism, 4
music, ix, 52, 54, 56, 70, 72–73, 99

Nassau (The Bahamas), vii, xii, 81, 103, 153
Nassau Guardian, vii, xii
Nassau Tribune, vii
nation language, 20, 77–80, 83–84, 86–103, 335–336, 338
National Association of Teachers of English (NATE), 316
National Council of Teachers of English (NCTE), 31–32, 35, 51, 73, 217, 282; *College Composition and Communication*, 31–34, 177, 199–201, 217–218, 298, 341
native language interference, 256
native tongue, 29, 41, 258
naturalized double consciousness, 204
Nero, Shondel J., 7, 33–34, 48, 73–74, 166, 168, 177, 205, 215, 218, 289–290, 300, 322–326, 330, 331, 332, 333, 342
nonstandard Englishes, 6
North America, 3–4, 6, 22, 34, 157–158, 276, 343, 349

Obama, Barack, 57–58, 64, 75
Oenbring, Raymond, vii, 3, 6, 11, 15, 25, 27, 29, 34, 91, 103, 109, 121, 124, 160–161, 177, 234, 249, 271, 281, 284, 288, 300, 307, 312, 318, 325–327, 339, 342, 344, 346
Okara, Gabriel, 337
oppression, 98
oral communication, 57, 172, 179, 258
orality, 27, 77, 79, 93, 99, 272, 277, 281–282, 284, 339
oratory, 27, 272–274, 277, 281–282, 339
orthography, vii, 9, 192, 286–287, 293–294, 346
Othello, 214

pathos, 275
pedagogy, 5–6, 15, 24–25, 27, 32, 34, 39, 108, 111, 176, 185, 259, 266, 273, 275–276, 278, 296, 320, 325–327, 330–331, 339;

postcolonial, 332, 340; process pedagogy, 283
persuasion, 271–273, 275, 281
phonology, 9, 192, 215
pidgin languages, 8
plagiarism, 170
poetry, 20, 59, 65, 66, 71, 79, 92, 98, 103, 275, 326, 335
Polanyi, Michael, 43, 71
polis, 27, 271–273, 277, 281, 283; small island, 273, 281, 344
politics, 32, 70, 176–177, 205, 218– 219, 299
Pollard, Velma, 41, 51, 68, 74, 192, 193, 201
popular culture, 54, 56, 69, 73, 283
portfolios, 108, 263
postcolonial approaches to teaching writing, 29, 320–323, 328, 331, 333–334
postcolonialism, 4, 6, 27, 29, 76, 79, 97, 100, 287, 320–324, 328–335, 338–340, 347
post-process theories, 276
postsecondary writing instruction, 5, 14–18, 25, 28
poststructuralism, 24, 346
power relationships, ix, 83
preaching, 274, 283
privilege, 329, 346
process writing, 14–15, 99, see writing
procrastination, 107, 108, 110, 113–117, 119–124
professionalization, 16, 24, 304, 315
progymnasmata, 279
proverbs, 53, 54, 87
public sphere, 212, 271, 283
Puerto Rico, ix, 12, 291, 299

purpose, 64–65, 67, 76, 81, 98–99, 133, 198, 210, 215, 227, 292, 303, 308, 327

race, 216–218, 248
racism, 98, 207, 216–217, 323, 325, 327
reading, 39, 42, 45, 49, 51, 59, 61–64, 70, 73–74, 95–96, 142, 154, 160, 177, 213, 223–226, 233–234, 237, 241, 248, 253, 289, 294, 303, 305, 311–312, 322, 330–331, 340; reading and writing, 59, 62, 74, 95, 154, 223–226, 233, 234, 237, 294, 303, 305, 311, 331
reflective practice, 19
reggae, 54–56, 70, 275
remediation, 198, 254, 292
resistance, 48, 76, 79, 80, 83, 100, 140, 168, 203, 212–216, 320, 322, 325, 328, 331–332, 340
response to writing, 22, 31, 35
rhetoric, 3–7, 16, 20, 32, 33, 35, 100, 103, 122, 157, 160, 174, 176, 198, 200, 218–219, 252–253, 267, 271–273, 275–276, 279, 281–284, 298, 305, 307, 315, 323, 329, 345–347, 349
rhetoric and composition, 3–7, 16, 20, 32, 33, 35, 100, 103, 122, 253, 271, 273, 275–276, 282–283, 305, 307, 315, 345–347, 349
Rhetorica Ad Herennium, 280
rhetorical situation, 276
rhetorical strategies, 99, 215
rhetorical theory: black, 274
rhetorical tradition, 272–273, 276, 279, 280, 283
Richardson, Elaine, 176, 204, 208–209, 218

Roberts, Peter, 15, 34, 125, 127, 145, 153, 170, 177, 275, 284
Rosenblatt, Louise, 59, 61, 63, 64, 74

schema theory, 28
school: primary, 15, 41–43, 45–47, 49–50, 70, 72, 94–95, 143, 294, 300, 310, 335; secondary, 12–14, 20, 30, 39, 42, 44, 48, 53–54, 57–58, 68, 73–74, 77, 107, 120, 122, 125, 130, 150, 178, 180, 192, 197, 200, 233, 248, 250, 254, 274, 288–289, 311, 316, 318, 335
Searle, John, 161, 167, 169, 177
self-confidence, xi, 22, 126, 128–129, 131, 134–135, 138–139, 143–148, 151, 154
Selfe, Cynthia, 31
self-esteem, 108, 124, 128, 145
Seymour, Chanti, 96
Shields, Kathryn, 41, 46, 74
silence, 41, 70, 75, 80, 84–85, 90, 93, 216, 308
Sint Eustatius, 12, 299
Sint Maarten, 12
slavery, 9, 50, 78, 210, 291, 324
Smitherman, Geneva, 19, 35, 203–204, 207, 218–219
soca, 81, 275
social change, 95
social media: see media
Society for Caribbean Linguistics (SCL), 153, 248, 287, 299, 316–317, 348
Sommers, Nancy, 157–158, 177
speech act theory, 159, 161–162, 166–169
St. Croix, x, 291
St. Lucia, 11, 255, 257
St. Kitts & Nevis, 8, 11, 255

St. Vincent & the Grenadines, 8, 11, 255
Standard English, ix, 5, 7, 10–11, 15, 20, 23, 32, 34, 40, 47, 52, 58, 64, 66, 70, 74, 86, 96, 125, 128, 130, 149–150, 152, 158, 164–166, 178–180, 182–183, 188–189, 192–196, 199–201, 209, 223, 253–254, 256–257, 259, 278–280, 282, 293, 297, 309, 311, 327, 338; Caribbean, 10–11, 15, 252; Jamaican, 10, 40–42, 45–48, 53–58, 68–69, 165, 196, 199, 201
Standard Written English (SWE), 168
Standardized British English, 321
standards, 6, 150, 160, 163, 169, 174, 185, 212–213, 241, 260, 292, 299
STEM (science, technology, engineering, math), 294
Straub, Richard E., 22, 35, 161, 163, 177
Street, Brian, 304–306, 313, 317–318
Students Rights to Their Own Language (CCCC, 1974), 19, 208
style, 5, 11, 20, 53, 81, 147, 158, 163, 170, 177, 254, 259, 274, 277–278, 305, 330
subject position, 28, 203, 205, 321, 324, 328, 334–335, 338–340
subjectivity, 207, 326, 328, 337, 339, 342
syntax, 8–9, 67, 86, 143, 186, 188, 193, 337, 340
systemic functional linguistics (SFL), 159, 170–173

technology, 16, 58, 119, 143, 251, 259, 294

time management, 21, 107–108, 110, 112, 116, 119–123
Tompkins, Jane, 19, 35
total education (of the individual), 197, 230, 232
transactional theory, 59, 74
transfer, 88, 96–97, 128, 143, 148, 152–153, 192–193, 200–201, 226, 234, 247, 261, 313
translanguaging, 3–4, 23, 204–207, 216, 289, 341, 347
translingualism, 3–4, 175, 205, 289, 296, 335
transnationalism, 289, 341
Trimbur, John, 7, 23, 33, 173, 177, 289, 290, 296, 299, 326, 333, 341, 347, 349
Trinidad & Tobago, 4, 8, 11, 18, 26–27, 130, 248, 251, 255–256, 259, 267, 288, 299
Troutman, Denise, 203, 212–213, 216, 219
Turks & Caicos, 12

United Kingdom, ix, 3, 5, 12, 28, 30, 81, 288, 343, 349
United Nations, 225, 249, 285, 286, 300
United States, vii, ix–xi, 3–5, 7–10, 12, 16, 18–19, 23, 27, 29–30, 81, 95, 99, 109, 120, 128, 144, 147–148, 172, 203–205, 207, 211–212, 273–275, 277, 280, 282, 288–289, 291–292, 294, 303, 307, 310, 316, 320, 325–330, 337, 343
University of Technology, Jamaica (UTech, Ja.), 23, 155, 178–179, 181–183, 193, 195–201, 224–226, 229–233, 235–237, 247, 303, 307–310, 312, 314–315, 318

University of The Bahamas, xiii, 17–18, 20–21, 76, 79, 96, 107, 249, 277, 282, 307, 312
University of the Virgin Islands (UVI), 28, 288–289, 291–293, 300
University of the West Indies, St. Augustine, The (UWISTA), 25–26, 250–257, 259–262, 264–266
University of the West Indies, The, xiii, 17–18, 25, 58, 72, 125, 130, 144, 146, 154, 160, 179, 224, 251, 266–267, 274, 297, 309, 313, 322, 328
University of West Indies, Mona, 17, 179, 197, 224, 252, 254, 313, 315
US Virgin Islands, 288–289, 291–293, 298–299

videos, 51, 57–58
Virgin Islands (British), 8, 12
Virgin Islands (US), ix–x, 12, 18, 27, 288, 291–292
voice, 15, 20, 50, 59–62, 64, 89, 92–93, 99–103, 147, 158, 162, 170, 176, 236–237, 307, 336, 338–339, 341, 348; authentic, 276
Vygotsky, Lev, 290

West Africa, 77, 208
workshops, 47, 82, 91, 250, 252, 265, 294
writing: academic, xii–xiv, 6–7, 13, 15, 17, 19, 21–25, 34, 58–59, 64, 66, 108, 114, 125–126, 129, 130–134, 136–154, 158–160, 162, 164, 166, 170–172, 175–176, 178, 180, 185, 197, 199, 201, 209, 224–225, 227–228, 234–235, 238,

240–242, 245–247, 249–251, 253–254, 256–257, 260–266, 303–304, 307–309, 312, 315, 321, 325, 333–334, 338–341, 343, 345–349; argumentative, 108, 309; collaborative, 54; expository, 62, 63, 108; in-class writing, 153, 280; reflective, 263; writing assignments, 14, 58, 62, 91, 114, 115, 140, 149, 159, 174, 310, 320, 339; conventions of, 71, 142; writing courses, 5, 13, 17, 25, 42, 58–59, 62, 66–67, 76, 82, 96– 97, 108, 113, 129–151, 153, 180, 182–183, 193, 195–197, 224–226, 231, 234–238, 242, 245, 247, 252, 254–255, 259, 265, 273, 297, 303, 310, 313, 325, 333–334; writing instruction, xi–xii, 17, 24, 25, 27, 33, 72–73, 103, 138, 153, 161, 177, 200–201, 228, 249, 251–252, 255, 267, 287, 289, 300, 318, 321, 323, 330–331, 342; pedagogy, xii, 17, 64, 68, 184, 319, 341; practices, 305, 306; process, 54, 59, 111, 140, 234, 280, 283; programs, xii, 17, 20, 26, 28, 30, 33, 109, 123, 249–252, 255, 259, 261–262, 265, 267, 280, 303, 306, 310, 317, 345; samples, 215–216; studies, 7, 16, 17, 18, 23, 24, 28, 29, 30, 175, 204, 209, 289, 304, 344, 345, 346, 349; strategies, 179; teachers, 343

writing across the curriculum (WAC), 151, 224, 265, 305, 313

writing centers, 24, 110, 199, 203–204, 207–209, 213–218, 224, 238, 240, 247, 311

writing handbooks, 158

writing program administration, xii, 17, 26, 33, 109, 123, 251, 261, 267, 345

writing program administration/administrator, 25, 251–252, 257, 258, 265, 317

Writing Program Coordinator (WPC), 251–254, 258–259, 262–263, 266

Young, Vershawn Ashanti, 23, 28, 35, 209, 219, 326, 327, 333, 342

www.ingramcontent.com/pod-product-compliance
Lightning Source LLC
Chambersburg PA
CBHW020301240426
43673CB00039B/664